A-Z of Opera

Dame Janet Baker, singing the title role in *Julius Caesar*, by Handel. John Copley's production for English National Opera.

The Wordsworth
A-Z of Opera

–

Mary Hamilton

Wordsworth Reference

First published 1990 by Facts on File, Inc. New York.

This edition published 1996 by Wordsworth Editions Ltd.
Cumberland House, Crib Street, Ware, Hertfordshire SG12 9ET.

ISBN 1-85326-383-4

Printed and bound in Great Britain by Mackays of Chatham PLC.

Introduction

Those who have discovered the joys of opera over the last decade can count themselves part of a much discussed and, for the most part, greatly welcomed, phenomenon. During these years opera has ceased to be the exclusive preserve of the rich and knowledgeable. Now, as opera is performed in venues ranging from churches to school halls, attracting audiences in both jeans and tuxedos, the art form itself has progressed out of the music pages to become a nationally discussed pastime. If statistics are to be believed, more people go to opera in London than to the local football clubs. But that new audience may be missing out on something.

Like any good hobby, opera is more enjoyable if you know something about it. There are certainly plenty of operas which will be pleasurable enough on a first hearing with absolutely no background information. The majority of 'first timers' find they enjoy the atmosphere and the excitement of a performance, but they want to know a little bit more. Everyone talks about *Carmen* as the ideal beginner's opera, but what exactly is the story all about? What is 'producer's opera'? Where exactly does sponsorship money go? Is it shameful to admit that you actually enjoy operas more in English when there is a chance of understanding the plot? Why do counter-tenors sound like that? And if Glyndebourne is so wonderful, why can ordinary people never stand a chance of getting tickets. Many opera goers are constrained by time, rather than interest, from reading the weightier musical tomes on the subject which may contain more information than they need to take in. They do not want to be patronized but they want to be able to discuss the production with friends or colleagues who may be more knowledgeable than they are. They do not want to bluff, in what is the ultimate bluffer's territory. They simply want to extend their interest in a new subject.

This is particularly true for the corporate community who have been catapulted into the world of opera by the extraordinary rise in opera sponsorship. Invited by his senior manager to Glyndebourne, the junior executive may not be able to distinguish Berio from Borodin, but he does not want to appear foolish in front of his boss. The corporate host at a major function at a leading opera house may not have understood a word of what has been happening on stage for the last three hours, but he dare not let on to his prestigious clients and customers, particularly when his firm has sponsored the production. Sensing this dilemma, Martini and Rossi commissioned me to write this *A to Z of Opera*.

I came to opera first as an excited seven year old with enlightened (or foolhardy!) parents who took me to a performance of *Nabucco* at Welsh National Opera. I had no idea what was going on, but it all sounded so wonderful and the atmosphere was so exciting that I knew I was hooked. I carried on going as often as I could, frequently dragging recalcitrant friends and frequently wishing I had let them stay at home. Later, through happy years working for English National Opera, I real-ized that there was a great deal more to an opera performance than singing; that opera at its best could be the most exhilarating form of theatrical entertainment. I also realized that people who are passionate about opera can frequently alienate those who have never been, simply by using the jargon and sounding so extremely knowledgeable. This book is an attempt to redress that balance, written in the firm belief that opera does not belong only to those people who know a great deal about it. It is open to everyone, and anyone who tries to pretend otherwise is doing a great art form a grave disservice.

Entries have been selected on the following criteria. Operas have been chosen if they appear regularly in the core repertories of major opera houses, particularly in Britain and America. The comments associated with them are in no way intended to prejudge the works but rather to prepare first time attenders for the operas they are about to see. Opera houses are listed under the city in which they are located. Singers who are no longer alive, or those who are retired, have been chosen because of their outstanding contributions to the world of opera. I have taken a time span of 150 years to cover these, and hope that anyone interested in singers before that date may choose to look them up in any of the excellent musical dictionaries available. Contemporary singers, directors and conductors (whose birthdates are not included because many agents are unwilling to release this information) have been chosen, in consultation with the managing directors of national opera companies in Britain, to include those who are already established performers and those in the early stages of their careers. Any omissions reflect in no way whatsoever on the talents of the performers in question, but rather on constraints of space. Opera houses and festivals are included to make a representa-tive selection of the enormous number of venues where opera is currently performed and where the reader of this book should be able to attend.

Throughout the book there are what I can only term the idiosyncratic entries. These do not fall easily into any pre-set category but are included simply because they add an intriguing insight into the world of opera. In many ways they en-capsulate the image of the book.

It is my sincere hope that anyone whose enthusiasm for opera may be fired by my book will further his or her knowledge by reading one of the excellent delinitive guides to opera. The *A to Z of Opera* is intended to take the first-time opera goer into an extraordinary and fascinating world through straightforward, non-technical lan-guage. It aims to do no more than light a spark which I hope the opera companies of the world will fan into a flame.

Acknowledgements

I am indebted to numerous sources for the facts contained in the text; in particular, *The Metropolitan Encyclopedia of Opera*, edited by David Hamilton, and *Kobbé's Complete Opera Book*, edited by Lord Harewood. I have also referred to *The Oxford Dictionary of Opera*, edited by the late Harold Rosenthal, *The Bloomsbury Dictionary of Opera and Operetta*, by James Anderson, *Opera Today*, by Meirion and Susie Harris, and books on the individual opera companies of Britain and America. The magazine *Opera Now* has provided many insights, and two tongue-in-cheek volumes, *How to Enjoy Opera*, edited by Melvyn Bragg, and *How to Enjoy Opera without Really Trying*, by John Cargher, raised several laughs.

David Rutherford, Fiona Graham and Samantha Goggin, from Martini and Rossi, have given me much encouragement; as have John Stidolph of Antler Books, and Sheila Dallas of Facts On File, whose enthusiasm and knowledgeable input have really set the parameters of the book. I am most indebted to Helen Greenwood, not only for her work on the biographies of contemporary artists, but for keeping me going when the writing seemed a little arduous.

The Managing Directors and staff of every opera company I contacted have been unfailingly helpful; and special mention must be made of Sarah Lenton and Jane Livingston (at ENO), and Katharine Wilkinson and Francesca Franchi (at the Royal Opera House), who have provided great assistance. The book would also be much the poorer were it not for the enthusiasm of Donald Cooper, whose exciting photographs create such an impact.

Friends and family have taken a tremendous interest which I have appreciated enormously. My greatest supporter has been my husband, Michael, to whom this book is dedicated. His constructive criticism and unfailing humour made researching and writing the book a very happy experience.

Mary Hamilton
Lyddington
July 1990

Abbreviations which appear regularly in the text

FP — First performance
ENO — English National Opera
Covent Garden — The Royal Opera House, Covent Garden, London
The Coliseum — The London Coliseum, home of ENO
WNO — Welsh National Opera
The Met — Metropolitan Opera, New York, USA
NYCO — New York City Opera, New York, USA
Kobbé — *Kobbé's Complete Opera Book*, published by Putnam and revised regularly
Prom — Promenade Concert, part of the series held in the Royal Albert Hall, London between July and September every year
The Ring — *Ring of the Nibelungen*, Wagner's epic opera cycle in four parts, also referred to as 'The Ring Cycle'

Picture credits

All the photographs in this book were taken by Donald Cooper, except for those on pages 102 and 182, which were supplied through the courtesy of English National Opera, and the one on page 150 by Alan Wood. The posters on p. 166/7 are from the author's collection. None of the illustrations may be reproduced without the permission of the copyright owner.

Abbado Claudio Italian conductor. Abbado is known for his ability to combine passionate and personal interpretation with precise musical attention to each score he conducts. He was Principal Conductor, rising to Music Director and finally Chief Conductor at La Scala, Milan, from 1968 to 1986, where he introduced many contemporary works whilst maintaining his reputation as a fine conductor of the classics, particularly Verdi and Rossini. On leaving Milan, he became Music Director of the Vienna State Opera, one of the most notoriously difficult positions to hold in the entire classical music world. He has conducted at most of the world's major opera houses and is well known to British audiences as Principal Conductor of the London Symphony Orchestra, a post he held from 1979 to 1988. In America, he was formerly Principal Guest Conductor of the Chicago Symphony Orchestra.

Abduction from the Seraglio (Mozart) FP 1782. Based on a popular eighteenth-century play known in Italian as *Il Seraglio*, the plot is set in Turkey.

Belmonte is looking for Constanze who has been captured by the Pasha, along with her English maid, Blonde, and Belmonte's manservant, Pedrillo. The Pasha loves Constanze, and his servant, Osmin, loves Blonde. Belmonte tries to get them all out, fails, but the Pasha lets them go anyway. The Pasha is a non-singing role played by an actor. Osmin gives a good comic singer the opportunity to make much of the role. The opera does not have the pace of *The Marriage of Figaro* and is vocally very challenging, keeping the number of superb productions of the work to a minimum.

Academy of Ancient Music The Academy was founded in 1726 in London, the first orchestra dedicated to the performance and study of vocal works and was for some time directed by Pepusch who wrote *The Beggar's Opera* with John Gay. The Academy lasted until 1792, but was revived in the early 1970s under the direction of Christopher Hogwood, and now specializes in playing on original instruments and is in worldwide demand both as a concert ensemble and baroque opera orchestra.

Acis and Galatea (Handel) FP 1731. The love of Acis for Galatea enrages the giant Polyphemus who kills Acis. Galatea uses her divine powers to make Acis immortal by turning him into a stream. The opera is written in the style of an Elizabethan masque and is therefore not full of action. It was designed as a private ensemble piece for the days when opera could be brought into your home. The work contains the well known aria 'O Ruddier than the Cherry'.

Acoustics One of the biggest complaints about opera is not being able to hear the words. While this is frequently the responsibility of the singers and the orchestra, the acoustics of the building are also vital for the audience to enjoy a balanced performance. It is also true that if you can see well, you feel that you can hear well too. Post war concert halls and theatre have had thousands of pounds spent on achieving the best acoustics – with mixed results. The Festival Hall on London's South Bank, for example, presents singers with a sloping wall of audience which absorbs the sound produced. It is therefore frequently criticized for almost total inaudibility in the auditorium; whereas the St David's Hall in Cardiff, Wales, is generally credited – by both musicians and audience – with being an excellent place in which to perform and to listen. Ironically, some of the best acoustics for music are to be found in the massive auditorium of the London Coliseum, built in 1904, years before technological advances had sought to help the basic instincts of the theatre architect. Here singers can 'float the voice', allowing the sound to reach right to the back wall and therefore conveying to the performers some impression of the sound their voices are making. The reasons for such variations are numerous and technical, depending chiefly on the size of the performance space in relation to the number of people in it, and the overall shape of the hall or theatre. The ideal way for sound to reach our ears is at a 90 degree angle, when it is not deflected by surfaces between the singer and the audience. But this can rarely be achieved when singers are constantly on the move around the stage and pieces of scenery may act as barriers to the best transmission of sound. Of the large auditoria, the Teatro Colon in Buenos Aires is thought to have the world's best acoustics. Of the smaller spaces, many believe that Derek Sugden's design for the Benjamin Britten Theatre at the Royal College of Music, London, can hardly be bettered.

Acting Sir Peter Hall, ex-Director of the National Theatre and producer of several productions at Glyndebourne, recently expressed his perception of a singer's ability to act in scathing terms: 'The public is quite content to see someone who is fifty-five, fat as a tank and can't act, provided they have a good voice'. That may be an unrepresentative view, certainly for the more adventurous audiences supporting the best ensemble repertory companies. If a singer, cannot act, however wonderfully he or she might sing, a sizeable amount of the enjoyment of the performance is lost. Naturally, if the notes are not conveyed with musicianship or skill, the performance can never be good, but it is the ability to act as well as to sing that sets some singers apart. It is ironic how many singers who are not in the least abashed at laying bare their emotions in music are inordinately shy about accompanying that music with suitable – and believable – actions. But the essence of all opera is to convey immense emotion not only through music but through action. Only recently has the importance of acting ability been recognized as an essential component in the great opera star; and music colleges and opera schools are now beginning to develop acting classes which are compulsory for all students. As more theatre directors move into the world of opera production, so acting skill will become more integral and essential, not only for the lead singers in a production, but for each member of the chorus. It is a skill which directors who have moved from theatre into opera are sometimes impatient about. The Glasgow Citizens Theatre Director, Philip Prowse, remarked with some cynicism, having worked on an opera production, that to say opera singers could now act was rubbish, all that had changed was that they were thinner! A notable example of a more tolerant attitude is the work of Nick Hytner, whose productions have ranged from classic drama at the Chichester Festival in England to several ENO productions, and mega-musicals such as *Miss Saigon*. Hytner takes infinite care to give detailed direction to each individual member of his cast, creating a sense of cohesion in his productions, where music and acting fuse together in one highly satisfying performance.

Adams, Donald English bass. Donald Adams was for many years chiefly known for his performances of Gilbert and Sullivan operettas. He was principal bass with the D'Oyly Carte Opera Company for fifteen years and co-founder of 'Gilbert and Sullivan for All.' He now also sings the 'serious' repertoire and made his debut at Covent Garden in *Boris Godunov* in 1983, followed by *A Midsummer Night's Dream* in 1984.

Adler, Kurt (1905–1988) Adler worked chiefly at San Francisco Opera from 1943 to 1982, rising from Chorus Master to Artistic Director to General Director. Just before the Second World War Adler went from Austria to America where he assisted Toscanini. He is noted for lengthening the San Francisco season from five weeks to ten and encouraging new works, young singers and adventurous stagings.

Administration Opera companies of whatever size are enormously complicated organizations. The cost and scale of opera dictates that even the smallest company will need one full time administrator who must be able to deal with accounts, publicity, venues, technical specifications and a myriad of other duties; plus an artistic leader who will be in charge of planning, casting and rehearsing. Many of the most successful small scale touring opera companies depend heavily on overworked, badly paid, superbly flexible staff who are able to turn their hands to anything, from profit and loss accounts to selling ice cream in the interval. Little wonder then that such administrators look at the staff involved in the largest companies and gasp at the apparent overmanning. Large opera companies have separate departments for finance, personnel, planning and casting, box office, front of house and catering (if the company is resident in one theatre), sponsorship, press, publicity and marketing, perhaps an in-house graphics office, technical, costumes, props, wigs, lighting, company management and dramaturgy. Current economic stringencies have forced big opera companies to pare down their administrative staff to the bare minimum. Subsequent analyses carried out by impartial management consultants have proved that, on the whole, such companies are now efficiently run with the smallest number of staff necessary. The major opera companies are presented with a dilemma when it comes to choosing an overall director who needs to control both the artistic and administrative policies of a company which can be capitalized at several million pounds or dollars. The two London based companies, English National Opera and the Royal Opera House, have chosen administrative managers (both termed General Director) to head their organizations, with artistic and musical directors taking senior and influential roles in the management structure. In Europe, many of the leading opera companies are led by artistic figures, such as Gotz Friedrich at the Deutsche Oper or Joachim Herz at the Komische Oper, both in Berlin. In America, both aspects are represented too. The Metropolitan Opera has a General Manager with a strong administrative background while the Pittsburgh Opera, for example, is led by an opera director of international stature. Whether an artist or an administrator is chosen to lead the overall organization, it is crucial that he or she maintains a close and active contact with both the artistic direction and the administrative control, if the organization as a whole is to succeed in a competitive and oversubscribed marketplace.

Adriana Lecouvreur (Cilea) FP 1849. The opera depends entirely on the soprano role and is often produced simply as a vehicle for the name part. The plot is based on the life of a real actress, who was the mistress of a man called Maurizio, whose jealous former mistress, Princess Boullion, sends Adriana poisoned violets. Thinking the flowers have come from Maurizio, Adriana assumes she has been rejected. She inhales the poison and, as Maurizio arrives to propose to her, she dies in his arms.

Adventures of Mr Broucek (Janacek) FP 1920. A literally 'fantastic' opera, it is almost impossible to believe it is composed by the same man who created *Katya Kabanova* or *Jenufa*. Although it is reasonably popular now, particularly for student productions, it has never been considered to be mainstream

repertory. You can approach the plot in one of two ways. On one level, it is a simple parable of a man who, fed up with the bickering of his young tenants in Prague, transports himself to the moon, has conversations with a moonbeam about the moonbeam's love life, becomes the object of adulation by the artists in the Temple of the Arts and eventually finds himself back in Prague where he started. He then travels back to fifteenth-century Prague, gets caught up in the religious/nationalist conflict of the Hussites, confronts the poet whose work inspired the opera, and is eventually imprisoned and shot, only to wake from his dream back in the inn where it all began. On a deeper level, fully described in *Kobbé's Complete Opera Book*, the work is placed in its context as a nationalistic opera, in which Janacek made powerful criticism of Czech society in the late nineteenth century. Even Kobbé is willing to describe the plot as 'sheer peculiarity' but the music is, in places, lyrical and extremely beautiful and the action, if nothing else, highly inventive!

Africaine, L' (Meyerbeer) FP 1865. Vasco da Gama, en route to undiscovered lands, gets shipwrecked off the African coast. There he finds Selika who falls in love with him, and Nelusko, who is in love with Selika. But Vasco is torn with regret for his former love, Inez, and, unable to bear the unrequited love, Selika commits suicide. Vasco is thus free to return to Inez. Once Nelusko hears that his beloved Selika is dead, he kills himself. The work contains the tenor aria, 'O Paradiso'. It is a gloomy story, but hugely popular in the nineteenth century, and full of exotic colour!

Agents The increasingly complex international world of opera is impossible for new singers to negotiate on their own. Prestigious opera managements may beckon with tempting roles, realistic rehearsal periods and promises of flexibility in performance, only to make a singer sign a contract which provides little money, little security and little promotion. So agents have evolved as intermediaries – shrewd business people with sound artistic backgrounds who can nurture the financial and musical fortunes of their clients. Anyone fresh out of college or training who hopes for a career in the business has to rely on the representation of their agent who will book dates, negotiate fees and rights and promote their singers in an oversubscribed market, leaving the singer free to concentrate on the musical side of the work. That, at least, is the theory. In practice there are terrifying stories of young singers falling into the hands of unscrupulous money makers who promise them the best exposure in return for a substantial percentage of the takings – but fail to deliver, leaving the singer no better known and considerably poorer. The best agents are not afraid to stop their clients from taking even highly paid roles which may damage their long-term career prospects by forcing their voices too early.

Aida (Verdi) FP 1871. Commissioned by the Khedive of Egypt for the new opera house at Cairo and the opening of the Suez Canal in 1869, *Aida* was not in fact performed in Egypt until 1871, two years after the opera house and the canal were officially opened. Verdi was paid 20,000 American dollars to compose this work which has had lavish sums of money poured into it ever since! It was a huge and instant success after opening night, went on to tumultuous applause at La Scala, Milan, conducted by the composer who received thirty-two curtain calls and a diamond encrusted baton for his pains!

Both Amneris, daughter of the King of Egypt, and Aida, her Ethiopian slave girl, are in love with Radames, the Egyptian commander sent to wage war against Aida's people. Aida is in fact an Ethiopian princess whose father Amonasro is captured by the Egyptians. Returning from a victorious campaign, Radames is told he can marry Amneris, although he is in love with Aida – and Amneris realizes this. Amonasro persuades Aida to get Radames to reveal secrets of the next Egyptian campaign against the Ethiopians. Unwittingly he does so, is overheard by Amneris and the High Priest Ramphis, and is sentenced to burial alive. As Radames prepares for death in his tomb Aida joins him.

The reason for the enduring popularity of *Aida* is the blend of the 'big numbers' – the triumphal march as the armies return, the exotic dance sequences, and the final burial – with the immense pathos and power of the

personal relationships, particularly that between a father and his daughter. One of few natural roles for a black soprano to perform, the opera explores the themes of exile and loneliness centring on Aida's torment, as the man she loves is set against her father.

Aix en Provence Festival One of the most superb settings for an opera festival of international repute is the beautiful Provencal town of Aix en Provence in Southern France. The Festival is held in high summer, usually late July, ensuring excellent weather for the outdoor performances in the Theatre de L'Archeveche, creating a wonderful ambience, as the city gives itself over to the enjoyment of music and merrymaking. This is a serious opera lovers' festival, with repertoire classics interspersed with lesser known works, all performed to the highest of standards to a well-heeled audience easily able to distinguish the good performance from the great. While it is difficult to obtain tickets 'on spec', it is worth visiting Aix during the Festival if only to enjoy the convivial atmosphere of the street cafés where activity continues well past the hour when the lights have dimmed on the stage.

Akhnaten (Philip Glass) FP 1984. Philip Glass wrote three 'portrait operas', one based on Einstein (*Einstein on the Beach*), one on Ghandi (*Satyagraha*) and this last on the Egyptian pharaoh Akhnaten, who abandons polygamy for love of Nefertiti and builds a city to the god Aten. Failing to produce a male heir and oblivious to the suffering of his people, Akhnaten is overthrown and the old order restored. Opinion is divided about Philip Glass's music, which is described as minimalist. Some find it repetitive, others relaxing, others tedious. There is certainly a great deal of pretentious talk about this 'new wave' of opera. *Akhnaten* sold out in both its British runs, at the London Coliseum in 1985 and 1987, as well as enjoying great success in Germany and at Houston Grand Opera. The opera attracts an enormous cross-section of society in the audience, with many coming because of the cult following Glass enjoys outside the opera house.

Albery, Tim English director whom many believe to be one of the most inventive and incisive talents currently working in British

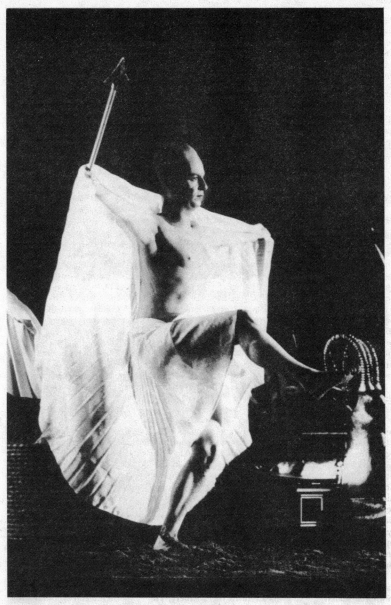

Akhnaten, by Philip Glass. Christopher Robson in the title role of ENO's London Coliseum production.

Albert Herring, by Benjamin Britten. John Graham Hall in the title role of Sir Peter Hall's 1985 Glyndebourne production.

Anna Bolena, by Donizetti. Dame Joan Sutherland and Suzanne Mentzer, at the Royal Opera House, Covent Garden.

theatre. His work is profoundly influenced by European theatre, and he has a particular admiration for the German director Peter Stein who, like Albery, has made an effective transition from directing plays to directing operas. Albery came to prominence with British opera audiences through his direction of *The Trojans* by Berlioz, a massive undertaking co-produced by three of Britain's opera companies. Shunning the histrionic acting styles which can so often accompany classic works, Albery created an intense drama where the individual characters came out strongly, albeit in a vast historical context. His production of *Billy Budd* for ENO was similar, as the scale of the set was matched by the power of the performances. Albery can adapt his style from the grand to the intimate, for example his oppressive *Mary Stuart* for the Greenwich Festival, by encouraging a sensitive intelligence from his performers, backed up by his own expansive imagination.

Albert Herring (Britten) FP 1947. An innocent grocer's boy Albert Herring, becomes the unwilling King of the May for the village of Loxton as there are no girls pure enough to be eligible for the prize. At the May Day celebrations, the worldlywise Sid, abetted by his girlfriend Nancy, laces Albert's drinks and the virtuous King becomes hopelessly drunk and disappears for the whole night to find out what he has been missing. Convinced he has died, the village unites to mourn him but he re-appears, hinting of nocturnal activities through which he has clearly lost his innocence.

Alboni, Marietta (1823–1894) Italian contralto. Leading lady for Rossini at whose funeral she sang, Alboni rivalled Jenny Lind for popularity in London, her salary reaching £2,000 pa. The late Harold Rosenthal, editor of *Opera* magazine for over twenty years, cites her in his *Oxford Dictionary of Opera* as, 'One of the greatest contraltos in operatic history'.

Alceste (Gluck) FP 1767. This opera is important chiefly for the preface written to the work propounding Gluck's ideas on operatic reform: that opera should be a music drama and not merely an elegant costumed concert. This theory was to have a profound influence on composers for centuries to come and is still hotly debated in the context of controversial new opera productions today.

Alceste offers to take the place of her husband Admere, King of Thessaly, who has been condemned to die by the Delphic Oracle. He is spared but cannot accept his wife's sacrifice and joins her at the gateway to hell. Admere's place is taken by Hercules who is raised to the status of a god because of his devotion to his king. Admere and Alceste are spared, thanks to their perfect love for each other.

Alcina (Handel) FP 1735. The opera is set on an island ruled by the sorceress Alcina who transforms her suitors into strange beasts. One such cursed suitor is Ruggiero who has abandoned his former love, Bradamante, for Alcina. Determined to win him back, Bradamante, with her guardian Melisso, sets off to find him, only to get caught in a web of confused identities and altered shapes! All comes out well as Alcina loses her magic powers and her suitors are restored to human form.

Alda, Frances (1883–1952) New Zealand soprano. Superb international soprano who sang in the Met's opening season in 1908 and married the Met's first manager, Gatti-Casazza. She sang twenty-one Met seasons, became famous for her fiery temperament and predilection to law suits, detailed in her autobiography with the telling title *Men, Women and Tenors*!

Aldeburgh The Aldeburgh Festival was started by Benjamin Britten in 1947 to bring professionals together with amateurs in a celebration of music making. At that time the only 'venue' in Aldeburgh was the Jubilee Hall which seats just 300 people. So close was it to the centre of the village that when a flare was sounded as part of a performance of *Peter Grimes*, the entire Aldeburgh lifeboat crew mustered on the beach thinking they were called to an emergency at sea! By 1967, the Festival had earned its reputation by premiering, amongst other works, *Let's Make an Opera, Noye's Fludde, A Midsummer Night's Dream* and the three Church Parables, all written by Benjamin Britten. The old malting house at the nearby hamlet of Snape was then converted into a superb concert hall, inspiring Britten's overture 'The Building of the House'. The luxury of a dedicated concert hall, not designed to be an opera house but adaptable for opera performances, was short lived. A devastating fire on the first night of the 1969 Festival reduced Ove Arup's original design to four, roofless walls. But within a year the building had been replaced – a measure of the strength of emotion felt by the public towards Britten's unique initiative. Now the building houses the opera festival in the autumn and the summer music festival, both overseen by Mstislav Rostro-povich who took over as Artistic Director of the festivals after Britten's death in 1976.

Allami Operahaz (see Budapest)

Allen, Thomas English baritone who graduated from the Royal College of Music and Glyndebourne Chorus, Tom Allen made his professional debut with Welsh National Opera in 1969 as Figaro in Rossini's *Barber of Seville* and now, over twenty years later, has won international acclaim not only for his wonderful voice but superbly sensitive acting ability and powerful stage presence. Accolades have ranged from descriptions as perhaps the best British baritone of all time and a CBE in the 1989 New Year's Honours List, to the general consensus from all who know and work with him that he is a very nice man. His notable roles include the title parts in *Eugene Onegin*, *Don Giovanni* and *Billy Budd* – all men of complex and romantic characters to which Allen brings insight and variety, never allowing two interpretations to be the same. Riccardo Muti described Allen's Don Giovanni in La Scala, Milan, in 1987 as 'probably one of the most interesting and subtle in the theatre today'. Such sensitivity is mirrored in Allen's life outside the opera house, where his commitment to the environment has prompted him to give sold out recitals at the Wigmore Hall in London, to benefit Friends of the Earth.

Alto A singer who can comfortably sing between the F below middle C and the A above the treble clef. In men, this is usually achieved by a bass singing falsetto, in women it is usually referred to as contralto.

Alva, Luigi Peruvian tenor who began his career singing 'zarauela' or gypsy songs. The enthusiasm needed for such performances has never left Alva who now enjoys an international career, bringing fire and energy to the roles he plays. He specializes in the romantic repertory of the eighteenth and early nineteenth centuries, such as Lindoro in Rossini's opera *L'Italiana in Alghieri*. He founded the National Opera Company of Peru in 1981, and remains their Artistic Director and Producer.

Amahl and the Night Visitors (Menotti) FP 1951. The first opera ever written specially for television, to a commission by NBC in America, this opera has remained a Christmas favourite, particularly for school performances.

The little cripple boy Amahl and his mother are visited in their poverty by the Wise Men on their way to the stable in Bethlehem. The mother cannot resist stealing some of their gold during the night and, when challenged, explains that it is for Amahl. The Wise Men allow her to keep the riches, believing that Christ will build his kingdom on love not wealth. When Amahl offers his crutch as a gift for the Wise Men to take to the Christ child, he realizes he has been cured and can join the Wise Men on their journey.

Amico Fritz, L' (Mascagni) FP 1891. Charming, very light piece about a confirmed bachelor, Fritz, who bets his friend Rabbi David he will never give up his bachelor life. Naturally, he immediately falls for the lovely Suzel but is too proud to let on. David hastens the romance by telling Fritz he has found a husband for Suzel. Fritz leaves town and Suzel is distraught. She appeals to Fritz to save her from the arranged marriage, giving him the ideal opportunity to declare his love but lose his bet.

Amore dei Tre Re, L' (Montemezzi) FP 1913. Intense political drama with shades of Shakespeare's *Romeo and Juliet*. The beautiful princess Fiora has been forced to abandon her beloved Avito and marry Manfredo, son of King Archibaldo. Fiora and Avito continue to meet in secret until they are discovered by King Archibaldo who tortures Fiora to reveal her lover's name. Rather than do so, she is strangled by her father-in-law who then poisons her lips, sensing that her lover will return to claim her. Avito finds Fiora dead, kisses her passionately and is poisoned as Archibaldo intended. Manfredo also discovers his dead wife and, rather than live without her, kisses her and dies. As the curtain falls, Archibaldo discovers that he has killed not only his intended victim but his own son as well.

Anderson, Marion American contralto. While the majority of her work has been on the concert platform, she is notable for being the first black singer to perform at the Metropolitan Opera in New York, thanks to the endeavours of the then Manager, Rudolf Bing. She played Ulrica in *A Masked Ball* by Verdi in 1955. Sadly, the unenlightened attitudes of many other opera houses prevented Anderson from using her extensive talents, and a voice which Toscanini described as coming 'once in a hundred years', more fully on the opera stage.

Andrea Chenier (Giordano) FP 1896. Hardly subtle but certainly exciting, the opera is set in the heart of Revolutionary France. Chenier, a poet, is loved by the wealthy Maddalena who in turn is loved by the servant Gerard. As the opera opens, before the Revolution, Chenier and Maddalena seem certain to enjoy their love together. But as the years pass, Gerard assumes a senior role in a post-Revolution tribunal and sentences Chenier to the guillotine. Attempting to save him, Maddalena offers herself to Gerard but he refuses her. She bribes the jailer to allow her to change with a female prisoner and joins Chenier to face the guillotine together.

Angel, Marie Australian soprano who is currently a leading member of the pioneering group Opera Factory, based in London and Zurich. Marie Angel has sung many of the major soprano roles, usually in experimental new productions which have called on her extensive acting ability as well as her powerful voice and striking stage presence. She sang Queen Tye in the British premiere of *Akhnaten* by Philip Glass for English National Opera. Further contemporary work includes Michael Tippett's latest opera *New Year* for Glyndebourne Touring Opera, and *Gawain* a new commissioned work by Harrison Birtwistle for the Royal Opera House, Covent Garden.

Anna Bolena (Donizetti) FP 1830. Donizetti's first major 'hit' in Italy. Basically the story of Henry VIII and Anne Boleyn with an Italian slant. Henrico is Henry, Giovanna is Jane (Seymour) and Riccardo is Richard (Percy). In order to further his romance with Giovanna, Henrico brings back Anna's former love Riccardo from exile, to keep Anna company. So strongly does Riccardo feel on seeing Anna again that he threatens to kill himself and although Smeton the page prevents this, all three are arrested and imprisoned. Anna learns to forgive her rival and goes to the scaffold pardoning the royal couple. The final aria and cabaletta is wonderfully dramatic.

Antefatto/Argomento An operatic device which can frequently confuse the new opera goer. Some very important parts of the plot will have happened prior to the action on stage. This information is either contained in a narration, as in *Il Trovatore*, or in a preface which should be made clear in the performance programme.

Arabella (Richard Strauss) FP 1933. An opera frequently set in the most lavish surroundings but with a very confusing plot! The impoverished Count Waldner has two daughters, Arabella and Zdenka but because of the cost of bringing a girl out into Viennese society, Zdenka has been brought up as a boy. Anxious that Arabella should make a good marriage, Waldner introduces her to the wealthy Mandryka and the couple immediately fall in love. At a lavish ball to bid farewell to her former suitors, Arabella spurns her former love Matteo, whom Zdenka has always secretly loved. Jealous of her sister's success, Zdenka peevishly offers Matteo a rendezvous with Arabella and passes him a key – only to see Mandryka throw a tantrum having overheard the whole interchange! Accusing Arabella of infidelity, Mandryka flirts outrageously with Fiakermilli, the ball mascot. Unable to hide her deceit any longer, Zdenka comes clean and Matteo accepts her anyway! If the story gets too much, just enjoy the music and the settings.

Archers, The (Benjamin Carr) FP 1796. This opera is based on the story of William Tell and was the first opera ever written by an American composer.

Argenta, Nancy Canadian soprano who now lives in England, Nancy Argenta has an international career which began as soon as she completed her studies with such notable teachers as Sir Peter Pears and Gerard Souzay. She excels in the earlier opera repertoire of composers such as Handel, Purcell and Rameau and is a frequent concert performer with groups such as the Monteverdi Choir and Academy of Ancient Music. She has made several recordings, including one of *Tamerlano* by Handel.

Aria A piece of music sung by one singer, the words of which do little to further the plot of an opera but are used to heighten one particular moment in the overall work. Highly descriptive, arias can be subdivided into many forms, describing the music as 'agitata', 'infuriata', 'cantabile' (gentle and sad). The arias are often used as a showcase for the singer as in Tosca's 'Vissi D'Arte', Leporello's Catalogue Aria from *Don Giovanni* or the Duke's 'La Donna è Mobile' from *Rigoletto*.

Arietta Shorter, frequently less dramatic version of an aria, often given to smaller roles particularly those of servants.

Ariadne auf Naxos (Richard Strauss) FP 1912. Originally designed to be performed after Molière's comedy-ballet *Le Bourgeois Gentilhomme* for which Strauss had written the incidental music, the opera was soon performed on its own rather than incur the cost of a theatrical and operatic troupe. The work is set in the 'house of a great gentleman' and opens with a prologue. The entertainers brought together by the great gentleman are concerned at the news that they will have to perform together rather than individually, in order to be finished by the time of the fireworks display. Thus the composer and principal singers of the opera vie for supremacy with the cunning of the clowns, led by Zerbinetta; an uneasy truce reigns as they all join together to perform 'Ariadne', the opera which forms the second part of the work. The opera is set on the deserted island of Naxos where, thanks to the efforts of Zerbinetta and the clowns, Ariadne (the prima donna of the prologue) overcomes her loss of Theseus and joins with Bacchus (the tenor

of the prologue) to rise to a new life in heaven.

Arlesiana, L' (Cilea) FP 1897. Federico is determined to marry a girl from Arles (l'Arlesiana) but his mother shows him letters proving that the girl has a lover, Metifio He reluctantly agrees to marry his mother's goddaughter, Vivetta, but overcome by jealous rage at the sight of Metifio, he kills himself on the night of the wedding. The opera's best known section is Federico's haunting aria.

Armide (Gluck) FP 1777. The sorceress Armide is one of Gluck's greatest characterizations, as well as being the subject of about forty other operas. She intends to slay Renaud, general of the Crusaders, but comes to love him. Ultimately, he is rescued from her supernatural powers by the intervention of other knights.

Arnold, David American baritone who has appeared extensively in America, particularly at the Metropolitan Opera, New York City Opera and San Francisco Opera. An energetic young singer, Arnold has made confident performances of new works including *A Winter's Tale* by John Harbison. He has performed with many European opera festivals and made his UK debut as Escamillo in *Carmen* for English National Opera in 1986.

Armstrong, Richard Richard Armstrong graduated from Cambridge University and progressed via the music staff at Covent Garden to an assistant conductor's role at Welsh National Opera in 1968. He assumed WNO's Musical Directorship in 1973 and remained there until 1986. He is credited with much of the prestige the company currently enjoys, particularly for his Verdi interpretations and his Janacek performances, for which he won the coveted Janacek Medal in 1979.

Arts Council of Great Britain The principal funding body for all British arts organizations, the Council was set up in 1945 to 'foster the practice, understanding and enjoyment of the arts in Great Britain'. The Council receives an annual grant from the Treasury which varies in size depending on the pressure exerted on behalf of the arts lobby by the Minister for the Arts. Every recipient organization then makes an application and may be awarded a grant based on an individual assessment made by the twenty Council members. The Royal Opera House currently receives approximately £12 million each year and English National Opera approximately £6.5 million – by far the biggest single grants given to any arts organization and therefore the subject of constant debate. The Council makes other awards through the Incentive Funding Scheme and numerous training bursaries, as well as overseeing the work of the Welsh and Scottish Arts Councils and the Regional Arts Associations.

Arundel, Dennis (1898–1988) English opera producer and translator who worked for Sadler's Wells Opera, producing performances of *Tosca* and *Katya Kabanova* and writing the definitive history of Sadler's Wells.

Atherton, David British conductor who was Resident Conductor for the Royal Opera House, Covent Garden, for twelve years whilst maintaining an active international career, performing regularly with the Metropolitan Opera, New York, San Francisco Opera, San Diego Symphony Orchestra and La Scala, Milan. In 1967, he co-founded the London Sinfonietta, created to perform contemporary works and now the regular orchestra for Opera Factory. The orchestra has an excellent international reputation for adventurous programming, superbly performed, and won the 1982 International Record Critics' Award for Atherton's performance of *King Priam* by Michael Tippett.

Atonal (see Stockhausen)

Auber, Daniel (1782–1871) French composer and Director of Paris Conservatoire from 1842 to 1871. While much of Auber's work is no longer performed, he is generally credited with initiating a French grand opera style, characterized by fine harmonies, great dramatic colour and powerful orchestral writing – themes which were taken up by Rossini and later Wagner who greatly admired Auber's work. His most notable opera

La Muette de Portici sparked off the Belgian revolt against the Dutch when it was premiered in Brussels in 1830. His epitaph is fittingly written by Rossini – 'A small musician but a great music maker'.

Audience Opera has an image of a particularly forbidding clientele – all highly knowledgeable, ready to curse at an innocent remark or action by someone who 'doesn't know the form'. Many opera goers have preserved this illusion of a clique, unwilling to break ranks and admit a newcomer who might dilute the elegance of the experience. Thankfully, however, opera companies have realized recently that they must pitch for that new audience for whom dress and behaviour is less important than the action on stage. Slowly the traditional audience is beginning to accommodate the new opera lovers.

Such 'rules' as apply to an opera audience will be readily observed by any music lover whether it be their first or fiftieth attendance – to arrive on time, not to talk through the overture, not to miss the start of an act and so on. The audience is the most vital component of any operatic production and has been known to condemn several premieres of works that are currently in the standard repertoire, including *The Barber of Seville*, *Norma*, *Traviata* and *Tannhauser* and to react with such ecstasy to others that they could hardly fail to succeed – *Aida* being a notable example. Reactions to some new productions at English National Opera have been loud and frequently critical. *Rusalka*, now accepted as a popular repertory piece, was booed throughout the house on the first night in 1983. *Mazeppa*, complete with chainsaws and decapitation, received an even more angry reaction as patrons stormed out, one hurling his programme across the foyer in fury. But such reactions keep opera a lively, changing force, provoking discussion throughout the audience and creating that 'buzz' around a theatre which separates the extraordinary production from the mundane.

Audition Nancy Gustafson estimates that a singer may have to undergo fifty auditions to secure perhaps three roles – 'if you're very lucky!' The auditioning process is necessary, but traumatic, which every opera singer has to face, promoting themselves in a competitive world where supply far outstrips demand. Peter Katona, Artistic Director of the Royal Opera House, estimates he will accept perhaps ten per cent of the 200 singers he may hear in a year. Judgments will be made not solely on the quality of voice but on temperament and presentation (both in person and on paper). The most wonderful voice in the world will be of limited value if its owner is unable (or unwilling) to take direction or get on with the rest of the cast. In his *The Art of Auditioning* (Rheingold Publishing, 1988), Anthony Legge's philosophical attitude ('it's luck that you have the right goods at the right time') must be small comfort to a young singer before the first round of auditions for the major companies, who hold on average three hundred auditions a year. Auditionees may find themselves singing before an illustrious panel in some draughty rehearsal hall before being allowed to step on to the hallowed stage at Covent Garden or the New York City Opera. An invitation for a singing audition may have come about as a result of an impressive letter of application, an excellent review in a respected paper or through a personal contact. End of year performances at the music colleges are also prime sources for talent spotting.

For new auditionees, Steuart Bedford, Artistic Director of the Aldeburgh Festival, wisely suggests that certain pieces can curse an audition almost before the first note is sung. Dido's Lament from Purcell's *Dido and Aeneas* is one such, as is 'Glitter and be Gay' from Berstein's *Candide*, 'Una Voce Poco Fa' from *The Barber of Seville* and anything by Menotti or Philip Glass. These are works that seem so impressive at a first glance but are in fact fiendishly difficult to make memorable in so short a time – and are best left to the established professionals. And from one such professional, Helen Field, comes another piece of advice – take your own accompanist as soon as you can afford to. At her first professional audition (for Scottish Opera), she was unable to sing a note because the resident accompanist refused to play from her photocopied score of *Der Rosenkavalier*.

Auger, Arleen American soprano who has made a speciality of the Mozart repertoire, performing almost more in Europe than in her home country. She is a particularly commanding Queen of the Night in *The Magic Flute* by Mozart, but covered an extensive repertoire as a member of the Vienna State Opera from 1967 to 1974. Now in international demand as a principal singer, she was chosen to sing one of the Mozart anthems for the wedding of the Duke and Duchess of York in London in 1986.

Bailey, Norman English bass-baritone, and one of the most respected and admired singers on the contemporary opera circuit. Bailey is known for his Wagner performances, particularly Hans Sachs in *The Mastersingers*, and for Wotan in the Ring Cycle, and has performed roles as diverse as the Forester in Janacek's *Cunning Little Vixen* and the Father in *Hansel and Gretel* by Humperdinck. He has achieved a considerable international reputation with acclaimed performances in all the major European opera houses and in New York and Chicago. Bailey's stage presence is as powerful and affecting as his magnificent voice, bringing dignity and sincerity to every role he plays.

Baker, Dame Janet English mezzo soprano. Her great dramatic intensity was suited particularly to Monteverdi operas but her versatility has enabled her to play comic roles with equal success. The sensitivity she brought to the characters of Orfeo (Gluck), Mary Stuart (Donizetti) and Dido (Purcell) has become legendary. These same qualities are evident in her numerous concert appearances. She retired from opera in 1982 and her autobiography *Full Circle* was published by Penguin in the same year. In the autumn of 1989, it was announced that Dame Janet had retired from all forms of public performance.

Balachine, Georges (1904–1983) Internationally renowned French choreographer who worked principally in America. His work for the Metropolitan Opera contributed enormously to the vitality of performances. While Director of New York City Ballet, he turned his hand to opera production, directing *Orfeo*, *The Golden Cockerel* and *The Rake's Progress*.

Ballad of Baby Doe, The (Moore) FP 1956. This opera uses the cultural traditions of the

America of the late nineteenth century, the era of the Colorado Gold Rush, to create a work which has increased in popularity in its country of origin but has yet to make an impact in Europe.

Elizabeth Doe, known as 'Baby' has abandoned her husband and followed a wealthy older man, Horace Tabor, to Colorado hoping to make her fortune from the new money there. Horace divorces his wife and marries Baby Doe, but she finds herself spurned by Colorado society. Horace's ex-wife Augusta warns him that he faces ruin as the price of silver is about to collapse. He ignores her but she is proved right and Horace dies a penniless man. Baby Doe retreats to the Matchless Mine which belonged to her husband to live out the rest of her life in solitude.

Ballad opera A style of opera prevalent in the eighteenth century where extensive spoken dialogue was included and words were sung to the music of popular songs. Frequently irreverent and satirical, the best known example is John Gay's *The Beggar's Opera*. Though the form threatened to eclipse classical opera for popularity in the eighteenth century, it has never been revived and only two notable twentieth-century ballad operas exist, Vaughan Williams' *Hugh the Drover* and Weill's *Threepenny Opera* which is a deliberate imitation of *The Beggar's Opera*.

Ballet Ballet was integral to forms of entertainment such as masques from which opera evolved and therefore many early operas have ballets written into them. It was primarily a French tradition, where ballets were often written at the start of the second act, totally irrelevant to the plot of the opera but serving the useful social purpose of allowing patrons who dined during the interval to arrive late. This rigid tradition was observed cunningly by Wagner in the French premiere of *Tannhauser* in 1861. Wagner included a ballet to placate French audiences only to infuriate them again by placing it at the start of the opera, and therefore the second act had no place to accommodate late-comers. Towards the end of the nineteenth century, Wagner, Verdi and Borodin were all including dance in their operas, (*Parsifal*, *Aida*, and *Prince Igor* for example) to complement rather than oppose the dramatic action. Nearly all Tschaikovsky's operas include some opportunity to dance. In modern times, dance has become central to many plots eg *Salome* by Richard Strauss, *Gloriana* by Benjamin Britten and *A Midsummer Marriage* by Michael Tippett.

Ballo in Maschera, Un (Verdi) FP 1859. The plot of this opera is based loosely on the assassination of King Gustavus III of Sweden at a masked ball, but Verdi was forced to change the setting of the opera from Sweden to Boston. He was forbidden by Italian censors to show an assassination which was still fresh in the minds of the crowned heads of Europe. By moving the setting to the New World, Verdi could still make the victim a nobleman without having any direct reference to politically sensitive matters. When the opera was premiered in Paris two years later, it was set in Naples, and for every setting, the characters take different names! With the passage of time, Verdi's original version has come back into favour and is now more commonly performed than the 'Boston' version. The 'Naples' version is rarely staged. Directors since the Second World War have developed the theme that Gustavus III was a homosexual who engineered his own downfall. The plot is fiendishly complicated but the music is so wonderful it is quite possible to ignore the plot and still enjoy every minute! 'Boston' characters are in brackets.

Gustavus III (Riccardo) is warned by a fortune teller Madam Arvidson (Ulrica) that he will die at the hand of a friend. That friend proves to be Ankarstroem (Renato), his close ally and advisor. Ankarstroem's wife, Amelia, and Gustavus III are in love and Ankarstroem suspects his wife's infidelity. He conspires to assassinate his king at a masked ball at the palace. As Gustavus dies, fulfilling Ulrica's curse, he swears Amelia's innocence and forgives Ankarstroem.

Baltsa, Agnes Greek mezzo soprano who is now in international demand due to her exciting voice and wonderful stage presence. Baltsa worked as a member of the companies in Frankfurt, Deutsche Oper, Berlin, and Vienna State Opera until 1976 when she left to concentrate on her solo career. She has since performed in major opera houses, creating sultry and fascinating interpretations of leading soprano roles, including Carmen, and Delilah in Saint Saens' opera *Samson and Delilah*.

Barber, Samuel (1910–1981) Prominent American composer, noted for his operas *Vanessa* and *Antony and Cleopatra*. Hardly dramatic and very romantic, Barber's work is now coming into the standard American operatic repertoire.

Barber of Baghdad (Cornelius) FP 1858. Written by an adherent of Wagner, this opera is totally un-Wagnerian in style. Set in Persia, Hassan acts as barber for Nureddin to prepare him for his secret assignation with his beloved Margiana. Abdul nearly lets his charge miss the important rendezvous and then proposes to accompany him, much to Nureddin's horror. But when Nureddin is forced to hide in a chest, having been discovered with Margiana, it is Abdul's cunning that gets him out and, naturally, the marriage of Nureddin and Margiana follows with everyone's blessing.

Barber of Seville, The (Rossini) FP 1816. Thought by many to be one of the all time greats of the classic opera repertoire, the enjoyment of a 'Barber' performance depends enormously on the production and on the singers playing Rosina and Figaro. At its slickest, it is highly amusing, fast paced and very attractive. Miss the mark and it can seem unbearably facile and dull. Rossini based this work on a play by Beaumarchais which was further developed by Lorenzo da Ponte, to create the libretto for *The Marriage of Figaro* by Mozart.

The beautiful Rosina is jealously overseen by her guardian, Dr Bartolo, and is thus unattainable to her would be suitor, Count Almaviva. The Count enlists the help of the local barber, Figaro, who dresses the Count first as a drunken soldier and then as an assistant to Rosina's music teacher, Don Basilio, in an attempt to be admitted to Rosina's room. With Figaro's help, the couple manage to evade Dr Bartolo's care and elope together. The story of Figaro's wedding to the maidservant Susannah is taken up by Mozart in *The Marriage of Figaro*. The overture will be familiar and Figaro has the other big tune in the opera, the fast paced aria 'Largo al Factotum'.

Barcelona – El Gran Teatro Liceo One of the earliest corporate membership schemes paid for the building of Barcelona's 3,500 seat theatre as 1,000 shareholders stumped up the not-inconsiderable sums to pay for a second opera house in Barcelona – the Santa Cruz Theatre was already staging operas with reasonable success and popularity. In true Latin tradition, rivalry flourished between the two houses, the Liceo being gutted by fire in 1861 to the delight of the Santa Cruz Theatre, only to be rebuilt within a year thanks to the generosity of her shareholders. Their descendants still hold exclusive rights to a large number of the Liceo seats and have enjoyed glittering social occasions as well as superb opera over the years. The house is permanently associated with the work of Victoria de Los Angeles who made her stunning debut there in 1945.

Barenboim, Daniel Israeli conductor who first achieved international acclaim as a pianist. From the mid 1960s he started to devote more time to conducting, making his London conducting debut in 1967. He first conducted opera at the 1972 Edinburgh Festival and since 1978 has been in charge of several new productions at the Deutsche Oper, Berlin. He has appeared regularly in Bayreuth since 1981. His other opera performances have tended to be concentrated in Paris where he created the Mozart Festival, conducting *Don Giovanni*, in 1982 and 1985, *Cosi fan Tutti* in 1983 and *The Marriage of Figaro* in 1984. He was Music Director of the planned Bastille Opera in Paris until his resignation in extremely bitter circumstances in January 1988. Barenboim was married to the brilliant cellist Jaqueline du Pré until her death from multiple sclerosis.

Baritone Range of voice between tenor and bass, at its best a velvety tone of great beauty. For a singer who can sing comfortably between the G below the bass clef to the F above middle C. In Germany, the range is further subdivided, hoherbariton, heldenbariton and the commonly used bass-bariton for roles such as Don Giovanni and Hans Sachs.

Baroque Description of the style of music prevalent between 1600 and 1750, characterized by Bach and Handel. Baroque operas developed the aria, as opposed to the recitative, and encompass a more elaborate musical style with complex harmonies and contrasting styles. In the eighteenth century, the term became pejorative, meaning old fashioned or coarse.

Barstow, Josephine English soprano who has pioneered the importance of sensitive acting in operatic roles as well as a masterly singing voice. After early work with Sadler's Wells and Welsh National Opera, she became in international demand but returns regularly to ENO where her best roles include Emilia Marty (*Makropulos Case*), Salome, and Lady Macbeth of Mtsensk, as well as many of the dominating, tortured heroines of Verdi's operas. Her voice is unusual but commanding and her stage presence contributes dramatically to the success of many of the roles she plays. She has an extensive international career, performing in Miami, Chicago, San Francisco, and in 1986 sang Tosca with the Bolshoi Opera in Moscow. She played Amelia in the new production of *A Masked Ball* at the 1989 Salzburg Festival. Away from opera, her passion is horses and she keeps a fine selection on her country farm in southern England.

Bartered Bride, The (Smetana) FP 1866. Light pastoral opera, often set in a colourful staging with much dancing and peasant antics – including a full scale circus! Opening with a well known overture, the work characterizes the nationalism in late nineteenth-century East European opera.

The peasant girl Marenka was long ago promised to the simple Vasek, son of Tobias Misha, in payment of a debt agreement between the two families. She is in love with someone else, Jenik, disguises herself to go to Vasek and, through outrageous flirting, persuades him to sign an oath rejecting his future wife. Jenik has meanwhile been persuaded by Kecal, the marriage broker, to accept a bribe of 300 gilder if he will let Marenka go to marry Vasek. Jenik agrees to reject his love, safe in the knowledge that he is in fact Misha's long lost son from a former marriage – he can thus claim his bride, pay off the family debt and get his 300 gilder back, and only the hapless Vasek comes off the loser.

Bartok, Bela (1881–1945) Hungarian composer whose later compositions are fiercely dissonant and challenging. But his only opera *Duke Bluebeard's Castle* is more rhythmical and tuneful, written when he was influenced by Strauss and Debussy.

Bass Range of singing for the lowest male voice, frequently subdivided in some European countries with Slavonic basses able to reach the lowest notes. The bass range sits comfortably between the F below the bass clef to the E above middle C.

Bassarids, The (Henze) FP 1966. While this is a fine example of a twentieth-century, one-act opera, a new opera goer should not be lulled by its brevity into thinking it might be a good one to start off with. It is written as a four movement symphony and deals with themes, rather than action, based loosely on Euripides' play *The Bacchae*. The action is connected by interludes sung by the chorus taking the role of Bassarids, or Bacchae, who are followers of the cult of Dionysus.

Semele, daughter of Cadmus, founder of the city of Thebes, has died, but her unborn child Dionysus has been rescued. Debate rages as to whether Dionysus' father was the god Zeus, making Dionysus a god, or simply a mortal man. Cadmus has abdicated his throne in favour of his grandson Pentheus. In Pentheus' first proclamation as leader, he denounces any idea that Dionysus could be the offspring of a god, thus hoping to crush the cult of Dionysus-worship that has developed among the people. The people will not accept this verdict, particularly when the ethereal voice of Dionysus is heard, and Cadmus, sensing rebellion, tries to re-assert his authority over his grandson. But Pentheus rejects his elders, imposes martial law and arrests many key subjects. These include his mother Agave, his aunt Autonoe, the old prophet Tiresias and a mysterious young stranger. All but the stranger give individual accounts of their allegiance to Dionysus and Pentheus realizes that, rather than managing to supress the cult, it has grown beyond his control. Only the advice of the stranger seems to offer him any comfort. In a strange intermezzo, the Theban characters play out a scene from mythology involving the gods Mars, Pluto, Jove, Venus and Prosperine. The stranger persuades Pentheus to dress as a woman if he is to evade punishment at Mount Cythaeron, centre of the Dionysus cult. Only Semele's old nurse, Beroe, has deduced that the stranger is in fact Dionysus and is leading Pentheus to certain death. Pentheus meets with a gruesome death, rejected even by his own mother Agave. When Cadmus finally persuades her of the awful deed she has just committed, she yearns for death but at that moment Dionysus re-appears and banishes all the mortal rulers of Thebes. The palace is set aflame and Dionysus has achieved the revenge he sought for his mother's death.

Bastille, Opera de la (see Paris)

Battle, Kathleen America soprano who has been a regular feature of the New York City Opera since her debut there in 1978. She brings charm and humour to many of the lighter roles such as Susannah in *The Marriage of Figaro*, but also shows greater depth in more serious pieces. Her European performances are becoming more frequent, both in opera and in concert appearances.

Battle of Legnano (Verdi) FP 1849. Verdi wrote this opera shortly before the declaration of the Roman Republic and its nationalistic themes brought the audience together in demonstrations against the current political regime. It does not have the imagination of *Rigoletto* or *Macbeth* and is now rarely performed.

It is set in twelfth-century Italy, when Frederic Barbarossa was threatening to invade Milan. While Arrigo has been at war, his loved one Lida has married Rolando. Distraught at the news, Arrigo vows to die in defending Milan. Lida tries to dissuade him and the two are discovered by Rolando who suspects infidelity. Arrigo returns to the war and kills the mighty Barbarossa, only to be mortally wounded himself. He dies protesting Lida's innocence to Rolando.

Bayley, Clive English bass, who came to national attention whilst still a student, for his portrayal of John Claggart in *Billy Budd*. As a result of this success he made his professional debut. He has a strong stage presence and dramatic ability and has gone straight in at the deep end of the repertoire,

tackling such roles as Schwarz (*The Mastersingers*), Banquo (*Macbeth*) and Pietro (*Simon Boccanegra*). So far he has shown much promise and ability, both vocally and dramatically.

Baylis, Lilian (1874–1937) An extraordinary character of enormous drive and principle whose legacy lives on through four of Britain's leading arts organizations, the Old Vic Theatre, Sadler's Wells Royal Ballet, the National Theatre and English National Opera. She took over the running of the Old Vic Theatre in 1898, pursuing her principle of the best arts for the greatest number at the lowest prices. With Ninette de Valois she opened Sadler's Wells Theatre to be 'the Old Vic of North London' in 1925, providing her with a better auditorium for opera and a chance to engage a full time opera company to work between the two theatres. It was Baylis who first introduced the idea of opera in English, received at first with scepticism but soon accepted as a superb means of reaching the widest possible audience – a policy still strongly adhered to by English National Opera which developed from her Sadler's Wells Opera Company.

Bayreuth More than any other composer, Richard Wagner believed the audience to be an integral part of any performance. In 1876, in a small town in Franconia in Germany, he opened an opera house dedicated to his ideal of 'Gesamkunstwerk', literally 'together art work' and meaning for Wagner's purposes the total integration of singers, production, orchestra and audience. Not for him the distracting social niceties associated with going to the opera. His audiences were there (and still are) for one thing only – the performance. Bayreuth is not an easy place to get to, tickets are extremely hard to find and the seats are not comfortable in the Festspielhaus. But you do have an uninterrupted view of the stage from everywhere in the auditorium and the acoustics are incomparable. The orchestra is completely hidden beneath the stage and as the house lights dim, no neon EXIT sign pierces the darkness. It is an intense, almost mystical experience – 'Art as religion and the theatre as a temple' as Stravinsky described it.

While Bayreuth now enjoys an international reputation, Wagner's early seasons were fraught with difficulty. When money to build the theatre ran out, over 3,000 prospective sponsors were sought and all refused. Many of Wagner's first Festival Orchestra in 1875 agreed to play without fees, and only the intervention of King Ludwig of Bavaria ensured that the Festival continued after Wagner's death in 1883, when it was led by his wife Cosima. It was she who transformed the house and the Festival into something like a shrine in her husband's memory – archly conservative in the staging of productions and interpretation of the music. His family continued to exert a strong influence over the artistic direction of the place, but realized that if a modern audience was to be attracted, some concession had to be made to the advances in stage design, lighting and production. Gradually 'star' names were introduced, the antithesis of Wagner's day when no performer was credited anywhere, everyone subjugating their own identities to the creation of one performance. In 1930 Arturo Toscanini became the first non-German to conduct at Bayreuth but such internationalism came to an abrupt halt with Hitler's domination of Germany. It was Hitler's insistence on using Wagner's music to promote the policies of the Third Reich, pouring money into the Festival and working closely with Winifred Wagner (Wagner's daughter-in-law), that tainted the Festival and much of Wagner's work in the eyes of the rest of the world for years to come. Strangely, the Festival achieved some of its highest artistic standards at this time, still attracting good audiences until the link between art and politics became too obvious.

It was the combination of Wieland and Wolfgang Wagner, Wagner's grandson's which brought the Festival back to international prominence after the war, as Wieland's more intriguing, thought provoking productions were backed by Wolfgang's immense administrative ability. Artists were employed who were already, or were about to become, world famous: singers such as Hans Hotter, Birgit Nilsson, Marti Talvela; conductors such as Pierre Boulez and Sir Colin Davis; directors like Sir Peter Hall and designers like Joseph Svoboda. While a new production at Bayreuth is now anticipated with all the fervour and gossip of any other opera house, the Festival still retains its special ability to bring together the best artists working together to achieve one single, unified performance where the music is celebrated more than the production.

Beat An opera performance is an extraordinarily complicated operation, with perhaps eight principal singers, a chorus of eighty, a similar number in the orchestra and a host of technicians all combining together and hoping fervently that the result will please the audience. Only one thing is common to all of them on the night of the performance – the beat set by the conductor. By watching the baton, every person concerned with the performance should be able to put their own role in context. Beats vary in complexity from a simple four-four, with each note signifying one beat, to a complex time such as twelve-eight, where each beat is divided into three parts. It is a measure of the confidence of any opera singer that he or she can perform in character, with a commitment to the drama of the piece, without having his eyes rivetted to the conductor for fear of missing the beat and throwing the entire performance out of cue.

Beatrice and Benedict (Berlioz) FP 1862. Based on the Shakespearean tale, this opera is very rarely performed. Berlioz lightened the proceedings by marrying Beatrice to Benedict and Hero to Claudio and omitting the ominous sub-plot with Don John. He also included a comic band-leader, Somarone, set as a critic of all types of pedantry. The overture to the opera is very popular in the concert repertoire.

Beecham, Sir Thomas (1879–1961) English conductor. He founded the Beecham Opera Company in 1915 and went on to create the London Philharmonic in 1932. He became Artistic Director of Covent Garden in 1932 rising to General Director in 1935 and remained there, overseeing the British premieres of *Ariadne auf Naxos, Der Rosenkavalier* and *Salome* before moving to America for the whole of the Second World War. On his return, he founded the Royal Philharmonic Orchestra which he conducted until his death. A prolific recording artist, many of his complete opera recordings have become definitive interpretations. He was an unfailing champion of the work of Delius, whose biography he wrote, and a central, controversial and colourful character in the British music circuit in the post war years.

Beethoven, Ludwig van (1770–1827) German composer. Despite his prolific musical output, Beethoven wrote only one opera, but one of such intensity and individualism that it represents him superbly in the standard operatic repertoire (see *Fidelio*). He contemplated writing other operas, and admired the stage work of Mozart and Cherubini enormously, but his perfectionism and lack of stage experience combined to frustrate his efforts.

Beggar's Opera, The (John Gay) FP 1728. The best known ballad opera, with music partly composed by Pepusch and text by John Gay, it reflects many of the social activities of the time. The central character, Macheath, is modelled on the Prime Minister, Sir Robert Walpole, and the rivalry between Lucy Lockitt and Polly Peachum is thought to reflect that of two eighteenth-century prima donnas. When the opera was produced by Frederic Austin at the Lyric Hammersmith in 1920, it ran for nearly 1500 consecutive performances – the longest single run for any opera anywhere in the world, proving that if the subject matter is right and the music tuneful, opera can retain its popularity throughout the centuries!

The work is introduced by a Beggar – a speaking role – who brings forward Macheath, leader of the highwaymen. Thrown into Newgate Gaol, Macheath becomes a target for the affections of Lucy Lockit, the jailer's daughter, and Polly Peachum, daughter of a notorious criminal. About to face execution, with Polly and Lucy begging to join him, Macheath is saved by the intervention of the Beggar on a very spurious pretext which only emphasizes the tongue-in-cheek nature of the whole work.

Begley, Kim British tenor with an established reputation which began with six seasons as principal tenor for the Royal Opera House, Covent Garden. There he performed many of the major tenor roles, with notable accounts of Achilles in *King Priam*, by Michael Tippett, and Pang in *Turandot* which was seen by American audiences at the 1984 Los Angeles Festival. He

appears frequently with Glyndebourne and sang the major role of Pellegrin in *New Year* by Michael Tippett in 1990.

Behrens – Hildegard German soprano. A renowned Wagner exponent, Behrens is at her best in the dramatic acting roles and created a sensational Salome in Salzburg in the mid-1970s. She was nearly lost to the operatic world from the start, having qualified as a lawyer in Freiburg before changing her career.

Bel canto A style of opera singing favoured by the Italians, from the seventeenth to the nineteenth century, where smooth tone, excellent breath control and technical virtuosity was achieved at the expense of realistic acting or characterization. At its most pronounced, bel canto singing represents all the worst images of opera – large ladies belting out their arias facing the audience and not moving an inch, best summed up by Harry Secombe's much quoted spoonerism 'can belto'! However, when a bel canto style is combined with an ability to act, the result, as typified by Pavarotti, is quite magnificent.

Belle Hélène, La (Offenbach) FP 1864. Helen of Troy set in the Paris of the Second Empire! Helen and Paris outwit Helen's husband Menelaus, King of Sparta, thanks to the help of Calchas, High Priest of Sparta. Woven into a simple story is all the gaiety of late nineteenth-century Paris with its loose morals and glittering social circuit, reflected by some immensely tuneful music.

Bellezza, Vincenzo (1888–1964) Italian conductor who conducted Dame Nellie Melba's farewell to the operatic stage at Covent Garden in June 1926 and the first English *Turandot* in 1927.

Bellini, Vincenzo (1801–1835) Italian composer. For a composer who died at the age of thirty-four, Bellini has left a formidable legacy, *I Capuletti e i Montecchi*, *La Sonnambula* and *Norma*, all written before he reached, thirty, are now classics of the grand opera repertoire, together with *I Puritani* which he finished in the year of his death from dysentery, borne of ill health from overwork. His operas have been criticized for their lack of dramatic content, with a tendency to be mere showcases for the performers. But as singers of the intensity of Callas or Sutherland have brilliantly demonstrated, his writing can be full of drama if passionately performed.

Bennett, Richard Rodney British composer. If the thought of late twentieth-century music makes you reach for the cotton wool, Richard Rodney Bennett's work could surprise you. He studied as a pianist with Lennox Berkeley at London's Royal Academy of Music before moving to the prestigious school of Pierre Boulez in Paris for a further two years. The strength of his music lies in its diversity, as he incorporates influences from the jazz and pop rhythms of the 1950s and '60s, as well as more classical aspects, encompassing traditional harmonies and atonal compositions. Thus his works have spread across a wide range of performances. He has written notable film scores, including that for John Schlesinger's 1967 epic, *Far from the Madding Crowd*, for which he won an Academy Award nomination. His ballet *Jazz Calendar* was widely acclaimed when choreographed by Fredrick Ashton for London's Royal Ballet in 1963, and his vocal, chamber and orchestral music have earned him a reputation as one of the leading composers of the late twentieth century. He has written five operas – *The Ledge* (1961), *The Mines of Sulphur* (1963–5), *Penny for a Song* (1966), *All the King's Men*, a children's opera, (1968–9) and *Victory* (1970).

Benvenuto Cellini (Berlioz) FP 1838. Originally devised as a comic opera, the initial productions of this opera failed until taken up at Weimar by Liszt who substantially revised the score.

Two sculptors, Cellini and Fieramosca, are in love with the same girl, Teresa, daughter of Balducci, the Papal Treasurer. During the Roman Carnival Cellini dresses up as a friar and plans to elope with Teresa. Fieramosca overhears them, dresses up as another friar and joins the general melée of carnival night. A fight ensues and Cellini is arrested for the murder of a man called Pompeo. Teresa is taken to Cellini's studio where his fate is to be decided – if he cannot complete the statue commissioned by the Pope by midnight, he will be hanged for murder. Fieramosca, determined to see his rival die, organizes a strike to prevent Cellini completing his task, but Cellini prevails and presents a statue of Perseus by the deadline, thus earning his pardon. The music from the Roman Carnival will be familiar as a concert piece.

Berg, Alban (1885–1935) Austrian composer. Berg's greatest theme was the suffering of the individual and his two best known works *Wozzeck* and *Lulu* are fine examples of the human plight set to music. The personal drama of the pieces is intended to be of paramount interest to the audience – the musical structure is made up of instrumental forms such as the rondo and suite and does not follow the conventions of classic opera. The music is intended to heighten the drama of the stage action rather than to be an entity of its own, and Berg's scores are detailed to the finest degree, including the speed at which the curtain is to be raised and lowered. While *Wozzeck* would be more accessible than *Lulu* for a new opera goer, Berg's individual style can be difficult to appreciate at a first hearing!

Berganza, Theresa Spanish mezzo-soprano. A fine mezzo voice complemented by great physical beauty and powerful acting ability make Berganza a popular and prestigious artist, particularly in the more tempestuous roles such as Carmen and Rosina in Rossini's *Barber of Seville*. She is also an excellent singer of 'zarzuela', Spanish gypsy songs.

Berghaus, Ruth German producer whose radical productions have shocked some British audiences and enthralled others. Originally trained as a choreographer, Berghaus worked with the Deutsches Theater, Komische Oper and Berliner Ensemble which she led as Intendant from 1971 to 1973. She is steeped in the inventive traditions of German opera production since the Second World War, and profoundly influenced by the legacy of Walter Felsenstein at the Komische Oper as well as work with such influential figures as Berthold Brecht, Gotz Friedrich and Harry Kupfer. Berghaus was given the opportunity to try her ideas on British audiences by Brian McMaster at Welsh National Opera, who asked her to direct a production of *Don Giovanni* in 1984.

It was an abrasive and austere account, highly symbolic and consequently rejected by many of WNO's regular audience. But Berghaus comes from a school which has pushed forward the frontiers of opera production and therefore it is unwise to ignore or condemn her work too quickly.

Bergonzi, Carlo Italian tenor, formerly a baritone. No important operation was required for Bergonzi to make the transition upwards in the musical range from baritone to tenor – just a period of training away from performance after his three years as a baritone. His success as a tenor proves the value of singers recognizing where their natural range lies, rather than forcing themselves to sing otherwise for the sake of landing bigger roles. Bergonzi's greatest performances were of the major Verdi roles. His limited public appearances now reveal the lyrical beauty of his voice is still very much apparent.

Berio, Luciano (1925–1990) Italian composer whose radical compositions for the stage were influential in the development of contemporary opera. He was Artistic Director of the Maggio Musicale in Florence. His most notable operas are *Opera* with a libretto written by the Italian writer Umberto Ecco and *Un Re In Ascolto*, first produced in Salzburg in 1984 and subsequently at the Royal Opera House Covent Garden.

Berkeley, Sir Lennox (1903–1989) English composer. Despite the failure of his first, highly romantic opera *Nelson*, produced by Sadler's Wells in 1954, Berkeley continued to write operas which subsequently met with more success, *A Dinner Engagement*, *Ruth* and *The Castaway*, though these too have been hampered by bad libretti.

Berlioz, Hector (1803–1869) French composer. Abandoning his study as a medical student, Berlioz turned to music and to Shakespeare, completing his artistic education by falling hopelessly in love with an English Shakespearean actress, Harriet Smithson whom he later married. Heroism and grand spectacle characterize Berlioz's first operas *Benvenuto Cellini* and *Les Troyens* followed by a more personal account in *Beatrice and Benedict*. The failure of 'Cellini' in Paris did not deter him from forming an even grander design for *Les Troyens* which has been described by the late Harold Rosenthal, editor of *Opera* magazine, as 'one of the noblest monuments of operatic imagination in the history of the art.' Berlioz adored the myth and heroism of Roman legend, the passion of their warriors set against the order and organization of their military compaigns. The lyrical and the spectacular come together in much of his work but his perceptions of personal relationships and wry humour are obvious too, in a work such as *Beatrice and Benedict*. During his lifetime, Berlioz found greater support in Germany and Russia than in France but only in the twentieth century have his operas enjoyed world-wide appeal.

Berlin Berlin's three opera houses suffered dreadfully during the Second World War and it is a tribute to the administrations on both sides of the now-defunct wall that all three opera companies housed in the city enjoy superb international reputations.

Die Deutsche Oper, the only one of the houses in West Berlin, was opened in its present form in 1961 under the leadership of Gustav Sellner. It has a policy of producing inspiring work, with plenty of contemporary premieres mixed with traditional pieces, though it is considerably more conservative than its East Berlin counterparts. Since 1981, Professor Gotz Freidrich has been General Manager, with Jesus Lopez-Cobos as Chief Conductor.

Die Komische Oper in East Berlin still thrives on the reputation it developed under Felsenstein. Those who are led by the name to expect a repertoire of light humorous opera will be surprised – the house adopts a policy of radical, controversial stagings of a range of classical and contemporary operas. While the musical performances never fall below an acceptable standard, people go to the Komische Oper to be shocked, awakened and inspired by the productions rather than wallow in the familiarity of their favourite opera melody.

Die Staatsoper the oldest of the three companies arrived in its current home Unter den Linden in 1955 and performs a more traditional repertoire than the other two houses. Contemporary work is not ignored, but the house seeks to serve those East Berlin opera lovers who cannot take the powerful inter-

Beatrice and Benedict, by Berlioz. Ann Murray and Philip Langridge in this rarely performed opera, based on Shakespeare's *Much Ado About Nothing*.

La Bohème, by Puccini. Placido Domingo and Ilona Tokody, as the ill-fated lovers Rodolfo and Mimi, in Covent Garden's 1987 production, relayed on a giant screen to thousands outside the opera house.

Harrison Birtwistle's *The Mask of Orpheus*. Premiered in 1986 by ENO; visually and musically stunning, featuring the latest acoustic technology and inspired designs by Jocelyn Herbert; the director was David Freeman.

pretations on offer at the Komische Oper and have hitherto been prevented from experiencing the more mixed programme available at Die Deutsche Oper.

Bernstein, Leonard American conductor and composer. Bernstein exemplifies the great transition between opera and musical theatre in his best known work *West Side Story*. Written for the Broadway stage and released as a film in 1960, everyone speaks of it as a musical, but in fact it has much that is operatic in its structure. Bernstein's two-part opera *Trouble in Tahiti* and *A Quiet Place* is an excellent introduction to the melodious, accessible side of late twentieth-century opera. He is likewise notable as a conductor and was the first American to conduct at La Scala, Milan, with a performance of *Medea* in 1953. As a conductor of opera, his performances have been limited, including a few at the Metropolitan Opera, New York, of *Carmen*, *Cavalleria Rusticana* and *Falstaff*.

Best, Jonathan English bass baritone whose exciting professional performances to date show him to be at the early stages of a promising career. Jonathan Best studied at Cambridge University and the Guildhall School of Music in London, winning the BP Opera Award in 1982. He has since made his debuts with Welsh, Scottish and English National Operas as well as performing with the English Bach Festival and Maggio Musicale in Florence.

Big Four, The All opera houses are subject to fashions. The current vogue for opera as musical-drama favours organizations such as English National Opera and New York City Opera. But for consistency of musical quality, prestige of international artists and glamour of overall surroundings, a contentious categorization of the 'Big Four' opera houses should include La Scala, Milan, The Metropolitan Opera House, New York, The Vienna Staatsoper and The Royal Opera House, Covent Garden.

Billington, Elizabeth (1765–1818) English soprano. Very popular in her day and thought to have been the mistress of the Prince of Wales, she is best known to today's opera audience as the subject of a lovely portrait by John Hoppner which hangs on the main staircase at the London Coliseum.

Billy Budd (Britten) FP 1951. Working from an unfinished story by Herman Melville, Eric Crozier and E. M. Forster wrote the libretto for Britten's intense and savage account of a young sailor aboard a Man O' War. Its overriding theme of the power of homosexuality in an all male environment – which is expressed or repressed depending on the production – currently makes the opera a subject of heated debate as to its suitability for a young audience.

Billy Budd is the naive young sailor, uncorrupted by the cunning of the world and press-ganged into service on a Man O'War. His goodness incites the resentment of his Master at Arms, Claggart, who taunts and harasses Billy, finally inciting him to mutiny, before denouncing him before Captain Vere. Attempting to defend himself and afflicted by a nervous stammer, Billy inadvertently strikes Claggart who dies of the blow. While Captain Vere knows how strongly Billy was provoked, he has to condemn the young sailor to death. The opera opens with Vere's remorseful prologue as he looks back on his life, weighing up the mysteries of good and evil, and is told in flashback. The brilliance of the piece is the subtlety in which the menace of power is introduced on a number of levels, not only sexual, making it a moving and involving drama.

Bing, Sir Rudolf An inspired opera manager, latterly and sadly the subject of outlandish tabloid newspaper articles because of his increasingly eccentric behaviour. Bing has worked at many of the leading opera houses, bringing the Metropolitan Opera House to worldwide attention during his tenure there from 1950 to 1972. Previously he worked as General Manager of Glyndebourne from 1936 to 1949 and as Founder and Artistic Director of the Edinburgh Festival. At the Met, he oversaw a vast improvement in stage design, the move to the Met's current Lincoln Centre premises and the employment for the first time of black artists.

Birmingham One of the best activists in bringing opera to the places other opera companies do not reach, City of Birmingham Touring Opera is firmly allied to the city of

Birmingham in the heart of England although the company tours extensively. It was created from the merger of English Touring Opera and Birmingham Music Theatre and regularly attracts artists of international calibre to work on productions which may be staged in school halls, gymnasia or in the aisles of parish churches. The Artistic Director is Graham Vick, known for his ability to persuade even the most recalcitrant performer to take a full and enthusiastic part in any opera he directs – particularly in his community works. 'We are a company who likes to surprise' he says – and proves it in his productions of *La Bohème*, *Falstaff* and *Cinderella*. All were masterpieces of small scale theatre, proving that opera could be as effective and affecting if played with conviction in even the least theatrical of surroundings.

The musical leadership is shared by Simon Halsey and Paul Herbert, both of whom have the gift of making a tiny orchestra sound like an eighty piece band – thanks in no small way to the orchestrations by Jonathan Dove. CBTO's repertoire encompasses the classics, with a production of the Ring Cycle planned for 1990, and the contemporary *Trouble in Tahiti* (Bernstein), *Eis Thanaton* (commissioned by the company from John Taverner) and *Ghanashyam – The Broken Branch* by Ravi Shankar, his first music theatre piece which tackles the contemporary problem of drug abuse. By putting their audience first and creating uncompromising excellence even on the smallest scale, CBTO have redefined the over-used word 'accessibility' by proving that opera can be performed anywhere with style, quality and commitment, given enough talent amongst its performers.

Birtwistle, Harrison English composer. Birtwistle's operas reflect many aspects of twentieth-century society whilst not abandoning classical forms or plots. Thus his opera *Punch and Judy* can be performed away from the opera house, relying on minimal staging and acknowledging the importance of a small budget for touring opera. Conversely, his *Mask of Orpheus*, based on the Orpheus legend, is on a massive scale, requiring huge and complex sound systems and the latest in acoustic techniques, as well as contemporary design and staging. His determination to involve our twentieth-century lifestyle in his operas makes his work fascinating to watch, though not immediately tuneful to hear.

Bizet, Georges (1838–1875) French composer. Perhaps one of the best known composers of opera, Bizet's entire reputation is founded on just two works *The Pearl Fishers*, which he wrote in 1863 and *Carmen*, composed in 1874. Their stature and lasting popularity have given him an image of a prolific and tuneful writer which is far from the truth. He was a talented pianist and made much of his income from arranging and accompanying. His relationship with the musical establishment in Paris was acerbic and unfruitful. Both *The Pearl Fishers* and *Carmen* were badly received and attended during Bizet's lifetime and his epic work *Ivan IV* was rejected by both the Lyrique and the Opera. Only after his death, and a successful production of *Carmen* in Vienna did Paris recognize the genius of his work, finally reviving *Carmen* in 1883.

Bjorling, Jussi (1911–1960) Swedish tenor. Attracted worldwide acclaim throughout the mid-twentieth century, having been taught by his father and sung in a quartet with his brothers until 1926. His numerous recordings prove the lyrical beauty of his voice, at its best in Verdi and Puccini roles.

Bjornson, Maria Stage designer who has done a tremendous amount to break through the barriers of classical opera, where she has done the majority of her work, by extending her range of colourful stagings to the West End and Broadway. She was commissioned by Andrew Lloyd Webber to design sets for *Phantom of the Opera*, and *Aspects of Love* whilst maintaining regular contacts with Britain's national opera companies. Examples of her opera designs include a radical new staging of *Carmen*, set in a disused car pound in a central American dictatorship (for ENO, 1985), a magical woodland setting for Janacek's *The Cunning Little Vixen* (WNO with other co-producers) and a powerfully futuristic vision for *Donnerstag aus Licht* by Stockhausen for the Royal Opera House.

Blake, David British composer of opera who studied with Hanns Eisler in East Germany and became influenced by his teacher to a very large degree. Blake joined the music staff at the University of York and progressed to become Head of the Department in 1981. His work has since developed from atonal, twelve note composition to more lyrical tuneful work. His first opera *Toussaint L'Ouverture*, based on a revolutionary coup in Haiti, was premiered at ENO in 1977 and *The Plumber's Gift* was first staged by the same company in 1989. Both update traditional stories to contemporary settings.

Bleeding chunks A disparaging term used to describe excerpts from certain operas which are played regularly as concert pieces and thereby gain disproportionate popularity to the opera as a whole, eg 'The Ride of the Valkyries' (*Die Walkure*), 'Habenera' (*Carmen*) and 'La Donna è Mobile' (*Rigoletto*).

Bliss, Sir Arthur (1891–1975) English composer whose two operas, *The Olympians* and *Tobias and the Angel*, have not been as popular as much of his other work. He did, however, write highly descriptive, dramatic music with operatic overtones for the film *Things to Come* and the ballets *Checkmate*, *Adam Zero* and *Miracle in the Gorbals* as well as arranging the score of *The Beggar's Opera* for the 1953 film version.

Blitzstein, Mark (1905–1964) American composer who brought the vernacular speech rhythms of 1920s' America into the opera house through his musical theatre piece *The Cradle will Rock* and his opera *No for an Answer*. Greatly influenced by Brecht and Weill, Blitzstein wrote a stunningly successful English-language version of *The Threepenny Opera* and pioneered the theory that music in general and opera in particular is an effective means of communication to the widest possible audience.

Bohème, La (Puccini) FP 1896. Initially unsuccessful, then acclaimed before falling out of fashion again, this most sentimental of Puccini's operas is once more back in favour. The music is lush, tuneful and extraordinarily beautiful in many places. The plot does not have the emotive pull of *Madam Butterfly* or the grandeur of *Turandot* but in its simplicity and romanticism, it can be very moving indeed. Much depends on the acting abili-

ties of Mimi and Rudolfo to bring across the genuine plight of the lovers without descending into sheer sentimentality.

Four young students are sharing a garret on the Left Bank of Paris. It is Christmas, bitterly cold and though they are penniless, they have their hopes and humour to keep them warm. Avoiding the persistent calls of their angry landlord, three of the young men repair to the Café Momus, leaving Rudolfo to continue his work. The enchanting Mimi, clearly suffering from tuberculosis, makes a timid entrance to the garret asking for a light for her candle. It is love at first sight and the couple sing rapturously of their passion before joining their friends at the café. They are joined by Musetta, the coquettish ex-lover of one of the other students, Marcello, whose romance is re-established after much argument. The two couples continue stormy relationships – Musetta and Marcello through constant bickering, Rudolfo through his concern that Mimi will worsen if she lives in poverty in his garret. Months later, Marcello and Rudolfo have ended up alone in their garrett and Mimi has returned to her wealthy former lover. Musetta rushes in to tell Rudolfo that Mimi is dying and needs to talk with him. The couple have just enough time to declare their true love for each other before she dies in his arms.

Bohm, Karl (1894–1981) Austrian conductor of international reputation, particularly in German and Mozart opera. Never flamboyant, Bohm was an accurate, authoritative leader, learning his trade from Bruno Walter and through work in all the leading European opera houses, finishing with a brief tenure as Generalmusicdirektor of the rebuilt Stadtsoper in Vienna before becoming a guest conductor throughout the world.

Boito, Arrigo (1842–1918) Italian composer and librettist. Boito's one completed opera *Mefistophele* is very long and rarely performed and his unfinished *Nerone* was performed only as a memorial to him in 1924. His legacy to grand opera survives through his libretti of Verdi's *Otello* and *Falstaff* and his encouragement of the young Puccini and Catalani.

Bolshoi (see Moscow)

Bolton, Ivor English conductor. One of Britain's most active and versatile younger conductors both in opera and concert work. Bolton works regularly at Glyndebourne with the Festival Opera having made his conducting debut in 1989 with Gluck's *Orfeo* and with Glyndebourne Touring Opera. He also conducts regularly for Opera 80. A baroque specialist, he founded the St James's Baroque Players (Piccadilly, London) in 1984, and he has recorded Handel arias for Virgin Classics and Purcell's *Dido and Aeneas* for ASV.

Bonynge, Richard Australian conductor who enjoys an international career, specializing in bel canto operas. He was Artistic Director of the Vancouver Opera from 1974 to 1977, and Musical Director of Australian Opera from 1976 to 1984 and is married to the great Australian soprano, Dame Joan Sutherland, whose performances he always conducts. Rarely do musical marriages succeed to the extent of Richard Bonynge and Dame Joan Sutherland, both of whom have maintained superb international careers whilst enjoying over twenty-five years of marriage.

Borge, Victor To describe Victor Borge merely as a Hungarian musical humorist barely does justice to his originality and brilliance. He lampoons the pretensions of grand opera in such a charming manner that aficionados cannot be offended and new opera lovers realize that, after everything, opera is there to give pleasure at a number of very different levels.

Boris Godunov (Mussorgsky) FP 1974 in full version. Several versions exist of Mussorgsky's towering, grim tale of dynastic Russia. His original version, consisting of only seven scenes from his full work, was rejected by St Petersburg opera in 1870. The full version was a public success and critical failure – it was withdrawn after only twenty-five performances in 1874 and the composer never saw his monumental work performed again in his lifetime. Rimsky-Korsakov then revised the work twice. The first was heavily cut and performed in 1896. He then restored the cuts for a new staging, premiered in 1908. This last has remained the most often-performed version, until modern tastes have

called for the full 1874 edition which has recently been revived with great success. Like all rattling good yarns, *Boris Godunov* is based on a true story. The scenes can almost stand alone, relating only generally to the overall historical context and are re-arranged or omitted for different productions

Prologue. Boris has murdered the young heir to the Russian throne, Dmitry, in order to clear his own path to the crown. When the crown is offered to him, he pretends not to want it, but the crowd persuades him to accept it

Sc 1. Years after Boris' coronation, things are not going well in Russia. Despite Boris' wise and kind rule, food is scarce, violence is rife and the people are unhappy. The monk Pimen is trying to comfort his young novice, Grigory, who has woken yet again from a recurring nightmare where he stands at the top of a high tower seeing Moscow at his feet. The crowd mocks him and he falls from the tower as he wakes from his dream

Sc 2. Grigory has escaped from the monastery and fallen in with two dishonest monks, Varlaam and Missail. At an inn he evades the guards who are pursuing him, by setting up Varlaam instead, and escapes

Sc 3. Boris joins his children in their nursery and, in a towering monologue, pours out the despair he feels in governing the vast and unruly country of Russia, still wracked as he is by the memory of having murdered Dmitry. Trouble is brewing in Poland – a pretender has gained the throne and been acknowledged as leader by the people and the Pope. Left alone, Boris is tormented by visions of the rightful heir he murdered and the thought of his own downfall

Sc 4. In Poland, the young girl Marina is preparing for a meeting with the man she believes to be Dmitry, heir to the Russian throne. The man is in fact Grigory, the escaped monk, who has called himself Dmitry and pretends to be the Russian heir. Embracing Marina as his love, Grigory/Dmitry makes plans to march on Moscow.

Sc 5. The Council members in Moscow are troubled first by the threat to their power from the pretender and secondly by Boris' increasingly anguished behaviour. Boris is further distracted by the story of a miracle that has taken place at Dmitry's tomb and finally, in one of the all-time-great scenes of all opera, collapses and dies, leaving Russia and her troubles to his son

Sc 6. Grigory/Dmitry and his followers are at camp in the Kromy Forest and divisions arise between the factions which support Boris and those supporting Grigory/Dmitry. After the passing of a massive procession the stage clears leaving only one old fool left to prattle on the fate of Russia as he sings 'Woe and sorrow always, lament, Russian folk, poor hungry folk'.

Borodin, Alexander (1833–1887) Russian composer whose earliest work for the stage was a lighthearted pastiche, *The Bogatyrs*, now hardly ever performed. As a complete change of mood, he worked sporadically for eighteen years on the Russian historical epic *Prince Igor* but died of a cardiac arrest before completing it, leaving Rimsky-Korsakov and Glazunov to finish the work.

Boulez, Pierre French composer and conductor. One of the twentieth century's most eminent musicians, Boulez has had a profound influence on classical music, pioneering the operas of Berg and bringing contemporary music into the concert hall as a regular feature, rather than a one-off event. He was Principal Conductor of the BBC Symphony Orchestra from 1971–1974 and of the New York Philharmonic from 1971–1978 before returning to France to head the Institute for Research into Contemporary Music Techniques (IRCAM). He now exerts a powerful influence over the controversial new opera house at La Bastille in Paris. He instils his performances and recordings with an intellectual challenge rather than any comfortable sense of familiarity and will probably be best remembered for his forthright declaration that all opera houses should be blown up!

Bowman, James English counter-tenor. Although his opera appearances are limited by the dearth of roles for a counter-tenor in the standard repertoire, Bowman has become well-known for his interpretations of baroque and twentieth-century works, in which there has been a great demand for counter-tenors of his calibre. He also has an active recital and concert career, and has made a series of highly successful recordings of the baroque counter-tenor repertoire.

Boxes Thought to be the smartest seats in any opera house, boxes are great for the intimacy they provide and the feeling that you are not quite part of the hoi-polloi in the audience. They have their drawbacks, as the sightlines are frequently dreadful (particularly some of the ones at the side at Glyndebourne, or in the horse-shoe auditoria at the Met in New York, or La Fenice, Venice) and you can feel very daft cheering an opera to the echo in splendid isolation. Some of the best boxes are situated at the back of the stalls area with a full view of the stage but near enough to the bar if needs be!

Brannigan, Owen (1908–1973) English bass. Brannigan enjoyed almost cult status as an interpreter of Britten's bass roles, his powerful stage presence heightening the impact of his magnificent voice. He created Swallow (*Peter Grimes*), Collantinus (*Rape of Lucretia*), Noye in *Noye's Fludde* and Bottom in *A Midsummer Night's Dream*.

Brecht, Bertholt (1898–1956) German playwright whose collaboration with Kurt Weill achieved some of the most politically aware and fascinating twentieth-century opera – *The Threepenny Opera, The Rise and Fall of the City of Mahagonny, Happy End* and *Jasager*.

Bregenz Festival Located in the Vorarlberg, Austria, the Festival was begun in 1956 and has risen steadily in importance to rank as one of Europe's most influential operatic enterprises. Performances are staged either in the large open air theatre beside the lake, which seats over 4,300, or in the smaller Theater am Kornmarkt. The size of the larger venue dictates the scale of Bregenz productions, which are thought to rival Verona in their magnitude. For example, Stefanos Lazaridis' design for *The Flying Dutchman* for the 1989 Festival included a lighthouse, from which Senta fell to her death, which was a massive thirty-two metres high and no doubt accounted for a large part of the £1,500,000 budget for set and costumes alone. Such generosity does not impair the musical impact of the festival, which attracts singers of excellent calibre as well as inventive and enterprising production teams.

Brindisi A drinking song. The best known example is at the beginning of *La Traviata* by

Verdi, which always sends a ripple of recognition around any audience.

British Council The cultural arm of Britain's Foreign and Commonwealth Office, devoted to promoting British arts abroad. It can give grants of substantial sums and enable touring companies to develop their foreign links through the Council's on-site offices. While the Council has made some impact, given its declared policy, it is frequently thought to be less effective than it might be, due to the overall control of its work by the bureaucracy of the Civil Service.

British National Opera Company Formed in 1921, this touring opera company was made up of leading characters on the British music scene who went on to prominence in the latter part of the century – John Barbirolli, Adrian Boult, Malcolm Sargent and Thomas Beecham who directed the group until its demise through lack of funds in 1929. It was briefly resurrected as the Covent Garden English Opera Group under Barbirolli's directorship, when it lasted for three seasons.

Britten, Benjamin (1913–1976) While Britten's output was extensive, embracing all musical forms, many think his best composition was for the voice. Throughout his life he encouraged the young and the talented, whilst befriending some of the greatest singers of the age, Galina Vishnevskaya, Dietrich Fischer-Dieskau, Janet Baker and, particularly his life-long partner, Peter Pears, all of whom inspired his work. His descriptive style became apparent at the age of twenty with the composition of a song-cycle 'A Boy was Born'. But it was the opening of *Peter Grimes* in 1945 that indicated to the public that a great new talent was emerging. He did not lead his life in the public eye, preferring to concentrate on the music festival he founded in the Suffolk village of Aldeburgh, dedicated to bringing amateurs and international artists together, often in the same piece.

Britten was fascinated with the outsider, the misunderstood, and with lost innocence featured in the personalities of Peter Grimes, Billy Budd, Owen Wingrave, Lucretia, Aschenbach in *Death in Venice* and throughout *The Turn of the Screw*. His wry comic observations created *Albert Herring*, *The*

Beggar's Opera (which he updated) and *A Midsummer Night's Dream*. He developed a perceptive knowledge of the type of music children could enjoy, the best example being *Let's Make an Opera*. In 1958, he wrote *Noye's Fludde* again for children and professionals, to be performed in a church setting. The success of this became the inspiration for an entirely new type of opera – the Church Parable – for small scale performances in churches. The first of the three parables, *Curlew River*, was based on the Japanese Noh Play. His opera written for the Coronation, *Gloriana*, aroused much discussion, chiefly because of its libretto, and was deemed a failure at first, though it has subsequently been performed by ENO to great success. Britten has an unjustified reputation for being 'difficult' for the new opera goer. But there can be few better introductions to opera than a work of the charm of *Albert Herring* and for those who dismiss the all opera plots as contrived or ridiculous, a performance of *Billy Budd* or *The Rape of Lucretia* would surely show an alternative view.

Broadcasting In Britain the authorities are pursuing an enlightened policy of broadcasting opera both on radio and television. Live radio relays are not so difficult for an opera house to accommodate. Television, on the other hand, incurs huge costs in setting up technical equipment, moving the audience to set up cameras in the best positions, and paying every singer and technician involved a very handsome television levy. It is possible to defray this expense by sponsorship and all sponsors greatly welcome the exposure television provides. Such commercial agreements have worked with great success in America, notably Texaco's sponsorship of performances 'Live from the Met' on Sunday afternoon. Currently, the BBC is prohibited by its charter from promoting sponsors, but, as the number of television channels increases in Britain and the new satellite networks provide whole channels dedicated to the arts, the number of operas on television will no doubt increase.

Television is the perfect medium to familiarize oneself with an opera plot but no new opera goer should be disappointed if left unmoved by a televised opera. The full wonder of opera is only apparent in a live

Benjamin Britten's most powerful operas are characterized by their sinister plots. Two particularly compelling examples are *Billy Budd* (above, with Thomas Allen, as Billy, and Richard van Allan as Claggart) and *The Turn of the Screw* (below, with Gillian Sullivan, as the Governess, Malcolm Green as Miles, and Robert Tear as Peter Quint).

performance. Operas commissioned for television include Britten's *Owen Wingrave* and *Amahl and the Night Visitors* by Menotti.

Brook, Peter English theatre and opera director. One of the most influential characters in the post-war theatre, his productions are avowedly controversial, mould-breaking and often become classics in their own right. He was Director of Productions at Covent Garden from 1947 to 1960, with the Royal Shakespeare Company from 1962 (where he produced the now-legendary *A Midsummer Night's Dream*) and works in Paris as Founder/Director of the International Theatre Research Centre. His production of *The Tragedy of Carmen*, produced in Paris in 1981 featured only six people, concentrating on the intense psychological drama of the work. It has joined 'The Dream' as one of the greatest theatrical productions of our times.

Brussels – Theatre Royal de la Monnaie Known by everyone as 'La Monnaie', this theatre reached its heyday in the latter part of the nineteenth century, having played a formative role in the creation of the modern state of Belgium. For it was at the theatre in August 1830, at a performance of *La Muette de Portici* by Daniel Auber, that the crowd was incited to revolt in an uprising which led to the Belgian Revolution. On a more musical level, the theatre hosted amongst other notable events, the operatic debut of Dame Nellie Melba in 1887. The current administrative and artistic team wishes now to recreate that sense of splendour which the theatre has lost for the greater part of this century. It is known chiefly as the home of Maurice Bejart's pioneering ballet company 'Ballet du XXieme Siècle'. The theatre's Administrator, Gerald Mortier, was appointed, in 1989, to succeed Herbert von Karajan as Director of the Salzburg Festival.

Budapest – Allami Operahaz Built in 1875 and costing only a little over £43,000, this beautiful theatre was called the Hungarian Royal Operal House until the advent of the Communist state changed its title to the Hungarian State Opera House. Until the mid-nineteenth century, the house strongly favoured Italian opera but throughout the century, the popularity of native Hungarian operas developed thanks to the nationalist composer Ferenc Erkel. The house has boasted some fine conductors and singers including Gustav Mahler (Chief Conductor 1888–1891), Otto Klemperer (1947–1951), and the soprano Eva Marton.

Buenos Aires – El Teatro Colon A huge, beautiful opera house originally seating over 2,500 and reckoned by many experts to have the best acoustics for the human voice of any opera house in the world. The first theatre on the site was built in 1856 and immediately attracted the best opera stars of the day, happy to perform in a town where the demand for opera outstripped any other form of entertainment. So high was the demand, in fact, that even a house of such capacity could not satisfy the potential audience wishing to attend, so a new house was built and opened in 1908. While the technical capacity of the house has remained the same, the theatre has frequently housed over 4,000 once all the standing allocation has been taken up. It is the great, dramatic works that have always found most favour with the discerning, predominantly young Argentinian audience. Mozart has never been established as a favourite but Verdi, Wagner and Richard Strauss have brought audiences to their feet clamouring their applause. Such enthusiasm encourages the best performers to return to such a lovely place, where the backstage facilities are said to rival the front of house opulence. But, as with many state funded institutions, the theatre's recent fortunes have been coloured by the unpredictable nature of Argentina's political administration.

Bumbry, Grace American mezzo soprano who was the first black artist to appear at Bayreuth. Now she has an international career in both mezzo and soprano roles – particularly Bess, Carmen, Salome and Amneris.

Burgess, Sally One of the few British opera singers glamorous enough to make the front page of a tabloid newspaper (*The Daily Mail*) for her performance as Carmen in David Pountney's controversial production, Burgess is a vivacious soprano turned mezzo with unusual vocal and dramatic versatility. She joined English National Opera straight from college but her career has really taken off since she became a mezzo, and she now concentrates chiefly on the dramatic mezzo repertoire. She has retained her versatility however and is competent enough to tackle the musical *Showboat* and *The Trojans* in a single season.

Burning Fiery Furnace, The (Britten) FP 1966. The second of Britten's Church Parables is based on the biblical tale of Nebuchadnezzar who condemns three Jews, Shadrach, Meshach and Abednego to death in a fiery furnace for refusing to worship the Babylonian god, Merodak. As they emerge unscathed, Nebuchadnezzar rejects Merodak and falls down to worship the God of Abraham. The spectacle involved in the plot (fiery furnaces etc) is virtually impossible to recreate in a church setting but the rare, fully staged performances of this work have been extraordinarily imaginative in conveying large scale drama in an intimate setting.

Burrows, Stuart Welsh tenor. A leading international lyric tenor, Burrows has an active recital and concert career as well as success all over the world on the operatic stage. He is very popular and a dependable performer who is more well known than many British singers of this generation because of his successful television series 'Stuart Burrows Sings'. He is particularly acclaimed for his interpretations of Mozart with some of the finest opera companies worldwide.

Bury, John English stage designer who evokes periods in the past by using the latest in scenic technology. Began work with Joan Littlewood's Theatre Company, moving to the RSC with Peter Hall before turning to full time opera design. His most successful work has been at Glyndebourne, particularly his designs for *La Calisto* and *Il Ritorno d'Ulisse in Patria*.

Busch, Fritz (1890–1951) German conductor who led the Dresden Opera through one of its most brilliant periods from 1922 to 1933. He left Germany in 1933, refusing to conform to the strictures of Hitler. After a brief spell in Buenos Aires, he came to England where with Karl Ebert, John Christie and Audrey Mildmay, he founded the Glyndebourne Festival in 1934, returning to

conduct it every year until the outbreak of war. He worked in America throughout the war, returning to Glyndebourne in 1950. His best performances were given conducting Mozart, Verdi and Wagner.

Butt, Dame Clara (1873–1936) English contralto. Dame Clara has retained her fame throughout this century as one of the greatest English sopranos. In fact she gave only one operatic performance of the role she had made her own on the concert platform, Orfeo, which she sang in 1920 at Covent Garden for Sir Thomas Beecham.

Buxton Opera House A tiny opera house is situated in the centre of a municipal park in the spa town of Buxton, one of the most attractive towns in England. The theatre was designed by Frank Matcham, who also designed the London Coliseum, and was built in 1903, seating barely one thousand people. The exquisite, ornate auditorium and foyer was allowed to fall into disrepair over the years but has been restored to its original glory. The theatre now hosts the annual Buxton Festival, begun in 1979 and currently one of Europe's most prestigious and popular gatherings. Each festival is based on a theme, usually a literary one, providing the audience with a wide range of activities around the operas which form its core. The 1989 Festival, for example, featured two rarely performed operas by Cimarosa, as well as recitals by musicians such as Thomas Allen and Margaret Price. The increasingly impressive artistic reputation which Buxton has gained, added to the beautiful setting in the heart of the Peak District, attracts singers and directors of high calibre, as well as encouraging those at the start of their professional careers.

Cabaletta A descriptive term referring to a section of an aria, the precise definition of cabaletta has changed over the years. When Rossini wrote cabalettas, he intended his sopranos to sing the first phrase as written, then embellish the repeated phrases as they saw fit. By the end of the nineteenth century, a cabaletta referred to the last section of an aria, written into the score but often taken at a quicker pace. It can, just to complete the picture, be used to describe the first section of an aria! One of the best examples is 'Sempre Libera' from *La Traviata*.

Caballe, Monserrat Spanish soprano. Critics have been scathing about Caballe's acting ability but few can question the sheer beauty of her voice. Her clarity of tone and effortless technique have created memorable performances both in opera and on the concert platform. Having trained in Barcelona and made debuts throughout Europe in prominent soprano roles such as Aida, Salome, Ariadne and a selection of Wagner heroines, she shot to international fame in 1965 in the role of Lucrezia Borgia in Donizetti's opera. She has specialized in the dramatic bel canto roles ever since, particularly in works by Bellini and Donizetti. While she has established herself in all the major roles, she has made a specialism of lesser known works by famous composers and her recordings prove the greatness of her voice. In a single year, 1965, she made her debut at the Carnegie Hall, the Met and Glyndebourne and has since maintained her place in the forefront of the international soprano singers. But it is for her home town of Barcelona that she feels a special affection, even agreeing, in 1986, to make a pop record and video, with the British rock star Freddie Mercury, to extol the virtues of the city to support its bid to host the Olympic Games!

Cadenza An opportunity for singers to embellish an aria, breaking off from the music as it is composed to add a section which acts as a showcase for their own virtuosity. In the early nineteenth century, singers were allowed to make up their own interpretations, to fit in before the end of the written aria but by the end of the century up to the present day, composers incorporated written cadenzas into their works. Usually contemporary singers choose a particular cadenza from a selection which may have been brought together in a volume such as *Variantes et points d'orgues* edited by Marchesi which includes, for example, nine different cadenzas for the aria 'Ah, fors'e lui' from *La Traviata* by Verdi.

Cahill, Teresa English soprano whose operatic career began at Glyndebourne where she won the John Christie Award. Since her Covent Garden debut in 1970, she

has sung in over one hundred performances there and is best known for her interpretations of Mozart and Richard Strauss. She also tackles contemporary works and sang the role of Elizabeth Zimmer in Henze's *Elegy for Young Lovers* in London and at the Alte Oper Frankfurt, conducted by the composer as part of his sixtieth birthday celebrations.

Cairns, Janice English soprano and an excellent singing actress, Cairns has brought excitement and dignity to many roles, particularly for English National Opera. She has featured in several of the more notorious productions, including *Mazeppa* by Tchaikovsky and *A Masked Ball* by Verdi, proving her ability to take direction which may not conform to the classic interpretation of the opera and produce a performance which is musically excellent and dramatically inventive. She has created a poignant Madam Butterfly and hard-edged Tosca, for which her former teacher, Tito Gobbi, gave her the accolade 'piccola Callas'.

Calisto, La (Cavalli) FP 1651. Based on Ovid's *Metamorphoses*, this opera hardly has an enthralling or original plot, but has been produced with great imagination and verve, which more than compensate, particularly by the experimental European opera group, Opera Factory in 1984.

The great god Jove loves Diana's nymph, Calisto, and disguises himself as Diana in order to be near her. Jove's wife Juno tries to thwart her husband by turning Calisto into a bear and Jove, recognizing when he is beaten, immortalizes his love as Ursa Minor, the star constellation.

Callas, Maris (1923–1977) If anyone, opera buff or not, is ever asked to name the first opera singer they can think of, it is often Maria Callas. She had every attribute of the classic opera singer – a voice of enormous range (up to a top E Flat), extraordinary stage presence, a colourful personal life which kept her in the constant eye of the media, not simply on the music pages, and a bad reputation for a 'prima donna' temperament which, on closer examination, was actually unjustified. Her capacity for hard work and her inability to compromise, even though her musical technique was not perfect, caused problems as a cast member – but with her talent, it soon became obvious that she would always be more than that.

Callas' special skill was not only the interpretation of the major roles, which took up her early career, but the way in which she developed her roles from Italian opera of the early nineteenth century, particularly Rossini, Bellini and Donizetti. Many of these works – *Anna Bolena, Lucia di Lammermoor, Armida* – are now in the standard repertoire, thanks to the prominence given to them by Callas. Her career on the opera stage was at its height between 1948, when she shot to prominence by covering for an indisposed 'Elvira' in *Il Puritani*, until the early 1960s when she began to concentrate on her concert work. By 1953, however, her personal and professional lives had become inextricably linked in the public mind. Her desperately quick weight loss gave rise to a vocal crisis which precipitated her retirement from the stage, and her liaison with Aristotle Onassis provided her with a consort who could reflect her power and glamour in his own lifestyle. While nothing can compensate for missing her definitive performances of, say, Tosca, Norma or Violetta, Callas made a vast range of recordings which still give ample evidence of her legendary contribution to the post-war opera world.

Calve, Emma (1858–1942) Italian soprano whose portrayal of Santuzza in *Cavalleria Rusticana* became her passport to international acclaim but was then surpassed by her performances of 'Carmen', a role she played sixty-one times at the Metropolitan Opera, New York.

Campanello di Notte (Rossini) FP 1836. One act opera by Rossini, now a popular choice for student or amateur opera societies.

A doddery old doctor, Don Annibale, is required to answer his door at any hour in case he is needed by a patient. He has recently married the lovely young Serafina whose former lover Enrico, keeps the doctor up all night by knocking his door, in order that he can spend time with Serafina. Hardly complex, but the tunes are very jolly!

Candide (Bernstein) FP 1956. Is it an opera, is it a musical? Bernstein's wonderfully colourful work started life as an operetta and is now accepted as part of the standard opera repertoire (although it is not in the definitive guide to synopses of operas, *Kobbé's Complete Opera Book*) and as a viable commercial piece which has recently played to packed houses at the Old Vic Theatre in London. It is full of 'numbers' rather than arias but demands operatic skills of its singers. As an introduction to the medium of opera, it would be perfect, provided it is cast and directed with panache and speed, maximizing the humour of the piece (which is plentiful as Dorothy Parker wrote the lyrics) rather than over-developing its philosophical side.

The story concerns Candide and Cunegonde on their journey through life. They wish to prove the theory of their philosopher Dr Pangloss who has taught them that 'this is the best of all possible worlds'. On their journey, they experience the Inquisition, betrayals, war, rape and exile, to arrive at the other end firm in the belief that they can only make the most of every day as it comes.

Can-can French dance performed at the Folies Bergère and immortalized for the opera stage in the last act of *Orpheus in the Underworld* by Offenbach.

Canadian Opera (see Toronto)

Capobianco, Tito Born in Argentina of Italian parents, Capobianco began his career as an opera producer at the Teatro Colon in Buenos Aires. He has since studied in Europe and now produces grand opera all over the world, as well as in Pittsburgh where he is Artistic Director of the prestigious opera company. His productions are characterized by lavish grandeur.

Capriccio (R. Strauss) FP 1942. A real insider's opera which the first time listener can enjoy for the music but may need to do some homework to appreciate the niceties of the plot. It is basically a discussion piece on the oldest argument in all opera – which comes first, the music or the words? Strauss constructs his plot out of this by placing Countess Madeleine as a central character with two suitors, a poet Olivier and a composer, Flamand in the time of Gluck's treatises on operatic reform, about 1775. No real conclusion is drawn and the musical high point is the Countess' final aria when she muses on the impossibility of finding a solution to the problem.

Capuletti e i Montecchi, I (Bellini)   FP 1830. Do not be beguiled into thinking this is the Shakespeare story of Romeo and Juliet. It certainly has similarities, but there are important differences which need to be understood to get the most out of the opera. The main differences are that Tebaldo equates to both Tybalt and Paris in the play and that Romeo is usually sung by a mezzo soprano. This last fact might account for the relative unpopularity of the opera.

Carmen (Bizet)   FP 1875. From disastrous beginnings (the French composer Saint Saens declared the work to be 'nonsensical'), it has become one of the most frequently performed operas in the entire repertoire with nearly 600 performances at the Metropolitan Opera, New York alone. It has been set in circuses, filmed on location in Spain, staged in the middle of Earl's Court, London, with a cast of hundreds and directed by Peter Brook with six singers and no set. As an opera it has everything – glamour, tragedy, humour, love, melodies, characters, colour, pathos. It is the proportion all these components are given in any production which brings the work from the realms of musical comedy to that of high and complex drama.

Carmen works in a cigarette factory in Spain. She has a phenomenal reputation among her compatriots – with men as being an untameable, irascible lover, with women as a powerful adversary in affairs of the heart. The soldier Don José appears to be unmoved by her alluring fascination and naturally she singles him out as a target for seduction. He is promised to the village girl, Micaela, the complete antithesis of Carmen and the choice of Don José's mother. But after Carmen's arrest at a brawl, Don José finds he cannot forget her and eventually releases her from prison. Carmen pursuades him to join her band of smugglers, increasing his devotion to her all the while and therefore increasing the likelihood that she will get bored of him. The dashing bullfighter Escamillo creates the distraction Carmen has been seeking. Rejecting Don José,

she follows Escamillo to the bullfight and is overwhelmed by his passion for her. But Don José cannot forget or forgive his tempestous gipsy so easily. In a powerful confrontation with the sound of the bullfight in the distance, he stabs Carmen to death before collapsing with remorse.

Carreras, José   Spanish tenor. One of the most striking presences on the opera stage, Carreras made his name in his early career singing the romantic lyric tenor roles such as Alfredo (*La Traviata*), Rudolfo (*La Bohème*) and the Duke (*Rigoletto*). Karajan recognized his ability to portray the 'heavier' roles with great force, and under him Carreras sang a towering Radames (*Aida*) at the 1979 Salzburg Festival. Carreras has made many excellent recordings both of the classics of opera and lesser known works, specializing in Spanish zarzuela (gypsy songs). After an almost miraculous recovery from leukaemia, he is returning to performance and is much in demand from the great opera houses. He has also recorded a number of lighter works, including a collection of songs by Andrew Lloyd Webber, *West Side Story* and *South Pacific* with Kiri te Kanawa.

Caruso, Enrico   (1873–1946) Italian tenor. *The Metropolitan Opera Encyclopedia* simply states – 'Probably the greatest tenor of all time' and Placido Domingo cites him as the tenor all other tenors idolize. It is unfair and unrepresentative that Caruso may be best known to today's young audience through the Mario Lanza film *The Great Caruso* which, although it is a perfectly acceptable film, only hints at the massive charisma and appeal of the first of the operatic mega-stars. Caruso was fortunate in developing his career at the time of the rise of the phonograph, which brought his magical voice to a huge audience through over 280 recordings. He was lucky too in his personality – easily communicative, generous, humorous, down to earth but with natural ebullience. His vocal technique was superb (despite never being without a cigarette, even just before going on stage) and his voice came not only from excellent musicianship but from that feeling which turns good singers into great singers.

His performing career began in Naples but developed through his association with the

Metropolitan Opera in New York, with whom he sang over 620 performances both in New York and on tour. He sang virtually every role in the mainstream tenor repertory, making a particular favourite of Canio (*I Pagliacci*) and Dick Johnson, which he created in the premiere of Puccini's *La Fanciulla del West*. In his own words (probably apocryphal but apposite), he assessed what a great singer needs: 'A big chest, a big mouth, ninety per cent memory, ten per cent intelligence, lots of hard work and something in the heart'.

Castrato It is a popular misconception that any man singing in a high voice must have undergone a major physical change for the cause of his art. The sound of such a voice is termed counter-tenor, or male alto, and is also virtually guaranteed to unnerve a new opera goer – particularly if he is male. Such fears no doubt stem from lurid stories of the 'castrati'. The voice of a castrato was quite different from that of a counter-tenor in terms of its physical production. The castrato was popular in the seventeenth and eighteenth centuries, both in religious music, as it was thought irreligious to allow women to open their mouths in church, and in the earliest 'opera seria'. Young male singers were castrated before puberty to preserve the brilliant, flexible, almost feminine tone of their voices for roles such as Monteverdi's Orfeo. Women were not allowed to perform on stage, so the roles of both male and female characters had to be sung by men. These castrati enjoyed superstar status, which encouraged them to behave with extraordinary vanity and sensitivity, creating the first impressions of the prima-donna type temperament which has ever since been associated with opera singers. By the mid-nineteenth century, however, the tradition of writing roles specifically for castrati had died out, the last major role being written by Meyerbeer in *Il Crociato in Egitto*, in 1824. The last known castrato, Alessandro Moreschi, died in 1922 having sung with the choir of the Sistine Chapel but never in opera.

Catalani, Alfredo (1854–1893). French composer whose only well known work – *La Wally* was brought to non-operatic prominence through the hugely successful French

thriller *Diva*. The beautiful melody in the film, sung by Wilhemina Wiggins Fernandez, is the soprano aria from *La Wally*.

Catalogue aria A style of aria popular in the eighteenth century where a singer runs through a list of some sort, to particularly descriptive music. Perhaps the most famous example is the great show piece for Leporello, the manservant in Mozart's *Don Giovanni* when he catalogues his master's extraordinary sexual conquests throughout Europe. For an effective staging of this aria, look to the Joseph Losey film of *Don Giovanni* where, unhampered by the usual constrictions of the stage, Leporello makes full and effective use of the magnificent grounds of the Palladian villas north of Venice.

Cavalleria Rusticana (Mascagni) FP Rome 1890. One-act opera, rarely performed without its lifelong partner, *I Pagliacci* by Leoncavallo. Written as a reaction to the heroic operas which bore little resemblance to real life 'Cav and Pag' have come to symbolize 'verisimo opera' – the everyday story of Italian country folk, their lives and loves set to rumbustious, tuneful music. The plots are hardly subtle but the sheer sentimentality of *Cavalleria Rusticana* makes a good performance extremely affecting.

The action, which takes place on Easter Sunday, centres on the homecoming soldier, Turiddu, who has lost his love Lola to the drover Alfio. Turiddu seeks consolation with his former lover Santuzza who is already pregnant by him. When Turiddu rejects her in favour of Lola, Santuzza pours her heart out to Alfio who challenges Turiddu to a duel in which Turiddu is killed. Between the two scenes is the famous Easter Hymn, beloved of amateur choral societies and male voice choirs throughout the world.

Cenerentola, La (Rossini) FP 1817. The plot is based on Cinderella, without the magic! Like *The Barber of Seville* by the same composer, *La Cenerentola* can be very amusing if it is played with speed and humour. If it loses pace, it can seem facile and longwinded. Everything depends on the soprano singing the leading role, which is punishing musically and demanding artistically, and on Dandini, the 'Buttons' character.

Angelina, the Cinderella character, suffers

at the hands of her stepfather Don Magnifico and her stepsisters Tisbe and Clorinda. In true fairy tale tradition, the handsome prince Ramiro and his valet Dandini are roaming the country looking for a bride for the prince. Before they arrive at Don Magnifico's, they swap clothes, thus enabling Dandini to enjoy the attentions of the ugly sisters, and Ramiro to fall for Angelina. The rest of the story follows the fairy tale, with a gold bracelet being substituted for glass slipper and the Prince's philosopher Alidoro taking the role of the Fairy Godmother. Needless to say, they all live happily ever after.

Chailly, Ricardo Italian conductor who studied with his father Luciano Chailly and made his debut at the Metropolitan Opera, conducting *The Tales of Hoffmann* in 1982, at the age of twenty-nine. Chailly promises to be one of the most exciting young conductors to have emerged from Italy recently, with particularly notable performances of Verdi to his credit. Since 1986, he has been Music Director of the Teatro Communale di Bologna, attracting stars of world calibre to perform there and bringing the chorus to a superb standard.

Chaliapin, Feodor (1873–1938) Russian bass, forever associated with the role of Boris Godunov. He worked with the Bolshoi Opera in Russia for over twenty years until emigrating to Paris after the Russian Revolution and never again returning to his homeland. He typifies the lowering Russian bass – huge in stature with a powerfully deep, resonant voice and overwhelming stage presence. In 1921, he commanded a fee of $3,000 per performance at the Metropolitan Opera, New York – the highest single fee paid to an artist until the 1960s. Some idea of his immense ability can be seen in the 1915 film *Ivan the Terrible*, directed by Ivanov Gay with music by Rimsky Korsakov.

Chamber opera Literally, opera to be performed in a room rather than on stage, chamber opera became increasingly popular in the 1980s. It is relatively cheap to produce and easy to tour, involving only small casts and minimal orchestras. Some of the best examples of the genre are by Britten whose English Opera Group was formed specifically to perform small scale opera. Increasingly, large scale operas are reduced to chamber opera size to bring them to as wide an audience as possible, although many classic works are also scaled down to enable them to tour at a minimum cost.

Chance, Michael English counter-tenor who is in increasing demand internationally as more roles are written for his type of voice, with its penetratingly clear tone complemented, in Michael Chance's case, by a handsome stage presence. He has appeared throughout Europe singing the major counter-tenor roles, balancing the work of composers such as Monteverdi and Handel with contemporary pieces such as *A Night at the Chinese Opera* by Judith Weir, in which he sang the Military Governor. In America he has so far appeared in concerts and oratorio only, but his acclaimed recordings will surely bring his superb voice to a wider public and ensure his American opera debut cannot be far away.

Chicago – Civic Opera, Lyric Opera Born as a result of the argument between Oscar Hammerstein and Otto Kahn about the right to produce opera in New York, the Chicago Civic Opera House was started in 1910 to create 'an opening wedge in the Great West' using many of the artists from Hammerstein's Manhattan Opera House, which had recently closed. Its productions soon rose to rival those of the Met, with premieres such as *The Love of Three Oranges* by Prokofiev in 1921, under the leadership of the prima donna Mary Garden who managed to leave a deficit of over $1,000,000 – quite a feat even by opera standards! The tenure of Samuel Insull as Chairman from 1924 to 1932 brought glamour and wealth to the house, now renamed the Lyric Opera of Chicago despite the savage effects many felt after the Wall Street Crash of 1929. But Insull's slightly shady business dealings forced him to leave America, and opera in Chicago fell into abeyance (save for a few unsuccessful attempts) throughout the Second World War. But by 1954, both Maria Callas and Renata Tebaldi had been signed up for a season at the new Lyric Theatre, thanks to the determination of the extraordinary Carol Fox. She led the company through twenty-five years of steady improvement, never particularly controversial but always strong musically. She was succeeded by another leading female figure in the opera world, Ardis Krainik, who still maintains a high profile for the company both in and outside America.

Children in opera While no-one would consider bringing a little child to the opera night after night, directors are frequently faced with the dilemma of needing to include one or more children in certain scenes of an opera. This necessitates entertaining these would be stars when they are not on stage. Some choose to make the production into a full scale children's event – *Carmen* produced by David Pountney for ENO in 1986 had over forty children on stage for most of the performance. Other directors, particularly those producing Britten operas where the children play a crucial role, need to select performers for their acting and singing abilities – notably the sailor boys in *Billy Budd*, or Miles and Flora in *The Turn of the Screw*.

Perhaps one of the best 'Never-act-with-children-or-animals' anecdotes belongs to Australian Opera and John Copley's production there of *The Magic Flute*. A child of three (not an age associated with compliance of any sort) was required to dress as a duck-billed platypus and crawl across the stage. Each night, the stage manager would gently whisper 'Kevin, Kevin' from the wings, hoping it would act as a homing device for the child who invariably became blinded by his unwieldy costume. But one night the child waddled out of range of his mentor and headed – much to the audience's amused horror – straight for the orchestra pit! The stage manager, torn between the wrath of his director or the child's mother, let paternalism prevail and rushed on stage to divert his charge, and stop the show with the resulting hilarity.

Chorus The ex-chorus master of one of Britain's national opera companies has described his chorus as 'made up of very nice individuals but stick them together as a unit and they seem to become a totally uncontrollable monster with no human feelings whatsoever'. That may seem strong, but choruses, particularly of the major repertory companies, have, over the years, developed a herd-like camaraderie which can overshadow their perfectly pleasant individual personalities. An opera chorus gets the blame when it all goes wrong and is rarely complimented when it all goes right. (A notable exception to this was the first chorus of Welsh National Opera which was amateur in the early days of the company and frequently received far better notices than their soloists!)

Choruses are trained by chorus masters who then hand them on to the behest of any one of several different directors. A good chorus member may know his role in every main repertory work by heart but is rarely given the artistic limelight (frustrating for the large numbers of would-be soloists in their ranks). As a group they are often called on to besport themselves in the name of contemporary productions which can be at best exhilarating and at worst excruciatingly embarrassing. Some like to be directed through every step, others prefer to be treated as a group, simply to support the soloists. But the level of concentration required is the same for every performance – eighty people making their musical entries any time other than exactly together makes for an appalling performance. And the level of musicianship is, in a first class chorus, extremely high. The chorus of a national repertory company will frequently be performing two operas in repertory each night; 'note-bashing' one in the rehearsal studio and trying yet another production for the first time on stage – perhaps with all four in different languages! A healthy voice and a healthy body are needed to maintain such a pace.

Christie, John (1882–1962) 'Impressario' hardly seems the correct way to describe this mild mannered English amateur opera fan and sometime organ builder who in 1934 opened his Sussex manor house to the public so they might enjoy performances of Mozart in the tiny theatre he had built for his wife, the lyric soprano Audrey Mildmay. The house was Glyndebourne and the Festival has continued to be the most successful British opera festival, each year playing to packed houses with an impressive international artistic reputation. Christie founded the Glyndebourne Arts Trust in 1954 and a year later was created a Companion of

Honour for his work. On his death, his son George Christie took over his father's role, taking the enterprise to its current stature and profitability.

Christoff, Boris Bulgarian bass. Sent by King Boris to study singing in Rome, having been 'spotted' in the Sofia Chorus, Christoff rewarded his first patron by developing an international career, failing to gain great popularity only in America, where he was prevented from entering at the height of the McCarthy era. He was regarded as the natural successor to Chaliapin as his portrayal of Boris Godunov was particularly noteworthy. He has also made excellent renditions of the heavier Verdi roles.

Chung, Myung Whun Korean conductor. Chung was thrust into the operatic limelight in the summer of 1989 because of his appointment as Music Director of the embattled Bastille Opera House in Paris. Not yet forty, Chung had the responsibility of steering the new house to its first performance of *The Trojans* by Berlioz in March 1990. Although relatively unknown amongst large audiences in Europe, Chung has developed an impressive reputation with his conducting, winning the Premio Abbiati, one of Italy's most prestigious musical prizes, for his leadership of *Boris Godunov* at Florence's Maggio Musicale. Word is that Chung, who does not yet speak French but is learning fast, has already gained the confidence of the Bastille orchestra and seems well placed to produce the first positive reactions from the hitherto troubled opera house.

Cid, Le (Massenet) FP 1885. Love and family honour in twelfth-century Spain! Don Rodrigue, the son of Don Diegue has challenged the father of his girlfriend to a duel. Don Rodrigue is victorious but Chimene, the object of his affections, is then torn between love for her dead father and love for the man who killed him. Only when Rodrigue returns home from a victorious battle against the Moors does Chimene realize how much she loves him. Not a patch on Massenet's great works *Werther* and *Manon* but a good tune is never far away with this composer.

Cilea, Francesco (1866–1950) Italian composer. Only two of Cilea's operas have survived into the contemporary repertoire *L'Arlesiana* and *Adriana Lecouvreur* chiefly because they provide such glamorous vehicles for their leading ladies. They are both melodic and 'sweet' but some might find them a little insubstantial.

Cincinatti Opera Association Drawing on a strong choral tradition in this industrial city, the Summer Opera Association was founded in 1920 to perform open air performances. But it was not until 1972 that the Association moved to its present home in the Music Hall and divided its season into Spring, Summer and Autumn sections rather than one six month period. It is now notable for spotting emerging talent amongst America's young opera singers in consistently strong performances of the repertory classics as well as more adventurous work.

Claque A tradition which has never really caught on in England but is still prevalent in Italy. A performer or producer will hire a number of people either to stimulate applause or start the booing. It all sounds very simple and somewhat informal but in the last century, claques were highly organized groups whose emotive outpourings could ensure the success of one performer at the expense of another. They were particularly prevalent in late nineteenth-century Paris, with the 'chef de claques' invited to the dress rehearsal to study the score and inform his 'claqueurs' when to laugh, cry, clap, boo, cheer and so on (all of which would be paid at a certain rate – five francs to applaud, fifteen francs to express alarm, etc). As late as the 1950s, a pro and anti Maria Callas claque at La Scala Milan had to be restrained by the police as riots broke out.

Clarissa (Robin Holloway) FP 1990. Although the composer finished this opera in 1976, it was not fully staged until the ENO production of 1990 when it formed the second opera in ENO's new programme. At first it seems an unlikely tale for an opera, being based on the novel written by Samuel Richardson in 1747. Richardson's tale runs into seven volumes, making it the longest novel in the English language. Undaunted by such an unwieldy basis for his work, Holloway wrote the libretto to his score, determined to bring out the stark nature of Clarissa's tragedy – that she is hopelessly tempted by the feckless Lovelace who ultimately rapes her after which she dies – interspersing the drama with surreal themes and images.

Clarissa's family, the Harlowes, have determined that she is to marry Screwtape – an unsuitable husband for all reasons other than being very rich! Clarissa's salvation appears to be Lovelace, a well known womanizer who attempts unsuccessfully to seduce Clarissa. Lovelace manages to rescue Clarissa from death at the hands of her father and takes her to a brothel – although Clarissa does not recognize it as such. Lovelace attempts to seduce Clarissa again by starting a fire but she escapes once more. She is brought back exhausted and, still rejecting Lovelace in her comatose state, is raped by him. As she dies, Clarissa's life is viewed from alternative perspectives – that she is saved by God, that her downfall was brought on by her family who pray for forgiveness at her funeral, and that she is now at last independent and secure.

Clark, Graham English tenor. A former sports teacher, consultant to the Sports Council, and a 'late starter' in opera, Graham Clark joined Scottish Opera in 1975. But his former career is not wasted. He brings an enormous amount of vocal and physical athleticism to his committed and energetic performances of demanding roles. He joined English National Opera in 1978 and has appeared in some notable productions there, including Busoni's *Doktor Faust* in 1986. Graham Clark has a successful international career, especially singing Wagner. He has appeared in Bayreuth annually since 1981. He made his Met debut in 1985/86, and sings Herod (*Salome*) and The Captain (*Wozzeck*) there.

Clemenza di Tito, La (Mozart) FP1791. At the height of his artistic powers, Mozart moved away from the jollity of *The Marriage of Figaro* to tackle a serious opera based on the drama of Ancient Rome. The action takes some concentration and is worth reading in Kobbé if it is your first Mozart opera. If you want to get to know Mozart's operas, however, don't start with this one – compared to the others it is very uninspired!

The Emperor Tito has decided to marry Berenice. This infuriates his former love Vitellia, who asks her admirer Sesto to assassinate the Emperor. Tito then strays from Berenice, wooing Sevilia instead but when he realizes Sevilia is already in love with Annio, who happens to be a friend to Sesto, Tito comes back to Vitellia – who can not stop her plans to have him assassinated! He escapes, but Sesto is arrested and tried for his assassination attempt. Vitellia eventually discloses her part in the plot, but Tito lives up to the title of the opera and forgives them both.

Colds A great dilemma is put before all opera singers who are feeling under par – should they go on and risk being booed for a bad performance or should they withdraw and risk losing their fans? There are numerous heroic stories of singers completing performances only to collapse in the wings, but opinion is divided between those who think that an announcement before the performance relating to the state of a singer's health reassures or angers the audience.

Coliseum (see London Coliseum)

Cologne The Oper der Stadt which opened in 1872, quickly made its name with performances of Verdi and Wagner operas but it was the arrival of Otto Klemperer as Director in 1917 which heralded the theatre's greatest period, staging performances such as the German premiere of *Katya Kabanova*. The current theatre was opened in 1957, following the demolition of the older one during the Second World War. Since then the theatre has staged many notable world and German premieres, including *The Fiery Angel* (Prokofiev) and Britten's *Billy Budd*. From 1978 until his death the Opera was led by Sir John Pritchard whose tenure there has been described as '(breathing) fresh air into the dour world of German opera'.

Coloratura 'The Twiddly Bits', which have in the past contributed to giving operatic sopranos a bad name; coloratura means the ornamentation sopranos can give to the highest notes in a melody. It is particularly prevalent in Rossini, in roles such as the lead in *La Cenerentola* or Rosina in *The Barber of Seville*. The best coloratura adds enormous excitement and bravado to a singer's performance. It can, however, be excruciatingly embarrassing if the singer is anything but artistically confident and musically accurate.

Commission 'We are in the position of an art gallery whose most modern pictures are by Sargent or a library whose newest novel is *The Forsyte Saga*.' Thus Tyrone Guthrie bewailed the lack of new opera in 1945 and many believe the situation is little changed nearly fifty years later. But the problem is not so much the writing of new operas as attracting an audience to them. Marketing managers for opera companies tend to believe that if 'New Commission' appears on promotional material, they can budget for a 25 to 50 per cent drop in Box Office takings. It is true that today's audiences tend to shy away from the new, the modern and often the controversial; but enlightened opera administrators rightly insist on developing new commissions such as ENO's four year programme, with a new work performed every year, now complemented by a workshop to encourage the writing and performance of new work, or the nationwide initiative currently running in America called 'Opera for the '80s and beyond'. Glyndebourne, for all its conservative audience, also pursues an active commissions policy and plans to stage *The Death of Klinghoffer* by John Adams (based on the terrorist attack on the ship, the *Achile Lauro*) with its Touring Company in 1991.

An opera house will approach a composer and make an offer of a fee for a new work, to be completed by a certain date (hardly ever adhered to) and put into performance. Negotiations are made regarding any 'cut' the composer might get from the box office takings and detailed discussions ensue on the transformation of a composer's concept to a workable technical specification. Working with a living composer (particularly one seeing a piece he may have worked on for years being cut, note-bashed and generally hacked around in rehearsal) can be a nerve racking experience for cast and crew. But opera companies will last into the next decade (let alone the next century) only if they are willing to take those risks and support the work of our contemporary composers.

Compton Verney The Compton Verney estate is just to the east of Stratford-upon-Avon in the heart of the Midlands of England. A powerful team of enthusiasts, backed by a combination of public enterprise and private sponsorship is undertaking a massive project on the estate – to build the first purpose built opera house Britain has had since the opening of Buxton in 1903. The Compton Verney Opera Project seeks to provide opera and ballet to the population of the Midlands who are at present badly served for large scale productions, coming between the tours of Opera North and Welsh National Opera and being just that bit too far away from London to attend performances there regularly. The comparisons with Glyndebourne are obvious – Compton Verney is in a beautiful situation with grounds landscaped by Capability Brown, will rely heavily on private support for its initial establishment and subsequent running costs, and will be an ideal venue for up-scale corporate entertaining. But it will be substantially larger than the rebuilt Glyndebourne, with some 1,300 seats, and will be a purpose built theatre as opposed to a less-formal appendage to a private house.

Eighty-five architects tendered for the contract, the winner being the Danish firm Henning Larsen whose design seems beautifully classical and complementary to the waterfront setting of the new building. Already Compton Verney has attracted a persuasive team of advocates to work on its behalf. Managers of the calibre of Sir John Tooley and Lord Harewood, artists of the prestige of Dr Jonathan Miller and Humphrey Burton, corporate supporters of the stature of Merrill Lynch and IBM, have contributed to the progress of the project so far. It says much for the confidence with which the future of opera is viewed in the UK. Compton Verney is due to open in 1993. The wise will sign up for the mailing list at the first possible opportunity.

Comte Ory, Le (Rossini) FP 1828. A fairly insubstantial plot, pretty music and often very lavish sets make this work hardly the greatest dramatic experience but pleasant for those not easily bored!

A Knight of the Crusades, Count Ory, and his manservant, Isolaier, are after the same woman, the Countess Adele, who is sworn to chastity while her brother is off fighting the crusades. By various devious means (the Count has something of an amorous reputation) both woo her and are only revealed when her brother's return from battle forces their immediate escape.

Conductor The conductor as we recognize him today is a relatively recent phenomenon. Until the middle of the nineteenth century, orchestras were led from the first violins or from the harpsichord, often by the composer himself. Only with the larger scale works of the Romantic composers, where more complex parts were written for more instruments, did it become essential to have one impartial time keeper easily visible to everyone in the orchestra and on stage. The conductor has since grown in importance in opera and even now, the heyday of the powerful director, the conductor has the final say by virtue of his or her being there on the night. Today's conductors are trusted with the musical management of an opera, the sensitivity to give singers and players the guidance they need without numbing their own ideas, the ability to balance an orchestra to achieve an overall sound which captures the character of the piece and the versatility to make each performance stand in its own right. While the conductor employs all the technical tools – baton, a method of counting which holds good for numerous musical styles, constant eye contact for sharp entrances and exits, sound musicianship to interpret a range of works – it is the personality that he, or infrequently she, possesses which colours the overall performance.

Connell, Elizabeth South African soprano who began her career as a mezzo but has since found international fame with roles in the higher register. She has worked with opera companies in Australia, Bayreuth, La Scala and New York and is a frequent performer at Covent Garden. Her interpretation of the punishing role of Lady Macbeth in Verdi's opera *Macbeth* is particularly notable.

Consul, The (Menotti) FP 1950. If you thought all opera plots revolved around men dressing up as women, a fair number of amorous maidservants and other generally daft activities, this is the opera to open your

eyes. This opera is about bureaucracy, pettymindedness and individual freedom. The Consul never appears, the city is not identified but the theme is so familiar to audiences that the opera became an immediate success.

John Sorel needs to leave the city after a brush with the Secret Police. He leaves his mother, his wife, Magda and their young child and heads for the mountains where they can join him and escape together once they get a visa. The Secretary to the Consul who is, as Kobbé so beautifully puts it, 'the embodiment of every form-ridden bureaucrat in every big city in the world' processes her daily round of applications with a soulless formality which leaves Magda – and her fellow applicants – desperate. The drama heightens as Magda pursues her quest to see the Consul and John refuses to move on without his family. Ultimately, after a series of nightmarish events, John returns to the city, minutes too late to prevent Magda, bereft of all hope of escape, from committing suicide. As the curtain falls, the last sound to be heard is that of a telephone ringing, unanswered.

Contes d'Hoffmann, Les (Offenbach) FP 1881. A complete change from Offenbach's other, lighter works, 'Hoffmann' is a peculiar work of great psychological complexity and, if the staging difficulties are adequately overcome, compelling theatricality. The Barcarolle, towards the end of the opera, is well known.

The poet Hoffmann is desperately in love with the prima donna Stella. While waiting to meet her, he tells Lindorf and Niclausse three tales, each representing one aspect of a woman's love. First, in Paris, his love for the automaton Olympia who is destroyed by her creator. Next, in Munich, the consumptive Antonia and Hoffmann plan to elope. Antonia is prevented from using her talent to sing, by her father who fears the exertion might kill her but, before she can escape with Hoffmann, she is tricked into performing by Dr Miracle and dies in the attempt. Finally, in Venice, Hoffmann sells his soul and murders a rival in his quest for the prostitute Guilietta. She rejects him for Pitichinaccio. In the Epilogue, Hoffmann is finally abandoned, exhausted and inebriated by his revelations, by Stella who leaves with Lindorf.

Continuo The full term is 'basso continuo' and describes an accompaniment played to a recitative. This accompaniment doubles the melody in the lowest violin part and in opera is played most frequently on the harpsichord. Occasionally it will be played by the cello or by the harpsichord and cello together. In small orchestras, it is common for the conductor to play the continuo part on the harpsichord and direct the orchestra from there. Recitatives with continuo are most frequently found in the 'opera seria' of the seventeenth and eighteenth centuries.

Contralto (see Alto)

Copley, John English director. John Copley started out as a performer and then a stage manager before becoming Assistant Producer at the Royal Opera House in 1961. He has maintained his long association with Covent Garden which has many of his productions in its repertoire. These tend to be traditional in style with elaborate sets and costumes, although it must be remembered that many of these productions are now more than twenty years old and have been revived time and again. Thus accusations that they are 'dated' are as inevitable as they are unfair. Copley has also worked with other British opera companies, in Europe, and in North America.

Coproduction An increasingly popular method of sharing production costs with other opera houses, creating one production to be shared between two or more theatres. Within Britain, it has been most successfully worked between ENO and Opera North, with the recent production of *The Pearl Fishers* for example, but it is even more effective when a foreign theatre is involved. These relationships extend the international experience of opera, bring opera companies to prominence overseas and introduce new and innovative techniques to theatres at home. For example, David Gockley at the Wortham Centre in Houston has co-produced some highly successful operas with ENO, including *Orpheus in the Underworld* with scurrilous designs by the British satirical cartoonist, Gerald Scarfe. In Europe the Maggio Musicale in Florence co-produced a recent production of *Tosca* with ENO, and the opera house at Amsterdam recently undertook a successful collaboration with the same company for *Lear* by Aribert Reimann.

Cosi fan Tutte (Mozart) FP 1790. Many people think this is one of the greatest of Mozart's operas. It is subtle in its inferences and has a more powerful contemporary relevance than any of his other works. It is not action-packed, like *The Marriage of Figaro*, or highly dramatic, like *Don Giovanni*, so is best approached as a relaxing, often amusing performance with some of Mozart's finest music. A good production will bring out the heartache, as well as the joy, of being in love. Because the action is slow, a bad production can render an intriguing work into a boring set of occurrences.

Dorabella is engaged to Ferrando, and Fiordiligi is engaged to Guglielmo. A cunning bachelor, Don Alfonso, has placed a bet with the two men that their fiancées could not be faithful to them while they are away. He pretends to send them off to war, but in fact dresses them up as two handsome Albanians and sends them back to Dorabella and Fiordiligi. Each man flirts with the other's fiancée. They face initial rejection but ultimately, thanks to the help of the wily maidservant Despina, the girls are persuaded to break off their engagements and marry the Albanians. As the double wedding approaches, the 'Albanians' make an excuse to leave and return dressed in their rightful clothes. Don Alfonso has won his bet, but reason and tolerance prevail and both pairs are reunited happily.

Costumes Janet Pullen, head of the Wardrobe Department of Covent Garden, sums up the problems facing the wardrobe department of a major opera house with characteristic good humour: 'One person is as much of a problem as one stage. A hundred people are very different sizes, they have mouths, they answer back, they spill coffee down themselves ... they break their arms they break their legs. The production team has only got one stage. I have a hundred people, all answering back and putting on weight!'

There is something inherent in most of us that dictates that dressing up in costume must be fun and when we put a costume on we must look better. But for singers to feel right is crucial to their performance. If a costume does not move or flow in the manner of the character, a king or a peasant, it makes it extremely difficult to sing the part convincingly. Arguments about costumes are far more important than mere questions of vanity. Thus wardrobe staff play an intensely diplomatic role between performer and designer, massaging the ego of the former, while representing the concept of the latter. A bad or inexperienced designer may ignore what the performers have to offer naturally – which is fatal, as Josephine Barstow describes: 'If you just put a costume on stage and expect the costume to make the right kind of noise, you've obliterated one of your dimensions.'

Costume making is a painstaking and expensive process for the biggest houses, where the repertory system may dictate that the costumes will have to last for many years. A prototype is always made, out of a reasonably inexpensive material, to see if the costume is practical on stage and leaves the singer's neck and chest unconstricted and ears free to hear the other sounds on stage. The finished garment may be made out of the finest cloth, particularly for principal singers, and is frequently the cause of overspent budgets. Such seeming luxury is in fact vital if the costume is to make an impact in a theatre the size of the Metropolitan Opera, New York, and is to be constantly cleaned and worn for up to ten years. The weight of a costume is also crucial to the success of a singer's performance – each light above the stage generates about as much heat as one bar on an electric fire and there may be up to 150 lights trained on a singer at one time. Add to that the padding that will go into a costume of, say, Falstaff, and the costume designer's task becomes one of safety as well as appearance.

Opera companies without the large resources of the big houses seek out costume designers whose inspiration rarely seems to be hampered by lack of money. Cheaper materials and contemporary clothing can be transformed into extraordinarily effective period costumes, not built to last but perfect for a small touring company. Such simplicity can actually engage the curiosity and imagination of the audience more powerfully than the sumptuousness of a lavish national company production, where over-indulgence on the part of the costume designer can sometimes detract from the overall message of the opera.

Cotrubas, Ileana Romanian soprano who has specialized in the gentle, sympathetic roles such as Manon, Mimi and Violetta. Such performances in some way contradict her personality, as she is the first to acknowledge in saying, 'I have never had a big voice, I have always had a big temperament'.

Coughing 'A real opera goer would have a heart attack or strangle himself, rather than cough at a key moment.' So speaks the great Wagnerian bass Gwynne Howell. This may seem harsh and dictatorial, but when the success of a performance lies in a sound that comes from the mouth, somehow the effect of a misplaced cough is almost greater than it is in the concert hall. If you feel a cough coming on, the best answer is to slip out then and there – the moment you start to stifle it, it will get worse. If a cough sweet can be unwrapped and sucked quietly, it often helps, but to rustle cellophane compounds the offence.

Counter-tenor The counter-tenor voice is entirely natural, commonly referred to as a male alto, and is beautiful in its tone and clarity. Every man has a natural falsetto range to his voice, and even the deepest bass can sing notes in the counter-tenor range for a short time. Some people find the sound of a man singing notes more usually associated with a woman disconcerting, but the best exponents can make a counter-tenor role sound quite beautiful. The work of Alfred Deller, James Bowman, Michael Chance or Christopher Robson has brought the counter-tenor to prominence in the latter part of this century, particularly in contemporary music (Oberon in Britten's *Midsummer Night's Dream* or *Akhnaten* by Philip Glass). On the concert platform, the search for authenticity in many of the major oratorios has led to many erstwhile contralto or tenor roles being assigned to counter-tenors.

Covent Garden (see London)

Cox, John English director and currently Production Director at Covent Garden. He shares responsibility with other members of the artistic/music team for the artistic de-

Carmen, by Bizet, possibly the best known opera of all. Sally Burgess as Carmen, with John Treleaven as Don José, in David Pountney's controversial production set in a used-car lot.

The Cunning Little Vixen, by Janacek. Rita Cullis (left) as the Fox, and Anne Dawson as the Vixen.

velopment of the house, stages revivals and produces new productions. Prior to this post, he had two notably successful long-term commitments. The first was for Glyndebourne Festival Opera where several of his acclaimed productions were filmed for television, including Strauss's *Ariadne auf Naxos*, *Arabella*, and *Cappriccio*, and where he engaged several distinguished artists including Erté, Sir Hugh Casson, and David Hockney as designers. The second was as General Administrator/Artistic Director of Scottish Opera, from 1981 to 1986. Although he is best known as an opera director, he has also worked extensively in the theatre, television and documentary films.

Craig, Charles English tenor whose career lasted for over thirty years, with a rendering of 'Nessun Dorma' from *Turandot* at the age of sixty being strikingly powerful in even the highest registers. Craig was thought to be one of the few British tenors able to convey the more demanding tenor roles such as Otello with conviction and confidence and though his career was truly international, he remained closely associated to the two London opera houses he always considered to be his home.

Crespin, Régine French soprano who dominated the Paris Opera during the 1950s singing a notable Tosca and Carmen, as well as the heavier Wagner roles and lighter comic parts. Such versatility ensured that her career lasted over two decades and took her to the world's greatest opera houses. Her pure tone and exquisite diction created powerful performances which relied on exemplary technique rather than expansive acting ability. These she continued to the end of her career in a dignified portrayal of Madam de Croissy in *The Dialogue of the Carmelites* by Poulenc.

Cross, Joan British soprano who performed extensively on the English opera scene from 1931 to 1950. A particularly fine singer of Britten, she created Ellen Orford (*Peter Grimes*), Female Chorus (*Rape of Lucretia*), Lady Billows (*Albert Herring*) and Queen Elizabeth (*Gloriana*). After retiring from the stage, she devoted herself to teaching at the opera school she founded and producing operas for Sadler's Wells and Covent Garden.

Cullis, Rita English soprano who is a firm favourite amongst audiences in Britain and is rapidly gaining an impressive reputation in Europe. She performs chiefly with the Welsh National Opera and her commanding stage presence and powerful voice have latterly brought her great praise for such roles as Ellen Orford in *Peter Grimes*, the Countess in *The Marriage of Figaro* and the Marschallin in *Der Rosenkavalier*. She is equally proficient in contemporary roles, singing Jenifer in *A Midsummer Marriage* by Michael Tippett and the Fox in Janacek's *Cunning Little Vixen*, each to great acclaim.

Cunning Little Vixen, The (Janacek) FP 1924. A seemingly innocent pastoral tale that has more profound psychological undercurrents for those who choose to look for them. It was produced with such vigour and charm by David Pountney for Welsh National Opera, with Helen Field in the title role, that the production seems likely to be unsurpassed by professional opera companies, although it continues to be very popular for amateur productions. It calls for young agile performers who can act as animals whilst being persuasive as singers.

The cunning little vixen Sharpears has evaded the Forester who tamed her, by inciting the animals of the forest to revolution! She marries the fox Goldenstripe and produces a large family; but, never able to resist trouble, taunts the local poacher who kills her. The opera ends as the Forester sees a vision of a young fox cub and reassures himself that in the forest, there are no endings, only new beginnings.

Curlew River (Britten) FP 1964. The first of Britten's Church Parables, *Curlew River* is closely based on the Japanese Noh play *Sumidagawa*. Britten moved the action (such as it is!) from Buddhist Japan to Christian England and retained the stylized form of performance, with introduction and chorus, minimal sets and simple musical motifs to symbolize each character. The beauty of the work lies in the gentle mixture of music, word and setting, rather than in strong action and melody.

The Ferryman is cautious about taking an old woman across the river because she is clearly mad. She is seeking her lost son and, as the ferryman tells the story of a young boy who died escaping from robbers, they both realize that the boy is her son. The Ferryman takes her to the boy's grave and the chorus conclude the opera with their ritual chanting.

Da capo A style of aria particularly popular in the eighteenth century when the first section of the aria was repeated again at the end of the piece, often with added ornamentation.

Dale, Laurence English tenor who made his operatic debut at ENO as Camille in *The Merry Widow* in 1981, and his Covent Garden debut in the same year, since when he has been constantly engaged in the UK, and in Europe, both with a varied operatic career and a very busy concert career. He was the original Don José in Peter Brook's extraordinary production of *The Tragedy of Carmen* in Paris.

Dalibor (Smetana) FP 1868. Highly nationalistic Czech opera set in fifteenth-century Prague, beloved by nineteenth-century audiences who saw it as the epitome of their national struggle. It is often compared with Beethoven's *Fidelio*, written many years earlier but conveying the same sense of heroism against oppression.

Dalibor has been sentenced to imprisonment for killing the Burgrave of Prague to avenge the death of his friend Zdenek. The Burgrave's daughter, Milada, disguises herself as a boy and seeks to help Dalibor escape but is wounded in the attempt. Dalibor, now facing a death sentence carries Milada from the prison and as she dies in his arms, he stabs himself rather than be captured by the armed guard.

Dallas Civic Opera In a city with resources similar to that of Houston, the Dallas Civic Opera has chosen a policy of safe, glamorous productions rather than the Wortham Center's more adventurous approach. International stars are attracted by superb facilities and healthy production budgets as well as a strong artistic reputation. Luigi Alva, Teresa Berganza and Dame Joan Sutherland all made their American debuts with the company, which performs at the State Fair Park Music Hall.

Damnation of Faust, The (Berlioz) FP 1846. The structure of this work rather defies description – part concert piece, part oratorio and certainly full of enough dramatic action to merit a full operatic staging, which was only done nearly twenty years after Berlioz' death.

It is in four parts, following the traditional story of the tortured Faust, who sells his soul to the devil after death, in return for perfect happiness while he is alive. In its concert version in America in the late nineteenth century, it caused a sensation but the opera version has hardly achieved any significance outside France.

Daniel, Paul English conductor. Paul Daniel has already established a varied and successful career at an early age and enjoys a considerable following. In 1981 he joined the music staff at ENO after assisting John Elliott Gardiner and playing continuo on David Freeman's production of Monteverdi's *Orfeo*. This introduction to David Freeman led to Daniel becoming one of the founders of Opera Factory in London and later its Musical Director. He has had some notable successes with performances of contemporary works including *The Mask of Orpheus*, *Akhnaten*, *Lear*, *Punch and Judy* and also with the standard repertoire. He first appeared at ENO at the age of twenty-six conducting *Fidelio* at less than a day's notice. He was appointed Musical Director of Opera North from the 1990/91 season. Everything he tackles is likely to be marked with the distinguishing features of his work to date – a fully integrated performance where music and production are given equal importance and which all participants approach without preconceived ideas.

Daphne (R. Strauss) FP 1938. A one-act classical opera with wonderfully rich, lyrical music and a final scene which challenges any technical director.

The beautiful Daphne, daughter of the fisherman Peneios and his wife Gaea, is more interested in the world of nature than in any of the suitors who pursue her, much to her mother's annoyance. She rejects the shepherd Leukippos and is bewildered by the advances of the god Apollo who has come to woo her in human form. Apollo kills Leukippos, but seeing that Daphne is genuinely distraught at this, asks Zeus to transform her into a laurel tree! As this transformation takes place, Daphne sings one of the most thrilling arias in all of Strauss's work.

da Ponte, Lorenzo (1749–1838) A Jew who converted to Catholicism, was expelled from the priesthood and banished from Venice for adultery, da Ponte had excellent credentials to write the libretto for Mozart's *Don Giovanni*! His witty style and sense of musicianship enabled him to write words of similarly lasting charm for *The Marriage of Figaro* and *Cosi fan Tutte*, but he himself died an immigrant teacher of Italian in New York City.

Dargomijsky, Alexander (1813–1869) Russian composer whose only work still recognized is *The Stone Guest*, based on the story of Don Giovanni.

Daughter of the Regiment (Donizetti) FP 1840. A total change of mood from Donizetti's previous works, *Lucia di Lammermor, Lucrezia Borgia* and *Anna Bolena*, this jolly romp tells of the life and loves of Maria who thinks she is an orphaned peasant girl brought up by the local regiment in the Tyrol, but turns out to be, first the niece and then, the daughter of the local Marquise. About to be forced into an arranged marriage with someone of similar birth, Maria is rescued by the regiment and reunited with her childhood sweetheart Tonio.

Davies, Arthur Welsh tenor whose ebullient presence, boyish good looks and attractive voice make him ideal for the romantic tenor roles in which he excels. He has recently moved into the stronger repertoire which he tackles with equal finesse and enthusiasm. Davies began his professional career with Welsh National Opera in 1973, singing a notable Nadir in *The Pearl Fishers* and Rodolfo in *La Bohème*, as well as several roles in WNO's Janacek cycle. He now appears regularly with English National Opera where he created the role of the Duke in Jonathan Miller's Mafia-style production of *Rigoletto* as well as an impressive interpretation of Faust and Alfredo in recent productions of *Faust* and *La Traviata*. Davies made his Covent Garden debut as Alfredo and is now increasingly seen in European opera houses and festivals.

Davies, Andrew English conductor and currently Chief Conductor of the BBC Symphony Orchestra. Much of Davies' career has been spent as an orchestral conductor. He is also particularly well-known for his interpretations of Richard Strauss operas including *Der Rosenkavalier* at the Paris Opera and Covent Garden, *Salome* and *Ariadne auf Naxos* at the Metropolitan Opera. Davies took over from Bernard Haitink as Musical Director of Glyndebourne Festival Opera in 1988. He conducted the British premiere of Michael Tippett's new opera *New Year* for Glyndebourne in 1990.

Davis, Sir Colin English conductor who has specialized in performances of Mozart but has also championed the staging of modern operas, including those by Stravinsky, Janacek and Kurt Weill. He came to prominence by standing in for Otto Klemperer barely a year after his professional debut at Sadler's Wells. A debut at Glyndebourne followed and Davis was thereafter appointed Music Director of Sadler's Wells Opera, a post he held from 1960 to 1965. As Music Director of the Royal Opera House, Covent Garden, from 1971 to 1986, he conducted the world premieres of *The Knot Garden* and *The Ice Break* by Michael Tippett and *The Mines of Sulphur* by Richard Rodney Bennett. During this time, he made his debut at the Metropolitan Opera in New York and became increasingly in demand as a fine, intuitive conductor, able to extract every aspect and detail of a work. In 1977, he was invited to conduct *Tannhauser* at Bayreuth, the first Englishman ever to conduct at the prestigious festival. He is still associated with many fine orchestras throughout the world, and his extensive recordings bear out his genius in the world of opera.

Dawson, Lynne English soprano who came to professional singing after training to be a translator and interpreter of French. Her exciting, vibrant voice is well suited to Mozart and she has performed Pamina (*The Magic Flute*) for Scottish Opera, to excellent notices. Her European performances have been extensive, particularly in the prestigious music festivals at Aix en Provence in southern France, Paris and Vienna. To date, her appearances in America have been in concerts rather than opera.

Death in Venice (Britten) FP 1973. Challenging in its musical structure, *Death in Venice* would not be an ideal choice for a first Britten opera, though it does have a peculiar dramatic power in its combination of ritual with intense personal feeling. It is based closely on the novel by Thomas Mann.

The German writer Gustav von Aschenbach becomes obsessed with the beautiful young boy Tadzio as he watches him play on the beach of the Venice Lido with his family. The two never meet, but Aschenbach's obsession becomes so powerful that he refuses to leave Venice in spite of the threat of an outbreak of cholera to which he eventually succumbs.

Debussy, Claude (1862–1918) French composer. Despite his prolific output in other areas of music, Debussy completed only one opera, *Pelleas and Melisande*, although his uncompleted version of the Edgar Allen Poe story *The Fall of the House of Usher*, has recently been produced to some acclaim. He is credited with writing the first modern opera in 'Pelleas', which was composed as a strong reaction to the rich, complex works of Wagner, who nevertheless influenced him greatly. 'Pelleas' also shows signs of the great influence Oriental music had over the composer.

Delibes, Leo (1836–1891) Best known as a composer of ballets, most notably *Coppelia*, Delibes wrote one opera which is still revived today, *Lakmé*, which includes a famous duet for two sopranos.

Delius, Frederick (1862–1934) British composer. Renowned for his interpretation of pastoral themes in much of his best work, Delius's only remembered opera is *A Village Romeo and Juliet* which is quintessentially English. He in fact wrote five other operas, including *Koanga* and *Fennimore and Gerda* which, with *Village Romeo and Juliet* were the only ones to have been performed in his lifetime and from which only excepts are now known.

del Monaco, Mario (1915–1982) Italian tenor. Del Monaco is reputed to have taught himself to sing from recordings, but a formal education at the Opera School in Rome prepared him for a successful international career which reached its peak in the 1950s. His repertoire encompassed all the heroic tenor roles – Don José, Andrea Chenier, Ernani, Samson – but he was best known for his Otello. By his own estimation he performed the role 427 times, and was buried in his Otello costume!

de los Angeles, Victoria Spanish soprano. Versatile and attractive both musically and physically, de los Angeles reached the height of her operatic fame in the 1950s, from a triumphant debut at the Paris Opera House, to performances in La Scala, Milan, and the Royal Opera House, Covent Garden, culminating in fourteen consecutive seasons at the Met in New York – in addition to appearances at Bayreuth and other leading European opera houses. She is particularly associated with the Teatro del Liceu in Barcelona, her home town where she made her operatic debut in 1944 as the Countess in *The Marriage of Figaro*. Her voice was strong in the lower register, but it was inadequate strength in the upper part which forced her relatively early retirement from performance. She continues to give concert recitals and has made numerous excellent recordings, including twenty-two complete operas. She was awarded, amongst numerous other accolades, the Golden Record for having sold more than five million records worldwide.

de Luca, Guiseppe (1876–1950) Italian baritone whose international career spanned an extraordinary forty-five years. Like Mario del Monaco, he specialized in one role – Rigoletto. It was a part which ideally suited his voice – which was not by any means powerful – and gave him the opportunity to show off his considerable dramatic and comic talent.

de Reszke, Jean (1850–1925), **Edouard** (1853–1917) **and Josephine** (1855–1891) Two brothers and their sister from one Polish family, all of whom enjoyed some measure of international fame on the opera stage. Edouard (bass) created the role of the King in *Aida* in Paris (1876) and went on to sing seasons in the world's major opera houses, often opposite his brother. After retirement he tried a teaching career in London – once that failed he returned to Poland to live in abject poverty until his death. It was Edouard who pursuaded his brother Jean to move from his early baritone roles to tenor parts – wise advice, as Jean's triumphant performance in *Herodiade* in Paris in 1884 proved. Jean went on to perform extensively in America and in Bayreuth, where he sang his Wagner roles in German after years of intensive language study. Both brothers were considered masters of their particular voices, Jean enjoying something of a matinee-idol reputation amongst audiences and Edouard renowned for his dramatic stage presence. Josephine enjoyed considerable acclaim at the Paris Opera and once sang with both brothers in a performance of *Herodiade*. She retired from the stage early, on her marriage to Baron Leopold de Kronenberg.

Designer The recent popularity – and occasional notoriety – of opera owes much to the creative imagination of the opera designer. It requires a special understanding of both music and theatre to design a set which will fascinate and enlighten the audience, but which will be practical for singers to use and companies to tour. The transition from design on paper to three-dimensional model via production workshop to creation on stage is often fraught and costly, as designers refuse to compromise on the materials they need to achieve exactly the right effect. Only the most experienced can envisage exactly what will happen when upwards of fifty people follow the directions of the producer all over the designer's carefully thought out ideas. One designer once described it as, 'watching marauding hoardes trample over your children'. Close liaison with the director is essential, and many directors will team up with designers whom they know to understand their concepts. The freedom allowed to a designer depends entirely on the director and the budget – many directors will only want to direct a piece because they already have a clear idea of what to do with it (Jonathan Miller and the ENO's Mafia *Rigoletto*, for example) and the designer is simply charged with realizing that vision. Other designers demand far more autonomy, devising sets and costumes which give a director a framework in which to work. Designers are often blamed for an overspend on a production

but, if sets and costumes are going to last in repertory or tour extensively, the audience would soon complain if the set appeared shabby or cheap. However, some of the most effective productions have been wrought from virtually nothing (dustbin liners and supermarket trolleys are the hallmarks of such), as any visit to a student opera will testify.

Detroit – Michigan Opera Theater Since 1986 Michigan Opera Theater, in the heart of one of America's most violent cities, Detroit, has reported a surplus at the end of its financial year. The current situation of the company is highly successful – good audiences, secure bank balance, praiseworthy artistic reputation. The company is run by David DiChiera who is credited with overcoming Detroit's inferiority complex about the arts by mounting events of national interest. Dr DiChiera has shown that there is an audience for grand opera, even in a town where no-one feels safe to walk ten yards to their parked car after twilight. He has not compromised on his artistic product and contracts international opera stars without apologizing for Detroit's reputation – and thereby enhances it. He scales large and lavish productions in a venue seating more than 4,000 and has proved that the audience will brave a trip downtown to see them. The company depends on the affluent middle and upper classes which live in the beautiful suburbs around Detroit. While the company's education programme is making great advances in attracting a minority audience to opera, the bulk of the mailings, programming and ticket pricing is designed to encourage those attracted by the intrinsic glamour of the product. Thus the audience is predominantly made up of over thirty-five year olds, affluent, loyal, conservative in their taste and willing to support MOT financially, contributing to an active programme of fund raising events. The current mix of traditional grand opera and Broadway musicals performed by the company creates a difficult marketing problem. As more British opera companies are encouraged to perform 'commercial' pieces (Scottish Opera's *Candide* or ENO's *Pacific Overtures* for example) it is interesting to note that such a policy has also clouded MOT's image without producing significantly higher box office returns. Now they face the future not knowing whether they are a grand opera theatre which can attract stars of the calibre of Dame Joan Sutherland or a musical comedy house, concentrating on shows such as *Kiss me Kate* and *Brigadoon*.

Deus ex machina One of those devices which only the theatre can get away with. When the plot has reached its most complex, and the less than fascinated among the audience are looking at their watches wondering how on earth it's all going to be resolved by 10.30, suddenly some act of God, or hand from heaven, or fairy godmother appears and puts the whole lot right in a matter of moments.

Deutsche Oper, Die (see Berlin)

Devils of Loudon, The (Penderecki) FP 1969. Save this one up for when you have explored the whole classic opera repertoire, you are a confirmed opera lover and very little could put you off! The best word for the music is abrasive, which is not necessarily a criticism for it suits the action admirably.

To the Ursuline nuns and their prioress Jeanne, the priest Grandier is the personification of the devil. After prolonged torture, he is burned at the stake. The opera has been professionally produced once in Britain – by ENO in 1973, directed by John Dexter.

Dexter, John (1925–1990). English director. Dexter was one of the few contemporary directors at ease with drama as with opera. His productions were intelligent, sensitive, and frequently controversial, born from a career which took him to many of the leading arts venues of the world – The Metropolitan Opera in New York, the National Theatre and Royal Court in London, Chichester Festival, Paris Opera, Hamburg Opera, Covent Garden and on Broadway, where he received two Tony Awards for his direction of *Equus* and *Madam Butterfly*. It was his tenure at the Met, from 1974 to 1984, that confirmed his international status, with notable productions of *Aida*, *Rigoletto, Billy Budd* and, perhaps best of all, *Parade* by Eric Satie, and the Stravinsky Triple Bills with gloriously colourful designs by David Hockney. Uncompromising in his standards, Dexter was thought by some to be a difficult man to work with, but such demands were justified given the brilliance of the productions he created.

Dialogues des Carmelites (Poulenc) FP 1957. The three operas written by Poulenc are quite different and it would be worth listening to some of his other music – the Gloria for example – before embarking on this, the most sentimental of his staged works. The music is unremarkable and the story hardly compelling, but it has been given some superb stagings.

The plot centres on a Carmelite convent at the time of the French Revolution, where the young, unstable Blanche has sought refuge from the mob. She and Constance, young novices together, witness the gradual death of the old Prioress and, together with the rest of the nuns, become increasingly aware of the danger they all face from the Revolutionary gangs. They take a vow of martyrdom and leave the convent in civilian dress – at which point Blanche escapes. On hearing the nuns have been arrested and face execution, Blanche cannot bear to renege on her vow, and joins her fellow sisters on the steps of the guillotine.

Dido and Aeneas (Purcell) FP 1689. Superbly beautiful music which will be enjoyed much more in performance if you can listen to a recording (or excerpts) before attending. Dido's final lament is well known and, in a good production, almost unbearably moving. It is among the few seventeenth-century operas which can still be fully enjoyed by modern audiences, particularly if performed in other than a theatre, perhaps in a magnificent church as part of a festival.

Dido, Queen of Carthage, is wooed by the Trojan Aeneas, despite the fact that Carthage and Troy have recently been at war. The dignified Queen finds it hard to accept the advances of someone who has killed so many of her countrymen, but is persuaded by her maid Belinda that their relationship would be of ultimate benefit to Carthage. Dido agrees to marry Aeneas but the evil Sorceress is intent on destroying their happiness. Aeneas is forced by one of the Sorceress' spirits, dressed as the god Mercury, to consider his life-long ambition of building a new Troy in Carthage. He can hardly resist the temptation, although it would mean leaving his new wife. He gives in, and as the fleet is prepared to leave, the Sorceress celebrates her victory (with one of the worst couplets ever written – 'Our plot has took, the Queen's forsook'!) Aeneas prepares to leave Dido who is embittered and broken hearted. In sending him away, she knows she cannot live without him. The last words of her lament, 'Remember me, but ah! forget my fate', equal, if not surpass, those in any other opera for their tragedy.

Dimitrova, Ghena Bulgarian soprano who began her career at Sofia Opera House in the late 1960s, and appeared all over France, Spain, central and South America in the next decade. She did not make her London debut until April 1983 and has since appeared at Covent Garden, and has also established a continuing relationship with several North American companies. Dimitrova is not afraid of taking on the unknown (she has toured with La Scala to Korea and Japan), or the potentially overwhelming – in 1987 she sang the title role in *Aida*, outdoors at the Pyramids in Cairo!

Director Like contemporary designers, today's directors (or producers, which means exactly the same thing, but is more frequently used in Europe) are responsible for much of the upsurge in the popularity of opera. They are becoming personalities in the same way as opera singers have always been and composers were. Purists will argue that it is wrong to speak of 'Jonathan Miller's *Rigoletto*' or 'David Pountney's *Rusalka*', neglecting the composer's contribution, and the argument will continue to rage about whether radical productions are true to the composer's original intentions. The director has overall say in all aspects of the production, except the music, telling the singers where to move, their exits and entrances, coordinating the input of the set and lighting designer, liaising with the management regarding budgets, but most importantly, conveying to everyone involved his (or, very rarely, her) idea behind the production as a whole. It is not always the most harmonious of relationships. A recent survey of the directorial profession in British theatre revealed the scathing contempt with which even leading directors may regard their singers.

A director/producer is very often caught in a cleft stick, particularly in opera houses where unusual, thought provoking productions are expected. If he produces a classic interpretation, he is labelled as unimaginative; if it veers towards the radical, it becomes gratuitous and self-indulgent. There is no doubt that unusual interpretations have attracted a new audience to opera – *The Mikado*, staged by Jonathan Miller for ENO in 1985, was the first ENO opera ever to be given matinees, it attracted such a wide audience. A director may make his name from constantly producing deliberately provocative stagings – the American Peter Sellars is one such, having set *The Marriage of Figaro* in a New York penthouse and *Don Giovanni* in the drug crazed sub-culture of Manhattan. Some stagings are so deeply symbolic that only someone reading every detail of the director's notes (and probably his mind too!) would have the first idea of the meaning of it all. Many contend that the future of opera depends on provoking the audience to think and to criticize but it also depends on the audience enjoying the experience. No-one wants to be preached at every time they go to a performance, but it is the director's responsibility to evince something more from the text than the factual details of the plot which may in themselves be insubstantial and unconvincing.

di Stefano, Giuseppe Italian tenor who reached the peak of his fame in the 1950s and '60s and joined Callas on her world concert tour in 1973–74 which brought the great diva out of retirement. Di Stefano was at his best in the tenor roles which enabled him to display his remarkable ability to sing extremely quietly, but with immense clarity and beauty.

Diva Now that 'prima donna' has become almost a term of criticism, world-class female opera singers are more happily referred to as 'divas'. The term expresses an elegance and aloofness (it comes from the Latin, meaning goddess) and should be used to describe only those singers who have reached the highest pinacles.

Doktor Faust (Busoni) FP 1925. Unfinished two-act opera which is rarely performed because of the extraordinary demands it makes on both the title role and the singer playing Mephistopheles, who has one of the most difficult musical entries in all opera. It was produced by ENO in 1986 in a chillingly futuristic interpretation which overcame the theatrical challenge of bringing a child to life on stage with fascinating effect. The final scene was completed by Busoni's pupil, Philipp Jarnach.

Faust has sold his soul to the devil and proceeds to pursue the newly-married Duchess of Palma, who eventually elopes with him. They separate, and, shortly before her death, the Duchess sends Faust the child she has borne by him. He rejects it and leaves the city, but on his return encounters an old beggar woman. As he approaches her, he realizes she is the ghost of the Duchess, holding their dead child in her arms. With supreme effort, Faust attempts to project his personality on to the child, enabling all his wrongs to be righted in the next generation. As he dies, a naked youth appears from his body and walks away.

Domingo, Placido Spanish tenor and conductor. To have a great voice is one thing, to match that with film star good looks is another; to add an intelligence which allows over seventy major roles to be learnt with consummate ease may seem greedy, and to top it all with a genuine concern for the ills of mankind seems to make up a paradigm of public performance who hardly seems real. Despite the occasional inevitable bad press nothing can really detract from the enormous popularity of this world class musician who has done more than almost anyone to bring the highest standard of opera within the reach of everyone through his films, recordings and television broadcasts. His work to raise funds for the victims of the Earthquake in Mexico City (where he was brought up) showed the compassionate side of his personality; and the increasing demand for his conducting skills proves that he is as competent in front of the stage as on it.

Don Carlos (Verdi) FP 1867. A complex Verdi plot and a very long performance (five acts and lots of drama). Not to be recommended for new opera goers, but if you do go, do lots of homework beforehand. Try, in advance of the performance, to buy a programme which should contain an idea

of the staging, and try to take in the basic idea that Don Carlos is in love with Elisabeth of Valois who has married Don Carlos' father, Philip of Spain and therefore Carlos is in love with his step-mother!

As part of the peace treaty between France and Spain, Elisabeth of Valois has been promised to Don Carlos which they are both delighted about. But before they can be married, the agreement is revoked and Elisabeth is persuaded to marry the King of Spain (Don Carlos' father) which is a better move politically. Heartbroken, Carlos seeks consolation at the tomb of his grandfather, Charles V, and there pours his heart out to his greatest friend, Rodrigo, Marquess of Posa. Rodrigo suggests that Carlos should get away from Spain and come and help him fight with the oppressed people of Flanders. But to do this, Carlos needs his father's permission and needs to see his step-mother in order to get to his father. Thus the former lovers, Carlos and Elisabeth, are thrown together and, with a moment on their own, declare their love for one another. Philip, although he knows nothing of this interchange, is suspicious of Carlos and Elisabeth, and asks Rodrigo to watch out for them. At a masked ball, Carlos tells all to a masked figure whom he believes to be Elisabeth. It is, in fact, Princess Eboli, her lady in waiting, who has always harboured a secret love for Carlos and is distraught to hear he loves her Queen instead. She threatens to tell all to the King.

The most lavish scene in the opera follows – the Auto da Fe. Heretics are about to be burned at the stake with great ceremony. Carlos is leading the Flanders contingent but his pleas that the King be merciful are ignored. The King returns to the Palace resolving to denounce his son for heresy and his wife for adultery and is joined by the Chief Inquisitor who wishes to denounce Rodrigo. One final element complicates the plot – the Princess Eboli confesses to the Queen that she has been the King's mistress ever since her rejection by Carlos! If you've managed to keep up so far, just sit back and enjoy the first scene of the fourth act where the emotional outpouring is magnificent! The King, rejected by his wife and son, turns to the Inquisitor for advice. Elisabeth, desperately in love with Carlos, is cursed by the King and retaliates to Eboli. Eboli can do nothing but

Doktor Faust, Busoni's interpretation of the Faust story. Thomas Allen (left) as Faust, and Graham Clark as Mephistopheles.

Don Giovanni. The final scene of Mozart's opera, where the Don finds that the price of philandering is a high one. William Shimell in the title role of the ENO production at the London Coliseum.

curse the fatal beauty which has brought her so much heartache. Carlos faces a death sentence for heresy and Rodrigo is murdered in prison. The whole saga is resolved in the tomb of Charles V, with the aid of supernatural forces.

Don Giovanni (Mozart) FP 1787. One of the all time greats – a good one to start with, because of its good story and wonderfully tuneful music. It has got everything – power, glamour, tragedy, ghosts, and, above all else, romantic intrique. It just goes to show that a handsome philanderer retains his popularity throughout the centuries.

Don Giovanni has attempted to seduce Donna Anna who is renowned for her purity. He is challenged by her father, the Commendatore, and in the ensuing fight, the Commendatore is killed by the Don. Don Giovanni escapes with his trusty servant, Leporello and finds a beautiful woman, Donna Elvira, crying in the shadows. Unaware of who he is, she tells him of the love she had and has lost – who is, of course, none other than Don Giovanni. Another hasty exit by Leporello and his master brings them to a peasant wedding, and a chance for the Don to seduce the nubile peasant girl Zerlina, would-be bride of Masetto. Don Giovanni engineers that the wedding celebrations take place at his home, and is joined there not only by the new bride and her husband but also by Donna Anna, Donna Elvira and Don Ottavio, Donna Anna's fiancé, all intent on revenge. Don Giovanni escapes by changing clothes with Leporello and, having tired of Zerlina, swaps her for Elvira's maid. Leporello is left to fend off the advances of Donna Elvira herself and the angry Massetto, who is out to kill the Don. Eventually, master and servant meet in the churchyard where the Commendatore is buried. From a gravestone, a statue appears to speak and Leporello is commanded to invite it to dinner! In the final scene – one of extraordinary tension if played to full power – the ghost makes his entrance at Don Giovanni's table and forces the dissolute hero into the hands of the Devil and into hell.

While the plot and music give the opera the ingredients of sure-fire success, only a good production will play up the contrast between the great comedy and high tragedy.

A less-than-sensitive staging will make the wronged trio of Donnas Anna and Elvira and Don Ottavio into hopeless wimps, and the final denoument can seem ridiculous if badly played. But the music saves everything, full of well known tunes, both orchestral and vocal, particularly for Don Ottavio who is an unsympathetic character compared with Don Giovanni but has one of the most wonderful arias ('Il Mio Tesoro') ever written for the tenor voice.

Donizetti, Gaetano (1797–1848) Italian composer. Donizetti produced six of his best operas, *Anna Bolena, L'Elisir d'Amore, Lucrezia Borgia, Maria Stuarda, Lucia di Lammermoor* and *Roberto Devereaux*, within a ten year period, making him into one of the most prolific and versatile composers of the high Romantic period. He was greatly influenced by Bellini and the French composers but developed an individual style for which he is still renowned. His works ranged from the intense drama of *Anna Bolena* to the light comedy of *L'Elisir d'Amore*. His writing was strong for the female voice, particularly when his leading lady was 'in extremis', facing her end with quiet tragedy, as in *Anna Bolena*, or more public anguish, as in the mad scene from *Lucia di Lammermoor*.

Donna del Lago, La (Rossini) FP 1819. Written as a deliberately light opera, 'Donna' does not have the varied charm of *The Barber of Seville* and its characters do not have the complexities of many of Rossini's other roles, so the piece has fallen out of favour recently. The lead characters have notoriously difficult music to sing, pitched extremely high for both soprano and tenor.

Ellen is the daughter of the famous laird Douglas who has been exiled from the Scottish court. She is in love with the young hunter, Malcolm, she is also betrothed to Roderick, the man of her father's choice and, to complete the confusion, is pursued by the mysterious Hubert. By one of those devices so beloved of opera librettists, Hubert gives Ellen a ring, telling her to take it to the King of Scotland who will grant whatever wish she desires. Naturally, when she does so, she finds that Hubert is in fact King James of Scotland and, because of his love for her, is willing to release her father from banishment and give her to the man she loves.

Don Pasquale (Donizetti) FP 1843. A jolly jape of mistaken identity, young love and old love, with lots of well known melodies, particularly the serenade towards the end. It was Donizetti's last opera, and the most comic of all his works.

The aged and wealthy Don Pasquale is angry with his nephew, Ernesto, for refusing to marry the woman Don Pasquale has chosen for him. Ernesto has chosen his own love, Norina. Don Pasquale decides to disinherit Ernesto by finding a bride for himself. He asks for the help of Dr Malatesta, a friend of all the family, who is more concerned with Ernesto's future than that of the cantankerous old man. Dr Malatesta suggests that Don Pasquale considers marrying the young, innocent Sofrina, whom Malatesta passes off as his sister. Sofrina is, in fact, Norina in disguise, part of a cunning plot put together by Malatesta and Ernesto. Demure and heavily veiled, 'Sofrina' marries Don Pasquale, but hardly is the ink dry on the marriage contract when her entire personality changes. No longer the dutiful ex-convent wife, she becomes nagging, shrewish and generally impossible to live with. Don Pasquale goes back to his old friend Malatesta and begs that the marriage be annulled (a comic duet which can reduce even the most sober opera audience to helpless mirth!). Naturally, he is able to oblige and the two young lovers are united, this time with Don Pasquale's approval.

Donnelly, Malcolm Australian bass who came to Britain from Australia on a scholarship in 1970. Well known in Britain, having been a member of both Scottish Opera and English National Opera, for whom he sang, amongst many other roles, the title role in the company's infamous production of Tchaikovsky's *Mazzeppa*, he left ENO in 1985 and started to work more internationally, including a return to the Australian Opera in Sydney, although he still performs regularly with British companies.

Downes, Edward English conductor. Anyone who has been to opera performances at Covent Garden on more than a couple of occasions is almost bound to have seen Edward Downes conduct. He spent seventeen years as a member of Covent Garden, during which time he conducted hundreds

of performances embracing a wide repertoire, and including world premieres of *Taverner* by Peter Maxwell Davies and *Maddalena* by Prokofiev. He then moved to become Music Director of Australian Opera from 1972 to 1974, and now enjoys a regular association with Covent Garden again, having conducted there every season since 1952.

D'Oyly Carte, Richard (see Gilbert and Sullivan)

Dramaturg Common in all German opera houses and increasingly prevalent elsewhere, the dramaturg oversees all literary aspects of the repertory, programme notes, opera guides and so on and is frequently involved in repertory planning discussions.

Dress Despite everything that has been written and said about the accessibility of opera, it is useful to have some idea of the guidelines relating to dress. It would be possible to feel out of place in jeans and a tee-shirt at Glyndebourne and highly overdressed wearing a dinner-jacket for a first night at the Coliseum. It is actually unfair to say to a new opera goer, 'oh wear anything', if he happens to be taken as a corporate guest and is sitting in the orchestra stalls for a first night at the Royal Opera House. So the following is a highly opinionated view, based on a number of potentially awkward and embarrassing experiences!

For gentlemen, black tie is preferred at Glyndebourne ('customary but not obligatory' as the programme quaintly puts it). Be warned too that the Sussex police keep a special watch for anyone wearing a black tie driving after about 10.30 pm during the Glyndebourne season! Unless your host requests otherwise, dinner jackets are not usually worn to any of the national companies except for Gala performances, when dress should be specified and theatre staff should give you clear advice if you call beforehand to ask. Dinner jackets are more regularly worn to the Royal Opera House, particularly if you are a member of a party, in which case take the advice of your host. Otherwise, it is simply a question of where you are sitting. Roughly speaking, if your ticket is within the top three price brackets, jacket and tie should be worn, otherwise, open collars are fine. Bear in mind the physical conditions as well. Many of the older theatres have absolutely no effective air conditioning and the further from the stage you are (both upwards and back) the hotter it will be, not only in the summer. If you need to remove your jacket, by all means do so if you will enjoy the performance more as a result, but better still, anticipate the problem and wear a lightweight suit.

The whole question is altogether more complicated for women. It is not obligatory to wear long dress for Glyndebourne, but it is the most perfect occasion to dress up, if you enjoy to do so. Remember, too, it can get very cold at the end of even the most perfect summer evening and Glyndebourne is usually a long way home for everyone. It's amazing the number of sensible jumpers that get pulled over the most elaborate dresses in the car park at the end of the performance – which is far better than shivering to death all the way home. By far the biggest proportion of the London week-day audiences come straight from work, so everyday clothes are fine. A Saturday performance is a good excuse to go for more glitz if you want to. Out of London, audiences are usually smarter during the week and particularly smart at the week-end. In Cardiff or Glasgow, for example, you could feel distinctly under-dressed in a blouse and skirt, particularly if you are in the more expensive seats. If you are part of a corporate party, smart/short is usually fine – your invitation should specify otherwise if not. Make sure your shoes are comfortable – theatres can have the same effect as airlines in making your feet swell up; and it is fatal to take your shoes off and risk losing them down the seat in front!

The situation is much the same in America. For galas and first nights in the major cities, 'dressing up' is the order of the day. Midweek audiences in the same cities will come straight from work and therefore the style will be more casual. Out of town audiences will be somewhat smarter during the week and considerably smarter for weekend performances. But with characteristic directness, American opera companies will often advise patrons as to the best mode of dress. For example, this quote from a New York City Opera programme for the summer of 1988, directed at New Yorkers sweltering in one of the hottest summers on record – 'Slip into something more comfortable. Wear your summer dresses and seersucker suits. Or dress more casually if you prefer. At City Opera, *we* worry about the lavish costumes so *you* won't have to.'

Due Foscari, I (Verdi)   FP 1844. The two Foscari of the title are father and son, and the plot, such as it is, really concerns only them, plus the son's wife and one other. It is very grand and musically dramatic and the Venice setting allows for some very beautiful stage effects. It really can not be transposed anywhere else as Venice is crucial to the story. The only trouble is that very little happens.

Francesco Foscari, the good but misguided Doge of Venice, is over eighty and knows he is approaching death. Three of his sons have died in infancy and the fourth, Jacopo, has been exiled, accused of murder, but has now returned to the city. His wife Lucrezia pleads to the Doge that he should overrule the judgement of the Venice Council and play the father, not the Doge, in allowing his son to return. Torn between public duty and private will, Francesco realizes he is trapped. Loredano, the evil character, who has sworn hatred of the Foscari family, is unmoved even by the pleas of Jacopo's children and Jacopo is exiled once again. By the time another man comes forward admitting to the murder of which Jacopo was originally accused it is too late – Jacopo has died of a broken heart on the ship taking him from his home city. Bereft of family and stripped of his title of Doge, Francesco also dies.

Duesing, Dale American baritone who trained to be a pianist but changed course while at the Lawrence University in Wisconsin and has since enjoyed an increasingly successful international singing career. He has performed at the leading opera houses of America and Germany, as well as European festivals including Edinburgh, Salzburg and Glyndebourne. It was at Glyndebourne in 1989 that he sang a superb Figaro in a brilliant production of *The Marriage of Figaro* by Sir Peter Hall, conducted by Simon Rattle, which found an ever wider and more enthusiastic audience at the 1989 'Proms' in London. Duesing is an enthusiastic and credible actor on stage, bringing humour and energy to his comic roles, complemented by intelligent sensitivity in the more complex parts such as Billy Budd and Peter Grimes.

Duet Music written for two voices of any pitch where both singers have an equal part to perform.

Duke Bluebeard's Castle (Bartok) FP 1918. Bartok was very influenced by Hungarian folk music when writing this opera – the more melancholic aspects rather than the jolly side which Smetana showed in *The Bartered Bride*. The almost dirge-like style of some of the chant-singing can add to the intensity of a very dramatic story. It does not, however, make for a very tuneful evening of foot-tapping Slavonic melodies. If you have to go and are slightly dubious, take comfort in the fact that it lasts under an hour, and that the work lends itself to the most fantastic (in the literal sense of the word) stagings. The only thing the stage has to contain are seven doors.

Duke Bluebeard has brought his new wife Judith home to his castle. She sees the seven doors and is curious. Through the first she hears the sound of the wind and, on opening it, finds the walls streaming with blood. It is the torture chamber. The second door leads to the Armoury, the third to the Treasury, the fourth to the garden and the fifth to Bluebeard's Kingdom. Each one is characterized by the colour of the light which comes from it and by the different musical instruments which introduce it. They all contain some drops of blood. Despite Bluebeard's protests, Judith opens the sixth door which reveals tears, and the seventh, through which appear three of his former wives symbolizing the morning, noon-day and evening of his life. Judith's pleas are ignored as she, the end of his life, is forced behind the seventh door and Bluebeard remains alone.

Eaglen, Jane English soprano. Jane Eaglen was recognized early in her career as a very talented young soprano who became a principal member of English National Opera on leaving college. She has a very big voice and personality to match. She has tackled some of the major roles whilst still very young, including Elizabeth I in *Mary Stuart*, with great success and her stage presence and dramatic ability continue to improve. She has been careful not to push on too quickly and many think she will become one of the best Wagnerian sopranos that Britain has

produced for some time if her career continues on its present course.

Ear, playing by One of those very clever talents by which musicians can impress their friends, if only when sitting at a piano at a party or in the pub. It is the ability to play an instrument without instruction, rehearsal or music, instinctively knowing how it should be played by listening to the sound. The best jazz musicians do it instinctively and many classical musicians develop an ability to do it after long sessions in ensemble rehearsal. But it is basically a gift acquired at birth which many musicians, no matter how talented and proficient, are never able to master.

Ebert, Carl (1887–1980) Actor turned producer who spent his early career in the opera houses of Darmstadt and Berlin but refused to work under Nazi rule and came to Britain. With Fritz Busch, he started the Glyndebourne Festival, becoming its first Artistic Director. He stayed there from 1934 to 1959, living in America for the years of the Second World War. In 1951, he staged the premiere of Stravinsky's *The Rake's Progress*, in Venice. After Glyndebourne, he became Director of the Deutsche Oper in Berlin. Long and intense rehearsal periods enabled him to create detailed, dramatic productions, particularly of Verdi and Mozart.

Ebrahim, Omar English baritone who has specialized in performances of contemporary works to which he has brought insight and conviction as well as an excellent singing ability. Much of his work has been with Opera Factory, including performances as Punch in *Punch and Judy* by Harrison Birtwistle, Mel in *The Knot Garden* by Michael Tippett, and Mercury in *La Calisto* by Cavalli. The radical and inventive productions staged by Opera Factory suit Ebrahim's stage presence, proving he is an accomplished actor as well as singer. For Glyndebourne Festival Opera he took the lead role of Sereza in the 1988 world premiere of *The Electrification of the Soviet Union* by Nigel Osborne. Performances in *Don Giovanni, Die Fledermaus, Ariadne auf Naxos* and *The Barber of Seville* prove that Ebrahim is as comfortable with the 'conventional' repertoire as he is with the contemporary.

Edinburgh Festival Started by the prime movers behind Glyndebourne, Audrey Christie and Rudolf Bing, it is hardly surprising that this international festival has a fine reputation for attracting notable opera productions, particularly from overseas. Such cultural barrier breaking started in 1952 with the first visit of the Hamburg State Opera, and has been continued through visits from the opera companies of Belgrade, Milan, Stockholm, Prague, Florence, East and West Berlin (only a smattering of the total number). The Festival has also produced its own operas, including a highly successful *Carmen* in 1977, as well as staging British premieres of, amongst others, *The Love of Three Oranges* (Prokofiev), *From the House of the Dead* (Janacek) and *The Rake's Progress* (Stravinsky). Such a powerful profile has attracted some of the world's greatest singers to give performances in Edinburgh which are still talked about – Callas in *La Sonnambula* in 1957, Dame Janet Baker in *The Trojans* (1973) and Sir Thomas Beecham's conducting of *Ariadne auf Naxos* in 1950, to name but a few.

Edgar (Puccini) FP 1889. Early Puccini opera, with hints of the musical brilliance that was to come but only an inkling of the great dramatic talent Puccini had.

Edgar loved Fidelia but abandoned her for the winsome Tigrana, for whom he has to duel with Fidelia's brother, Frank. Full of remorse at wounding Frank, Edgar leaves Tigrana, joins the army and is thought to be killed. At his funeral, a monk recites Edgar's crimes but is revealed to be none other than Edgar himself. He embraces Fidelia, who is stabbed to death by the jealous Tigrana.

Edwards – Sian English conductor. She won the Leeds Conductor's Competition in 1984. She has conducted at Scottish Opera, Glyndebourne and the Royal Opera House – the first female opera conductor at Covent Garden! Her name is well known abroad through work with the Orchestre de Paris and an American debut with the St Paul Chamber Orchestra.

Einstein on the Beach (Philip Glass) FP 1976. If you do not know Philip Glass' music and haven't been to one of his operas before, be prepared for something very different. Opinion is divided as to whether his work is extremely affecting for its novelty, or downright tedious. Certainly, no clearly defined plot emerges from 'Einstein' – it is rather a series of tableaux on recurring images – a train, a trail, a spaceship, and Einstein himself, who watches the action (such as it is) while playing his violin.

Elder, Mark English conductor and Music Director of English National Opera since 1979. Under his leadership, the company has achieved an enviable reputation for its high musical standards, and adventurous, theatrical productions. Elder's fruitful collaboration with ENO's Director of Productions David Pountney has led to some memorable work, including Busoni's *Doctor Faust*, Bizet's *Carmen* and Humperdinck's *Hansel and Gretel*. His own performances of the Verdi operas, including *Rigoletto* and *Simon Boccanegra* have been much acclaimed. Sometimes critics do not like the rather daring and adventurous production styles adopted at the Coliseum, but it is rare for Elder's conducting to be criticized.

Despite his responsibilities at English National Opera Elder has not neglected his international career, nor his career as an orchestral conductor. In 1989 he became Music Director of the Rochester Philharmonic Orchestra in the USA, and in Britain he has conducted annually at the Proms, including the internationally televised Last Night of the Proms in 1987.

Electrification of the Soviet Union, The (Nigel Osborne) FP 1987. Even the most regular attenders found this opera a surprising, if refreshing, choice for the generally conservative Glyndebourne Festival. The extraordinary title of the work gives an indication that the piece is firmly set in the 'real world', in a manner not unlike *The Consul* by Menotti. But for those willing to put aside their traditional expectations of Mozartian glamour, 'Electrification' proved itself to be an intriguing modern opera, not perhaps an ideal choice for the first time opera goer, but a brave and imaginative new work.

The opera is written from the perspective of Boris Pasternack who is seen in the prologue. He looks back on his life through the eyes of a young poet called Serezha Spectorsky, tutor to Harry the young son of Mr and Mrs Frestln. A series of images conveys

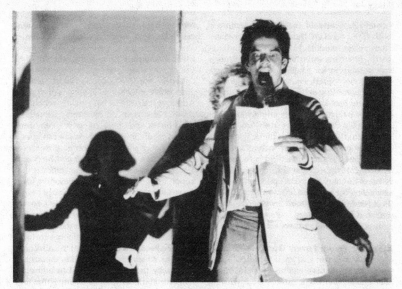

The Electrification of the Soviet Union. Omar Ebrahim as the poet Serezha, with Elizabeth Laurence and Henry Herford, in Nigel Osborne's dramatic opera, given its world premiere at the 1987 Glyndebourne Festival.

Eugene Onegin, by Tchaikovsky, in a production at Covent Garden. Peter Dworsky as Lensky (left), Jean Rigby as Olga, and Wolfgang Brendel as Onegin.

Serezha's feeling of inadequacy compared with those who are fighting for the socialist cause. He is reluctant to give up his academic work, however, particularly as he becomes emotionally involved with Harry's governess, the embittered, recently widowed Anna Arild. He continues his relationship with the prostitute Sashka, who becomes a victim of police brutality. Serezha eventually proposes to Anna but then becomes so absorbed in his mission to right the wrongs of the world that he takes no notice of her answer and she leaves. The Frestln household is in turmoil, symbolic of the upheaval to come with the Russian Revolution. In the epilogue, the main characters are reunited four years later, Anna as a revolutionary guard threatening to be avenged for her former lover for his association with the middle class Frestlns.

Elegy for Young Lovers (Henze) FP 1961. One to leave until you are a confident opera goer, this work has elements of the hilarious, the banal, the tragic and the downright weird. A colleague and keen music lover described the score as the most erotic he had ever heard, Henze himself stipulated that the libretto incorporate 'tender beautiful noises', complemented by a 'small subtle orchestra'. But the basic theme of a great poet taking two young lovers up a mountain and allowing them to die there in order to inspire his poem is hardly the recipe for a jolly evening of theatre!

Elektra (Richard Strauss) FP 1910. Immensely powerful one-act opera which makes enormous vocal demands on the leading ladies and is written in such a way as to make the audience feel immediately involved in the psychological pressure and personal anguish the chief protagonists are experiencing. It is not a comfortable performance to watch but it can be inspiring.

It is based on the Greek tale of Klytemenestra who is suffering under the guilt of murdering her husband Agamemnon. Their daughter Elektra is determined to avenge her father's death and enlists the help of her gentle sister Chrysothemis, thinking that their brother Orest, who is best placed to help them, is dead. But Orest returns and, with Elektra, succeeds in killing both Klytemenestra and her lover Aegisth. Even though Elektra has achieved all she set out to do, the

mental strain proves to much and in her final, crazy dance of vengeance, she falls dead.

Elisir d'Amore, L' (Donizetti) FP 1832. All the elements of a classic comic opera contained in one terrific piece, full of humour, good tunes and charm. There is a pretty girl, Adina, whose riches have made her choosy about her choice of husband. There is a good-but-simple peasant boy, Nemorino, who is madly in love with Adina but knows he will never get a look in because she is the daughter of a wealthy farmer and he is only a poor peasant. There is the buffoon of a suitor, Sergeant Belcore, whom Adina agrees to marry to spite Nemorino. There is the quack doctor who promises Nemorino a love potion (nothing more sinister than red wine) and an old uncle who dies off stage, fortunately leaving Nemorino his fortune. Thus he becomes the target of the affections of all the village girls, Adina gets jealous and eventually the two get round to admitting what the audience knew all along – that they were meant for each other. There is also one of the best 'tunes' in all opera – Nemorino's aria 'A furtive tear'.

Ellis, Brent American baritone who studied in Italy before returning home to masterful performances of the Italian repertory heroes at the Met, Santa Fe, San Francisco and Boston. He appears regularly in Europe, particularly in Vienna, and at Covent Garden.

Encore Literally 'again'. A singer may respond to particularly appreciative applause at the end of a concert by singing another piece or occasionally repeating a piece from the repertoire he or she has just performed. While individual arias may command massive applause in the course of an opera performance, 'encores' as such are now rarely performed during or after a staged performance.

Enfant et les Sortileges (Ravel) FP 1925. This opera calls for imaginative staging, as it concerns a small boy's antics with a teapot, a squirrel, a cat, a fire, a clock and a book, all of which come to life to teach him a lesson. Confined to his room by his mother after a temper tantrum, the boy smashes the clock, hurts the squirrel, pulls the cat's tail, stirs up the fire, damages the clock and tears the book. As the objects turn to attack him in their turn, the squirrel is injured. The boy tends to the squirrel's wounds, and, having learnt his lesson, harmony is restored again.

English National Opera Britain's biggest opera company in every sense, ENO employs over 600 people, produces a staggering 200 performances of opera in every ten month season, running a repertory of up to twenty productions, five nights a week, from September to June, in a theatre which seats over 2300 – the London Coliseum. The company in its present form has been at the Coliseum since 1968 and before then at Sadler's Wells when it was known as Sadler's Wells Opera – a name many find it difficult to forget. As Sadler's Wells Opera, the company had a fine reputation for excellent performances, all in English, using the same singers regularly and attracting a loyal, steadfast audience. Seat prices were deliberately low, choice of repertoire deliberately adventurous and accessibility – particularly through an active touring programme – a key part of the company policy. During its Sadler's Wells tenure, the company presented the world premiere of Britten's *Peter Grimes* and the British premiere of Verdi's *Simon Boccanegra* – now both standard in the opera repertory and a sound indication of the validity of the company's somewhat controversial programming policy. Sadler's Wells Opera never accepted the 'star' system, working instead with a core ensemble and regular principals. Looking through their old cast lists however, it is clear that plenty of 'stars' did work with the company – Joan Cross, Reginald Goodall, Peter Pears, Owen Brannigan, Colin Davis, Alexander Gibson, Tyrone Guthrie, Charles Mackerras – a list which established the company as a major force in British, if not yet in world, opera. It was a far cry from the earliest days of the company, which had been founded and led by the redoubtable Lillian Baylis and housed at the Old Vic theatre, a performing space totally inappropriate for opera.

Today, the company is riding on the crest of an artistic wave and has done much to bring the medium of opera to the massive popularity it now enjoys. Much of this success is due to the old tenets of the company's policy. The seats are still priced as cheaply as possible (it is still cheaper to get into the Coliseum than into the nearby cinemas). Every opera is still sung in English. The performers are an ensemble company, both resident and guest, and now include the likes of Jonathan Miller, Simon Rattle, Thomas Allen, Josephine Barstow, Helen Field, Arthur Davies, Nicholas Hytner, Norman Bailey and, as resident company members, Mark Elder and David Pountney. The productions are still controversial, perpetuating the great operatic debate by espousing the theory of 'drama per musica' by creating real music theatre. New productions generate immense comment, not only on the arts pages, which is clearly what the management of the company are trying to encourage. There is still a fine policy of commissioning new work and staging world premieres. And the ENO audience is growing. There is a friendliness about the Coliseum, where the new opera-goer need not feel abashed, where you can come in your jeans or your Jean Muir and still feel at home and where you can see operas which will attack your every sense, not simply stun you with their musical expertise.

Ehtfuhrung aus dem Serail (see Abduction from the Seraglio)

Ensemble Literally 'together', ensemble has varying meanings in an operatic context. It can refer to a number of people singing together, usually other than in a chorus, or the quality of sound produced by more than one singer (e.g. 'their ensemble singing was excellent'). When referring to a company such as ENO, a sense of democracy amongst the singers where roles are shared between members of an ensemble company, rather than 'importing' international stars for one production. This co-operative spirit is admirably summed up by Philip Glass who said, 'You can spend your life learning about opera – it would be silly trying to do it alone.'

Entr'acte Interval, but not one where you can go off for a drink. Entr'acte signifies a pause in the action when music which has been composed particularly for this moment in the production is played. Such a device sorts the regular opera goer from the first timer as the house lights usually come up about half way, and those who do not realize otherwise make a dash for the bar – and return looking somewhat sheepish. Read the programme if you do not want to be caught out.

Erede, Alberto Italian conductor specializing in performances of Wagner, conducting a notable *Lohengrin* at Bayreuth in 1968, as well as in the Italian repertoire. He was a regular conductor at Glyndebourne from 1934 to 1939 and at the Metropolitan Opera, New York from 1950 to 1955. As Music Director of the Deutsche Oper am Rhein (1958 to 1962), he conducted the premiere of *The Old Maid and the Thief* by Menotti.

Ernani (Verdi) FP 1844. Many of Verdi's operas thrive on personal conflict – *Aida*, *Rigoletto* and *Don Carlos* being the best known. But the plot of *Ernani*, which is performed relatively rarely, is perhaps the most pronounced in terms of personality clashes and can be gripping and exhilarating, with plenty of good melodies and rich orchestration. Verdi undoubtedly wrote better operas, but some homework on the complicated plot and some idea of Verdi's music should make a performance enjoyable to a relatively new opera goer.

Three men are in love with the beautiful Elvira – Don John of Aragon, who is disguised as a bandit Ernani; the elderly grandee de Silva, to whom Elvira is betrothed; and the King of Castile, Don Carlos. Elvira only loves one of them, Ernani, who is not the man she should marry. One night, Elvira and Ernani are disturbed by the King and only the intervention of de Silva (who, like a true gentleman, overlooks the fact that two men are in his fiancée's bedroom in the middle of the night!) saves Ernani from being killed by the King. Ernani flees, only to return on the eve of Elvira's wedding to de Silva, with the King in hot pursuit. The long suffering de Silva hides Ernani from the King, but challenges Ernani to a duel for Elvira's hand. Ernani refuses, recognizing all the old man has done to help him and plans instead to join forces with de Silva to defeat the King. He makes a pledge that if de Silva ever sounds his hunting horn, Ernani will take his own life, leaving de Silva free to marry Elvira. Don Carlos is crowned Emperor Charles V on the day Ernani swears to murder him. The new Emperor discovers the plot against him and forgives Ernani – who has by now revealed himself as a nobleman – so Ernani can be united with Elvira. But it is all too much for de Silva. Having lost both his beloved and his chance to overthrow the King, he sounds his hunting horn and Ernani, chivalrous to the last, stabs himself before his beloved Elvira.

Erwartung (Schoenberg) FP 1924. A one-act tour-de-force for a powerful singing actress, Schoenberg's drama deals with expectation (the literal translation of the title.) A woman is waiting for her lover in the forest. Using highly expressionistic music, Schoenberg creates an atmosphere of almost unbearable intensity which is shattered when the woman stumbles upon the corpse of her lover's body.

Esham, Faith American soprano who had her first successes in the USA in the mid 1970s and by the time she made her European debut in 1980 had been widely acclaimed internationally. She is noted mainly for her interpretation of the French repertoire – Marguerite, Manon, Leila, Melisande, Michaela (*Carmen*) – as these roles suit her personality and her rather delicate and romantic voice. In 1983 she appeared as Michaela in the popular film of *Carmen* with Placido Domingo and Julia Migenes-Johnson.

Esposito, Valeria Italian soprano who won the 1987 Cardiff Singer of the World competition, impressing the jury with her excellent musicianship as well as beautiful singing voice.

Estes, Simon American bass Simon Estes was the first black male artist to sing at the Bayreuth Festival. He sang *The Flying Dutchman* there for six successive years. His repertoire includes nearly ninety roles, but he is particularly associated with Wagnerian roles and it is a measure of his ability and world standing that he has been so successful in this area where, sadly, there still remains a certain amount of prejudice against black singers, which hides behind decisions purporting to be based on 'historical' or 'artistic' accuracy. Estes is to take the lead role in *King*, a commercial musical based on the life of the Black civil rights leader, Martin Luther King.

Eugene Onegin (Tchaikovsky) FP 1879. A real treat for a first time opera goer. A romantic tear jerker with wonderful melodies, perfect for anyone who enjoys curling up in front of an old movie with a large box of tissues! There is not a tremendous amount of action, but good actors can make the personalities so endearing that you can hardly bear it to end. It was a work with which Tchaikovsky became immensely involved. His reaction on reading the Pushkin poem on which the story is based was to call Onegin 'a cold, heartless coxcomb' for rejecting Tatiana and, so anxious was Tchaikovsky not to be like him, that he went as far as marrying a young girl who had written him a mad, passionate love letter. The marriage was not a success, Tchaikovsky being by nature a homosexual, but the experience did leave us with a superb opera! Try to see a version in English because the words really do matter.

The young, naive Tatiana has fallen desperately in love with the worldly-wise poet, Eugene Onegin. Full of the anguish of first love, she pours out her feelings in a letter (one of the greatest operatic arias of all time!) only to be crushed when she receives the all-too-common put-down: that he could never love her but would be happy to be her friend. Tatiana's sister Olga is engaged to Onegin's greatest friend, Lenski and it only increases Tatiana's anguish to see Onegin flirting outrageously with Olga at Tatiana's birthday party. Lenski challenges his friend to a duel and is killed. Several years pass, Onegin having opted out of St Petersburg society and Tatiana having married the fabulously wealthy Prince Gremin, who happens to be Onegin's cousin. A dance is in progress at the Gremins' house – the Polonaise will be familiar to everyone. From Gremin's magnificent aria, it becomes clear how he worships his wife, now grown to be elegant and beautiful, the toast of society. Naturally, it takes all this to make Onegin realize what he lost in rejecting Tatiana and begs her to leave Gremin for him. She refuses, but only after she has whispered that she still loves him. Distraught at this final emotional twist, Onegin departs.

Evans, Anne English soprano who has confirmed her position as one of the world's leading singers with her triumphant performances as Brunnhilde at the 1989 Bayreuth Festival and performances at Covent Garden, Paris, Nice and in Berlin and Washington. She is in great demand all over the world and, as her international status increases, she does fewer performances with the smaller companies although she has enjoyed happy associations with both English and Welsh National Operas. In addition to her operatic work Evans enjoys an extensive concert career both in Great Britain and abroad.

Evans, Damon American bass with a charismatic stage presence that demands attention and is fortified by a rich, velvety voice. He came to prominence in Britain as Sportin' Life, the drug dealer in Gershwin's *Porgy and Bess*, in the superb Glyndebourne production in 1986, where his athleticism and acting ability created a memorable character in a production full of unforgettable moments. A finalist in the 1989 Cardiff Singer of the World, Evans proved that his repertoire ranges from powerful interpretations of Gershwin to a sensitive performance of Handel and Mozart. He seems marked out to be one of the most exciting opera performers for years to come.

Evans, Sir Geraint Welsh baritone who soon realized that he could excel at the character roles in opera and went on to build a superb international career with a wide repertoire of such parts. A sparkling personality with a constant 'twinkle', Evans was an ideal Falstaff, Leporello or Figaro, maximizing the humour in every role while never compromising his high artistic standards. He complemented such comic roles with character parts from the more intense works, creating a memorable Balstrode in *Peter Grimes*, the title role in Berg's *Wozzeck*, and Beckmesser in *The Mastersingers of Nuremberg*. A regular performer at Covent Garden, he sang in the world premieres of *Billy Budd*, where he created the role of Flint, and *Gloriana*, playing the first Mountjoy. He sang six seasons with the Metropolitan Opera in New York and appeared regularly at San Francisco Opera and at Glyndebourne. When he retired from performance the world of opera lost one of its greatest and best loved characters. He now gives occasional concerts for charities with which he feels a particular affinity.

Ewing, Maria English soprano. Maria Ewing's sultry appearance and startlingly dramatic stage presence give her all the appeal of a modern pop star, far removed from the old image of the female opera singer. Her 'Dance of the Seven Veils' in a recent production of Strauss' *Salome* (directed by her former husband Sir Peter Hall) left no-one in any doubt about her sex appeal. But Ewing is also a highly accomplished musician and in 1985 she sang with great success at Glyndebourne Festival Opera in *Carmen*, a role with which she has become associated, singing it at the spectacular production set in London's Earl's Court Exhibition Centre, in Tokyo in 1989, and at the Royal Opera House, Covent Garden, in 1990.

Faery Queen (Purcell) FP 1692. Hardly an opera in the accepted sense of the word, Purcell's work was originally composed as a masque to be performed at the court of Queen Elizabeth I, and therefore does not depend on full staging in the same way as a usual opera. It is made up of a series of five scenes with a prologue. The score was lost for 200 years and only re-discovered in the early part of this century when it was performed in San Francisco. It is based loosely on Shakespeare's *A Midsummer Night's Dream*.

Falsetto Technique used principally by counter-tenors to sing in the highest range of the voice, often with a penetratingly pure tone.

Falstaff (Verdi) FP 1893. Verdi's last opera and the one which may consider to be the height of his achievement. It combines virtually every emotion in the human spectrum, humour, pathos, love, hatred, jealousy, grandeur, and simplicity, all wrapped up in a battle of wits between young and old. Several composers have taken Shakespeare's *The Merry Wives of Windsor* as an opera text but no other has succeeded in characterizing Falstaff so well. Although *Falstaff* is perhaps most fully enjoyed when you realize that it is the culmination of Verdi's long and brilliant composing career, it is not the best choice as an introduction to the operas of Verdi. It is a work which he kept close to himself, not intending it to be performed in public but only for the enjoyment of his friends.

In the tavern of the Garter Inn, Windsor, Falstaff tells his drinking cronies Pistol and Bardolph that he has sent two love letters to the 'merry wives' Alice Ford and Meg Page. Unbeknown to Falstaff, the wives have compared letters, realize they are identical and plan their revenge, with the connivance of Mistress Quickly and Alice's daughter, Nanetta. Meanwhile, Pistol and Bardolph tell Alice's jealous husband Ford what Falstaff has done. Thus a male team and a female team are made up to seek revenge on Falstaff. There is also a gentle sub-plot of the young love developing between Nanetta (whose father wants her to marry the aged Doctor Caius) and her suitor Fenton. Mistress Quickly meets Falstaff in the tavern and tells him Alice can receive him between 2 and 3pm when Ford is away. No sooner has she gone than a mysterious stranger, Master Brook, arrives at Falstaff's table. He tells Falstaff that he too is madly in love with Alice Page and offers money if Falstaff can bring them together. Falstaff delightedly agrees, telling the stranger of his planned rendezvous and pouring great scorn on Alice's stupid husband. Of course, 'Master Brook' is none other than Alice's husband in disguise and Falstaff has played right into his hands. Falstaff keeps his meeting with Alice but is disturbed by the return of her husband, mad with jealousy. In the famous scene, Falstaff is bundled into a laundry basket and is thrown out of the window into the river below. In one of the funniest scenes in the opera, Falstaff recovers back at the Garter Inn where the earnest pleas of Mistress Quickly pursuade him to try for another rendezvous in the forest that evening. As all the protagonists meet together in the haunted forest, the confusions are endless and eventually Falstaff is shown up for the fool that he is. He is finally made to see reason, the young lovers are successfully paired up and all ends happily.

Fanciulla del West, La (Puccini) FP 1910. Puccini was nothing if not varied in the settings he chose for his operas. From the depths of Imperial Japan, the garrets of Paris and the high society of Rome, he moved to California during the Gold Rush, made his hero as close as the opera stage has ever had to John Wayne, added a tough 'Annie-get-your-gun' type heroine and gave it all a happy ending. The modern setting also brings out some of Puccini's more dissonant music which, rather than being difficult to listen to, only adds to the pace and fire of the production.

Minnie is the saloon keeper of the Polka Saloon. She acts as guide, confidant and friend to the tough mining community. Two very different men are after her heart – the Sheriff of the town, Jack Rance, and the newcomer who calls himself Dick Johnson, but is in fact the bandit Ramerrez. Dick is shot in a skirmish and, promising to mend his ways, is given sanctuary by Minnie. Jack discovers them and plays Minnie at poker with Dick's life as the wager. By cheating, Minnie secures Dick's life but not his freedom. The Sheriff continues to hunt Dick down and finally captures him, threatening him with the hangman's noose. In a famous aria, 'Let her believe that I have gained my freedom', which was sung as a troop song in the First World War, Dick pleads that Minnie should be told he has escaped, rather than know the truth of his cowardly fate. But just in time, Minnie arrives, pleads with the miners to release her love and the couple ride off, as they say, into the sunset.

Farrar, Geraldine (1882–1967) American soprano who sang the first *Madam Butterfly* at the Met. She was best known not only for her lovely lyric soprano voice but for her enormous beauty, giving her a cult following amongst the 'Gerryflappers' of 1920s America.

Fassbaender, Brigitte German mezzo soprano whose father Willi Domgraf-Fassbaender was a professional baritone. Fassbaender began her career with the Munich Opera in the trouser-role of Nicklaus in *The Tales of Hoffmann* by Offenbach. She has come to specialize in these roles, performing a notable Octavian in *Der Rosenkavalier*, as well as creating powerful, musically superb, renditions of the major Wagner roles.

Fauré, Gabriel (1845–1924) French composer known chiefly for his beautiful Requiem, Fauré wrote only one true opera, *Penelope*, and one major work full of operatic components, *Promethee*. Even those who extol Fauré's work as that of a major-league

French composer cannot describe either work as a lasting classic.

Faust (Gounod) FP 1859. Critics dismiss it as sentimental but a good performance of Gounod's best known opera can be an uplifting experience. It sounds, as does *Hamlet*, as if it is full of quotes, or in this case tunes, has a story-line which has fascinated audiences in many forms for years, and is highly romantic, as it is chiefly concerned with the Faust-Marguerite relationship rather than any of the other aspects of Goethe's story.

Dr Faust is old, lonely and contemplating suicide. He is faced by Mephistopheles who conjures up the vision of a beautiful young woman, Marguerite, whom Faust can have in return for selling his soul to Mephistopheles. Faust finds himself amongst a crowd of young people including Valentin, Marguerite's brother who is about to go to war, and Siebel, who has promised to look after Marguerite in Valentin's absence. Faust and Marguerite meet briefly but it is only after he gives her a magnificent casket of jewels – to outshine the gift given to her by the lovesick Siebel – that their love begins to develop. Marguerite's husband is conveniently despatched by Mephistopheles and soon Marguerite is pregnant with Faust's child. But Faust disappears, leaving her alone and increasingly desperate. She finds no comfort in church, being constantly pursued by the taunting Mephistopheles. Valentin returns with his soldiers from the war at the same time as the hapless Faust. Furious at his sister's predicament, Valentin challenges Faust to a fight which Valentin loses, Faust having supernatural forces on his side. Marguerite slowly descends into madness, murders her child and ends up in prison, where, despite Faust's pleas, she chooses to remain until her death. Her soul is saved and the opera closes with a massive choral hymn glorifying the resurrection of Christ.

Favola d'Orfeo (see Orfeo)

Favorita La (Donizetti) FP 1840. Leonor is the mistress of the King of Castile but in love with a young novice monk, Ferdinand, for whom she has secured a key place in the army. Ferdinand saves the life of the King and asks to marry Leonor as a reward. The King realizes he is about to be revealed as an

Fidelio, Beethoven's only opera.

The full chorus of ENO in the final chorale.

adulterer and Leonor tries to tell Fernand of her other love. But the marriage goes ahead, and only afterwards does Ferdinand realize he has married the King's mistress. Distraught, he takes holy orders and becomes a monk. Just before taking his final vows, Leonor comes to plead for his forgiveness. Realizing that he still loves her, Ferdinand takes her in his arms, only to find that she has died.

Felsenstein, Walter (1901–1975) Mould-breaking Viennese actor turned opera producer who brought the Komische Oper in East Berlin to prominence as one of the world's most notable opera houses. He was the first of the opera producers to add his name to a production and thereby supercede the composer – people still talk about the Felsenstein *Otello*, Felsentstein's *Carmen* or Felsenstein's 'Bluebeard'. Sadly his productions were never seen in Britain, but the work of his disciples, such as Gotz Friedrich, Joachim Hertz and Ruth Berghaus has been seen in opera houses all over the world. He demanded that his singers should utilize their entire psyches in whatever roles they play, demanding more concentrated, intense acting ability than ever before, with extraordinarily long rehearsal periods (up to 200 times the playing length of any opera, he once decided). He always claimed that his was never a personal interpretation, more one wrought from long discussions with the cast and dramaturg to get to the literal meaning of a piece. Anthony Peattie, writing in *Opera Now*, summed it up thus: 'If you care about drama in opera, as opposed to mere vocalism, if you believe, as Mozart, Verdi and Wagner did, that composers are dramatists – you soon hear the name of Felsenstein'.

Ferrier, Kathleen (1912–1953) British contralto adored by her loyal following, particularly through the Second World War. Her operatic performances were rare compared with her numerous concert recitals, most notably of the Angel in Elgar's 'Gerontius' and Mahler's 'Das Lied von der Erde'. She created the role of Lucretia in Britten's *The Rape of Lucretia*. Her only other operatic role was the title role in Gluck's *Orfeo*.

Fidelio (Beethoven) FP 1805. Beethoven's only opera, which took him ten years to write, driven throughout by the subject matter rather than his desire to write for the human voice which had never come easily to him. Over 340 pages of sketches exist of his drafts of the opera. He wrote four different overtures to the work and he tried to write the hero's entrance sixteen times! The opera is punishingly difficult to sing, but the passionate commitment the composer felt to the opera's overall themes of freedom and devotion are obvious the moment the overture starts. Such seriousness can provide for a performance of excitement and tension, making *Fidelio* an opera which demands involvement in its cause and an understanding and sympathy of the motives of the main characters. It is also one of those operas where an important part of the action happens before the curtain rises (see 'antefatto').

A Spanish nobleman, Florestan, is imprisoned by Pizarro who has told the world that Florestan is dead. Leonora, Florestan's wife, is determined to prove her husband's innocence and have him released. She dresses as a man, calls herself Fidelio and is taken on by the chief jailer, Rocco, as an assistant at the prison. The jailer's daughter, Marcellina, sees Fidelio as a nice young man and better marriage prospect than her intended, Jacquino. When the opera starts, Marcellina is trying to evade Jacquino's advances. Pizarro is becoming increasingly worried that he will be found keeping Florestan in the deepest dungeon unlawfully and decides to kill him. Rocco refuses to help him, agreeing only to dig Florestan's grave which he does with Fidelio. At this point, the prisoners are released for a brief moment in the sunlight to celebrate the King's birthday. Their chorus is one of the most moving choral moments in all opera. From then on the action picks up as Pizarro comes to murder Florestan, is intercepted by Fidelio who reveals herself by challenging 'First kill his wife'. A trumpet call startles everyone as the Minister of State approaches, demands that Florestan be released and Pizarro be taken instead. Leonora and Florestan are reunited and the opera closes with a massive chorale rejoicing the devotion of a wife to her husband.

Field, Helen Welsh soprano. One of a number of talented singers with burgeoning international careers whom one might label

'Made in Wales'! Born near Wrexham, Helen Field won the 1976 triennial young Welsh Singer Competition, arranged by the Welsh Arts Council, and as a result became closely associated with Welsh National Opera, singing important roles in notable productions including Janacek's *Cunning Little Vixen*. She now appears regularly with Opera North and English National Opera, with whom she made her Metropolitan Opera debut, substituting at very short notice to sing Gilda in *Rigoletto*, during the company's American tour in 1984. Helen Field is slim, feminine and elegant and her undoubted acting ability and tendency to become totally involved in a role make her a compelling and touching performer.

Fielding, David English designer whose productions have divided audiences at many of Britain's leading opera companies. His work has been seen in Los Angeles in a new production of *Wozzeck* by Berg. Fielding does not have a clearly definable style, working closely with his director to transfer concepts to the stage which will be unique to each production he works on. His designs for *Xerxes* (ENO, 1985) for example, drew gasps of delighted admiration from the audience, as the stage was suffused with bright light, illuminating the colourful elegance of the Vauxhall Pleasure Gardens of the eighteenth century. For the same company, Fielding horrified audiences by setting Tchaikovsky's *Mazeppa* encased in four stark white walls, resembling a Siberian labour camp, and added a cubicle to house a decapitation by chainsaw, complete with blood-spattered carnage. Seen by some to be deliberately provocative and gratuitous, Fielding's designs always add a new aspect to productions, frequently lifting discussion of opera out of the music pages and encouraging wider debate.

Fiery Angel, The (Prokofiev) FP 1954. Weird, sinister, dissonant and not for first timers, this opera is highly symbolic and can be taken on a number of different levels. Only a part of it was performed in the composer's lifetime, as he lost the score and used some of the music in his third symphony. The work re-appeared in Paris after Prokofiev's death and is now regaining popularity amongst the more adventurous

opera houses. Many regard it as the composer's greatest operatic masterpiece – it is certainly intensely dramatic but not immediately enjoyable for those who are new to opera.

Renata, the heroine, saw visions of an angel as a child and, once grown up, found the personification of that angel in Count Heinrich with whom she shared a year of perfect happiness. As the opera opens, she is distraught at being abandoned by Heinrich and pours her heart out to a young man, Ruprecht. Together they look for Heinrich, encountering on the way an extraordinary philosopher-magician, Agrippa, and Ruprecht eventually succumbs to a duel with Heinrich. Although Ruprecht recovers his health, Renata cannot regain her sanity and becomes increasingly possessed by evil spirits. Even entry to a convent cannot calm her and she is finally denounced as a heretic and sentenced to death.

Fille du Regiment, La (see Daughter of the Regiment)

Film – opera on The current vogue for opera is thought by many to stem from the number of opera films which have been released. Film certainly makes the best of all the wonders of technology which can enhance an opera score, taking performers to locations to get the visual impact whilst adding a soundtrack of spectacular quality. Watching an opera film can give you that special excitement usually associated only with a live performance in a far more satisfying way than watching performances on the television. A director of the calibre of Zefirelli can bring the change of mood in opera to the fore in a far more exciting way on film than can ever be achieved in a theatre. Look, for example, at *La Traviata* which ranged from the vast and glittering balls of Paris to the simple intimacy of Alfredo and Violetto alone on a walk in the woods.

In many ways, opera on film is an excellent introduction to the medium – the pace is quicker, the locations are usually fabulous, the singers of top quality. Some of the best examples include Joseph Losey's *Don Giovanni*, where the lapping waters of Venice seem to be part of Mozart's score; *Carmen* with Julia Mignes Johnson and Placido Domingo where you can feel the heat of the

Spanish sun; and *Otello*, again with Placido Domingo, which was panned by the critics but gives a wonderful inside-view into this difficult and complex role. Don't be tempted to think, however, that seeing a film is like spoon-feeding opera. It takes just as much concentration, possibly more, because it can reach even more of your senses than a live performance. And, despite all the arguments about accessibility, it is far preferable for new opera goers at least to see an opera film at a cinema, with an audience, rather than on the video at home. So much of the satisfaction of opera depends on total involvement with the characters, which simply cannot be achieved when it is possible to nip outside and make a cup of tea during the boring bits.

Finnie, Linda Scottish mezzo-soprano and a versatile performer, as often found on the concert platform as on the opera stage. She sings with all the major British opera companies and in Frankfurt, Paris, and Bayreuth, where her success is such that she has been invited back each season in the same roles until 1992. She also performs extensively in concerts and recitals.

First nights The glitter, the glamour and the gossip which used to constitute the first night of an opera is now gone for the most part and sorely missed by many. First nights are now often picked to suit the press (the optimum night being Thursday in order to get a review in the Sunday papers), thus proscribing elaborate dress, as many people have to come straight from work. But there is a new excitement emerging at the first nights of new productions in many of the world's opera houses, not on who's with who, or who wears what, but on the production and set design. There is an undeniable buzz which circulates around a theatre as the curtain rises on a new set, sometimes appreciative to the point of spontaneous applause (the case with David Fielding's set for *Xerxes* – ENO 1985), sometimes aghast with horror, to the point of walking out before a note has been sung, (the case with *A Masked Ball* – ENO, 1989, by the same designer!). There is a tension about first nights (chiefly because the theatre is full of critics) which means that singers often do not sing their best, and many eminent musi-

cians would choose any other night to see a performance.

Fischer Dieskau, Dietrich German baritone. He has deservedly enjoyed a stunningly successful international career, the like of which has been experienced by very few artists this century. He made his operatic debut in the late 1940s at the Berlin State Opera, and within a few years was singing at all the most prestigious festivals and opera houses, often in contemporary works, in which he has always been interested. This interest has continued up to the present day. Aribert Reimann wrote *Lear* (first performed 1978) for him. Recital work has always been important to him and this, together with recording, takes up most of Fischer-Dieskau's time now. He has recorded the complete Schubert Lieder and won many prizes. Always fascinated with the academic side of music, he has researched and written several books and been awarded honorary doctorates by Oxford, Yale, and the Sorbonne.

Flagstad, Kirsten (1895–1962) Norwegian soprano. A 'late-developer' who incurred unfavourable reaction particularly in America for her husband's brief collaboration with the Nazi party during the Second World War. Her voice was admirably suited to the weightier roles, with emphasis on Wagner and it is her recording of *Tristan and Isolde* that marks her out as one of the all time greats for quality of voice.

Fledermaus, Die (J Strauss) FP 1874. One of the lightest, prettiest, funniest operas in the repertoire, beloved of amateur operatic societies, but like so much comedy, quite difficult to achieve a really stunning performance that does justice to all the elements of the story. The music is so tuneful and the settings often so glorious that the finer nuances of the plot really do not matter at all. The title actually means 'The Bat' – hardly an appropriate name for such a flirtatious piece of music! It refers to the disguise that Dr Falke was wearing when his old friend Eisenstein left him to sleep off a particularly vicious hangover and then find his way home in the cold light of day in his fancy dress! The plot of this opera concerns Dr Falke's revenge on Eisenstein.

Eisenstein is due to go to prison for five days but Falke persuades him that he might as well go the next morning and enjoy Prince Orlovsky's ball that night. As the men leave to plan their evening, Eisenstein's wife Roselinde receives her admirer, Alfred. By chance donning his rival's dressing gown, Alfred is mistaken for Eisenstein and whisked off to prison by the Governor, Frank. The main characters (including Frank) meet at the ball, but Roselinde is dressed as a Hungarian countess and Adele, Roselinde's maid, has come in one of her mistresses dresses. Eisenstein, not recognizing his wife, attempts to seduce her with his chiming watch. Resolutely refusing to prove her real identity, Roselinde launches into a wonderful display of coloratura singing, matched with Hungarian dancing, all finally resolving into the glittering 'Fledermaus waltz'. As the party reaches its height, the clock strikes six and Eisenstein realizes he is due in jail. Surrendering himself to justice, he encounters the jailer Frosch (a non-singing role, usually taken by a well known comic actor) who has had as good a time with the champagne in prison as his boss the governor has had at the ball. Such drunken stupors are further confused when Frosch, who thinks he already has Eisenstein in jail, when in fact it is Alfred, is faced with the real Eisenstein, on the arm of the prison governor. That only leaves Eisenstein to work out who was arrested in his place, accept Roselinde's explanation and join her in putting it all down to the influence of 'King Champagne'!

Fliegende Hollander, Die (see Flying Dutchman)

Florence – Maggio Musicale One of the most exciting festivals in the opera calendar, the Maggio Musicale usually runs through May and June each year and is housed at the Teatro Communale. It attracts some of the world's greatest singers, matched by enterprising directors whose productions are designed to provoke, surprise and stimulate. The Festival is truly international – the 1990 programme included a new production of Mozart's *Don Giovanni*, produced by an Englishman, conducted by an Indian and starring an American, as well as a complete staging of a work by Rimsky Korsakov,

designed by an Italian, conducted by a Korean and sung by an entirely Russian cast! The repertory is enormously varied, extended to superb recitals and a matchless atmosphere of excitement throughout the beautiful Tuscan city.

Floyd, Carlisle American composer whose first opera *Susannah*, written in 1955, was deliberately popular and enjoyed enormous success. Since then Floyd's operas have been more intellectually based and have marked him as one of the most important operatic composers currently writing in America. His work includes *Wuthering Heights*, based on the novel by Emily Bronte and *Of Mice and Men*, based on the work by Steinbeck.

Flying Dutchman, The (Wagner) FP 1843. Opinion is divided as to whether this is the ideal introduction to Wagner for a first timer because, unlike all his other works, it is a manageable length! Indeed, it was written to be played without an interval and is frequently performed thus. This either makes it an absorbing experience or a stunningly dull one, guaranteed to put you off Wagner, and possibly off all opera for life. The music is glorious, so it is probably sensible to listen to all or part of the score before investing in a ticket. If the music does not spur you on to want to see the action which accompanies it, do not bother, because 'action' is really too strong a word for the slow, painstaking process by which the Dutchman works out his destiny.

The Dutchman of the title accepted the help of the Devil when sailing around the Cape of Good Hope. In return, he has now been condemned to sail continually until he can find a woman who will love him until death. He is allowed to come into port every seven years and on one such occasion meets the beautiful Senta, daughter of the sea captain Daaland. Senta has always had romantic notions of the myth of the Flying Dutchman and spurns her other admirer, Erik, in order to be with the sailor. The Dutchman discovers Senta trying to explain to Erik how she feels about the Dutchman and, unable to hear their conversation properly, assumes that Senta has returned to her original lover. Once more, he sets out to sea, heartbroken. Senta is distraught and throws herself off a cliff, reunited in heaven with the Dutchman who has drowned in a storm.

Forza del Destino, La (Verdi) FP 1862. Somebody once described this opera as soft, strong and very, very long. Soft because rather than relying on destiny it makes a great deal out of some rather improbable co-incidences; strong because it incorporates some wonderful and very well known Verdi melodies, and the individual characters are interesting; and very, very long – no longer than *Don Carlos* or *Boris Godunov*, but it can seem interminable!

By accident, Don Alvaro has killed the father of Leonora, the girl Alvaro intends to marry. As the lovers flee, they become separated and Leonora, disguised as a man, ends up in a convent under the safe keeping of Padre Guardino, who allows her to live in complete isolation. Meanwhile, her brother Don Carlo is roaming the country trying to track down Don Alvaro to avenge his father's death and his sister's honour. In true operatic fashion, Don Carlo and Don Alvaro meet when both are heavily disguised and, not recognizing each other, Don Alvaro saves Don Carlo from certain death. The two swear undying allegiance and true friendship. As both men fight on the same side in battle, Alvaro is mortally wounded and the duet they sing as he lies dying is one of Verdi's finest and best known melodies – a perfect example of the conflict a singer faces when asked to sing a soaringly wonderful melody when the character is meant to be close to death! As Alvaro is carried away, believed dead, Carlo opens the box Alvaro gave him, sees Leonora's picture and realizes his former friend was in fact his sworn enemy. A further twist reveals that Alvaro's life has been saved, thus giving Carlo an opportunity for revenge. Carlo finally tracks down Alvaro in a monastery – conveniently near Leonora's isolated cell – where Alvaro is posing as Padre Raffaello. Alvaro is ready to make peace, even offering to kneel before his old enemy, but Carlo's taunts prove to much and their long awaited duel begins. Leonora overhears the fighting and arrives to find her ex-lover delivering the fatal blow to her brother and, in bending over to comfort Carlo, is herself stabbed by the dying Carlo, still intent on revenge. Alvaro is left along on the stage, cursing the

destiny which brought such tragedy to his life.

Fra Diavolo (Auber) FP 1830. An opera by a French composer about an Italian bandit, featuring an English lord, now rarely performed except in Germany! Perhaps this light little opera comique will become a favourite in the single Europe, post 1992!

In a tavern in Italy, Lord Cockburn declares he has been robbed and offers a reward for the return of his wife's jewels. His wife, Lady Pamela, is more interested in the attentions of the Marquis of San Marco. The soldier Lorenzo is anxious to win the reward so he can prove his wealth to Matteo, the father of Zerlina whom Lorenzo wants to marry. Fra Diavolo, the bandit who is causing all the problems, appears at dead of night with his accomplices Beppo and Giacomo, but rather than robbing anyone, he causes complete turmoil by pretending to Lorenzo that he had an assignation with Zerlina, and to Lord Cockburn that he was after Lady Pamela. At the Easter procession the next day, the accomplices give away a vital clue to prove what Fra Diavolo was up to, Lorenzo organizes his capture and justice prevails.

Francesca da Rimini (Zandonai) FP 1914. Rarely performed today, this opera is one of about thirty based on Dante's *Inferno*. It concerns three brothers – Paolo, Gianciotto and Malatestino. Francesca has been tricked into marrying the deformed Gianciotto, thinking he is the more handsome Paolo with whom she has genuinely fallen in love. The one-eyed brother Malatestino harbours an unrequited love for Francesca. Malatestino betrays Francesca and Paolo to Gianciotto, who kills them both.

Frau ohne Schatten, Dia (Richard Strauss) FP 1919. Some operas are about action, some are purely about emotion. This is certainly of the 'emotional' category, and while it is recommended with caution for a complete new-comer to opera, chiefly because it is very long, it actually has a peculiarly engrossing plot and some heartrendingly beautiful music. It has been given some sympathetic productions recently, so could be a surprisingly enjoyable evening if you are prepared to concentrate and become involved.

The opera is set in a mythical time and place but deals with emotions which many audiences may find immediately recognizable. The Emperor of a mythical land has married a supernatural woman whose father has decreed that if the couple cannot produce a child, the Empress must return home and her husband be turned to stone. The Empress' barren state is symbolized by her inability to cast her own shadow (a technical challenge for any lighting designer!). The Empress and her nurse seek out the dyer Barak and his wife. They have no children but the wife has a shadow she is willing to sell to the Empress in return for great riches, thus rendering the couple childless for life. But seeing Barak's heartache at this decision, the Empress feels unable to go through with the agreement and is finally rewarded for the compassion she showed to the mortal couple by the gift of a shadow.

Freeman, David Born in Australia and now in demand internationally, David Freeman is without doubt one of the most influential directors working in opera today. He demands total commitment from his cast, insisting on long and intense rehearsal periods and works through improvisation and workshop-style rehearsal to bring the highest acting standards to his productions. The results are intelligent, superbly motivated stagings, maximizing the human drama from the plots and making each event totally believable. Freeman is the guiding light behind Opera Factory, the first of which he founded in Sydney in 1973, followed by Zurich in 1976 and London in 1981. Encouraging these uncompromising standards of artistic dedication, Freeman has created numerous notable productions for Opera Factory including premieres of *Punch and Judy* and *Yan Tan Tethera* by Harrison Birtwistle as well as *La Calisto* by Cavalli and *Cosi fan Tutte* by Mozart. He has produced Philip Glass' *Akhnaten* for ENO and *La Bohème* for Opera North, as well as productions in Paris, Germany, Houston and New York. His exacting style is admired by many singers who welcome the opportunity to work on his thoughtful productions.

Freischutz, Der (Weber) FP 1821. The supernatural comes to a little German peasant community. There is a good deal of talking which tends to dilute the effect of the music and causes the action to seem rather disjointed. The hero is not heroic in the traditional sense, and all the characters are deliberately ordinary – Weber was trying to convey a picture of the effect the supernatural has on real people. There is one scene in the middle of the opera – set in the Wolf's Glen – which can be spectacular in a good production. In historical terms, the opera is important because it represents the beginning of the German Romantic movement which reached its height with Wagner and ended with Richard Strauss. The overture, which is well known out of context, was the first to use whole themes from the opera itself, rather than be a separate piece of music altogether.

Max wants to marry Agathe and in order to do so must win a sharpshooting contest. Anxious to improve on his previous record, he asks for the help of the sinister Caspar who offers him magic bullets which always hit their target. Max is persuaded by Caspar to go into the eerie Wolf's Glen in order to have seven magic bullets forged. Six are for Max's use – the seventh can go wherever Samiel (who represents the Devil) wants it to. On the day of the contest Max is left with this one bullet which he shoots, knowing he has no control over where it goes. To his horror, his beloved Agathe falls, but only in a faint. The bullet has in fact struck a fatal blow to Caspar who lured the innocent Max into the clutches of the Devil.

Freni, Mirella Italian soprano who developed from the lyric roles such as Susannah in *The Marriage of Figaro* to the dramatic parts such as Desdemona in *Otello* with ease and conviction. Freni enjoys a superbly confident technique, borne of extensive training in Italy and a gradual debut into the professional world, accepting only those roles of which she felt confident, rather than pushing herself too early. She is in international demand and has created memorable performances of the dramatic soprano heroines, having been encouraged to do so by Herbert von Karajan. She is married to the Russian bass Nicolai Ghiaurov.

Friedrich, Professor Gotz German producer who assisted Walter Felsenstein at the

Komische Oper in East Berlin until Felsenstein's death in 1959 when Friedrich took over. He moved to the West in 1972 and in 1981 became Intendant of the Deutsche Oper, West Berlin. Now only stages two productions a year away from this house which he has developed to be among the most influential opera houses in the world. A prime example of the ability of fine artists to cross political borders, he staged a free matinee performance of *The Magic Flute* on the day travel restrictions between East and West Berlin were lifted in November 1989, welcoming anyone from the divided city to come and see it. He therefore seems well placed to be highly influential in the cultural re-unification of Berlin which boasts three world class opera houses. Friedrich is renowned for his strongly conceptual productions, the symbolism of which is not always apparent to those of a less formidable intellect than his own.

From the House of the Dead (Janacek) FP 1930. Rather like Menotti's *The Consul*, this opera will convince you that not all operas are about women dressed as boys, and men moping around in a lovelorn state. It is set in a Siberian labour camp and really has very little plot. Rather it tells the stories of several different prisoners, beginning and ending with the tribulations of Gorjancikov, a political prisoner who is savagely beaten by the guards. In Janacek's original version, which he left uncompleted before his death, the end of the opera saw the prisoners returning to their cells. The version more regularly performed today is that completed by Bakala and Chlubna, where the prisoners sing a final, optimistic chorus of freedom. Perhaps the overall theme of hope in the opera is best summed up by Janacek's own epigraph for the score – 'In every creature a spark of God'.

Funding Any sanguine accountant, however musical, begins to smart when he or she realizes quite how expensive opera is to produce. It is extraordinarily labour intensive and almost impossible to rationalize or economize in any way. If one even starts to question whether opera is worth the money, one becomes caught in a spiral of justification and counter-argument, leaving true opera lovers to accept that their beloved art

form is an unashamed luxury. It is a popularly held myth (usually put about by those who know no better and have rarely been inside a theatre in their lives) that opera houses are profligate and wasteful of the enormous amount of funding they receive. In fact every cost cutting measure that can be made usually has been, to the extent that salaries are pared to their lowest minimum, resources – both human and physical – are stretched to the maximum and revenue is generated from virtually every possible area. If opera companies were expected to survive on their box office income alone, as many critics suggest, the productions would be so few and so sparse or the ticket prices so ridiculously high that the public outcry would be considerable in either case. It is impossible too for opera managers to exploit the potential of a highly successful production by asking the singers to extend their contracts and similarly curtail a loss maker in the same way that commercial producers are able to do. Opera singers simply cannot sing major roles night after night and therefore companies are limited to various methods of organization; repertory where different works are performed each night; 'stagione', where major stars are brought in for a limited number of performances; or touring.

Glyndebourne Festival Opera in southern England is acknowledged in Britain to be amongst the best at making the most of its income and receives no state funding. The Festival takes 65 per cent of its income from the box office and the rest from sponsorship. But the cheapest Glyndebourne seat price is well over £30 and accessibility is hardly the cornerstone of its policy. In Britain the companies who rely on state funding may only get confirmation of the bulk of their working capital six months before the beginning of their financial year, by which time they will have had to contract artists, plan set designs and fix seat prices. Sponsorship (see separate entry), while having increased massively in the last few years, can never be relied upon to make up any pre-agreed total. Very many opera houses play to more than 80 per cent full houses already, so the potential for increasing revenue from the audience is limited. The current vogue is to maximize income through sharing production costs with other opera houses, selling recording and video rights and exploiting the merchandizing potential of such a glamorous art form through calendars, address books, posters – and perhaps less subtle items such as 'Elisir d'Amore' perfume. A further growth area is that of 'special events' – galas, balls, recitals, and so on – which, for those who have ever worked on them, usually means the amount of money raised is in inverse proportion to the amount of work put in! When it comes to self-generated income of all types (ie everything that does not come in grant-aid from the state), Britain has a good deal, both good and bad, to learn from America where opera has been big business for far longer than it has in Europe. The American companies, however, look to the European form of state support for the arts with as much longing as Europe looks in admiration at the massive corporate and individual support American opera companies receive.

Furtwangler, Wilhelm (1886–1954) German conductor, most notably of Wagner, Brahms and Beethoven during his long tenure at the Berlin Philharmonic. Highly individual in his interpretations, his two recordings of the Ring Cycle are thought by many to be the definitive interpretations.

Gadski, Johanna (1872–1932) German soprano who specialized in Wagner and Italian roles, and reached the height of her career in America before the First World War. By 1917 war fever had reached America and she was forced to return to Germany with her husband who was wanted on charges of spying. She returned to the USA and ran her own company for two years before meeting an early death in a car accident. Her voice was fluid and expressive, with a beauty apparent on the recordings she made.

Galli-Curci, Amelita (1882–1963) American soprano who became one of the first American singers to achieve state-wide popularity, due mainly to the large number of excellent recordings she made. Largely self taught, she made an exciting debut as Gilda in Chicago in 1916 and went on to perform virtually every major soprano role. A throat tumour cut short her career in 1930.

Galli-Marie, Celestine (1840–1905) French soprano who created the roles of Mignon and, most notably, Carmen in 1875.

Gambler, The (Prokofiev) FP 1917. Set in the wonderfully named German town of Roulettenburg, which is in fact Wiesbaden. The General is waiting for his maiden aunt to die so he can inherit her fortune and marry his beloved Blanche. Blanche is a keen gambler, as is Alexey, tutor to the General's children. Alexey has lost all the money his girlfriend Pauline (who is the General's stepdaughter) has given him prior to their marriage. The General, infuriated by his aunt's continuing good health, has borrowed money from a rich French Marquis to continue his gambling. A further twist reveals that Pauline once had an affair with the Marquis, but now she only wishes to prove Alexey's devotion to her and stop his gambling. The maiden aunt arrives, in a wheelchair but otherwise in sterling good health. She makes for the gambling tables and proceeds to lose the General's inheritance. Insulted at the Marquis' offer to give more money to Pauline, Alexey heads back for the tables and begins a run of remarkable luck, providing him with the fortune he always wanted in order to marry Pauline. But she is fed up with being attached to a compulsive gambler. She takes Alexey's money only to hurl it back in his face. As the curtain falls, Alexey is irresistibly drawn back to the gaming tables where all his problems began.

Garden, Mary (1874–1967) Scottish soprano who worked chiefly in America and sang a remarkable number of first performances of works which are now standard in the repertoire. She created Melisande in *Pelleas and Melisande* (Debussy) at the Opéra Comique in 1902, the title role in Saint Saens *Helène*, had *Cherubin* written for her by Massenet and reintroduced *Salome* (Richard Strauss) to the USA in 1909. She went on to lead the Chicago Opera for one season in 1921 which was artistically wonderfully and financially disastrous. She nevertheless continued her artistic association with the company until 1931, retiring fully in 1934. She was regarded as an excellent singer/actress, perhaps amongst the first to excel in both talents.

George Gershwin's *Porgy and Bess*, staged by Trevor Nunn at Glyndebourne in 1986, has all the compelling interest of grand opera. Willard White plays the crippled Porgy, with Cynthia Haymon as Bess.

Gardiner, John Elliott English conductor who founded the Monteverdi Choir in London in 1964 and shot to fame in 1968 as the youngest conductor ever at the Proms in London. He made his operatic debut at English National Opera a year later with a performance of *The Magic Flute* and has since conducted many of the world's greatest orchestras including those in Dallas, San Francisco and Toronto as well as directing the Opéra de Lyon for five years. Chiefly known for his superb interpretations of the baroque repertoire, Gardiner has made a significant contribution to the performance of baroque opera. His performances include a complete staging of *Les Boreades* by Rameau, part of which Gardiner discovered as an abandoned score in a Paris library. He reconstructed the opera to give a performance in the 1982 Aix en Provence Festival. Gardiner also conducted a production of Debussy's *Pelleas and Melisande*, which he again put together from the original 1901 score. His academic ability is combined with a talent to make seemingly obscure works come to life and attract a contemporary audience, and his recordings of operas such as *L'Étoile* by Chabrier, *Comte Ory* by Rossini and *The Damnation of Faust* by Berlioz have found widespread popularity. His plans include a recording of all seven of the great operas by Mozart.

Garrett, Lesley English soprano. Lesley Garrett stared out at travellers from posters on the London Underground as part of English National Opera's autumn 1989 advertising campaign, enticing many people into the Coliseum who would not normally go. She has a very lively and vivacious stage personality and lots of sex-appeal. Although she is a member of ENO she also sings regularly with other UK companies and abroad and in 1991 sings *Peter Grimes* with Geneva Opera.

Gatti-Casazza, Guilio (1869–1940) Italian opera manager who became the first salaried, opera specialist to manage the Metropolitan Opera House, New York. In his thirty-seven year tenure he transformed the Met from a small conventional operation to an internationally ranked house with an impressive string of premieres to its credit, including *Fanciulla del West* by Puccini,

Goyescas by Granados and *Konigskinder* by Humperdinck. Only the years of the Depression curbed Gatti-Casazza's reign which was as successful financially as it was artistically. His reputation in the opera world was further enhanced when he married the Met's prima donna, Frances Alda in 1910 and after her, the Met's prima ballerina Rosina Galli in 1930.

Gay, John (1685–1732) English composer. Gay wrote the libretto to *Acis and Galatea* by Handel but made his name with the phenomenally successful *The Beggar's Opera* which he composed in 1728.

Gazza Ladra, La (see Thieving Magpie).

Gedda, Nicolai Swedish-born tenor of Russian/Swedish parents, Nicolai Gedda spent much of his early childhood in Leipzig. This cosmopolitan background perhaps explains Gedda's great facility for languages, fluency and perfect diction in at least five, and his huge repertoire of over seventy roles. Gedda is renowned for his versatility, and over the years he has sung most of the great tenor roles, from the Russian (Dimitri, *Boris Godunov*, Hermann in *Queen of Spades*), to the baroque (*Orfeo ed Euridice*) to contemporary (Kodanda in Gian-Carlo Menotti's *The Last Savage*). He has also sung and recorded operetta – *Die Fledermaus*, *The Merry Widow*, *The Singing Baron* – all for EMI. Recently Gedda has tended to concentrate more and more on teaching and concerts, so nowadays you are as likely to see him giving a 'Celebrity Recital' as on the lyric stage.

Gentele, Goran (1917–1972) Successor to Rudolf Bing as Manager of the Met in New York, Gentele introduced two new posts to the senior management of the house – Music Director and Principal Conductor. For the former, Gentele chose Rafael Kubelik; for the latter, the relatively unknown James Levine who has gone on to attract worldwide acclaim. Gentele was killed in a car accident shortly before the opening of his production of *Carmen* in 1972, but the production was still staged using Gentele's original notes.

Gershwin, George (1898–1937) Gershwin really wrote only one opera which up until recently hovered in the foggy territory which divides opera from music theatre. But Glyndebourne's 1986 production of *Porgy and Bess* made the music world sit up and realize that this work had every right to be in the repertoire of every leading opera house. Gershwin's distinctive style began with musical comedies like *Lady be Good* and *Girl Crazy*, developed through more thoughtful works like *Rhapsody in Blue* and *An American in Paris*, and finally flowered with *Porgy and Bess* which was written in 1935. His music has an energetic tunefulness which conjures up the extraordinary fascination of America in the Twenties and Thirties, blending the free forms of jazz with the structure of superb musicianship. Gershwin's music is a wonderful bridge between classical and popular and therefore cannot be recommended too highly for a new opera goer.

Gesamkunstwerk Literally 'together art work', this term was used by Wagner to describe opera as the perfect fusion of music, drama and poetry.

Ghiaurov, Nicolai Bulgarian bass in great demand internationally, with a repertoire ranging from *The Barber of Seville* to *Boris Godunov*. This in spite of very humble beginnings in his native Bulgaria. He entered the Sofia Music Academy in 1949 and won a state scholarship to study in Moscow until 1955. His first appearances were in Bulgaria and the USSR, but since his 1959 debut at La Scala he has performed a very wide repertoire, in all languages, all over the world.

Gianni Schicchi (Puccini) FP 1918. One act opera which forms the last part of Puccini's Trittico (three part work). It is chiefly known for one stunningly beautiful soprano solo 'O My Beloved Father' which was used as the theme music for the highly successful Merchant Ivory film *A Room with a View*. The opera is rarely performed and has a rather extraordinary plot, but the famous soprano aria is typical of the tuneful and evocative music throughout.

The scene is the bedroom of Buoso Donati who has recently died. His relatives are furious when they discover that all his money has been left to a monastery and Rinuccio suggests that the wily Gianni Schicchi, who happens to be the father of Rinuccio's girl-friend Lauretta, be brought in to sort out the problems. Schicchi hits on a plan but warns the others of the devastating consequences if they are found out. Sworn to secrecy, they agree Schicchi can go ahead with disposing of the body, and then he climbs into the death bed and impersonates Donati by dictating a different will. Each relative comes in turn to bribe Schicchi to favour them, but he outsmarts them all. The new will reveals that Schicchi is the sole benefactor of the best possessions, with the house going to Lauretta and Rinuccio.

Gibson, Sir Alexander Scottish conductor who played a leading role in the formation of Scottish Opera in 1962, and remained with the company for twenty-five years as its Music Director. He appeared with many of the world's finest orchestras including those in Detroit, New York, Los Angeles, Pittsburgh and Houston where he was Principal Guest Conductor from 1981 to 1983. In Washington in 1974 he presented the American premiere of *The Return of Ulysses* by Monteverdi and has recently worked with the Kentucky and Los Angeles opera companies on performances of *Aida*, *La Traviata* and *Madam Butterfly*.

Gigli, Benjamino (1890–1957) Italian tenor, still ranked as one of the greatest ever – the most common word used to describe his voice is 'beautiful'. He had absolutely no acting ability but with a voice like his, it hardly mattered at all, particularly as he reached the height of his career when opera singers were judged entirely by their voices and nothing else. His was one of the first truly international careers, beginning in Italy, transferring to the Met, returning to Italy rather than accept the Met's Depression-inflicted pay cut, but continuing to perform at leading houses all over the world. He concentrated on the lyrical romantic roles like Cavaradossi (*Tosca*), Alfredo (*La Traviata*), Pinkerton (*Madam Butterfly*) and Rodolfo (*La Bohème*). Singing this last role, he took part in a particularly notable production at Covent Garden in 1946 when his daughter sang the role of Mimi.

Gilbert & Sullivan (W S Gilbert 1836–1911, English librettist; Arthur Sullivan (Sir) 1842–1900, English composer.)

Recent audience research undertaken by a small amateur opera society, recorded that a substantial proportion of the audience thought Gilbert-and-Sullivan was one person. These two eminent Victorians have a strong claim to be the most indivisible of musical partnerships, achieving little of note separately but together providing a series of works which are uniquely British, perennially popular and extraordinarily adaptable. Their collaborative works are known as the Savoy Operas (see entry), and started with *Trial by Jury* (1875), followed by *The Sorcerer* in 1877, *HMS Pinafore* (1878), *The Pirates of Penzance* (1879), *Patience* (1881), *Iolanthe* (1882), *The Mikado* (1885), *Ruddigore* (1887), *The Yeomen of the Guard* (1888) and *The Gondoliers* (1889). Gilbert and Sullivan's pieces are strictly termed operetta, being lighter and funnier than even the most comic opera, and are therefore omitted from many opera anthologies. This is a tremendous shame because, for the new opera goer, they are an almost perfect introduction, bridging the gap between spoken and sung theatre with deliberate ease.

Gilbert had the ability to write lyrics which were apposite, charming (occasionally lapsing into the sentimental), highly satirical and often fairly cruel. His treatment in particular of the middle-aged spinster as a figure of fun verged on the merciless. But in late Victorian England, gentle fun-poking at the Establishment proved enormously popular. Sullivan's music matched his partner's words for accessibility, hummable tunes and an ability to heighten the description of a character with his music – which after all is what opera is all about. The pair's association with Richard D'Oyly Carte, a Victorian impressario, began when he commissioned 'Trial' in 1875 and continued throughout Gilbert and Sullivan's writing careers. All the works were performed at the Savoy Theatre, which D'Oyly Carte owned and, on Gilbert's death in 1911, the D'Oyly Carte family assumed sole rights to the performances of the operas. The family's insistence that the works be performed in their original Victorian style for the duration of the copyright period, together with the development of a more sophisticated theatre-going audience for whom the works were almost unbearably silly and sentimental, caused 'G & S' to become the preserve of a few hardened aficiandos until 1961 when the

copyright expired. Since then, modern producers have taken massive liberties with the original productions, altering music and words as well as staging, and have received the inevitable brick-bats from the purists. But they have brought the operettas to a new young audience and, with the revival of the D'Oyly Carte Company after some years absence, Gilbert and Sullivan's popularity seems set to continue in a myriad of different interpretations.

Gioconda, La (Ponchielli) FP 1876. Lots of very well known tunes, most of all 'The Dance of the Hours'. It is very grand and lush, but not performed very often, partly because much of the singing is extraordinarily difficult. Also, having two important female roles can lead to terrific 'artistic difficulties' (roughly interpretted as temper tantrums!) both off and on-stage.

'La Gioconda' means a ballad singer and she is referred to as such throughout the work, never having a Christian name. She is madly in love with the exiled-nobleman-disguised-as-fisherman, Enzo Grimaldo. Grimaldo is in love with another woman, Laura, wife of a leading councillor and La Gioconda has another admirer – the spy Barnaba. Thinking it will increase his chances with La Gioconda, Barnaba tries to get his rival out of the way by denouncing him to the Council. La Gioconda meets Enzo and Laura enjoying a secret tryst on a boat, and, rather than hating her rival, La Gioconda recognizes Laura as the woman who once helped La Gioconda's blind mother. La Gioconda helps Laura escape from her councillor husband who has come to arrest Enzo and she goes on to save Laura's life, finally reuniting Enzo and Laura as lovers with La Giocanda's blessing. Rather than carry out her promise to marry Barnaba, La Gioconda takes the poison originally intended for Laura and falls dead just as her new husband is about to embrace her.

Gioielli della Madonna, I (Wolf-Ferrari) FP 1911. Most of Wolf-Ferrari's output falls in to the jolly little opera catagory, but he obviously wanted to be remembered for one great serious work and penned 'Gioielli' as a real-life drama. It did not entirely work, and he went on to suffer a nervous breakdown during World War One and not compose anything else really notable for the rest of his life.

Two men – the gangster Rafaele and the blacksmith Gennaro are after the same girl, Maliella. Rafaele boasts that he loves her so much, he would steal the jewels off the Madonna's statue and give them to her. Gennaro overhears Maliella who seems to be impressed by Rafaele's daring, and goes off to steal them himself. His plan works – Maliella falls into his arms, but then tells all to Rafaele who rejects her completely. Maliella throws the jewels back at Gennaro and drowns herself. Distraught, Gennaro replaces the jewels back with the Madonna and stabs himself.

Girl of the Golden West, The (see Fanciulla del West)

Giulini, Carlo Maria Italian conductor who was Chief Conductor at La Scala, Milan, from 1953 to 1967, after which date he has concentrated on a successful concert career. At the height of his opera career, his performances of Mozart and the Italian repertory were thought to be unsurpassed.

Glass, Philip American composer who completed work with Nadia Boulanger in Paris and at the Julliard School in New York, before studying Eastern music in some depth. This prompted him to reject the complex musical forms of the West and concentrate on radical and simple ideas instead, termed 'minimalist' music. This consists of music centred on a limited number of notes frequently repeated in different combinations which may be added to or subtracted from, but consistent in the style of sound they produce. All of Glass' operas are written in this style. They include the trilogy *Einstein on the Beach, Satyagraha* and *Akhnaten*, a work for children, *The Juniper Tree, The Making of the Representative for Planet Eight*, based on the novel by Doris Lessing and *The Fall of the House of Usher*, based on Edgar Allen Poe's novel. Glass enjoys a cult following internationally, through performances of his operas and concert performances of his pieces. He has brought an entirely new audience to the opera house and is slowly being accepted by older opera goers who have hitherto criticized his work for its apparent repetition and monotony.

Glinka, Mikhail (1805–1857) Russian composer whose unusual combination of Italian and French opera styles with Russian folk music was to become very influential to later Russian composers like Tchaikovsky and Mussorgsky whose own operas have remained better known than Glinka's. He wrote only two of note, *A Life for the Tsar* and *Ruslan and Ludmilla*, from which the overture is frequently used as a concert piece.

Gloriana (Britten) FP 1953. To compose an opera for the Coronation of a Queen must lead to expectations which it is almost impossible to fulfil. When *Gloriana* was premiered on June 8th 1953, in the presence of the new Queen Elizabeth II, it sank like a lead balloon. The first audience – which Tyrone Guthrie described as preferring a performance of *Iolanthe* with an all star cast – stormed at the inappropriateness of the theme. The beautiful young Queen who was to lead Britain into the latter part of the twentieth century, they said, should not be compared with a wizened Elizabeth I, sorting out the political intrigues in her incestuous court, with the odd bit of dancing thrown in here and there. But as the production toured round the country, it met with more and more approval – though not enough to bring it back to London until 1963, with a new production staged by Sadler's Wells in 1966. That production is occasionally revived by ENO, and formed a central part of their American tour in 1984.

Glover, Jane English conductor and a leading exponent of Mozart, Jane Glover has succeeded in a traditionally male-dominated world. She is currently Artistic Director of the London Mozart Players and was Music Director of Glyndebourne Touring Opera from 1981 to 1985. She has conducted all Britain's major orchestras and for Glyndebourne has led performances of many of the major Mozart operas, as well as works by Britten and Rossini. She conducted the 1986 performance of *A Midsummer Night's Dream* given by Glyndebourne at the Hong Kong Festival. For ENO, she has conducted *Don Giovanni* and plans to conduct *The Magic Flute*. Her Covent Garden debut was *Die Entführung aus dem Serail*. Well known to British television audiences through her presentation of well-researched, accessible series on classical music, Jane Glover is also familiar to audiences in Canada.

Gluck, Christopher (1714–1787) German composer who had a profound influence on the development of opera when, in 1762, he composed *Orfeo ed Euridice*. In this opera, he abandoned the traditional conventions of opera writing and went for real, human drama. It marked a turning point in opera, proving that the art form could describe the human condition with direct realism rather than through the conventions which had been observed by all composers until then. It was in the preface to *Alceste*, which he wrote in 1769, that he spelt out these ideas more fully: 'I have striven to restrict music to its true office of serving poetry by means of expression and by following the situations of the story, without interrupting the action or stifling it with a meaningless superfluity of ornaments.'

To a certain extent, Gluck capitalized on a trend, as many composers were beginning to abandon the regulation forms of composition in their operas. But it took someone not only of his musical genius but of real psychological awareness to transfer his characters on to stage, making them truly believable because of the music they sang and the words they used.

Glyndebourne Imagine an opera house in the middle of the countryside, appallingly badly sign-posted from such roads as there are, and miles away from any roads that are useful. Start all the performances at about 5p.m. so everyone *has* to take the afternoon off work or make special domestic arrangements to get there in time. Suggest that men wear dinner jackets and ladies wear long dresses, involving extraordinarily complicated sartorial planning for audiences across the country. Price the tickets well above the market rate for a West End show and make them so infernally difficult to get hold of that the Box Office Manager reckons she must be the most popular woman in British arts. Don't expect any money from the government and put your finances entirely at the mercy of the notoriously vague sponsoring community. Perform for a short period every summer and expect the majority of your audience to bring their own food and brave the vagaries of the British climate.

And, above all, have the sure and certain – and undeniably English – confidence that people have such a time that they want to keep coming back.

The success of Glyndebourne could be thought to encapsulate the popularity of opera across the world. It is a real event – exclusive, glamorous, unashamedly elitist, and as such tremendously exciting. There is a real sense of 'well, we made it', amongst a proportion of the audience, who then get understandably rattled by the non-opera-loving corporate members who go each year out of duty not enthusiasm. No-one can deny the importance the corporate community has had on Glyndebourne – it would simply not exist without corporate support and opera lovers should be grateful for such generosity. But it is galling to see how little appreciation many corporate members have of their considerable investment. For a singer to say wryly that, after the supper interval at Glyndebourne, 'you could turn cartwheels and most people wouldn't notice', seems to me very sad – and also the height of bad manners to deny the hard work and talent that makes Glyndebourne such a pinnacle of excellence both musically and financially. Anyone who fails to be excited by the sheer eccentricity, beauty and magic of this extraordinary place, or impressed by the high standard of musicianship and dedication that goes into every performance, should relinquish his seat to someone who might genuinely appreciate it. If you cannot be assured of tickets through a business connection but you are still desperate to go, how do you set about it? The following is not a fool-proof guide, but may throw some light on the most elitist of Britain's opera houses.

Getting tickets. Glyndebourne is run as a Festival Society and, consequently, first choice for tickets is given to members. At present, the waiting time to be an individual member is about twenty-one years. (Put your godchildren down now as a christening present and ensure they take you when their membership comes up!) Hence the majority of performances are technically sold out before the general public gets a chance to try. But if you are really keen to go and are not particularly choosy about what you see, a number of tickets are always returned and the Box Office staff are extremely patient about persistent callers. Simply keep ringing from the moment the booking opens (usually April) and go for the first tickets available. They are expensive but you are paying for much more than the performance.

Getting there. The rule about Glyndebourne is that it always takes at least half-an-hour more by car than you think. From London and the South East, it is an awful road, particularly towards the end. But going by car is really easiest, as you will be all togged up and carrying a picnic. Be warned too that the Sussex police look for people driving in bow ties during the Glyndebourne season and are very hot with the breathalysers. The train is actually rather fun if you go with a lot of people – and for those who can, Glyndebourne does have a helicopter pad.

Getting dressed. See the section on dress, with two extra provisos. It does get very chilly at the end of the performance; and do not be tempted to go in your jeans and change in the loo. You will feel extremely silly!

Getting fed. The best combination is to go in time for tea (they do a wonderful iced coffee) and then take a picnic for the long supper interval. Unless you have a butler and a Bentley, it is actually far better to keep the food simple. The grounds are lovely and large, so put your hamper down wherever you fancy before the performance – it has never been known for picnics to be nicked or muddled up! There is also a very good restaurant but you must book well in advance and it is fairly pricey. Champagne and Pimms are the staple Glyndebourne liquid fair. If you're an all female party, be warned that the barman will studiously ignore you if you queue up for a drink at the interval. Much better to take your own.

Getting read. One of the best things about Glyndebourne is the programme which covers all productions in the Festival. Considering how expensive everything else is, it is extremely good value, so do seek one out.

Getting home. Glyndebourne is a real event and takes up most of one day. Although the performance begins at about 5pm, you will not be out much before 10.30pm (the intervals together last over two hours). With a drive home afterwards, it can be a very tiring midweek experience for workers – but well worth every minute.

For those unable to get to Sussex, Glynde-

bourne runs a superb touring company throughout Britain.

Gobbi, Tito (1913–1984) Italian baritone. Gobbi's voice was not world class, but the power of his personality and his ability to characterize brought him to the forefront of the opera world throughout the 1950s and 1960s. His early career took him into films, but by 1942, he had established himself on the opera stage by singing the first Wozzeck for the Opera House in Rome. He was particularly strong in the later Verdi roles such as Falstaff and Iago and, with Maria Callas, made a formidable Scarpia to her Tosca. The majority of his work in America was with the Chicago Lyric Opera where he not only sang most of the major baritone role but also began to direct, starting with *Simon Boccanegra* in 1965 in which he sang the title role.

Gomez, Jill British soprano whose early training at London's Royal Academy of Music led to early roles with Glyndebourne both at the Festival and with the Touring company. Her Covent Garden debut took place in 1970 when she created the role of Flora in the world premiere of *The Knot Garden* by Michael Tippett. Her commitment to contemporary work continued with her interpretation of the Countess in the world premiere of *The Voice of Ariadne* by Thea Musgrave for the 1974 Aldeburgh Festival. As well as an outstanding performer of the modern repertoire, Jill Gomez excels in Mozart roles and appears internationally, being recognized for her excellent musical ability as well as convincing stage presence.

Goodall, Sir Reginald (1902–1990) English conductor, admired and respected throughout the opera world, particularly for his interpretations of Wagner. To see the diminutive Goodall leading a large Wagner orchestra was an extraordinary experience. His gestures were barely perceptible, his beat almost inexorably slow and his quiet passages barely audible. Yet the orchestra followed him with devotion, creating sounds of exquisite beauty as he conveyed exactly the emotion he required with the minimum of explanation. The resulting performances were intense, almost mystical sensations, relieved only by the tumultuous applause, long moments after the final notes had died away. He worked at all the world's major opera houses and conducted the world premiere of *Peter Grimes* by Benjamin Britten at Sadler's Wells in 1945.

Gotterdammerung (see Ring des Nibelungen)

Gounod, Charles (1818–1893) French composer whose operatic reputation rests primarily on *Faust* but also on *Mireille* and *Romeo and Juliette*. In his early life, Gounod was influenced by religious music and it was to remain an important part of his most successful compositions. He used the harmonies and melodies, so prevalent in earlier church music, to heighten character and emotion without making his works unnecessarily grand or ostentatious. He was at his best with the simple emotions, but his later music became increasingly sanctimonious, losing much of the charm of his earlier pieces.

Goyescas (Granados) FP 1916. In 1911 Granados wrote a set of seven scenes for piano, based on the life of the Spanish painter, Goya. He later rearranged this suite into the form of an opera in three short tableaux.

The beautiful Rosario is in love with the young officer Fernando. Their happiness is threatened by the toreador Paquiro who rejects his former girlfriend Pepa in favour of Rosario. Matters come to a climax at a ball where Fernando challenges Paquiro to a duel. After a brief moment with Rosario, Fernando goes to meet his adversary and is murdered by him, finding Rosario just in time to die in her arms.

Graham, Colin English producer whose work was widely seen in Britain after the Second World War. He was Director of Production for English National Opera from 1975 to 1978. His style was characterized by effective use of crowds, particularly in large scale productions such as *War and Peace* and by classic settings which heightened the drama of individual characters rather than producing a radical concept for the entire piece. His work was also seen in America, particularly his productions of the world premiere of *Death in Venice* by Benjamin Britten.

Granados, Enrique (1867–1916) Spanish composer. Granados was best known as a pianist, and his only opera, *Goyescas*, was originally written as a piano suite. He was popular in his homeland as an arranger and performer of 'zarzuela', the vivacious style of Spanish gypsy music. It was intended that *Goyescas* be produced for the Paris Opera but with the outbreak of the First World War in 1914, the opera had to be transferred to America for its premiere at the Metropolitan Opera in New York. Returning from this event, Granados was drowned on the *SS Sussex* which was sunk by German submarines in the English Channel in May 1916.

Grand opera Nowadays, grand opera tends to describe productions rather than the operas themselves. The recent production of *Carmen* in Earl's Court, London, complete with flamenco dancers and massive choruses was certainly grand opera. Peter Brook's production *The Tragedy of Carmen*, with the same music, six performers, a piano and two chairs is a less likely candidate for the description. Such variations mean that the term is less and less used today – it originated in France when describing operas on a historical theme that observed all the traditions of opera writing fashionable at the time – large choruses, full ballets, elaborate sets and so on.

Groves, Sir Charles English conductor. From early training at London's Royal College of Music, Charles Groves was appointed Chorus Master of the BBC Opera Unit for two years leading up to the Second World War. He returned to professional music after the war years, conducting the prestigious regional orchestras in Manchester and Bournemouth before being appointed Music Director of Welsh National Opera in 1961. There he conducted the British premiere of Verdi's *La Battaglia di Legnano* as well as notable performances of other major Verdi operas. In 1963 he moved to Liverpool where he conducted the Royal Liverpool Philharmonic Orchestra for nearly fifteen years, bringing the orchestra to a superb standard, extending the repertory and gaining praise from all quarters, including a CBE in 1968 and a Knighthood in 1973. In 1977, he became the full time Music Director of

English National Opera, having made guest appearances there since 1971, a post he held until 1979.

Guerre des bouffons One of those jolly little incidents which makes the history of opera fascinating and is an impressive anecdote to drop at a dinner party. In Paris between 1752 and 1754, a massive rivalry broke out between those who supported the serious opera of Lully, Rameau and so forth, and those who found the Italian opera buffa more appealing. It was an opera buffa by Pergolesi, *La Serva Padrona* which started the trouble, with factions behaving with utmost elegance and decorum, siding with one another in corners of boxes at the opera but having the added fascination that the King took one side of the argument (the serious one) and the Queen the other. The French went some way to compromising by introducing a form known as 'comédie melée des ariettes' where light comedy was interspersed by song.

Gui, Vittorio (1885–1975) Italian composer and conductor, founder of the Florence Maggio Musicale, now rated as one of the most exciting opera festivals in Europe. He was Music Director at Glyndebourne between 1952 and 1964, where his special aptitude for conducting Mozart and Rossini became apparent. Back in Italy, he was responsible for re-introducing several notable works into the standard repertory, including *Comte Ory* and *Cosi fan Tutte*.

Guillaume Tell (Rossini) FP 1829. An almost unbearably well-known overture preludes a very well-known story, full of apples and arrows and thigh slapping lederhosen, if given its most traditional production. It has not been particularly popular as a repertoire piece, partly because if played without cuts it lasts over five hours, and partly because the name part is written extremely high in the tenor voice and there are few tenors around who can do it justice.

The action is set in Switzerland when it was under Austrian domination in the thirteenth century. William Tell is a Swiss patriot who encourages his fellow Swiss to rise up against their oppressors. He is caught by the Austrian governor and forced to inflict near-certain death on his own son by shooting an apple from the top of his head. Naturally our hero succeeds and goes through several more adventures before leading his troops to victory over the marauding Austrians.

Gustafson, Nancy American soprano Nancy Gustafson continues to fulfill the promise of the early years of her career, when one critic described her as a real find, displaying a secure, beautiful soprano. She made her Metropolitan Opera debut in their 1989 season and her debut at Covent Garden as Freia in a new Lyubimov/Haitink *Das Rheingold*. Freia was also her first important role at the San Francisco Opera, where she was a member of the Adler Fellowship programme for young singers. She has a serene and graceful stage presence, and is a very successful recitalist in the United States. Her portrayal of Katya Kabanova at Glyndebourne won great acclaim.

Guthrie, Tyrone (1900–1971) English producer who ran the Old Vic/Sadler's Wells throughout the Second World War before moving to America to found the Shakespeare Festival in Stratford, Ontario. He developed a reputation as a controversial producer, being one of the first to depart from the traditional, accepted ways of staging and was therefore criticized for not doing justice to the music. He produced the premiere of *Peter Grimes*, by Benjamin Britten, at the Royal Opera House in 1947. He also produced two operas for the Met in New York, *Carmen* in 1952 and *La Traviata* in 1957.

Habanera As well as being the very famous tune from the first act of *Carmen*, it is also a full length verisimo opera by Laparra, all about an eternal triangle in Castile.

Hadley, Jerry American tenor. Jerry Hadley is a persuasive interpreter of the Mozart, French Romantic, and Italian bel canto repertoires with an affinity for the French romantic hero he usually sings. He was a stalwart member of the New York City Opera for some years, and has since appeared in major opera houses throughout North America and Europe. He is also a successful recitalist, accompanied by his wife Cheryll Drake Hadley, and a regular concert performer and recording artist.

Hagley, Alison English soprano, born and educated in London, and winner of several prizes and scholarships. She made her Glyndebourne Festival debut from the National Opera Studio, as the Little Owl in Ravel's *L'Enfant et les Sortileges* in 1987. She sang Susannah for Glyndebourne Touring Opera's 1989 production of *The Marriage of Figaro* and received excellent notices throughout the tour. Highly thought of, she is fully booked by British opera companies for the whole of the early part of the 1990s.

Haitink, Sir Bernard Dutch conductor who admits to having 'quite a healthy career on the whole', and is numbered among the most eminent (and most modest!) musicians in the world. He is currently Music Director of the Royal Opera House, Covent Garden, a post he has held since 1987. It is a role charged with responsibility, as the house has recently been criticized for its lacklustre productions, particularly of the Italian repertory, and has also to get used to a new General Director, Jeremy Isaacs. For the ten years before this appointment, Haitink was Music Director for Glyndebourne Festival Opera, graduating from the Directorship of the London Philharmonic, Glyndebourne's regular orchestra. There, his performances of the Mozart operas were particularly acclaimed, many recorded now for posterity on video and record. He has performed with the world's leading orchestras, conducts regularly at the Metropolitan Opera in New York and is a frequent guest conductor at prestigious European music festivals.

Halevy, Frommenthal (uncle) **& Ludovic** (nephew). Dynamic musical pair, the former writing *La Juive* in 1835 and teaching (amongst others) Gounod and Bizet at the Paris Conservatoire. The latter wrote the libretto to *Carmen* and to Offenbach's operettas.

Hall, Sir Peter English theatre director whose opera productions have been notable for their clarity of vision and sense of purpose. For the Royal Opera House, Covent Garden, he directed numerous productions, with his versions of *Tristan and Isolde*, Tippett's *Knot Garden* and Schoenberg's work *Moses and Aron* being outstanding. Since 1986 he has been Artistic Director of the Glyndebourne Festival, the culmination of a long and happy partnership which began in 1970. Amongst a range of hugely popular work he has directed there, his 1985 production of *Albert Herring* and *The Marriage of Figaro* which he directed for the 1989 Festival will be difficult to surpass. Outside Britain, his productions have not been greeted with such acclaim. His Ring Cycle for the Bayreuth Festival in 1983 was poorly received and the two productions he directed for the Metropolitan Opera, *Macbeth* in 1982 and *Carmen* in 1986, were not rated as popular.

Hall, John Graham English tenor who showed star quality while a student at Cambridge University, taking a leading role in the Cambridge Opera Group's production of *The Burning Fiery Furnace* by Benjamin Britten. Hall came to national attention when he was cast in the title role of Britten's *Albert Herring* in a new production by Sir Peter Hall for the 1985 Glyndebourne Festival. The role suited Hall's expressive voice and sensitive acting ability perfectly, bringing out both humour and pathos in a delightful production which was also seen at Covent Garden. He has worked with Peter Stein in Welsh National Opera's acclaimed production of *Otello*. His career will doubtless develop from the character roles in which he now specializes to the more complex tenor parts.

Halsey, Simon English conductor who specializes in choral works and has also led some highly successful performances of small scale opera with the City of Birmingham Touring Opera of which he is co-Music Director. Halsey is an energetic and committed conductor, dedicated to creating the best possible performances even if the surroundings are not immediately conducive to opera – church aisles, school halls, gymnasia and so on. He is much in demand from some of the finest orchestras in Britain and Europe, including the City of Birmingham Symphony Orchestra, the Academy of Ancient Music, the Opera de Lyon and the Stadtische Musikverein in Dusseldorf as well as holding the Artistic Directorship of the Salisbury Festival. As Chorus Master of the City of Birmingham Symphony Chorus, he has toured extensively in America though has yet to make his operatic debut there. Forthcoming projects for the City of Birmingham Touring Opera include a version of Wagner's Ring Cycle in the autumn of 1990.

Hamilton, Iain Scottish composer, educated in England and for many years a resident of New York. He has been an influential and prize winning composer since the late 1950s. Hamilton's stage works form a major part of his output. *The Cataline Conspiracy* (1974) was commissioned, premiered, and revived by Scottish Opera; *The Royal Hunt of the Sun* (1968) was premiered and revived by English National Opera; *Anna Karenina* (1978) was commissioned, premiered and revived by English National Opera and received its American premiere in Los Angeles. *Lancelot* (1982/83) was commissioned and premiered by the Arundel Festival in 1985.

Hamlet (Thomas) FP 1868. Yes, the Dane set to music but this time with a happy ending and a much bigger part for Ophelia. It has nothing of the grandeur of the other Shakespearean operas by Verdi (*Falstaff, Macbeth, Otello*) and is therefore hardly ever performed.

Hammerstein, Oscar (1846–1919) American impresario who made his fortune as an immigrant by inventing a cigar-making machine (as well as having extensive realestate interests). His theatre in New York, the Manhattan Opera House, was positioned to rival the Met, attracting top rate stars and performing an interesting, somewhat controversial repertory, including the premiere of Debussy's *oelleas and Melisande*. After four years, the Met could not stand the competition and bought Hammerstein out for the amazing sum (in 1910) of $1.2 million, on the condition that he would not produce opera again in the city for ten years. A year later he opened the Stoll Theatre in London, calling it the London Opera House (not to be confused with the London Coliseum) but that too failed because of the competition from Covent Garden. Hammerstein was poised to make a return to New York at the end of his ban, but died within a few months of it expiring. His grandson, Oscar Hammerstein II, had an illustrious career in musicals with his partner Richard Rogers, perhaps being best known for *The Sound of Music*.

Hammond Stroud, Derek English baritone who has sung with ENO and the Royal Opera since 1961 in a variety of roles from Alberich in Wagner's Ring Cycle to Rossini's Dr Bartolo to Gilbert and Sullivan, where he attracted perhaps his most loyal and appreciative audience. Guest appearances in Europe and the USA have taken him to the Met, Netherlands Opera, Bavarian State Opera, and Buenos Aires. He is a noted lieder singer (memorably with the pianist Gerald Moore on the occasion of Moore's last public performance of Shubert's *Wintereisse*) and regularly performs concerts. He was awarded the OBE in 1987 for services to music.

Handel, George Fredrick (1685–1759) German composer. Handel reaches his biggest, most popular audience with *The Messiah, The Arrival of the Queen of Sheba* and the Coronation Anthems, but recent productions of his operas have shown that they can be accessible, enjoyable and even humorous for a modern audience. They do not have fascinating plots nor is the music powerful or dramatic, as are, for example, the operas of Verdi; but a clever production will bring out the wit and elegance that runs through them and will use the music to highlight the charm of most of his work. Handel was, first and foremost, a court composer, writing opera at a time when conventions and traditions dictated much of the content of an opera – broadly defined as 'opera seria'. His early operas, which he wrote in Italy, show signs of him trying to develop his own style by enlarging the orchestra and giving his characters as much depth and personality as conventions permitted. His move to the court of George I in London in 1714 came to fruition with *Julius Caesar* and *Tamerlano*, both of which he wrote in 1724, and *Rodelinda*, written a year later. All of these include characters that audiences of today would find it easier to identify and sympathize with. But by 1728, Handel's tenure at the Royal Academy of Music came to an end as the Academy was closed and Italian opera, of which Handel was a fervent disciple, began to fall out of fashion. This was the time of *The Beggar's Opera* by John Gay – a sharply satirical study of the Italian opera conventions which Handel supported so strongly. Of the works Handel composed during this period only

Hansel and Gretel, by Humperdink, is set in a world of witches and gingerbread houses. David Pountney's production for ENO updated it to 1950s English suburbia. Ethna Robinson as Hansel and Cathryn Pope as Gretel.

Orlando, written in 1733, finds any regular place in the modern repertory.

Handel became increasingly isolated from musical society in London, being forced to move from the King's Theatre where his company had performed and losing many of his best artists to the newly formed 'Opera of the Nobility' (no pretence of easy-access-for-all in eighteenth-century English opera!). He was based at Covent Garden from 1734 where he produced *Ariodante*, *Alcina* and *Atalanta* before suffering a stroke in 1727. From then on, he concentrated primarily on writing oratorios, with only the lighter *Serse* (*Xerxes*) which he wrote in 1738 remaining in today's opera programmes. His operas were rarely performed anywhere in Europe until the 1920s when a revival began in the German opera houses which has continued throughout this century. His popularity has risen steadily in Britain in recent years, with the formation of the Handel Opera Society in 1955, and excellent productions of his major works by the national companies. His music is never difficult or abrasive but is not the ideal introduction to opera for a new-comer, simply because of the 'opera seria' conventions which he followed. Individual passages are exquisitely beautiful, and many of his best works are now available on excellent recordings of excerpts.

Hansel and Gretel (Humperdinck) FP 1893. Humperdinck wrote this work as a lavish, lyrical opera with a large orchestra making the most of some dramatic melodies and wonderful orchestration. It would make an excellent introduction to opera because, like all fairy tales, it has the charm of a simple story with the added dimension of somewhat macabre overtones. An intriguing twist was added in the ENO production, staged in 1987, by casting one singer as both the mother and the witch.

Hansel and Gretel have been sent by their mother Gertrude to a forest to pick straw-berries, little knowing that the forest is home to a wicked witch who cooks and eats chil-dren. Their father Peter is horrified when he realizes where their callous mother has sent them, but the children have been looked after by the Sandman and Dew Fairy who protect them while they sleep. When they wake up, they are mesmerized by a ginger-bread cottage which has appeared, together with gingerbread children. Tempted into the cottage by the witch, they are im-prisoned and Hansel is fattened up in preparation for his demize. But together he and Gretel turn on the witch, forcing her into her own oven and turning her into gingerbread. Victorious, Hansel and Gretel free the gingerbread children and are re-united with their parents.

Harewood, Earl of A first cousin of Queen Elizabeth II, Lord Harewood may well have inherited his immense love for music from his great-great grandparents, Queen Victoria and Prince Albert. But his contribution to the opera world has never been confined to the realms of the nobility – indeed he has done more than almost anyone else in Britain recently to bring the best opera to the greatest number. In 1950, he founded *Opera* magazine, still considered the definitive monthly accompaniment to opera across the world. As an ideal complement to a monthly magazine, he is also editor and revisor of *Kobbé's Complete Opera Book* which is an in-dispensible and virtually timeless guide for any serious opera lover.

Lord Harewood was Director of Opera Planning for the Royal Opera House from 1953 to 1960 before heading the Edinburgh Festival from 1961 to 1965, contributing greatly to the international stature it now enjoys. From 1972 to 1985 he was Managing Director of English National Opera during a formative period in the company's history. Under his guidance the company consoli-dated its tenure at the London Coliseum and grew to become a major, respected force in the opera world both nationally and inter-nationally – as proved by the company's artistically acclaimed American tour which took place in 1984. Unafraid to place the young in positions of responsibility, to en-courage new artists to try out their ideas at the Coliseum and to back it all up with a sound administrative structure.

Harper, Heather Irish soprano who came to stardom virtually overnight by taking the place of Galina Vishnevskaya at the first performance of Britten's *War Requiem* in Coventry Cathedral in 1962. Her dark and dramatic voice suits the female leads in Brit-ten's operas perfectly and she has created memorable performances of Ellen Orford in

Peter Grimes and Helena in *A Midsummer Night's Dream*. She has sung extensively with Britain's national opera companies, appearing in the world premieres of *Owen Wingrave* by Britten and *The Ice Break* by Michael Tippett. She also has a strong command over Wagnerian roles and made her Bayreuth debut in 1967. In America, she has sung the Countess (*The Marriage of Figaro*) and Ellen Orford (*Peter Grimes*) at the Metropolitan Opera.

Harrhy, Eiddwen Welsh soprano whose early career was spent working with Welsh National Opera. She is now in international demand with a wide repertoire which her persuasive stage presence and lyrical voice can tackle with ease. She has sung roles as diverse as Katya Kabanova for Opera North, Mimi for ENO and Poppea for Welsh National Opera, as well as taking part in modern works such as *The Plumber's Gift* by David Blake, when she sang the role of Marian in the world premiere in 1989. Her work abroad has taken her to many of the opera festivals and houses of Europe as well as to the Teatro Colon in Buenos Aires where she sang the Governess in *The Turn of the Screw* by Benjamin Britten.

Harwood, Elizabeth (1938–1990) English soprano whose career was prematurely curtailed by illness. Particularly adept at Mozart roles, Harwood's beautiful voice was noticed by von Karajan who launched her international career in the late 1960s.

Hary Janos (Kodaly) FP 1926. Very jolly suite full of Hungarian folk songs which is often performed at concerts rather than fully staged in the opera house. In its full version, it tells the tale of an old soldier who recounts his exploits coming home from the Napoleonic Wars.

Haydn, Joseph (1732–1809) For all his success at writing symphonies, oratorio and chamber music, Haydn's operas have never really established themselves in the late twentieth-century repertoire. Many of his opera scores were lost and those which survived are generally thought to have weak librettos but extremely tuneful music.

Hayward, Robert Young, promising British bass-baritone who went straight from studies to sing Don Giovani on the 1986 Glynde-

bourne Touring Opera tour. He sings with all the British companies and made his USA debut at Houston singing the Don in 1988/89. Hayward is also developing a successful concert and recital career, and although to date he has mainly performed Mozart on the lyric stage, he sings Verdi, Beethoven and Elgar on the concert platform, and no doubt his repertoire will expand to include the operatic 'heavy-weights' as time goes on.

Heldentenor The range of tenor voice described as 'heldentenor' can also be termed 'heroic tenor'. The voice is characterized by enormous power and clarity in its best exponents and therefore many of the major classic roles in Wagner are written for the heldentenor voice. These include Lohengrin, Tannhauser, Tristan and Parsifal – all demanding parts where the singer needs physical stamina as well as excellent technique to cope with the long phrases and sheer quantity of singing required. In addition, much of the heldentenor's music is written high in his register, placing an additional strain on the voice. It is therefore hardly surprising that truly great heldentenors are relatively rare. Lauritz Melchoir was acclaimed as one of the greatest from past generations, while contemporary singers such as Jon Vickers and Siegfried Jerusalem have proved how exquisite and powerful a great heldentenor voice can be. Other major heldentenor roles include the title roles in Handel's *Samson*, Britten's *Peter Grimes* and Verdi's *Otello* as well as Radames in *Aida*, and Florestan in Beethoven's *Fidelio*.

Henricks, Barbara American soprano who is a Maths and Chemistry graduate from Stephens University, Arkansas. Barbara Hendricks subsequently studied music at the Julliard School in New York with mezzo-soprano Jennie Tourel. Almost as well known as a recitalist and concert artist as an opera singer, she has performed with all the leading orchestras and conductors in Europe and made many recordings of both the concert and opera repertoire. She is very popular in Japan where she toured with Karajan (1977), Bernstein (1985) and with the Vienna State Opera as Susanna in *Figaro* and Sophie in *Der Rosenkavalier* (1986). In 1987 she undertook a major recital tour to Japan, culminating in three sold out recitals in Tokyo.

Henry the Eighth (Saint Saens) FP 1883. Saint-Saens 'other' opera, far less well known than *Samson and Delilah*, telling the story of Henry VIII and his love for Anne Boleyn.

Henze, Heinz Werner German composer whose operas have always been profoundly influenced by contemporary society and particularly the ways in which that society affects the artists working within it. His works also show a distate for the increasingly militaristic society which began to develop in Europe in the late 1950s and early 1960s. But such torment is tempered by beautifully lyrical writing, influenced by the romance and culture of Italy, where he has lived since 1953. His work is not to be recommended for complete opera novices but for those developing a wider interest in the art form, operas such as *Konig Hirsch*, *The Bassarids* and *Elegy for Young Lovers* should be approached, ideally through recordings first, and subsequently in productions which can do justice to the multi-layered meanings of his work.

Herbert, Jocelyn English stage designer with a distinguished portfolio of productions for both plays and opera. Her theatre work has been particularly effective for the modern playwrights such as Beckett, Ionesco and Wesker, and she has maintained this contemporary theme with some of her opera work. She staged a startling *Mahagonny* for the Metropolitan Opera in 1979 and an equally incisive *Lulu* for the same house two years earlier. Her work for the older operas is not less inventive and she has designed superb stagings for works such as *Orfeo*, *The Force of Destiny* and *Manon Lescaut* for opera houses all over the world.

Herincx, Raimond English baritone whose powerful physique and strong voice have suited the major baritone roles admirably, backed by an excellent music technique which has enabled him to sing contemporary roles with ease and confidence. He has sung in numerous world premieres, creating the part of Faber in Tippett's *The Knot Garden*, the White Abbot in *Taverner* by Peter Maxwell Davies and the Governor in *We Come to the River* by Hans Werner Henze. His career was no less acclaimed in Wagnerian roles which he sang with many of the British national companies and leading opera houses in Europe.

Herz, Joachim German opera producer who, like Ruth Berghaus and Gotz Friedrich, was profoundly influenced by the work of Walter Felsenstein. His working career has been spent on the eastern side of the now-demolished Berlin Wall, as Director of, first, the Leipzig Opera (1957–11), and then, Komische Oper in Berlin (1977–81). Enlightened managers have invited him to direct in the West, where his productions have included *Salome* and *Fidelio* for English National Opera and *Madam Butterfly* for Welsh National Opera as well as work in Paris and Vienna. His productions always have a strong political message and are criticized by some for their abrasive, intrusive atmosphere. But Herz demands commitment from his audience, aiming to involve them wholeheartedly in the drama of the characters rather than allow them to watch the spectacle from a safe distance.

Heure Espagnole, L' (Ravel) FP 1911. A real joy of an opera – short, funny, romantic, pretty with lyrical music demanding very little concentration! The clock maker Torquemada has left his clock shop in the charge of his winsome wife, Conception. Used to such days on her own, Conception has developed the habit of entertaining her lovers in her husband's shop. This day, however, she appears to be thwarted by the presence of Ramiro the Muleteer who has been ordered to remain in the shop until Torquemada's return. Conception is entertaining Gonzalve, one of her lovers, when a second admirer, Don Inigo Gomez turns up and the muleteer is put to use carrying Gonzalve upstairs in the body of a grandfather clock! As Conception's whims change, so Gonzalve comes back down and Gomez is carried upstairs, but finally she decides that she prefers the muleteer after all and disappears upstairs with him, sans-clock! The two suiters are left in the shop to discuss business with the returning Torquemada.

Higglety Pigglety Pop (Oliver Knussen) FP 1984. Maurice Sendak's fable for children, set to an exciting musical score which brings out the fantasy and brilliance. The 'plot' is only an excuse for the illustrator's dynamic imagination.

Hill-Smith, Marilyn English soprano whose tall bearing and distinctively powerful voice have made her a recognizable feature on the British opera and concert platforms since her debut with English National Opera in 1978. She remained with that company for six seasons making her debut at Covent Garden in the meantime and performing a wide range of major soprano roles such as Adele (*Die Fledermaus*), Susanna (*The Marriage of Figaro*) and the Fiakermilli (*Arabella*). She has since sung for WNO, Scottish Opera and the English Bach Festival, as well as appearing in Canada as Yum Yum in *The Mikado*. She is as popular on the concert platform as on the opera stage, making frequent performances, particularly of operatic highlights in sold-out concerts regularly broadcast on British television and radio.

Hindemith, Paul (1895–1963) German composer. So contemporary were Hindemith's arias that one, when a soprano sings the virtues of electric heating over gas, compelled an injunction from the local gas company! His early works are largely forgotten, with *Cardillac* (described by Kobbé as 'muscular and purposeful') being the first of his works to maintain a position in the contemporary repertoire. In 1935 he wrote perhaps his best known work *Mathis der Maler*, based on the life and work of the painter Mathias Grunewald, as a response to the rise of Nazi power in Germany. It was immediately banned, not receiving a performance until 1938. After this, he veered from overtly political subjects with *Die Harmonie der Welt*, a more gentle account of the life of the astronomer Kepler. His final work *The Long Christmas Dinner* had a libretto written by the American dramatist Thornton Wilder and concerns the confrontation of several generations over the Christmas table. As so often, Kobbé has a superb assessment of the gravity which runs through all Hindemith's works when he talks about Hindemith's 'lofty conception of the artist's responsibility'. These works are, in all senses of the word, 'heavy' – and (again from Kobbé) 'intense seriousness of purpose does not in itself secure artistic

results'. Hindemith is one of those composers whom serious opera lovers class as 'important', but should be left until new opera goers feel totally confident of their love of the art form.

Hockney, David British painter who has transferred his imaginative designs and brilliant technique to the opera stage with enormous success. Colourful, full of action and brimming with life, Hockney's stage designs assume almost as big a role as some of the characters on stage and are usually greeted with delighted applause by audiences who are all too used to monochrome sets. Amongst his best known works have been *The Rake's Progress* and *The Magic Flute* for Glyndebourne and the triple bills of operas by Stravinsky and *Parade* by Eric Satie for the Metropolitan Opera, New York. *Parade* featured the design of Harlequin doing a handstand surrounded by ladders, frequently reproduced on posters all over the world.

Hoddinott, Alun Welsh composer. Professor of Music at University College, Cardiff and Artistic Director of the Cardiff Festival, he has had considerable influence in awakening interest in contemporary music in South Wales. Operas include *The Beach of Falesa* based on a short story by Robert Louis Stevenson, first performed by Welsh National Opera in 1974; two one-act operas *The Magician* (first staged in 1976 and broadcast as *Murder, the Magician*) and *What the Old Man Does is Always Right* with libretto by Myfanwy Piper. Myfanwy Piper is also the librettist for his opera *The Trumpet Major* based on the novel by Thomas Hardy, and first performed in 1981.

Hofmannsthal, Hugo von (1874–1929) Austrian poet who wrote the libretti for many of Richard Strauss' best known operas, including *Elektra* (where Strauss wrote music for Hofmannsthal's finished poem), *Der Rosenkavalier*, *Die Frau ohne Schatten* and *Arabella*. The two men had extraordinarily different temperaments and rarely met, but catalogued their work together through a series of highly revealing letters. These provide a fascinating insight into the interplay between a romantic, reserved poet and a fiery, impetuous composer.

Hogwood, Christopher English conductor who enjoys a prolific international career specializing in the conducting and recording of Chamber music. In Britain, Hogwood founded the Academy of Ancient Music in 1973 and has brought the orchestra to a standard of international excellence which is admired worldwide. The Academy had, in the late eighteenth century, been dedicated to the performance and study of vocal works and was therefore important in the development of opera. Although the Academy now concentrates primarily on concert performances, the operatic output under Hogwood has been highly acclaimed. He is currently embarking on a major project with the orchestra – to perform and record all the operas written by Mozart. Hogwood has also conducted operas in La Fenice in Venice, the Deutsche Oper in Berlin and the Opera Comique in Paris, and enjoys an extensive performing career in America. He is Director of the Boston Haydn and Handel Society, the oldest performing artistic organisation in America and has also conducted performances at the St Louis Opera.

Holst, Gustav (1874–1934) British composer whose operas are not themselves well known and rarely performed professionally. They were, however, influential forces for Benjamin Britten and Michael Tippett whose contribution to the opera repertoire is unquestioned. Holst's first work was a one-act opera *Savitri* which is based on the Hindu legend 'Mahabarata' – a far cry from the composer's native Cheltenham! His subsequent works were more English in their tone – *The Perfect Fool*, *The Wandering Scholar* and, based on the Falstaff stories, *At the Boar's Head*.

Horne, Marilyn American mezzo soprano who came to prominence without ever showing her face during the performance! She was chosen to sing the role of Carmen Jones in the 1954 film while Dorothy Dandridge performed the part on screen. She has since risen to become one of the most popular and prolific artists in the opera world, specializing in the ebullient, attractive mezzo soprano leads which she injects with fire and humour. She performs all over the world and is a superb exponent of coloratura singing. Horne has a flawless technique which allows her to concentrate on sensitive acting of every part she plays. Her 'pet' composer is Rossini and an opportunity to see her as L'Italiana, La Cenerentola or Rosina in *'The Barber of Seville'* should be grasped as a superb introduction to opera.

Hosenrolle Literally 'trouser role', this term describes roles which are written for female performers who take on the characters of boys, such as Cherubino in *The Marriage of Figaro* or Octavian in *Der Rosenkavalier*.

Hotter, Hans German bass-baritone, one of the all time great singers of Wagner, particularly the roles of Wotan and the Dutchman, which he virtually made his own in the post-war Bayreuth seasons. Hotter has delighted audiences all over the world with his intelligent, sensitive portrayals of some operas most complex characters. He also produced a fine Ring Cycle for The Royal Opera House between 1961 and 1964.

House Manager Together with TV newsreaders, house managers are frequently asked 'And what do you do during the day?'. The reality may find a house manager unblocking sinks (or worse), pacifying irate conductors when rain pours in on their orchestra, or juggling fearsomely complicated schedules to accommodate pneumatic drilling for vital maintenance work whilst not disturbing that equally vital principal's rehearsal. In short, a good house manager will be at the hub of his or her theatre, an ever flowing font of answers for everything from complimentary tickets to fire-safe sets. He or she is responsible for the overall safety not only of the audience at performances but whoever uses the building during the day – which, for the larger companies, may be a considerable number.

The specific duties will vary from company to company, with the common link of the responsibility of being omnipresent to sort out the numerous problems which attend the theatre-going public. These too can be enormously varied – 'I'm blind, could you find someone to look after my dog during the performance?', 'I bought these tickets through an agent and there's someone sitting in my seats' (very common, particularly at one minute to curtain up), 'My wife's just had a baby and she'd love to see me singing the lead role tonight. Do you think you could...?', 'I've just had a man with an Irish accent on the phone who advises us to get everyone out now'. From royalty to rat catchers, from clamped cars to curtain calls, the House Manager has to be there with an answer and, if he or she is to retain sanity, with a smile.

Houston Houston is new money. The money was made from oil which hit the American South West within the last twenty-five years. In the same way as Rockerfeller and Vanderbilt had to support the establishment of the Metropolitan Opera in New York last century, so this new money has poured into Houston's new opera centre, the Wortham Center, to confer on its donors the social respectability and cachet they seek as an alternative to their business dealings. So money is no problem and the building itself is as much a tribute to Mamon as to St Cecilia – arches modelled on Tewkesbury Abbey, roofs which imitate the Pantheon in Rome, music which comes not from speakers but from a specially commissioned sculptured cellist in the foyer. And, as the ultimate tribute to personal giving, anyone who donates more than $25,000 can press a button and see their name light up on an electronic screen. In the balcony, reserved for the non-glitterati, the audience has been known to link hands in a human chain to get them downstairs because the rake is so steep. When it comes to programming, all Houston's conservatism flies out of the window. Houston Opera's general director is David Gockley, one of the most inspired men on the opera circuit, who simply refuses to feed his audience with the diet of Domingo-Pavarotti-te Kanawa he knows they would be content with. He premieres adventurous new American works (like *Nixon in China* by John Adams), imports radical productions from overseas (ENO's *Orpheus in the Underworld* for example), has recently launched the new Michael Tippett opera *New Year*, produced a truly operatic *Porgy and Bess* in 1976 only to see it transfer to Broadway, and co-produced (with ENO) *Akhnaten* and *Planet Eight* by Philip Glass. It is an extraordinary policy which, if you read a demographic profile of the town, you could never believe would work. But it does work, be-

cause Gockley and his team have positioned these pioneering events as the ultimate in classy opera going, by combining sound business acumen (he has an MBA from Columbia) with the very best musical standards. It is refreshing to discover that the substantial sums of money he has at his disposal are being used to further the frontiers of opera, rather than revert to yet more lavish productions of the old favourites.

Howell, Gwynne Welsh bass. One of the 'Welsh Mafia' of singers born, brought up and educated in Wales who have achieved international status. But he has never forgotten his origins and still returns as a guest singer with English National Opera and Welsh National Opera. Like many of his fellow countrymen, Howell performs every role with great feeling and dramatic involvement. He is a member of the Royal Opera House, Covent Garden, and has sung most of the major bass roles with the company. His extensive international career, particularly singing the major Wagnerian roles, has taken him to the Metropolitan Opera, Chicago, San Francisco, Santa Fe, Hamburg, and all over Europe and he also enjoys a highly successful concert career in Europe and the United States.

Hugh the Drover (Vaughan Williams) FP 1924. If you enjoy opera only if it is full of tunes then this is the work for you! Vaughan Williams was heavily influenced by the English Folk Song tradition and incorporates many of them in this ballad-opera. The plot centres on the everyday story of country folk in early nineteenth-century England. It is all very pastoral and jolly, concerning Hugh the Drover and John the Butcher who are both after the village girl Mary.

Huguenots, Les (Meyerbeer) FP 1836. Originally written in five acts, this massive undertaking is more usually performed in three, combining acts one and two and leaving out act five. If it is the full version, which is still occasionally performed, be prepared for a very long evening and do some reading up beforehand. But it is likely that only a seasoned aficiando will get to see the work as it is rarely performed, requiring seven top rank principals trained in French grand opera style to do justice to the main roles.

Rita Hunter achieved international acclaim for her performances in the great Wagner roles. Here she sings Brunnhilde in the Ring Cycle staged by ENO. *(photo: courtesy of ENO)*

The plot is set in France during the conflict between the Huguenots and the Catholics and concerns the love between Raoul, a Protestant nobleman and Valentine, a Catholic. Unable to go through with their marriage because he believes Valentine has been unfaithful, Raoul overhears the Catholics planning the St Bartholemew's Day Massacre and is torn between saving his fellow Protestants and Valentine, whom he has always loved.

Hugo, Victor (1802–1885) French author whose rich and fascinating stories inspired a number of composers, particularly Verdi (*Ernani* and *Rigoletto*) and Ponchielli (*La Gioconda*). He is also responsible for the story behind one of the most successful stage productions in many years, *Les Miserables*, now a musical playing to packed houses the world over.

Humperdinck, Engelbert (1854–1921) German composer whose first opera *Hansel and Gretel* is the only one of the five operas he wrote to maintain a place in the popular repertoire. Not to be confused with the popular crooner.

Hunter, Rita English soprano whose strong physique and rich voice make her a natural to play the demanding soprano leads in the operas of Wagner and Verdi. While she has created excellent performances of Aida, Leonora, Norma and Santuzza for opera companies all over the world, it is for her Brunnhilde in the Ring Cycle staged by English National Opera that she is best remembered. She has sung the same role at the Metropolitan Opera in New York, combining it with a memorable performance of Norma in the same season – a feat demanding immense technical prowess to cope with two vast roles. Her imposing figure was thought by some to prevent her from being cast in more attractive roles but the quality of her voice is so outstanding as to render this irrelevant. Always ready to see the humour in any situation, Hunter entitled her autobiography, published in 1986, *'Wait Till The Sun Shines Nellie'*.

Hvorostovsky, Dmitri Russian baritone and another 'find' from the increasingly prestigious Cardiff Singer of the World Competition. Hvorostovsky won the title in 1989 at the age of twenty-six, stunning audience and jury alike with his magnificent voice and handsome presence. He seems to have the makings of a fine international career ahead of him. He moved from a choral conducting course to the study of solo singing, choosing to concentrate on Verdi for his competition pieces (singing Italian with barely a trace of a Russian accent). Having sung in the Wigmore Hall in December 1989, he made his Carnegie Hall debut in February 1990.

Hytner, Nicholas English director who is most sought after for his work both in the opera house and the theatre. His breakthrough in opera came in 1979 with a hugely successful production of *The Turn of the Screw* for Kent Opera. Productions for ENO of Wagner's *Rienzi* in 1983 and Handel's *Xerxes* in 1985 led to international recognition. He works extensively in the straight theatre and therefore he works best with the new type of actor-singer for opera productions, concentrating on the ensemble, rather than with the star names who want to slot their own performance into every new production. Recently he combined opera and theatre directing very successfully in the West End musical *Miss Saigon*.

Ice Break, The (Tippett) FP 1977. Modern music, modern setting, somewhat improbable set of circumstances and a natural for an imaginative director to create a highly dramatic piece of theatre – but not one with lots of hummable tunes!

Lev and his wife Nadia are in a contemporary American airport. Their son Yuri and his girlfriend Gail are there too, as are Olympion the athlete and his girlfriend Hannah. These six represent a microcosm of modern society and as such act out in small scale a wide gamut of human experiences, including a race riot.

Idomeneo, King of Crete (Mozart) FP 1781. Though this was not the first opera Mozart ever wrote, it was the earliest of his to hold its place in the current opera repertoire. But this has only been the case since the Second World War. *Idomeneo* was not performed in America until 1947 and Kobbé describes it as never having been a repertory opera. The music is glorious but the subject is not as attractive as say, *Don Giovanni* or *The Marriage of Figaro*. It is strongly in the tradition of 'opera seria' and the music takes precedence over the action with many arias following one another with little or no activity in between. It is therefore recommended with caution for an absolute first timer – better to start with either of the two mentioned above but be sure to come back to *Idomeneo* in time. Broadly, it concerns emotion and destiny, rather than action and fact, in the lives of the royalty of Crete in mythological times.

Idomeneo has survived a storm at sea, thanks to a bargain he made on board with Neptune – to sacrifice the first person he saw on reaching land. That person is Idemeneo's son, Idamante (sung by a soprano, but originally by a castrato) who has fallen in love with the Trojan Princess Ilia whom his father has brought home from his victorious campaign over the Trojan people. Hoping to divert his son, Idemeneo takes the advice of Arbace and sets Idamante up with the Greek Princess Elektra who is desperate for Idamante's love. The island of Crete is ravaged first by storms and then by a sea monster and the people realize Neptune is angry at not having had his promised sacrifice. They demand to know who was promised and Idamante, hearing of his father's bargain, first slays the sea monster and then offers himself for sacrifice. Neptune relents and decrees that Idamante should survive and succeed his father as King and marry Ilia, leaving Elektra alone and distraught.

Illica, Luigi (1857–1919) Italian librettist who wrote the words to *La Wally* by Catalani and *Andrea Chenier* by Giordano, before teaming up with Puccini to work on *Manon Lescaut*. This led to his most successful work in collaboration with Guiseppe Giacosa and Puccini on *La Bohème*, *Tosca* and *Madam Butterfly*. Illica devised the structure of each drama, Giacosa wrote the verses and Puccini the music. Illica introduced the practice of adding detailed stage directions to Italian operas – a habit already prevalent in France.

Impresario From the Italian 'impresa' meaning undertaking, impresario has different connotations everywhere in the world. It can mean the overall head of an operatic enterprise equivalent to 'schauspieldirector' in Germany or managing director in Britain. In the UK, it has recently been more associated with commercial productions, most often applied to figures such as Victor Hochhauser and Raymond Gubbay, rather than to heads of a single artistic enterprise.

Incoronazione di Poppea (Monteverdi) FP 1642. This is one of Monteverdi's finest works, written in the baroque style but not conventionally staid as many other baroque works are. It deals with the Roman Empire and all the licentiousness that is usually associated with it! Some modern productions have tried to play up the sensual nature of the piece, with the ultimate effect of making a sensitive and erotic work rather crass and vulgar. A sympathetic production will allow Monteverdi's beautiful music and Tacitus' story speak for itself.

Ottone's mistress Poppea has been taken by the Emperor Nerone in Ottone's absence. The philosopher Seneca gives advice both to Nerone and to Nerone's long-suffering wife, Ottavia, despite a warning from Pallade, goddess of wisdom, on the dire consequences of his interference. To Ottavia he counsels patience, to Nerone restraint in his plan to divorce Ottavia and marry Poppea. Nerone rejects Seneca's advice and decrees that Seneca must die. Ottone meanwhile has been spurned in his attempt to get back with Poppea and turned his affections to Ottavia's slave-girl, Drusilla, who is madly in love with him. Seneca carries out his own death sentence by bleeding to death in the bath. Ottavia, unable to stand her husband's philandering any longer, orders Ottone to kill Poppea which he can only bear to do when Poppea is asleep and he is disguised as Drusilla. But Poppea wakes before the knife is stabbed and accuses the real Drusilla of attempted murder. Her pleas of innocence are ignored and she is sentenced to death – but Ottone is moved to confess his crime and is banished, followed by the lovelorn Drusilla. Nerone completes Poppea's triumph by banishing his wife and crowning Poppea Empress.

Intendant Title used in Germany and Austria to describe the administrative head of an opera house.

Iphigénie en Aulide (Gluck) FP 1774. Rarely performed by contemporary companies, Gluck's first opera, written for the Parisian audience, contains passages of lovely music but is not recommended for any but the most devoted early music lover. It is surpassed in all aspects by *Iphigénie en Tauride*.

Iphigénie en Tauride (Gluck) FP 1779. Written five years later than *Iphigénie en Aulide* and a stronger piece in every way, but still not a good one for a new opera-goer.

Iphigénie is a priestess on the island of Tauride, unaware of the awful disasters that have befallen her family. Her mother Clytemnestra has killed her father Agamemnon, and her brother Oreste has killed her mother. Oreste and his friend Pylade arrive in Tauride and are recognized by no-one. The King, Thoas, orders that they be executed. Facing death, Oreste tells his sister (who does not recognize him) that all her family, including her brother, are dead and the urge she feels to save him should be directed to his friend Pylade, who is released forthwith. As the moment of sacrifice approaches, Iphigénie realizes who Oreste is and Pylade arrives with Greek soldiers to free him.

Italiana in Algeri, L' (Rossini) FP 1818. Written in twenty-seven days when the composer was only twenty-one, 'L'Italiana' is all about youth and love. It was written in the style of 'commedia del arte', a type of stage performance which allowed the artists to improvise and make of the general plot whatever suited them. While this is impossible with music, the overall impression is one of spontaneity, happiness and great good humour.

Isabella, the heroine, is similar to Rosina in *The Barber of Seville* - plenty of fire and spirit, with a huge capacity to love and be loved. Her lover Lindoro has been kidnapped and she has looked for him everywhere. She eventually finds him in Algiers where they are both captured by Mustafa, Bey of Algiers. Isabella uses all her feminine wiles to charm Mustafa, making him promise to eat and say nothing, observing the old Italian order of 'Pappatacci'. Isabella meanwhile marshals all his courtiers, together with Lindoro and her travelling companion Taddeo, and escapes.

James, Eirian Welsh soprano. Eirian James sings regularly with all the English opera companies, ENO, Opera North, Sadler's Wells and made her Covent Garden debut in 1987 in *Der Rosenkavalier*. She is beginning to work more extensively in Europe and the United States, and is also heard frequently on the concert platform in Britain. She is especially popular in Wales, has appeared on many occasions with the BBC Welsh Symphony Orchestra and has hosted her own television series on the Welsh television channel.

James, Henry (1843–1916) American novelist whose works transferred to the opera stage with a particular power and force. Notable are the two Britten compositions, *The Turn of the Screw* and *Owen Wingrave*.

Janacek, Leos (1854–1928) Czech composer. Janacek's operas had received only rare performances in Britain and America until the mid-1970s when Welsh National Opera in conjunction with other British opera companies embarked on a series of productions of his major works - *Jenufa*, *From the House of the Dead*, *The Makropulos Affair*, *Katya Kabanova* and *The Cunning Little Vixen*. They all became classics, winning their conductor, Richard Armstrong the coveted Janacek Medal, and ever since these, and Janacek's other works (*Osud* and *The Adventures of Mr Broucek*) have featured in the mainstream repertory of most leading opera houses on both sides of the Atlantic. His music is not all lyrically tuneful and his plots are, on the whole, dark and macabre; but if you have been to one or two operas, you should give Janacek a try. He combines music with drama in a highly compelling manner, leaving the audience reeling from the sheer emotion of it all. His main exception to this is *The Cunning Little Vixen*, which is as close to bitter-sweet pantomime as opera gets. Janacek was influenced by Czech folk music throughout all his work and used the clipped short speech rhythms of his Lachian dialect in many of his musical phrases. His further inspiration came from an unrequited passion for a young woman, Kamila Stosslova, when he was sixty-three and she was twenty-five and already married. While the folk music influences are not always obvious to our Western ears, his female obsession comes out clearly in *Jenufa*, *Katya Kabanova* and *The Makropulos Case*. The three works show an extraordinary perception of the female character when faced by unbearably tragic events. Janacek had to wait until he was fifty before his first opera, *Jenufa*, became a success.

Janowitz, Gundula German soprano who trained at the Graz Conservatory and made her debut with the Vienna State Opera in 1959. She stayed with the company from 1968 to 1972, singing many of the leads in the major Mozart operas with which she became closely associated. She is also particularly strong in the Strauss and Wagner repertoires, having a rich fluid voice which can be powerful or delicate thanks to her exemplary breath control. She has performed with most of the major European opera companies.

Jarvefelt, Goran (1948–1989) Swedish director whose early death in November 1989 was felt with sadness by many in the opera world, particularly those at Welsh National Opera for whom Jarvefelt had directed several superb productions. Trained as an actor, Jarvefelt began directing plays as assistant to Ingmar Bergman, coming to opera director only in the late 1970s. His work was austere, penetrating and directed with a conviction of the moral importance of opera, most obvious with his Wagner operas for WNO. This led to occasional criticisms about 'lecturing' and his double bill of *Erwartung* and *Duke Bluebeard's Castle* for the Metropolitan Opera in New York in 1988 was not generally liked.

Jenkins, Graeme English conductor who graduated from Cambridge University and became Musical Director of the Glyndebourne Touring Opera. For the Glyndebourne Festival, he has conducted performances of *Falstaff*, *L'Heure Espagnole*, *L'Enfant et les Sortileges*, *Carmen* and *Capriccio* and has made his debut with English National Opera. Energetic and intuitive, Jenkins is tipped to be one of the major operatic conductors of the 1990s.

Jenkins, Terry English tenor. A former boy chorister and electrical engineering graduate, Jenkins has been a member of ENO since 1972 and sung over 1100 performances with them in a wide variety of roles from Monteverdi to Iain Hamilton. He has appeared in many operetta productions with the company and sang in the British premiere of Stephen Sondheim's *Pacific Overtures* and was a notable Orpheus in Offenbach's *Orpheus in the Underworld*. A true ensemble singer and actor, his appearances outside the Coliseum have tended to be with ENO, for example on their 1984 United States tour, and in numerous radio and television relays.

Jenufa (Janacek) FP 1904. The plot concerns the Kostelnicka, wife of the Sexton, her stepdaughter Jenufa and the stepbrothers Steva and Laca. Jenufa, Steva and Laca are all children of two brothers, but from three different marriages, meaning there is barely any blood relationship between any of them. Jenufa is pregnant by Steva, a fact she has concealed from her stepmother. She is frightened that Steva will abandon her to join the army and that she will be left alone to reject the advances of Steva's jealous step-brother Laca. A drunken Steva treats Jenufa appallingly as her stepmother looks on and, unaware of the pregnancy, the Kostelnicka declares that Jenufa and Steva cannot marry until Steva has stayed sober for a year. Thinking his chance has come, Laca once more advances on Jenufa first with tenderness, then with a knife when she rejects him, but he is immediately remorseful and begs Jenufa's forgiveness. Eventually, the step-mother realizes Jenufa is carrying a child and keeps her in complete confinement, telling everyone that Jenufa has found work elsewhere. Steva becomes engaged to the daughter of the Mayor and, after much persuasion from the Kostelnicka, agrees to support Jenufa and his child with money but nothing else. Turning to Laca, the Kostelnicka encourages him to pursue his idea of marriage with Jenufa, telling him Jenufa's child is dead. Back at home, the Kostelnicka administers a strong drug to Jenufa and, alone, takes the baby out to the frozen river and drowns him. When Jenufa recovers, the Kostelnicka tells her that her baby has died. Distraught and seeing no other option for her future, Jenufa agrees to marry Laca as her step-mother planned. On their wedding day, the ice begins to melt on the river and the corpse of Jenufa's baby is revealed. Jenufa is accused of murder, but the Kostelnicka is overcome with grief and admits to her crime, leaving the tragic Jenufa alone with the faithful Laca.

Jeritza, Maria (1887–1982) Czech soprano who sang the first Jenufa in America and was chosen by Richard Strauss to create the first Ariadne and the first Empress in *Die Frau ohne Schatten*. The majority of her career was spent in Vienna and in New York, becoming the leading prima donna at the Metropolitan Opera House after the retirement of Geraldine Farrar. Her popularity, particularly between the wars, was legendary and encouraged her to take greater and greater risks with her performances. She created a memorable Tosca, singing the great aria from the second act, 'Vissi D'Arte', lying on the stage – not so remarkable now but a sensation in the mid-1930s! She was above all a great theatrical artist whose lovely voice complemented an exciting stage presence.

Jerusalem, Siegfried German tenor. Since his Bayreuth debut in 1977 he has returned regularly. Many in the audience there would be surprised to hear him tackle the more popular repertoire with equal zest. He has made video films of, amongst others, *The Merry Widow*, and *The Bartered Bride*. Jerusalem made his Covent Garden debut in 1986 as Erik in *The Flying Dutchman* and made a sensational ENO appearance, as a last minute stand-in, in *Parsifal*. International audiences have been thrilled by his bravura performances and handsome charismatic presence.

Jones, Della Welsh mezzo-soprano whose bubbling personality has made her a natural performer for the flirtatious soprano roles in operas such as *The Barber of Seville*, *La Cenerentola*, *The Merry Widow* and *The Marriage of Figaro*. She takes these roles with superb confidence, maximizing all the humour and nuance in the roles, in productions for every major opera company in Britain. However, this does not prevent her from applying herself to more serious roles. She played in *Salome* and in *Don Giovanni* to great acclaim but was particularly notable in *The Trojans*, a massive production mounted jointly by Scottish Opera, Opera North and Welsh National Opera. She brought a simi-

lar sincerity and insight to the role of Dido in *Dido and Aeneas* which she sang for the English Bach Festival. She performs extensively in Europe and in New York she has appeared in the 'Mostly Mozart' Festival. She has also appeared in Los Angeles as Ruggiero in a recent production of *Alcina*.

Jones, Dame Gwyneth Welsh soprano who trained as a mezzo-soprano but established her soprano range while resident at Covent Garden and has risen to become one of the greatest singers of our age. A classic opera heroine, Dame Gwyneth has a voice of consummate power and beauty which is complemented by her distinguished good looks and poised stage presence. Her repertoire is wide and she has performed in opera houses all over the world, but she is perhaps best known for her Wagner and Strauss heroines, notably Senta, Kundry, Brunnhilde, Sieglinde, Isolde, the Marschallin and Salome, in performance at the Vienna State Opera and at the Bayreuth Festival. She has sung over fifty performances at the Metropolitan Opera, New York, where her superbly integrated performances have won her as much acclaim as they have in Europe.

Jones, Richard English director who started directing on the London theatre fringe and became involved with opera when in 1982 he was awarded an Arts Council director's bursary to work with Scottish Opera. Very successful as an opera producer (notably the world premiere of Judith Weir's *A Night at the Chinese Opera* for Kent Opera), he also works in the straight theatre. As a result Jones treats opera as part of the contemporary theatre scene, and not as a museum piece. His acclaimed production of Prokofiev's *The Love of Three Oranges*, designed by the Brothers Quay, complete with scratch and sniff cards was described by one critic thus: 'If there were any single current UK production capable of broadening the appeal of opera this... would be an ideal candidate'. The production was recorded in 1989 for transmission by BBC television.

Jonny spielt auf (Krenek) FP 1927. In English, *Johnny Strikes Up*, this is a 'jazz opera' which is worth going to see if the musicians are real jazz musicians rather than orchestral players who can be a little restrained in their interpretations! It is not as effective as *Porgy and Bess* in using jazz to describe a situation – it uses the jazz medium satirically, poking fun rather than using it for its own sake.

Jazz band leader Jonny steals Daniello's violin and masters it to such an extent that when he plays a performance at the North Pole, the whole world starts to dance the Charleston.

Judge, Ian English director. Judge has made the transition from drama to opera with great success, demonstrating his versatility by producing such popular works as *The Wizard of Oz* for the Royal Shakespeare Company as well as a complex and brilliant production of Gounod's *Faust* for English National Opera. He describes his passions as Shakespeare, musical comedy and opera, and has recently brought all three together in a production of *Showboat* by Jerome Kern, co-produced by Opera North and the Royal Shakespeare Company. His productions are not deliberately provocative or shocking but are designed to make the audience think – 'reacquainting people with why they like a piece, to see it clearly for the first time and shed the sentimental gloss of other producers' ideas', as he says.

Juive, La (Halevy) FP 1835. Halevy's only work to survive into the modern repertory, it is still fairly rare to find in performance. It is typically French grand opera, lush in melody and choruses with one of those very confusing 'antefatto' which happens before the curtain rises. The character of Brogni, who is now a Cardinal, was once a civic official in Rome, When away on business his house was ransacked by the Neapolitans and his wife and child were presumed murdered. Stricken by these events, Brogni gives up public life and joins the Church. Rachel, a Jewess and daughter of the Christian-hating Eleazar, eventually realizes that the lover she has always called Samuel is in fact Prince Leopold, a Christian, and that he is already married to Eudoxia. Before the Emperor and Cardinal Brogni, Rachel denounces Leopold for consorting with her as she is a Jewess, a crime punishable by death for them both. Rachel refuses to renounce her faith to save herself, despite the

constant entreaties of Cardinal Brogni to her father. Eleazar tells Brogni that he knows of the loss of Brogni's wife and daughter in Rome, but that his daughter was saved by a Jew and is alive and well – but he refuses to tell Brogni where she is. As Rachel is hurled to her death in the execution cauldron, Eleazar turns to Brogni with the dreadful words – 'Your daughter died in those flames'.

Julius Caesar (Handel) FP 1724. If all you know about Handel is *The Messiah* and you come along to one of his operas expecting the same wonderful tunes, you may be in for a surprise. The music in Handel operas is usually very tuneful, lovely to sit back and listen to, with plenty of well known bits, but there does tend to be rather a lot of it! This is due to the tradition, prevalent at the time when Handel was writing, of repeating large chunks of arias which were not particularly short first time round. It is becoming increasingly fashionable not to play the repeats, thus speeding up the opera considerably and, if you are planning to go to a Handel opera, check some of the reviews first of all because they usually mention this fact. It is particularly relevant to *Julius Caesar* which has some stunningly beautiful music but is not the most fascinating plot. It is a good choice for someone who has seen and enjoyed the standard repertory and wants a bit more of a challenge – particularly if the production plays up the regal nature of the piece and the costumes are extraordinarily sumptuous. It has the extra dimension of the name part either being sung by a woman or a counter-tenor and one character who has two names – Tolomeo or Ptolemy. Here, he is referred to as Tolomeo.

Julius Caesar has won his battle against Pompeo, who is killed by Cleopatra's brother Tolomeo, thinking this will please Caesar; but Caesar is furious at this unnecessary murder and Pompeo's son Sesto swears to avenge his father's death. The power-hungry Tolomeo continues to plot – this time against Caesar himself whom he plans to usurp with the help of the counsellor Achilla who is promised Pompeo's widow Cornelia in return for his help. Cornelia and Sesto are arrested. Caesar meanwhile has been pursued by the winsome Cleopatra (in disguise) and they are about to declare their

Julius Caesar, by Handel. Valerie Masterson (left) as Cleopatra, with Dame Janet Baker as Caesar.

Katya Kabanova, by Janacek. Nancy Gustafson in the title role of the Glyndebourne Festival production.

mutual love when it is announced that Tolomeo's troops are about to ransack the palace. While Caesar escapes and is presumed dead, brother and sister (Tolomeo and Cleopatra) amass forces against each other, Tolomeo wins and Cleopatra is imprisoned. But in the nature of all good stories, Caesar returns, enlists the help of the betrayed Achilla, frees Cleopatra, has Tolomeo killed by Sesto and is proclaimed Emperor.

Jurinac, Sena Yugoslavian soprano who trained in her home country but made her Viennese debut in 1945 and has since been closely associated with the young, attractive roles written by Strauss and Mozart. A delightful Cherubino, Octavian and Dorabella, Jurinac has also achieved affecting performances of the 'heavier' roles including Madam Butterfly and Desdemona which she has sung both in Europe and America.

Katerina Ismailova (see Lady Macbeth of Mtsensk)

Katya Kabanova (Janacek) FP 1921. More of Janacek's menacing mothers and distraught daughters, woven into a score of terrific drama and tension, not comfortable to watch but with an almost Hitchcock-like fascination.

Katya and her husband Tikhon live with Tikhon's mother Kabanicha who hates her daughter-in-law. Katya harbours a guilty secret which she pours out to Barbara, a foster-child in the Kabanov home: Katya is in love with another man, Boris, and he feels the same about her. Taunted by her mother-in-law's constant bickering and with her husband away, Katya succumbs to temptation and meets Boris, at the same time as Barbara meets her peasant lover, Kudrjas. Tikhon returns and, with Kabanicha and Katya, meets Boris in a summerhouse on a neighbouring estate at the height of a tremendous storm. Torn with emotion, Katya confesses her adultery to a disbelieving audience, naming Boris as her lover. She runs away from home, meeting Boris briefly before throwing herself into the Volga River. As her lifeless body is lifted out, Tikhon accuses his mother of murdering his young wife.

Kempe, Rudolf (1910–1976) German conductor, for fifteen years Music Director of the Royal Philharmonic Orchestra. He conducted extensively for the Royal Opera House and Metropolitan Opera, New York, creating his reputation for his interpretations of Wagner and Richard Strauss.

Kenny, Yvonne Australian soprano, and one of the leading sopranos of her generation, she is a member of the Royal Opera House, Covent Garden. She also appears all over Europe and with other UK companies including Glyndebourne as Alice in *Falstaff*, and Donna Anna in *Don Giovanni*, at the 1990 and 1991 Festivals. Yvonne Kenny broadcasts regularly with the BBC and has made a number of records including the Solti/Decca recording of *The Marriage of Figaro* in the role of Barbarina.

King Priam (Tippett) FP 1962. While no-one disputes Michael Tippett's place in the forefront of English composition this century, beginners should be very keen on Greek mythology and possess a burning desire to see their favourite characters set to music before tackling this one. It is based on the well-known story of Homer's *Iliad* with Helen of Troy madly in love with Paris, son of Priam and brother of Hector with whom he is always quarrelling. Hector is finally killed by Achilles, and Priam by Achilles' son, Neoptolemus.

Kipnis, Alexander (1891–1978) Russian bass who studied in Germany through World War One, though categorized as an enemy alien! He went on to specialize in the major German roles, singing with great success at Glyndebourne before emigrating to America in 1940 and obtaining citizenship there. He became the grandee of the Met over the next decade, still creating his best performances in the Wagner roles of Gurnemanz and King Marke (*Parsifal*) as well as a splendid Boris Godunov (in Russian) in 1943.

Kirov (see Leningrad)

Kitchen, Linda English soprano whose career in Britain has developed very quickly! Became a principal member of the Royal Opera House, Covent Garden in 1983 only two years after her professional debut. Also appeared with all the major British companies. Sings a wide variety of vocal and production styles from Papagena to Zerlina to Satanio/Destiny/Fury/ in Cavalli's *La Calisto* for Opera Factory and a Daughter in Philip Glass's *Akhnaten* for English National Opera. Such versatility will ensure that it cannot be long before she sings on the international circuit, in Europe and the United States.

Kleiber, Carlos German conductor, son of Eric Kleiber who at first discouraged his son from a musical career. The son succeeded however, making debuts in German opera theatres and moving ultimately to the Stuttgart opera where he concentrated on performances of Verdi and the German composers. While in demand all over the world, Kleiber is known as a reclusive, enigmatic and intense personality, bearing out Verdi's phrase that what makes a good conductor is 'a hot heart and a cool head'. He does not record extensively and his repertory is not huge. He insists on long and intense rehearsal periods, working with the same orchestral players from first to last and never willing to accept substitutions in the pit. Such a dictatorial attitude achieves superb results, as cynical orchestral players treat him with something akin to hero worship, and singers and managements leap at the opportunity to work with him. He has created a notable *Otello*, *Der Freischutz* and *Tristan and Isolde* among many wonderful stagings, perhaps best assessed by John Copley who worked with him on a production of *La Bohème* at Covent Garden: 'One's brief is to keep him happy at all times and even if it drives us all mad for a while, his magical performance makes you forget everything'.

Kleiber, Eric (1890–1956) German conductor who was appointed Director of the Berlin State Opera in 1923, virtually on the strength of one stunning performance of *Fidelio*. There he conducted the premiere of *Wozzeck* before escaping from the Nazis in 1934. He continued his career in London and New York, returning to Germany to head up the East Berlin State Opera from 1951 to 1955. A firm disciplinarian, Kleiber was known for his hatred of any form of showiness or theatricality, disciplining his musicians with an army-like regime.

Klemperer, Otto (1885–1973) German conductor who spent a considerable part of his early career in his homeland, where he premiered *Oedipus Rex* for the Kroll Opera, Berlin, before emigrating to America in 1933, working primarily with the Los Angeles Philharmonic. Back in Europe, he made his name first with the Budapest Symphony and then with the London Philharmonic. Klemperer will always be known as a fine and thorough musician who had a particular liking for conducting everything extremely slowly. Fans think the technique brings out the very best in the music and critics think it far too ponderous to be enjoyable. But any serious opera lover recognizes him as one of the greatest opera conductors of the century and his recording of *Fidelio* is quite superb.

Knapp, Peter English bass/director. From a highly acclaimed performing career, Knapp moved to direct his own opera group, Travelling Opera. A passionate advocate of opera in English, Knapp has brought live opera to many areas hitherto unserved by the national companies.

Knot Garden, The (Tippett) FP 1970. 'The *Knot Garden* is about the loves and hates of seven people in modern England', wrote the composer in the original programme – and there can be hardly any better explanation for this complex psychological and emotional drama. Tippett also referred to Shakespeare's *All's Well that Ends Well* in describing his work – 'Simply the thing I am shall make me live'. Now that is all very high minded and totally obvious if you understand the workings of Tippett's mind – but for us mere mortals who want to get to grips with contemporary opera, it is too evasive. Knowing the story of *The Knot Garden* will not actually help you very much when it comes to understanding it, but some idea of the characters and the overall structure might start you off. It is also notable for two other facts – the first homosexual kiss ever to be shown on the opera stage and the first opera ever to be conducted by a woman – Sian Edwards – at Covent Garden.

The seven characters are Faber and his wife Thea, their foster daughter Flora, Thea's sister Denise, a homosexual couple called Dov and Mel and an analyst called Mangus. Mangus has been invited to Faber and Thea's house to help Flora, who imagines that Faber has sexual desires towards her. But Mangus soon realizes that it is Faber and Thea's marriage that needs the help. Mangus often refers to himself as a character like Prospero in *The Tempest* – a still, wise force amongst whirling emotions. They are joined by Mel and Dov, who keep up the analogy as Caliban and Ariel, and finally by Denise. She has been horribly tortured in her campaign for world rights and attempts to convey her suffering to the others. The 'Labyrinth' act which follows pairs all the characters up in different combinations, with Dov finally showing great affection to Flora. The following 'Charade' is scored like a film script with the action happening simultaneously and 'dissolving' like a series of film takes – further complicated by the fact that the following characters have now assumed parts from *The Tempest* –

Mangus = Prospero
Dov   = Ariel
Mel   = Caliban
Flora   = Miranda
Faber   = Ferdinand

with only Thea and Denise remaining themselves. By the end of the opera, Thea and Faber are enjoying a newly strengthened marriage and Mel and Denise have found comfort together, Flora remains alone and Dov follows after Mel and Denise.

Knussen, Oliver British composer who is among the best known and most widely performed of his generation. Also a much sought after conductor of contemporary music at home and abroad. Made his conducting debut in April 1968, conducting his own First Symphony. Knussen's works for the stage were written in the early 1980s, in collaboration with Maurice Sendak (*Where the Wild Things Are* and *Higglety Pigglety Pop!*). 'Wild Things', since its London Premiere by Glyndebourne Festival Opera and the London Sinfonietta at the National Theatre, has been seen in productions at Glyndebourne, Amsterdam, St Paul (Minnesota Opera) and New York City, as well as in concert performances by the London Sinfonietta and City of Birmingham Symphony Orchestra conducted by the composer, and the New York Philharmonic under Zubin Mehta. Works in progress (1990) include a new version of *Higglety Pigglety Pop!*, a new work

for the London Sinfonietta, and a cello concerto for Yo-Yo Ma.

Kobbé, Gustave (1857–1918) American musicologist whose legacy to opera appears on the shelves of every serious opera lover. Educated in New York and Germany, Kobbé wrote extensively on opera for American magazines and for the *New York Herald* for which he was music critic for eighteen years. He combined this work with his other great love, sailing and, tragically, it was in a sailing accident that he was killed in 1918, just months before the completion of his massive undertaking – *Kobbé's Complete Opera Book*. This massive tome – now approaching two thousand pages – is still the definitive reference book for opera plots, offering detailed explanations of each work with many musical insights and knowledgeable asides. The work is now revised regularly by its editor Lord Harewood and is without doubt the most thorough and accurate introduction to the core of the opera repertoire.

Kodaly, Zoltan (1882–1967) Hungarian composer whose chief contribution to the operatic world was the work he did with Bartok on cataloguing Hungarian folk songs which influenced both their stage works.

Komische Oper, Die (see Berlin)

Konigskinder (Humperdinck) FP 1910. Very similar to the composer's other great hit, *Hansel and Gretel*, this is a pure fairy tale with some beautifully pretty music. The Princess has been turned by a witch into a Goosegirl and in this disguise she meets and falls in love with the Prince, The Fiddler helps bring the pair together but the girl is rejected as Queen. Poisoned by the witch, the couple die in each other's arms.

Krenek, Ernst German composer whose best known work is *Johnny Strikes Up*, but who also wrote *Karl V* in a more abrasive style. He now works in California using the very latest electronic techniques in his compositions.

Kubelik, Rafael Czech conductor who left the Communist bloc after the coup at the end of World War Two and has since worked in the West. His allegiance to his homeland is proved however by his superb interpretations of Czech composers such as Janacek. He moved from the Directorship of the Chicago Symphony Orchestra to the same post at the Royal Opera House, Covent Garden, which he held from 1955 to 1958. There he conducted the first British performances of *The Trojans* by Berlioz and *Jenufa* by Janacek. He repeated his performance of *The Trojans* for the American premiere at the Met in 1973 while he was Music Director of the house. He also wrote five operas, the most notable of which is *Cornelia Faroli*.

Kupfer, Harry East German producer who has been Artistic Director and Chief Producer of the Komische Oper in Berlin since 1981, having moved from the same roles in Dresden. His work is controversial, continuing the radical school of production initiated by Walter Felsenstein and carried out also by Gotz Freidrich and Ruth Berghaus. Greatly in demand as a producer throughout Europe, Kupfer has directed work for Welsh National Opera (*Elektra* and *Fidelio*) and *Pelleas and Melisande* for English National Opera. In the summer of 1989, be brought two Komsiche Oper productions to the Royal Opera House for the first time ever in Britain, for a lamentably small number of performances.

Lady Macbeth of Mtsensk (Shostakovich) FP 1934. This opera has been through several incarnations before being performed in its original version in Britain in a powerful new production by ENO in 1987. Its full title is *Lady Macbeth of the Mtsensk District* and in its revised version it is known as *Katerina Ismailova*. It has nothing whatsoever to do with Shakespeare's Lady Macbeth, being based instead on a Russian folk tale written by Leskov in 1865. When it was premiered in Russia in 1934, it was hugely successful but two years later it was barred from performance after a notorious article in *Pravda* entitled 'Chaos instead of music'. In this article, the Communist hierarchy unleashed a full blooded attack on Russian contemporary arts in general and on the music of Shostakovich in particular. It was nearly thirty years before the opera was played again in Russia, under its new title of *Katerina Ismailova*.

Katerina is married to the rich merchant Ismailova, but through boredom and frustration has taken a lover, Sergei. Her father-in-law Boris becomes suspicious of her infidelity and his interference provokes the lovers to murder him with rat poison. Believing their true happiness will only be attained with Katerina's husband out of the way, they throttle him and run away together. But the murder is discovered and the lovers are exiled to Siberia. On the way, Sergei, who has become bored of their liaison, flirts with a female convict. Katerina can stand the insult no longer and, angrily grabbing her rival, jumps with her to their deaths in the river below.

Lady of the Lake, The (see Donna del Lago)

Lakmé (Delibes) FP 1883. Fairly insubstantial light French opera based on variation of the Madam Butterfly story. There is a very famous duet for two sopranos. The British officer Gerald and an Indian girl Lakmé, have done the unforgivable and fallen in love. Lakmé's father Nilakantha, a Brahmin priest, is furious and demands to know the identity of his daughter's lover. Unwittingly she lets out her secret and Nilakantha stabs Gerald – but not fatally. Lakmé takes her lover away to nurse him back to health but their happiness together is brief. In Lakmé's absence, Gerald has a conversation with fellow-soldier Frederic who persuades him of his duty to the army. Realizing he would be happier if she were no longer around, Lakmé kills herself.

Langdon, Michael English bass. Former Director of the National Opera Studio in London and an established performer in the major opera houses during the 1950s and 1960s, particularly in the role of Baron Ochs (*Der Rosenkavalier*). His pioneering work at the Studio has brought his professional experience to benefit new generations of performers, placing great emphasis on the ability to learn a role accurately and convey the whole character in the context of the production rather than relying solely on vocal technique.

Langridge, Philip English bass and a 'British International', much in demand all over the world both as an opera singer and for recitals and concerts. His performances in Britain are always eagerly awaited. He is associated with the twentieth-century opera repertoire, notably *The Rake's Progress*, *Peter Grimes* and was particularly outstanding in the recent world premiere of *The Mask of Orpheus* (Birtwistle) at English National Opera. The staging of this work required Langridge to sing with a throat microphone and a half-mask on his face – something many performers, even contemporary music specialists, would baulk at. But his open minded approach to new works and new productions make him a very convincing performer as well as a great singer. In complete contrast to these performances of contemporary operas, Langridge has embarked upon a long term project with Graham Johnson of *The Songmaker's Almanac* to record Schubert's entire song output for Hyperion records. He is married to the soprano Ann Murray.

Language One of the greatest problems facing any relatively new opera goer is how to work out what's going on. To say that the words, or even the plot, do not matter, and that you should just sit back and listen to the music, denies you an enormous part of the enjoyment of the whole world of opera. You have to have an idea of who is who and what is happening, even if it is not possible to hear each individual word. The opera fraternity itself is divided over what language to use when performing. You will find many extremely experienced opera goers who simply hate to have everything sung in English and far prefer to listen to an opera in its original language, that is the language of its original performances. So dialect coaches are employed to bring a cast together in the performance language – no mean feat when some of the international houses may cast performers from numerous different countries in one production. Try teaching a Spaniard to be romantic in German or a Scotsman to be aggressive in French or an Italian to be pastoral in English. It becomes even more complicated with the chorus, who may, in one season, be asked to sing in Italian, French and German, when they may all be native English speakers. Add to that the fact that even a native German speaker may not really understand the true meaning of Wagner's plays on

words, written over one hundred years ago, in the same way that complex Victorian English looks somewhat foreign to us now. But if the coach achieves his or her task, or better still, a singer performs in his native tongue (Pavarotti in Italian for example) the effect can be staggeringly powerful. To many, then, a policy of singing everything in English, as ENO has, is not satisfying. But there are advantages, particularly for the new opera-goer and thanks are due to the work of superb translators who can make, say, the Italian of da Ponte realistic and lively for a modern audience without losing any of the original meaning.

Lauri-Volpi, Giacomo (1892–1979) Italian tenor who began his career in Italy before moving to America as a resident of the Metropolitan Opera for the 1920s. He sang all the major tenor roles with consummate ease, particularly those pitched high in the voice. His hold over the audience was still evident when, at the age of eighty, he sang a towering performance of 'Nessun Dorma' from *Turandot* at a gala at the Teatro Liceo in Barcelona.

Lawton, Jeffrey English tenor who came late to the world of opera but has now achieved an impressive reputation, particularly for his notable performances of Otello with Welsh National Opera and the Royal Opera House, Covent Garden. A commanding stage figure with a voice to match, Lawton came to prominence with WNO in the role of Siegfried in the company's Ring Cycle. He remained with the company to sing many of the major heroic tenor roles such as Florestan (*Fidelio*), Aeneas (*The Trojans*) and the Emperor in *Die Frau ohne Schatten*. But it was his portrayal of Otello in Peter Stein's magnificent production that brought Lawton to national attention. The production was staged again in Brussels with Lawton in the name part and has since been shown on British television. As a result of this acclaim, Lawton was asked to take the role at short notice in January 1990 at Covent Garden, deputizing for an indisposed Placido Domingo, playing opposite Katia Riccarelli as Desdemona in a production conducted by Carlos Kleiber. Future plans include more Otellos with WNO and the lead role in *Lear* by Aribert Reiman, Lawton's debut with English National Opera.

Lady Macbeth of Mtsensk, by Shostakovich, was banned in Russia for over thirty years. Even today it is rarely performed. Josephine Barstow and Jacques Trussel as the lovers Katerina and Sergei.

Lear, by Aribert Reimann, is the only one of the composer's works so far performed in Britain. Left to right, Vivian Tierney (Regan), Monte Jaffe (Lear), and Phyllis Cannan (Goneril).

Lazaridis, Stefanos Ethopian designer, now based in London, Lazaridis is an Associate Artist for English National Opera for whom he has designed over twenty productions. His work has also been seen at the Maggio Musicale in Florence, the Deutsche Oper in Berlin, the Bregenz Festival and in the opera houses in Los Angeles and San Francisco. His designs are highly inventive, ranging from the domesticity of a 1950s kitchen for a new production of *Hansel and Gretel* for ENO, to the charm of an elegant hotel for *The Mikado*, full of flappers and bell boys, to a massive, futuristic concept, floating in several metres of water, for a vast production of *The Flying Dutchman* for the 1989 Bregenz Festival, where the budget for sets and costumes alone was £1.5 million! Lazaridis is not phased by such dimensions, having designed the large scale performance of *Carmen* staged at London's Earl's Court in the summer of 1989, playing to an audience of 15,000 with a cast of several hundred. But his more intimate productions are no less effective, creating, for example, a chilling intensity for Dvorak's *Rusalka* which was set in a children's nursery (ENO 1983), and a sombre fatalism for Jonathan Miller's production of *Tosca*, updated to the Fascist dominated Italy of the 1940s.

Lecca, Marie-Jeanne Romanian designer who began her career designing for theatres in her home country and now enjoys a considerable reputation all over Europe. Her most inspired work has been for small scale, small budget opera, including *La Bohème* for what is now City of Birmingham Touring Opera, *La Wally* for Wexford and *Noye's Fludde* for the Brighton Festival. She has made the transition to larger venues effectively, creating a politically relevant setting for *Moses in Egypt* by Rossini (ENO 1987) and a colourful interpretation of *Falstaff* for the same company in 1988. She is equally skilful as a costume designer, with work including the vibrantly coloured clothing for *Pacific Overtures* by Stephen Sondheim, presented by ENO in 1986.

Legato This term describes a smooth, uninterrupted sound, achieved by singing a phrase in one breath.

Leggate, Robin English tenor. One of the great Cassios in the Royal Opera House's *Otello* – he has sung this role under Mehta, Kleiber, von Dohnanyi and Davis. Also regularly sings the Mozart tenor roles at Covent Garden where he has been a long time member of the company, and with the other British opera companies. Leggate has sung many important and varied concerts throughout the UK and in Europe.

Lehar, Franz (1870–1948) Hungarian composer whose best known work is *The Merry Widow* which he wrote in 1905. While Lehar did write more serious operas, particularly in the early part of his career, it is for operetta that he is best remembered, and for his ability to include some glittering dance in each of his works. His partnership with Richard Tauber resulted in a number of works which concentrated heavily on the vocal talents of one (usually female) singer.

Lehmann Lilli (1848–1929) German soprano who enjoyed a long, varied and influential career lasting over forty years and encompassing some 170 roles. She was a superb Wagnerian soprano, possessing the dramatic intensity needed for a truly persuasive Isolde or Brunnhilde – indeed even Kaiser Wilhelm intervened to arrange for her to return to sing in Berlin in 1891 after breaking her contract there to work in America. At the age of sixty, her voice was still as powerful and her recordings made at that age stand strongly in comparison with younger singers. Amongst her pupils were Geraldine Farrar, Germaine Lubin and Olive Fremstad.

Lehmann Lotte (1888–1976) German soprano who was no relation of Lilli Lehmann and quite different in her choice of roles. Her voice was not perfect but she injected a humane and essentially feminine quality into her work, which made her a popular and internationally acclaimed singer. Her 'pet' role was the Marschallin (*Der Rosenkavalier*) but she encompassed a wide range of other parts from the Dyer's Wife (*Die Frau ohne Schatten*) to Tosca.

Leiferkus, Sergei Russian bass and a leading singer at the Kirov Opera. Unlike many singers from the Eastern bloc, Leiferkus has managed to keep a successful career going in Russia whilst at the same time performing regularly in the West. With the emergence of cultural glasnost, his visits will no doubt become more frequent. He made his western debut at the Wexford Festival and has returned there many times subsequently. He was the first Soviet singer to appear with English National Opera (*Pearl Fishers* 1987) where he returned to sing in *Carmen* amongst a number of other roles. Debuts in America (San Francisco), at Covent Garden, Toronto, Chicago, and Glyndebourne are lined up for the early 1990s.

Leitmotiv The term literally means 'leading motive' and describes a phrase of music which represents a person, place or thing and recurs throughout an opera to describe its object. Although there are suggestions of leitmotifs in Mozart and Gluck, they are most prevalent in the works of Wagner, who used them in his massive operas to suggest influences and psychological changes in his main characters. Leitmotifs are a development of the Reminiscence motive, when a character thinks back and the music echoes his thoughts.

Leningrad Opera of an international standard came to Leningrad in 1860 with the opening of the Maryinsky Theatre. This was the site of notable premieres such as *Forza del Destino* by Verdi in 1862, *Boris Godunov* by Moussorgsky in 1874, and *The Queen of Spades* by Tchaikovsky in 1890. By 1935, after the tumult of the Revolution, the theatre was renamed the Kirov, and is now perhaps better known outside Russia for its ballet, though its highly nationalistic opera performances are stirring occasions. The smaller Theatre Maly has an excellent international reputation, and has staged the premieres of *Lady Macbeth of Mtsensk* by Shostakovich and *War and Peace* by Prokofiev.

Lenya, Lotte (1898–1981) German singer who defied the usual boundaries of soprano and alto with a voice which could be boy-soprano-pure at one minute and sensually husky the next. Lenya was trained as an actress but it was her marriage to Kurt Weill that brought her to prominence on the operatic stage. Her performances in *The Rise and Fall of the City of Mahagonny* and *The Threepenny Opera* were in every sense definitive and her unique voice has been captured very successfully on record.

Leoncavallo, Ruggero (1857–1919) Italian composer. Leoncavallo wrote several operas but is remembered for only one, *I Pagliacci*, which he wrote in admiration of *Cavalleria Rusticana*, with which it has been teamed ever after. He also wrote a version of *La Bohème* a year after Puccini's interpretation and lost out to Puccini in popularity.

Leppard, Raymond English conductor who has conducted many of the world's finest orchestras and made an impressive range of recordings. Particularly associated with Glyndebourne, he conducted the premiere there of *The Cunning Little Vixen* by Janacek as well as undertaking extensive work in America, with opera houses in New York, San Francisco and Santa Fe.

Levine, James American conductor who trained as a pianist who took conducting as a second study and is now one of the most highly acclaimed conductors in the world. He made a series of international debuts in the early 1970s, making a particular specialization of the operas of Verdi. He made his debut at the Metropolitan Opera in 1971, when he was under thirty, and within five years has risen through the post of Principal conductor to that of Musical Director. At the time the Metropolitan Opera management were criticized for 'risking' such an important artistic reputation on so young and relatively inexperienced a musician. But Levine has repaid their confidence many times over, bringing the orchestra of the Met to a superb standard and now, as Artistic Director, expanding the repertoire of America's greatest opera house with a bold programming policy which favours the new without neglecting the classics.

Libretto In a little over four hundred years, the subjects on which opera have been based have developed from the besporting of gods, demi-gods or personalities from ancient Greece and Rome to the impact of President Nixon's visit to China. How a composer chooses his subject matter varies enormously, but there are two prime areas. Either he sets existing words to his music or he uses his music as a starting point for a new libretto. In either case, the words largely reflect the time of composition rather than the period in which the opera is set. Conventions in the time of Monteverdi dictated that the characters should speak and act with the minimum of human feeling or emotion, but with *The Coronation of Poppea* and later with the reform operas of Gluck, audiences began to realize that the words could mean something to them, as they described simple emotions felt by kings and shepherds alike. Thus the librettist began to make an impact on the world of opera, developing his role as a complement to the composer, rather than letting the music alone do all the descriptive work.

With the work of Lorenzo da Ponte came libretti that had wit, elegance and realism, perfectly matched by the musical genius of Mozart in *Don Giovanni, Cosi fan Tutte* and *The Marriage of Figaro*. Here were words on themes any audience could identify with – the agony of unrequited love, the cheek and courage of a young servant, the insatiable sexual appetite of a handsome man. But the work of Richard Wagner prompted a shift in the need for contemporary relevance as he transported his audiences on to a completely different plane of time, place and emotion, exercising complete control over every aspect of his stagings from the words to the music to the stage design as he carried through his theories of Gesamkunstwerk. Through such total immersion, he hoped to make his audience feel the greater powers of destiny and all consuming passion, rather than the more homely emotions expressed by Verdi or Puccini. Verdi nearly always used existing texts for his operas, frequently working with Arrigo Boito who adapted *Falstaff* and *Othello* from Shakespeare to give Verdi a libretto he could set to music.

Libretto always means the words originally written for the opera; to speak of a 'new, English language libretto' for a non-English work is incorrect. There have been superb English language libretti written by, for example, W H Auden for *The Rake's Progress* by Stravinsky or Myfanwy Piper for several of Britten's operas. As the demand for opera in the language of the audience increases, and opera-goers realize how much understanding each word can add to their enjoyment, so the need for expert and sympathetic translators will develop from that of librettist to ensure that the words continue to convey equal meaning with the music.

Liebermann, Rolf German manager and composer whose tenure at the Opera in Paris from 1973 to 1980 brought the house to international prominence.

Liebsverbot (Wagner) FP 1836. Stun and amaze your Wagner-loving friends with the knowledge of this two-act opera which he wrote, based on Shakespeare's *Measure for Measure*. It was Wagner's only foray into opera in an Italian style and was a total failure!

Liebestod If you do not know any Wagner at all, find yourself a recording of this, the final passage from *Tristan and Isolde* and prepare to be converted. Isolde has come to be with her lover Tristan only to find him dying. Knowing she cannot exist without him, she can only be transported into the love-death they had both longed for and falls lifeless on his body. Wagner writes a towering, heart-breaking passage which is rich in melody and sensual in construction. It is, quite simply, one of the most moving pieces of music ever written.

Ligeti, Gyorgy Rumanian composer who uses contemporary electronic techniques in his works which have included presentations for small numbers of singers using an artificial language. His one music theatre piece *The Grand Macabre*, was staged by ENO in 1982

Lighthouse, The (Peter Maxwell Davies) FP 1980. Modern one-act opera by one of Britain's great contemporary composers. It is based on the true story of three lighthouse men who disappeared mysteriously in the Hebrides in 1900. The plot explores the psychological intrigues of their last hours, climaxing as the singers and the audience are blinded by an extraordinarily powerful white light, leaving everyone to draw their own conclusions.

Lincoln Center, New York What was once a derelict 'no-go' area of New York, popularized by Leonard Bernstein in his musical *West Side Story*, has been transformed into an elegant and thriving cultural centre. Around three sides of the vast square and magnificent fountain which forms the heart of the complex are the headquarters of New

York City Opera, the Metropolitan Opera and the Avery Fisher Hall, with the prestigious Juilliard School of Music and Vivient Beaumont Theatre completing the centre. (see under New York.)

Lind, Jenny (1820–1887) Swedish soprano, known as the Swedish Nightingale. Who says we push our young singers too early? By the age of twenty-one Jenny Lind had sung Agathe (*Der Freischutz*), Donna Anna (*Don Giovanni*), Lucia (*Lucia di Lammermor*) and the title role in *Norma*. Such a ridiculous schedule led to an enforced break from the stage between 1841 and 1842, but by the age of thirty she had sung in every major opera house in Europe – and had officially retired. Acclaimed by audiences throughout Europe for her sweet voice, she toured America (managed by the circus impressario P T Barnum) to similar popularity and at the time of her death was on the staff of the Royal College of Music in London.

Liszt Franz (1811–1886) Hungarian pianist who tried his hand at composing a one-act opera at the age of thirteen but never developed his talent beyond that, preferring to impress with his virtuoso piano playing. He was also the father of Cosima, who married Richard Wagner.

Lloyd, Robert English bass who began a career as an academic historian, turning to singing at the age of twenty-eight. Principal bass at Covent Garden from 1972 to 1982 during which time he sang an enormous range of repertoire and was best known as Sarastro, Gurnemanz and Boris Godunov. He has made many records and videos, and written and presented several highly successful BBC Radio documentaries on the human voice, and a TV documentary on the bass voice. But this does not mean that he takes an overly academic approach to his own singing.

Lloyd-Jones, David English conductor who was Artistic Director of Opera North, a post he held for the first twelve years of the company's existence. Lloyd-Jones can be credited with establishing the company as a major force in opera in Britain, leading some forty-six productions, including the world

premiere of *Rebecca* by Wilfred Joseph, commissioned by the company. Particularly adept at the Russian repertoire, Lloyd-Jones is a fluent Russian speaker and has conducted notable performances of *Boris Godunov* at the Royal Opera House, Covent Garden, *Prince Igor* for Opera North and was the first non-Russian to conduct *Boris Godunov* in the USSR. He has appeared extensively in Europe and conducts *Albert Herring* for Canadian Opera in 1991.

Lloyd-Webber, Andrew English composer. Purists will no doubt argue at the inclusion of this composer in a book about opera when his output is firmly placed in the world of musical theatre. But Andrew Lloyd-Webber has contributed significantly to the revival in the popularity of theatregoing in general and of musicals in particular, and this has, without doubt, had a knock-on effect for the world of opera. His phenomenally successful works began with *Joseph and the Amazing Technicolour Dreamcoat* in 1968 and have run through the next two decades with increasing popularity, including *Evita* (1976), *Tell Me on a Sunday* (1979), *Cats* (1981), *Starlight Express* (1984), *Phantom of the Opera* (1986) and *Aspects of Love* (1989). While critics may condemn his works for their lack of variety and possible plagiarism from classical pieces, he has succeeded in giving the public what they want and proving that words set to music can be a powerful and affecting means of communication at all levels.

Lockhart, James Scottish conductor who is currently Director of the Koblenz Opera, having worked with many of Europe's leading opera houses. He joined Covent Garden in 1954 and went on to work for Welsh National Opera during that company's formative years. He did much to bring the company to national prominence, his engaging personality making the transition from amateur to professional status easier than it might have been. In 1972 he became the first British musician to hold a full-time post in a German opera house when he undertook the leadership of the State Theatre at Kessel. He has since conducted extensively in Europe and America and has recently made his Japanese debut with the Osaka Opera Orchestra.

Lohengrin (Wagner) FP 1850. A mixture of tenth-century dynastic struggle and Saxon myth and legend is woven together by Wagner in a work which proved immediately popular to his Bayreuth audience. Newcomers to opera are often wrongly advised to avoid Wagner. While *Lohengrin* is long and the action is fairly static, it contains some wonderful melodies (including the famous wedding march) and, for the serious minded, may make a more satisfying evening than the lighter 'beginners' operas'.

In Antwerp, there is a struggle brewing between Friedrich of Telramund and Elsa for the right to the throne. Friedrich believes that Elsa has murdered her brother Gottfried, who is the rightful heir. King Heinrich of Germany arbitrates between the two parties, declaring that the matter will be solved by a combat between Friedrich and whoever fights on Elsa's behalf. That champion appears in a boat drawn by a swan, fulfilling Elsa's dream of a knight in shining armour. He will fight on her behalf, he says, but she must never ask his name. The mysterious knight defeats Telramund, who departs with his wife Ortrud to plot the overthrow of Elsa and her new consort. At Elsa's wedding, they accuse the knight of using supernatural powers to win the fight and gradually they build up Elsa's curiosity about her enigmatic new husband. Finally, she can stand the mystery no longer and asks the dreaded question. Before he can answer, Telramund appears, intent on murdering the knight, who is too quick and kills Telramund instead. Turning to his new wife, he tells her his name is Lohengrin, that he is a knight of the Holy Grail and his power rests entirely on his anonymity. Once she knows his identity he can no longer stay among men. The swan reappears, and is transformed back into human form, revealing none other than Gottfried, Elsa's brother and the rightful heir.

Lombardi, I (Verdi) FP 1843. The full Italian title is *I Lombardi alla Prima Crociata* (The Lombards at the First Crusade.) For its performances in Paris, Verdi revised the whole work and called it 'Jerusalem'.

The Lombards of the title are two brothers, Arvino and Pagano who, in their youth, had loved the same girl, Viclinda. Arvino had won the struggle and married her, producing a daughter Giselda. Pagano had been banished for attempting to wound his brother in a jealous rage. But his banishment is now over and, although everyone pretends to forget their old differences and unites together to fight in the Crusades, it is clear that Pagano still feels he has a score to settle. In attempting once more to kill his brother, Pagano realizes he has killed their father Pirro instead and is banished again. The scene moves to Antioch where Pagano is living as a hermit and Arvino is leading the Crusades. In the course of battle, Arvino encounters his daughter Giselda who has been taken prisoner by the Muslims and fallen in love with Oronte, son of the Muslim leader. Faced by both his daughter and his estranged brother, Arvino sees his troops kill Oronte and then Pagano, who is forgiven by Arvino as he dies.

London, George (1920–1985) American bass baritone who worked throughout Europe and America, and, in 1960, was vested with the honour of being the first American to sing on the stage of the Bolshoi – in no less a nationalistic opera then *Boris Godunov*! His career, which specialized in the great Russian roles and characters exuding menace and cunning, was curtailed in 1967 by paralysis of the vocal chords, after which he moved into management roles in theatres in Washington and Seattle, USA.

London England's capital has two major opera houses and serves as the administrative base of many smaller companies.

The London Coliseum is the home of English National Opera which has been based in the theatre since 1968. It is the largest auditorium in London, seating over 2,300 people and was opened in 1904 to designs by Frank Matcham, under the leadership of the acclaimed impresario, Oswald Stoll. Nearly ninety years later, the theatre remains a tribute to Stoll whose vision of a 'popular theatre' was realized by this massive building, built at his instruction away from the glamorous end of town but near the station so his audience could return home easily by train. The Coliseum was for many years a music hall and variety house, hosting performances by such 'greats' as Vesta Tilley, Gracie Fields, W C Fields, Noel Coward and Sophie Tucker, as well as staging spectacular dance shows, to choreography by Diaghilev amongst others. Its massive stage and technical innovations (it was the first theatre ever to have a revolving stage) allowed Stoll to realize his theatrical fantasies – lavish galas with the Tiller Girls, live horses on stage to recreate the Derby and frequent visits by members of the Royal Family. Indeed, the facilities for the Royal Family showed the imagination of Stoll's mind, including a 'Royal Car' which travelled along its own track to fit at the back of the stalls and become a Royal Box!

By the 1930s, the theatre was given over to major musicals, including the British premiere of *Annie Get Your Gun* and a spectacular production of *White Horse Inn* where the foyer was converted into an Alpine Inn and every programme seller wore Tyrolean costume. After a period as a canteen for ARP workers during the Second World War, the Coliseum became the venue for yet another innovation – this time less successful. The American technique of Cinerama, intending to surround the audience with sound and vision, involved extensive adaptations to the building which are still in place on the Dress Circle level. The experiment was a failure, and it was only the drive of Stephen Arlen that saved the theatre as a venue for live performance. Arlen was convinced that the Sadler's Wells Opera Company could take up residence at the Coliseum and create in the process an English National Opera company. It was a bold venture and the failure of the company's first production at their new home (*Don Giovanni*, directed by John Gielgud) made it seem a foolhardy one. But the success of the company has grown over the last twenty years and now its eccentric, somewhat shabby home, known with great affection as 'The Coli', once more bears out Oswald Stoll's original purpose of the greatest art for the greatest number.

The Royal Opera House, Covent Garden, was built in 1858. It is the third theatre to have occupied the site, the first two being destroyed by fire in 1808 and 1858 respectively. The public areas of the current building are sumptuously elegant and a fitting venue for the upper echelons of Britain's opera audiences, who may today have to pay approaching £100 for each ticket. But lamentably inadequate and potentially dangerous technical facilities have hampered produc-

tions in recent years. Now, exciting, though controversial, plans are in train to develop all areas of the house into a major new complex, with substantial commercial development offsetting the costs (estimated to be in excess of £175 million) of modernizing the whole northern corner of the Covent Garden area. These plans, by architect Jeremy Dixon, include restoring the roof of the old Floral Hall (though destroying the remainder of this historic building), to create larger public areas and bringing the complex into the heart of the thriving Covent Garden piazza. Technical innovations include bringing all the operations involved in staging an opera together under one roof (at present they are housed all over the city), installing powerful machinery to enable the stage to be raised, lowered or raked at the touch of a button and creating massively increased storage areas, with an integrated system, so sets can be assembled quickly and therefore cheaply. There are also plans to build a second theatre, to open with the rest of the new complex in 1996.

Although the theatre on the Covent Garden site has hosted opera since 1732, it was only in 1949 that the Royal Opera began to present regular seasons of opera throughout the year, interspersed by performances by the Royal Ballet, with other opera companies presenting their work at the house on very rare occasions. Now that the Royal Ballet are moving their base to Birmingham, and if the ambitious development scheme goes ahead according to plan, the Royal Opera House will be in a position to consolidate and extend its current policy of contracting world class singers, directors and designers to provide internationally rated opera in the centre of London. It is to be hoped that improved technical facilities will allow for a more inventive, exciting style of production, the lack of which has attracted valid criticism of the Royal Opera in recent years.

London International Opera Festival From modest beginnings in 1986, the London International Opera Festival has grown to become an established feature of musical life in London, attracting a new, predominantly young audience to a variety of opera-orientated events in the city each May. The Festival includes performances already scheduled by the major companies at the

Coliseum and Royal Opera House as well as smaller works in a variety of venues all over the city. These may range from rarely performed baroque operas, to world premieres of contemporary works, to a season of opera films, to a selection of pre-performance talks and workshops. Prices are kept deliberately low, with a variety of package deals on offer to encourage the first time opera goer to taste a range of different works.

Los Angeles Although Los Angeles has always featured on the touring schedules of the major companies in America, only in 1986 did the Los Angeles Music Center Opera Association present its first full season, under the administrative direction of Englishman Peter Hemmings. In true Californian style, it was a glittering occasion, located in the Dorothy Chandler Pavilion which seats 3,250 and commanded some of the greatest artistic talent available, with an opening production of *Otello* starring Placido Domingo and Sherrill Milnes. Subsequent productions have included *Tristan and Isolde*, directed by Jonathan Miller, with sets by David Hockney, and *The Mikado* in a co-production with English National Opera. The development of the well-resourced, well-attended company which seems unafraid to take artistic risks will be an exciting one to watch.

Lott, Felicity English soprano. A soprano can have a loyal and enthusiastic following throughout the world, achieve great critical acclaim, and be in demand constantly from companies wishing to make use of her elegant and sensitive performance style. But it is not until she sings at a Royal Wedding that the non-opera public may realize her extraordinary talent! This description fits Felicity Lott, who sang at the wedding of the Duke and Duchess of York at Westminster Abbey in 1986. She has a formidable international reputation as one of Britain's most successful sopranos, particularly in the distinguished roles such as the Marschallin in *Der Rosenkavalier* and the Countess in *The Marriage of Figaro*. She also performs extensively as a concert artist.

Love of Three Oranges, The (Prokofiev) FP 1921. This wonderful fairy tale of a piece lends itself to superbly imaginative and colourful stagings. The music is not immediately tuneful but the action is very intriguing. The work attracted one of the most appropriate sponsorship deals ever when Cointreau supported it at Glyndebourne!

The opera opens as the characters discuss which form of theatrical entertainment should be performed. The decision is finally made by masked intruders who insist on an opera. The Prince is very ill and his life can only be saved if someone makes him laugh. If he dies, the dreadful Clarissa will accede the throne. Two factions emerge – one to bore the Prince to death, the other to make him laugh so he will recover. In the end, much to everyone's amazement, it is the old hag of a witch, Fata Morgana, who makes the prince laugh when she inadvertently topples over. Furious that her evil schemes have been thwarted, she curses the Prince, saying he will fall in love with three oranges. The little devil Farfarello accompanies the Prince and his jester Truffaldino on their quest to the desert to look for the oranges. When they find the oranges, they contain beautiful princesses, two of whom perish of thirst in the desert but the third, Princess Ninetta, survives. Despite the continuing machinations of Fata Morgana, Ninetta and her Prince are married to general rejoicing.

Lucia di Lammermoor (Donizetti) FP 1835. The satisfaction of a performance of this opera depends almost entirely on the skill of the soprano singing Lucia. It is a role with which Dame Joan Sutherland will always be associated, having made an overnight sensation with her performance at Covent Garden in 1957. The role demands of the singer the almost impossible mixture of power of voice with vulnerability of character. The character is a young girl, torn between the lover of her choice and loyalty to her brother, but the music requires the performer to have considerable musical experience in order to convey Lucia's emotions adequately. And what a range of emotions they are – as Dame Joan herself says, 'His (Donizetti's) glorious melodies express every emotion, from happiness to bewilderment, melancholy, despair and, finally, madness.' Do not come to 'Lucia' expecting an evening with any humour in it, but do not be put off if you can take a profoundly dramatic and romantic tale with some of the most wonderful music in all nineteenth-century opera.

The family of Aston have held a long and bitter feud with the family of Ravenswood. Secretly, Lucia Ashton and Edgardo Ravenswood have met and fallen in love and now, as Edgardo prepares to leave for France, have exchanged rings and vows of faithfulness. But Enrico, Lucia's brother, intercepts Edgardo's love letters to Lucia and is furious. He forges a letter which reveals to Lucia that Edgardo has been unfaithful to her. Desolate and persuaded by her brother to save the family name (and his own fortune) Lucia agrees to marry Lord Arturo Bucklaw. As she signs the marriage contract, Edgardo rushes in, (in one of the most exciting entrances in the opera repertoire) returned from France to claim his love moments too late. He hurls his ring at her and declares her faithless. Enrico challenges Edgardo to a duel which Edgardo is determined to lose. But that same night, Lucia is overwhelmed by her plight. In a virtuoso scene she loses all sense and murders Bucklaw before killing herself. The news of her death reaches Edgardo as he waits for his duel with Enrico and he stabs himself.

Lucrezia Borgia (Donizetti) FP 1833. It seems almost unavoidable that the infamous Borgia family who held sway in sixteenth-century Italy should not at some stage find themselves the subject of an opera. Strangely, for all its fascinating subject matter, this is not one of Donizetti's best known operas, although it has some fine music.

Gennaro has fallen in love with a woman at the Venetian Carnival not realizing that she is not only Lucretia Borgia, but also, more important, his mother from whom he was separated at birth. Maffeo Orsini (a man sung by a mezzo-soprano) tells Gennaro that the lady is Lucrezia but knows nothing of the parentage. Gennaro plays down his love in front of his friends, and is imprisoned for taunting the Borgia crest. Lucrezia's husband Alfonso administers poison to Gennaro but Lucrezia, who realizes Gennaro is her son, relieves him with an antidote. But Gennaro turns up unexpectedly at a banquet where his mother has poisoned the wine of all the guests in revenge for insults to her name. Horrified when he realizes this murderous woman is his mother,

he rejects the antidote she offers and dies with his friends.

Ludwig, Christa German soprano who was born in Berlin and taught by her mother, Eugenie Ludwig – a distinguished singer in her own right. Ludwig appears as a guest artist at all the world's major opera houses, but her closest association has been with the Vienna State Opera of which she was made an honorary member in 1981. She has made numerous recordings, solo, oratorio works, and many operas, including *Fidelio*, *Lohenghrin*, and *Norma* with Maria Callas and Franco Corelli.

Luisa Miller (Verdi) FP 1849. A forerunner of *La Traviata* and *Rigoletto*, *Luisa Miller* shows Verdi's ability to write music for individual characters as well as epic, dynastic events.

The Duke Walter has planned an aristocratic marriage with Countess Federica for his son Rodolfo, without realizing that Rodolfo has already fallen in love with the young village girl Luisa Miller, who only knows Rodolfo by the name of Carlo. Count Walter puts his manservant Wurm to the task of winning Luisa from Rodolfo by imprisoning Luisa's father. He will be released only on condition that Luisa writes a letter professing her love for Wurm and her abhorrence of any relationship with Rodolfo. Luisa writes the letter to save her father and vows to leave the village with him, unable to face the distraught Rodolfo who has read the letter. Even when confronted by her former lover, she sticks to what she wrote and it is only when she has shared a cup of poison with Rodolfo, and both lovers are facing death, that she dares reveal the truth of her feelings. Just before he dies, Rodolfo stabs Wurm to death.

Lully, Jean-Baptiste (1632–1687) Italian composer who worked in residence at the Court of Louis XIV, perfecting the art of the stately court opera. He founded the Academie Royale de Musique in 1672, which was to become the Grand Opera, and pursued his own operatic style, known as 'tragedie lyrique' where chorus, ballet and aria were integrated into the plot of an opera, rather than standing as elements on their own. Such a formal style created one side of the 'guerre des bouffons', opposing the lighter, Italian operas which were increasingly gaining favour at this time. Lully's twenty operas still have a dignified elegance about them, but their adherence to such strict conventions prevents them from gaining general popularity today.

Lulu (Berg) FP (Acts one and two) 1937; First full performance 1979. Berg left this work unfinished and act three was only completed by his widow some forty years after his death. It is certainly original, both in its subject matter and style of composition, and will stand as one of the masterpieces of twentieth-century opera. But it is not to be recommended for first timers as the music is abrasive and inaccessible and the subject gruesome.

Lulu is introduced as a prize exhibit in a menagerie. Her husband is Dr Goll (a speaking role) and her lover is Dr Schon. Lulu leaves Schon for the Painter, whose seduction of Lulu provokes Dr Goll to have a heart attack. Having married the Painter, Lulu discovers that Dr Schon is also planning to marry and incites a quarrel with him. Schon tells the Painter of Lulu's lurid past and the Painter commits suicide. Lulu achieves her goal of marrying Schon, but taunts him with an extraordinary variety of explicit flirtations, Schigolch, who may be Lulu's father, the lesbian Geschwitz, the Athlete and Alwa, Schon's son. Schon tries to get Lulu to commit suicide by handing her a gun but she turns it on him. Convicted of murder (which is shown on film as part of the stage action), Lulu escapes, thanks to the help of Geschwitz whose obsession with Lulu prompts her to take Lulu's place on a cholera ward. Teaming up with Alwa and Schigolch, Lulu avoids prostitution in Paris but turns to it in London, using her earnings to support her friends. But one client turns out to be Jack the Ripper who murders both Lulu and Geschwitz.

Lunt, Alfred (1892–1977) The great actor/manager who created a superb duo when teamed with his wife Lynn Fontaine. He directed *Cosi fan Tutte* at the Met in 1951 and returned there in 1966 to produce *La Traviata*.

Luxon, Benjamin English bass who has established a varied and international career in opera, concerts and lieder. Widely known as one of Britain's most popular classical singers, and as a television performer, with his own programmes for Westward TV and BBC2. He has made over eighty recordings with all the major companies and in 1986 was awarded the CBE for his services to music. Although his TV appearances give the impression of a singer who is a master of the popular classics, excelling in roles such as Papageno in *The Magic Flute*, there is more to Luxon than this. His very wide repertoire encompasses such diverse works as *A Child of Our Time*, Britten's *War Requiem*, *Eugene Onegin*, *The Marriage of Figaro* and all roles are convincingly acted and meticulously sung.

Maazel, Lorin American conductor who was the first American to conduct at Bayreuth, leading a performance of *Lohengrin* at the tender age of thirty! He has held two of the most prestigious jobs in European opera, Artistic Director of the Deutsche Oper, Berlin from 1965 to 1971 and Director of the Vienna State Opera from 1982 to 1984. This last was not a happy appointment as Maazel suffered at the hands of a critical Austrian music press. He has since concentrated on opera performances in America and is now Music Director of the Pittsburgh Symphony Orchestra.

Macbeth (Verdi) FP 1847. 'He is one of my very special poets and I have had him in my hands from my earliest youth, and I read and re-read him continually.' Thus Verdi countered accusations that he did not understand Shakespeare when the Paris premiere of *Macbeth* met with extensive criticism. Its unsuccessful reception during Verdi's lifetime continued to grieve the composer but since his death, it has steadily gained in popularity. It now stands not as his most popular work but certainly one which showed early signs of his genius. Rather than take Shakespeare's play literally, he concentrates on three main characters – Lady Macbeth who is cast as the generator of all the troubles, Macbeth himself and the three witches.

As the witches foretold, Macbeth has become Thane of Cawdor and King of Scotland by murdering the present King Duncan at the insistence of Lady Macbeth. She further convinces Macbeth that he must murder Banquo who will otherwise be father to all future kings of Scotland, if the witches are to be believed. Banquo is murdered and his ghost returns to haunt Macbeth, but Banquo's son Fleanzio survives. On the other side of the Scottish border, troops are massing to oppose Macbeth, led by Macduff, Lord of Fife, and Malcolm, son of the murdered King Duncan. The witches return to warn Macbeth of this threat but tell him that no man born of woman can harm him. Believing he will be safe if Banquo's son and Macduff's family are dead, Macbeth undertakes a gruesome series of murders, encouraged by his wife who is suddenly overcome by the horror of what she has instigated and dies. But it is Macduff who poses the threat to Macbeth, as he was not born naturally but 'untimely ripp'd' from his mother's womb. He leads his troops to murder Macbeth and proclaim Malcolm, rightful heir as son of King Duncan, the new leader of Scotland.

McCormack, John (1884–1945) Irish tenor whose career began in London, spread to Europe but really came to fruition in America, where he took up citizenship in 1917. He was criticized because of his uninspiring stage presence and relative lack of acting ability but his voice was supple and elegant and well represented on his numerous recordings.

Mackerras, Sir Charles Australian conductor who was born in America, has performed extensively in England and has held the Music Directorship of Welsh National Opera since 1987, as well as enjoying an active international career! A specialist in the works of Handel and Mozart, his performances of *The Marriage of Figaro* and *Don Giovanni* are particularly notable. He has also done much to champion the performance of the operas of Janacek in Britain (influenced no doubt by his conducting training in Prague). His recordings of three Janacek operas with the Vienna Philharmonic Orchestra have won the coveted 'Operatic Recording of the Year' title from *Gramophone Magazine*. Sir Charles was formerly Musical Director of English National Opera, a post he held for eight years. He conducts regularly with opera companies in Paris and Vienna.

Madam Butterfly (Puccini) FP 1904. A lovely opera for new-comers, desperately sad with marvellous melodies which will all seem familiar even to someone who has never darkened the doors of an opera house. The plot of the opera retains a contemporary interest, as the cultural differences between East and West are fundamentally not greatly changed today. Different productions tend to exploit or play down the political tension which runs through the work, but the popularity of shows such as *Miss Saigon* prove that audiences continue to be intrigued by the relationship between the brash Western man and the mysterious Eastern girl. Western women may find Butterfly frustratingly naive when she professes her blind faith in Pinkerton, but surely such blinkered devotion has its counterparts in Western relationships?

The beautiful Geisha girl, Cio Cio San, has renounced her religion, family and background to marry the American naval officer Lieutenant Pinkerton, in a union arranged by the unscrupulous marriage broker Goro. She is delighted, believing her future is secure. Pinkerton is more casual, making off-hand asides about the real wife he will find when he returns to America. He brushes away the advice of the American Consul, Sharpless, who cautions that, for a Japanese woman, a failed marriage can be the end of everything. After a passionate love duet and one night together, Pinkerton sails to America, promising to return 'when robins nest'. Three years pass and there is still no sight of Pinkerton, but Butterfly is adamant that he will come back to collect her and their young son. Sharpless tries to warn Butterfly that Pinkerton is returning with an American wife but she refuses to accept his word. Pinkerton's ship is sighted approaching the harbour and Butterfly stays up all night to wait for him (as the chorus performs the haunting Humming Chorus). But Sharpless is proved right and Butterfly comes face to face with the new Mrs Kate Pinkerton. With great dignity, Butterfly concedes that her son may go to America if his father will come to collect him. As Pinkerton approaches her house, Butterfly blindfolds the little boy and stabs herself to death, leaving Pinkerton to call out her name as the music dies away and the curtain falls.

Madam Butterfly, by Puccini, Norman Bailey in the role of Sharpless and Janice Cairns in the title role.

The Magic Flute, by Mozart, lends itself to imaginative stagings because of the complexity of its themes. Here Thomas Randle, as Tamino, wrestles with a snake in the opening scene of Nicholas Hytner's ENO production.

Maestro The Italian word for 'master', this term is often used in America to describe a conductor for a performance. Outside America, the word is used more loosely as an adjective describing anyone who is eminent in the field of professional music.

Magic Flute, The (Mozart) FP 1791. One of Mozart's most important operas because it can be taken on various levels. Some see it as a comic opera which Mozart wrote in the first instance to accompany a puppet show, to a libretto by his friend the actor manager Schikaneder. Others read it as a deeper study of good against evil and it is on this level that the opera is proved to have clear associations with the subject of freemasonry. This was a highly topical subject when Mozart and Schikaneder were working on the piece. The rituals of freemasonry were much discussed but technically forbidden by Royal Command in eighteenth-century Vienna and violence had been used to break up masonic lodges. Freemasonry has lost little of its mystery or controversy today and although different producers may choose to understate this theme, there is no doubt that it has contributed to the lasting popularity of the opera.

Prince Tamino has been rescued from a serpent by the Queen of the Night and her Three Ladies and has been shown a picture of the beautiful Princess Pamina, the Queen's daughter. Tamino has instantly fallen in love with Pamina and willingly obeys the Queen when she asks him to save her daughter from Sarastro whom the Queen describes as a wicked captor. With the help of the birdcatcher Papageno and a magic flute, Tamino reaches the temple of Isis where Pamina and Sarastro are living. Tamino and Papageno become separated and Papageno finds Pamina in the clutches of the ghastly slave Monostatos who lusts after her, while Tamino realizes that the Queen's accusations about Sarastro were false and that Sarastro is in fact a wise and good man. Papageno brings Pamina to meet Tamino but before they can start their life together, Sarastro insists that Tamino and Papageno undergo trials of endurance. Tamino succeeds far better in these than Papageno and Sarastro welcomes him to the temple and to the arms of Pamina. Papageno does less well, though in a very endearing fashion,

and is rewarded with the love of the delightful Papagena. There is one final chance for the forces of evil – Monostatos, the Queen of the Night and the Three Ladies to try to wreak revenge but, as the stage is flooded with a clear bright light, it becomes obvious that good has triumphed over evil.

Mahagonny (see Rise and Fall of the City of Mahagonny)

Mahler, Gustav (1860–1911) Mahler is best known today for his compositions, including his magnificent symphonies, though none of the three operas he wrote is still available today. But his contribution to the opera world is considerable because of his extensive conducting ability. His work ranged from the Musical Directorships of the State Operas in Budapest, Hamburg and Vienna to leadership of notable performances at the Metropolitan Opera New York, including the American premieres of *The Bartered Bride* and *The Queen of Spades*. He was appointed Music Director of the New York Philharmonic two years before he died.

Making of the Representative for Planet Eight (P. Glass) FP 1988. Doris Lessing adapted her novel of the same title. The plot tells of the people of Planet Eight, who are forced to adapt to living in a desolate frozen waste as the result of a cosmological accident.

Makropulos Case (Affair) (Janacek) FP 1926. This is one of Janacek's most bizarre operas which can be enormously powerful in performance if the lead singer, playing the role of Emilia Marty, can portray the agony of a woman who is over three hundred years old!

Elena Makropulos appears to have discovered the secret of eternal youth by taking a potion given to her by her scientist father. While she is really over three hundred years old, she has lived her life in various disguises and never appeared to grow older. She is now assuming the role of opera singer Emilia Marty but has a strange foreboding that the potion is beginning to lose its effect as she feels signs of ageing. Desperate to find the papers containing the secret formula to make up more of the liquid, she starts an affair with Jaroslav Prus who can give her access to the information she needs. But she cannot convey any passion to him and he rejects her, accusing her of being cold. She now has the secret of the elixir but realizes that death would be preferable to a life where she can feel no emotion. She hands the paper with the formula written on it to a young couple shortly before her death, but seeing the grief her extended life has brought her, the couple burn the formula to ashes.

Malibran, Maria (1808–1836) Spanish mezzo-soprano. One of Europe's most famous mezzo-sopranos, Malibran was known for her fiery temperament and uneven performing ability which, when at its best, rivalled any other singer of her age. She started her public performances at the age of six and her extended repertoire encompassed all the major roles for her voice including Norma, Fidelio, Rosina and Mary Stuart. She died before reaching thirty as a result of a riding accident complicated by her pregnancy.

Mamelles de Tiresias, Les (Poulenc) FP 1947. After the carnage of the First World War, the authorities in most European countries encouraged their populations to reproduce in large numbers, in order to make up for the massive numbers each country had lost. This totally non-operatic fact provided the basis for an extraordinary opera by Poulenc. It is light, tuneful, outrageous and very popular in modern repertories, partly because of the opportunities it allows an inventive stage designer!

In an imaginary town on the South Coast of France, Therese has become disenchanted with her life and announces that she has become a feminist. To prove her devotion to her new cause, she decides to get rid of her breasts, believing them to be a cause of sin. (This is always staged by the popping of two large balloons, usually coloured and shaped appropriately!) She then drags her unwilling husband into her fight, declaring that he must now assume all the traditionally female roles of housework, child rearing and (amazingly!) child bearing. Belief is totally suspended as her husband takes to his new job with alacrity, producing some forty thousand children in just one day! Therese

(who now calls herself Tiresias) dresses up as a fortune teller and appears to him extolling the virtues of procreation before resuming her original character and relieving her grateful husband of his onerous duties.

Manaus – Teatro Amazonas Perhaps the most eccentric situation for an opera house anywhere in the world, this 650 seat theatre is located in the heart of the Amazon jungle, 1600 miles north-west of Rio and therefore fairly inaccessible! The story of the eccentric Irishman Fitzgerald, who pursued his extraordinary vision to build an opera house in the jungle, has been vividly told in the 1982 film *Fitzcarraldo*, directed by Werner Herzog. Fitzgerald's project was finally completed in 1896 and decorated to perfection thanks to the vast resources of the Brazilian rubber tycoons, but the theatre fell into disrepair when the rubber industry collapsed in 1907. However, in the late 1980s, the Brazilian government injected £7 million into their most unlikely tourist attraction, restoring it to its full glory, opening with a performance of Brazilian music and talking of contracting Pavarotti to perform there. Placido Domingo is signed up to sing Don Jose in *Carmen*, so opera lovers on a South American holiday, who are willing to brave the less than congenial environment, can now look forward to world class opera in the middle of the jungle!

Manon (Massenet) and **Mannon Lescault** (Puccini) Unusually, two operas on this same subject have both maintained their place in the mainstream opera repertoire, each attracting as wide and appreciative an audience as the other. A third opera on the subject, by Auber, has not managed to retain such popularity. The operas by Massenet and Puccini were premiered within ten years of each other and each one was the composer's first opera. They both show the romantic beauty that was to become characteristic of the composers' later works, particularly Puccini who used Manon as a model for his later heroines, Mimi (*La Bohème*) and Madam Butterfly.

Massenet's work, which was premiered in 1884, opens as the beautiful Manon Lescaut is being taken to a convent. On her way, she is intercepted by the Chevallier des Grieux whose advances she cannot resist. The

The Making of the Representative for Planet Eight was adapted from the novel by Doris Lessing, to music composed by Philip Glass. Lesley Garrett (right), as Alsi, and Andrew Shore as Doeg in a co-production between Houston Grand Opera and ENO.

The Marriage of Figaro, by Mozart. Francis Loup (Dr Bartolo), Joan Rodgers (Susannah) and William Shimell (the Count), in Sir Peter Hall's 1989 Glyndebourne production.

couple ride on to Paris where they encounter the fury of the des Grieux family. In order to separate the couple, the Comte des Grieux has his son abducted, and Manon chooses to abandon life in Paris for a luxurious liaison with the Comte de Bretigny. Unable to face life without Manon, des Grieux plans to become a monk but shortly before he takes his vows, Manon pleads with him to return to her and once more the couple are reunited. A gambling quarrel results in both Manon and des Grieux being arrested and, while he is released thanks to the intervention of his father, she is sentenced to deportation and dies in des Grieux's arms on the way to Le Havre.

Puccini's version, first performed in 1893, follows much the same lines before the couple reach Paris, but more is made of Manon's new lover, called Geronte. He represents the wealth and security the young des Grieux cannot provide for Manon, and showers her with jewels and fine clothes. Still drawn to a life with des Grieux, Manon attempts to steal the jewels Geronte has given her in order to finance her new life but in doing so she is arrested and deported to New Orleans. Des Grieux is allowed to sail to America with her and aids her escape on arrival, but she proves too weak to survive in the harsh surroundings and dies before they can reach safety together.

Marking During rehearsals, principal singers may choose to save their voices and not sing out fully, particularly when accompanied by a large orchestra. They will, however, mouth the words, or sing them very quietly, so the rest of the cast can work with them and the conductor can pace the opera correctly – a technique called marking. This arrangement works very satisfactorily for everyone except for those who have attended the dress rehearsal to form an audience and cannot hear a word mouthed by the principal singers.

Maria Stuarda (Donizetti) FP 1834 in a version entitled 'Buondelmonte' because Donizetti's original version had been censored in Naples. First performance of the re-instated version in 1835 in Milan. The German playwright Schiller had created a historically inaccurate but dramatically wonderful moment by placing Mary Stuart in direct confrontation with Elizabeth I in his play *Maria Stuart*. For Donizetti to develop the play into an opera was almost irresistable, given his specialization in powerful female roles, including Anna Bolena and Lucrezia Borgia. Placing two top ranking sopranos on stage in roles of equal calibre is a calculated risk, however, and there are numerous anecdotes about the rivalry on stage being continued into the wings (and beyond), even resulting in physical violence by some accounts. But such tension makes for thrilling performances and Donizetti's music gives every opportunity for each soprano to indulge in magnificent displays of bravura singing.

Maria Stuarda is imprisoned in Fotheringay Castle where the courtiers Leicester and Talbot are concerned about her welfare. Elizabeth I has, up to now, enjoyed a close relationship with Leicester and is infuriated when she realizes his interest in her greatest rival. She agrees to meet with Maria, who is advised by Leicester to act in a conciliatory way towards the Queen. But although the interview begins well, Elizabeth cannot resist provoking Maria, whose dignity and regal bearing infuriate her. Maria's defences are smashed as she hurls insults at Elizabeth including the distinctly un-regal description 'vile bastardess'. Supported by Lord Cecil, Elizabeth slams down Maria's death sentence. As she prepares for death, Maria is comforted only by the loyal Leicester, who has always loved her.

Marriage of Figaro, The (Mozart) FP 1786. From the moment the overture starts, with its very well known melody, you can feel the excitement mounting in Mozart's comic masterpiece and a good production will never let the action lapse from that moment to the magnificent finale at the end of the final act. The interplay between the intriguing characters is closely examined and creates a wholly believable and engrossing situation – if a little confusing by the end when disguise is the order of the day. It is a long work, and therefore should be approached early in an opera-going career but probably not right at the beginning. The music is amongst the finest ever written by Mozart, beautifully expressive as the comedy is never lost but the poignancy of many of the situations is highlighted. The work was based on a play written by Beaumarchais in 1778, first performed in 1784. The play aroused controversy because of the apparent supremacy that the servants Figaro and Susannah gained over their master, the Count, and was banned from performance in France, lest it incite the lower classes to revolt. Such anxiety on the part of the nobility was proved to be justified – within the decade the French Revolution had occurred and the seemingly innocent activities of Figaro and Susannah were put in a far more serious context.

The Count's servant Figaro is planning to marry the Countess's maid, Susannah. Susannah is doing all she can to prevent the Count from exercising his rights as Lord of the Manor to make love to her before Figaro has a chance to marry her. Susannah has also attracted the young servant, Cherubino, with whom she enjoys a delightful platonic relationship. Cherubino is keen to attract the Countess and the Count's ensuing jealousy has prompted him to enlist the cheeky young servant in the army. But Susannah is determined that the Count will not be allowed to flirt with her whilst depriving his wife of any extra-marital fun and plans to show him up for the hypocrite that he is. The Count attempts to enter his wife's locked bedroom, convinced he will find the Countess there with Cherubino, but by the time he has broken down the door, Cherubino has escaped through the window and only Susannah is there, in the closet where the Count hoped to find Cherubino. At Figaro and Susannah's wedding, Susannah takes the opportunity of starting her plot against the Count. She slips him a note offering to meet him in the garden that evening, telling the Countess of her plan but not Figaro. Figaro begins to suspect that Susannah is already unfaithful to him and hides in the garden to see what's happening. That evening in the shadows of the garden, the Countess and Susannah change clothes and the Count begins to flirt passionately and outrageously with a woman he believes is Susannah but is in fact his wife. Figaro, believing he has been wronged, pours his heart out to the 'Countess' until he realizes that she is Susannah and begins to see the funny side. But they continue their flirtation to provoke the Count into thinking that his wife is having an affair with Figaro. Furious,

the Count summons everyone to witness the depravity of his wife, at which point Susannah and the Countess reveal their true identities. The Count has no other choice but to beg his wife for forgiveness.

Martha (Flotow) FP 1847. Light, romantic and full of melodies, *Martha* is extremely influenced by the light French operas written at the time and retained its popularity in Germany though less so internationally. Its plot veers on the sentimental and anyone wishing to be challenged or engrossed may leave a performance unsatisfied.

Lady Harriet, lady in waiting to Queen Anne, is bored with her life at the English court and hatches a plot with her maid Nancy to visit the fair at Richmond. Disguised as peasant girls, with Harriet calling herself Martha and Nancy calling herself Julia, they are taken on by two farmers, Lionel and Plunkett, and taken back to the boys' farms to work as domestic servants. Life at court has taught the girls nothing about housework but everything about charm, and though Harriet and Nancy are hopeless at their domestic chores, the boys fall in love with them and are devastated when they return to court. Harriet realizes that what she felt for Lionel was more than a passing affection but, in the tradition of all good fairy tales, Lionel discovers that he is no mere farmer, but heir to a massive fortune in the north of England. Thus elevated to an acceptable status, he is free to pursue his love of the Lady Harriet.

Martinelli, Giovanni (1885–1969) Italian tenor who came to prominence at the same time as the great Enrico Caruso, with whom he was inevitably compared. Early in his career, Martinelli specialized in the romantic tenor roles, particularly Dick Johnson in *La Fanciulla del West*, and made his debut all over Italy and at Covent Garden. He moved to America in 1913 and rapidly became a key part of the Metropolitan Opera season, both in New York and on tour. As his voice developed, he took on the more heroic roles including Samson and a notable Otello. He was best known for his ability to project his none-too-strong voice right to the back of any auditorium, a technique which helped his career last until he was over eighty.

Marton, Eva Hungarian soprano whose powerful voice and build gave her excellent credentials to sing the demanding soprano roles such as Tosca, Leonora in *Il Trovatore*, Fidelio, and several of the Wagner heroines. Her performances have been seen chiefly in Europe, where she has worked at all the major houses including La Scala, Milan, and Bayreuth. She made her Metropolitan Opera debut in 1976 and sang a notable Brunnhilde in San Francisco in 1985 and has since enjoyed an increasingly appreciative American following.

Mary, Queen of Scotts (Thea Musgrave) FP 1977. Thea Musgrave is remarkable not only for being a composer of contemporary opera whose works have been performed and acclaimed in her lifetime, but for being one of the very few women in the field of opera composition in the twentieth century. This is one of the most popular of her seven operas, an intensely dramatic account of the tale of Mary, Queen of Scots, and her reign over Scotland before her downfall at the hands of Queen Elizabeth I. The opera is written from Mary's personal standpoint, making it a powerful theatrical piece with stirring music to highlight the drama.

Mary Stuart (see Maria Stuarda)

Mascagni, Pietro (1863–1945) Italian composer who wrote sixteen operas in total but only one, written at the start of his career, remains in today's repertory – the phenomenally popular *Cavalleria Rusticana*. This one act piece was an immediate success, won the coveted Sonzogno prize for its composer and initiated a trend for writing 'verisimo' operas. It was a success Mascagni was never able to repeat, despite frequent attempts, the most enduring of which is *L'Amico Fritz*. By the 1930s, Mascagni had become closely allied with the Fascist regime in Italy and wrote an extraordinary opera, *Nerone*, as a tribute to the achievements of Mussolini. The Italian musical establishment shunned Mascagni thereafter, and he died penniless and disgraced.

Mask of Orpheus, The (Birtwistle) FP 1986. One vast orchestra, two conductors, miles of electronic tape, more than a decade in composition – the statistics surrounding Birt-wistle's epic opera are staggering. Using the Orpheus legend as its core, the work interweaves dance, mime, voice and instrument in an extraordinary piece of music theatre which stunned its first audience. The imaginative should seek out a performance.

Masked Ball (see Un Ballo in Maschera)

Masnadieri, I (Verdi) FP 1847. One of Verdi's early operas in which he tried out his ideas for a truly evil character (Francesco), which he was to develop into more enigmatic and complex personalities such as Iago. This is not the most tuneful or attractive of Verdi's operas, although the role of Amalia (written for Jenny Lind) has some wonderfully colourful and impressive arias. The opera has found relatively little support amongst the leading opera houses of today.

Count Massimiliano Moor has two sons, Carlo and his younger brother Francesco. Carlo is in love with Amalia and, whilst at university, has fallen in with a wild crowd of friends. This gives Francesco the opportunity to achieve what he has always longed for – to usurp his older brother's postion, inherit his father's fortune and marry Amalia. Carlo's bad company has enticed him to join a band of robbers and Francesco tells his father that Carlo has died. Grief stricken, the father also collapses, apparently lifeless, and Francesco imprisons him. Rejecting Francesco's advances, Amalia happens to meet Carlo and tells him of Francesco's reign of terror. Carlo's robbers swear to avenge these wrongs and Carlo releases his father from prison but is then torn between his family loyalty and his allegiance to his new life of crime. Rather than involve Amalia still further in his sordid world and refusing to go back on his oath of allegiance to the robbers, Carlo stabs Amalia and gives himself up to the authorities.

Mason, Anne English mezzo-soprano. Student of Royal Academy and National Opera Studio, and prize-winner whilst still a student, Anne Mason's career has followed the pattern of a successful young British singer, starting out with a regional company (Welsh National Opera), then joining Glyndebourne Festival Opera and on to Covent Garden where her roles have included Mercedes on their tour of *Carmen* to the Far East.

Mastersingers, The (see Meistersinger von Nurnburg)

Masterson, Valerie English soprano and one of the most popular singers in British opera, a particular favourite of Gilbert and Sullivan audiences. Her repertoire is extensive, ranging from the roles of Susannah and the Countess in *The Marriage of Figaro* to Anna-who-Steals in the British premiere of Sallinen's opera, *The King Goes Forth to France*. Much of Miss Masterson's work has been with English National Opera where her striking good looks and delicately expressive voice have created memorable performances in *Der Rosenkavalier, Carmen, Xerxes, Rigoletto, The Pearl Fishers* and *La Bohème*, to name only a few. She has sung extensively at the Royal Opera House, Covent Garden, including the world premiere of *We Come to the River* by Hans Werner Henze, and at Glyndebourne and Opera North. She has performed at the Aix en Provence Festival as one of a number of European engagements. In America she has been seen in Chicago Lyric Opera's production of *The Tales of Hoffmann*, as Violetta in *La Traviata* in San Francisco and at the Metropolitan Opera as part of the English National Opera American tour in 1984. She is shortly to be seen in Houston in *Julius Caesar* by Handel.

Matheson-Bruce, Graeme Scottish tenor. Graeme Matheson-Bruce is well established in Europe and appears regularly at Darmstadt. He has taken an increasing interest in the study of the heldentenor repertoire and this is obviously an area of future development for this talented singer. Appearances as Florestan in *Fidelio* and a last minute substitution as Walter von Stolzing in *Die Meistersinger* with English National Opera have received considerable critical acclaim.

Mathias, William Welsh composer who is Head of the Music Department at the University College of Wales in Bangor, North Wales. His first opera, *The Servants* with a libretto by Iris Murdoch, was premiered by Welsh National Opera in 1980. He is perhaps best known for his choral compositions for royal occasions, including *Vivat Regina*, for the Queen's Silver Jubilee, and *Let all the people praise Thee O God*, commissioned for the wedding of the Prince and Princess of Wales in July 1981.

Mathis, Edith Swiss soprano. Mathis has sung at all the major opera houses in Europe and made both her Met and Covent Garden debuts in 1970 as Pamina (*Magic Flute*) and Susanna (*Marriage of Figaro*) respectively. Apart from her operatic work, Edith Mathis is one of the world's most distinguished leider and oratorio singers, and has, since 1967, recorded extensively.

Matrimonio Segreto, Il (Cimarosa) FP 1792. A jolly little piece which its first audience enjoyed so much that they asked for the whole opera to be played once more as an encore. The music is influenced by Mozart and Rossini although not as brilliant as either. The plot is fairly silly as a father tries to marry off his two daughters, one of whom has secretly married someone else, but they all live happily ever after.

Mattila, Karita Karita Mattila won the 1983 Singer of the World competition in Cardiff. She has appeared on the concert platform with conductors such as Abbado, Albrecht, Sir Colin Davis and Sinopoli. She has also given celebrity recitals in Brussels, Geneva, and throughout her native Finland. She made her Covent Garden debut as Fiordiligi in 1986, and her US debut with the Chicago Lyric Opera. She has a full engagements book and an exclusive recording contract with Philips.

Mauceri, John America conductor who has contributed significantly to bringing a new audience to opera through splendid performances of works by Bernstein and Weill, as well as exciting interpretations of the classic works. Currently Music Director at Scottish Opera, Mauceri has worked with opera companies in San Francisco, New York, La Scala, Milan, and at the Royal Opera House, Covent Garden, as well as conducting successful musicals such as the London run of *On Your Toes* starring Tim Flavin and Natalia Makarova.

Maw, Nicholas English composer who studied at the Royal Academy of Music in London from 1955 to 1958, a period when young composers were breaking away from traditional English idioms. He was influenced by this development, although his first major composition *Scenes and Arias*, recognized as one of the most outstanding British works of its decade, is in the traditional style of melodic writing. He wrote his opera *The Rising of the Moon*, described by one critic as 'practically neo-Straussian', during the 1960s. It received international success, particularly in the USA where he has since spent much of his time.

Maxwell Davies, Peter English composer, recognized as one of the most gifted British composers to have emerged since Benjamin Britten and Michael Tippett. Maxwell Davies has written for his own performing ensemble, *The Fires of London* which is made up of virtuoso performers who allowed Maxwell Davies to stretch their instruments to the limits of their capabilities, and also give vent to his vivid musical-dramatic imagination. Works for staged performance include *Eight Songs for a Mad King* although a recent interpretation of this work, by the radical group Opera Factory, was disowned by the composer. His opera *Taverner* was composed over a long period (1962–70) on a theme of much of his work: 'religious honesty. . . serving or traducing spiritual (and artistic) impulse'.

Maxwell Davies goes to Hoy, a virtually uninhabited island in the Orkneys off the north coast of Scotland, to compose. The influence of these surroundings is noticeable in many of his works, including the children's opera *Cinderella* and the adult chamber opera *The Lighthouse*, based on a true story from the Outer Hebrides. Many of his recent works have had their first performance at the St Magnus Festival in Orkney which he founded in 1977. In 1988 he was commissioned by Darmstadt for a new opera *Resurrection*.

Mazeppa (Tchaikovsky) FP 1884. The most nationalistic of Tchaikovsky's operas, this work is set in the Ukraine in the early eighteenth century. Its plot has a strange contemporary relevance, dealing with one man's quest to devolve the Ukraine from the rule of the Tsar and set up a separate state. The opera is rarely performed, particularly when compared with *The Queen of Spades* or *Eugene Onegin*, but has some dramatic music

and an engaging (if somewhat gruesome) story line. It was given a notoriously controversial production by English National Opera in 1985, which included a massacre by chainsaw.

The Cozack leader Mazeppa has plans to overthrow the Tzar and proclaim himself leader of the Ukraine. His chief obstacle in the quest is the General Kochubey, his erstwhile colleague who also happens to be Mazeppa's father-in-law. Seeing no alternative but to murder Kochubey, Mazeppa carries out the bloody deed but in doing so causes Maria (his wife and Kochubey's daughter) to lose her senses.

McEwen, Terry Manager of the San Francisco Opera House, 1982–89, having started his music career in Europe as a manager for Decca Records. McEwen arrived at San Francisco determined to raise the status of the house to one of the top six in the world. In the opinion of many, he achieved this with superb new productions, including a whole new Ring Cycle which was internationally acclaimed. He also developed the San Francisco Opera Center to encourage new, young talent and championed the work of Sir John Pritchard at the Opera, despite negative press reaction. His tenure at San Francisco was characterized by his immense and powerful personality taking an active role in all parts of the opera organization, bringing the house to international prominence and, largely through his individual efforts, keeping it there.

McIntyre, Donald New Zealand bass who started his career as a school teacher. He made his Covent Garden debut in 1967 and has since enjoyed a long association with the Royal Opera House in London. Since making his Bayreuth debut in 1967 he has returned there many times, most notably as Wotan in the centenary production of The Ring which was both recorded and televised. In 1989 he sang Prospero in the British premiere of Berio's *Un Re In Ascolto* at Covent Garden and his performance received outstanding reviews (although the opera and production had a mixed reception, as contemporary operas invariably do!).

McLaughlin, Marie Scottish soprano. One of the brightest young stars at the Royal

Opera House for whom she has performed almost all her major roles for her voice including Susanna, Zerlina, Despina and Micaela, McLaughlin is now in demand internationally although she remains determinedly Scottish. Vivacious personality, attractive appearance and stage manner, and a radiant voice, make her a popular choice for television and video performances.

Mefistofele (Boito) FP 1868. Best known for his libretti to operas by Verdi, Boito did compose one grand opera of his own. It is now rarely performed in Europe, though it is more popular in America and gives a starring role to a bass singer of exceptional quality. The work attempts to cover more than the usual story of Faust and Margherita by developing the second part of Goethe's play. Thus the opera has a straightforward story but also deals with the philosophical arguments which inspired Goethe, bringing the whole work to a great, and somewhat tedious, length of four acts with a substantial prologue and epilogue. This is a pity because it deprives modern audiences of what Kobbé describes as 'one of the most beautiful scores which has come out of Italy'.

The core of the plot mirrors Goethe's story, as Faust sells his soul to Mefistofele and comes to love Margherita who gives birth to their child and dies in prison, abandoned by Faust. But around this is written the bet between hell and heaven that Mefistofele can win Faust's soul and, after Margherita's death, see Faust with Elena (representing Helen of Troy) before he dies an old and disillusioned man.

Mehta, Zubin Indian conductor who studied in Vienna and now holds several prestigious conducting posts around the world, including Directorship of the Israeli Philharmonic and the New York Philharmonic. He has conducted operas at the Royal Opera House, La Scala, Milan, Vienna, Florence and Salzburg and has received particular accolades from Italy and India for the contribution he has made to music internationally.

Meier, Johanna American soprano who has established a loyal following at the Metropolitan Opera, New York, for her admirable performances of Ariadne auf Naxos, Ellen Orford in *Peter Grimes*, The Marschallin in *Der Rosenkavalier* and Wagnerian roles in which she is particularly adept. She has also been seen at Bayreuth, where she made her debut in 1981 in the role of Isolde.

Meilhac, Henri (1831–1897) French librettist who wrote the words for *Carmen* by Bizet, *Manon* by Massenet, and five of Offenbach's operettas. He was also a playwright. His work *L'Attache d'Ambassade* inspired Lehar to write *The Merry Widow* and his play *Le Reveillon* was Johann Strauss's basis for *Die Fledermaus*.

Meistersinger von Nurnberg, Die (Wagner) FP 1868. Probably the most popular choice for someone who wants to be introduced to the works of Wagner, *Die Meistersinger* has some marvellous melodies and an amusing, engaging plot. It is certainly the most accessible of Wagner's works, dealing with real life rather than heroic myths and legends. The overture and 'Prize Song' will be very well known even to first timers.

The beautiful Eva, daughter of the local goldsmith, Pogner, is to be married to the winner of the song contest to be held in Nuremberg. The contest has attracted great attention as nearly every man in the city appears to be in love with Eva, including the town clerk Beckmesser and the cobbler Hans Sachs. But Eva has already been attracted by a mysterious newcomer, the knight, Walther von Stolzing, who has resolved to enter the competition as well. The contest has some extraordinarily complicated rules which David, assistant to Hans Sachs, explains to Walter who attempts his first song. Beckmesser does not hesitate to be extremely critical, seeing this young man as a serious rival. But the more sanguine Hans Sachs realizes that Walther has all the commitment and passion of a true singer, if not yet the experience. That night, Beckmesser comes to sing his song to the girl he believes to be Eva. In fact 'Eva' is the nurse Magdalene in disguise, who has released Eva to elope with Walther. But Sachs criticizes Beckmesser's efforts so furiously that a fight breaks out and the young couple are prevented from escaping. Denying his own love, Sachs helps Walther construct a song of such beauty that it cannot fail to win the contest, despite Beckmesser's continued attempts, so Walther and Eva are finally united.

Melba, Dame Nellie (1861–1931) Australian soprano who still takes her place amongst the best singers in the world. Melba had everything – exquisite tone, an extraordinary range, a beautifully smooth and agile voice matched by sufficient acting ability to convey a range of roles from the pathetic Mimi in *La Bohème* to the tortured Lucia de Lammermoor. She also had something of the prima donna temperament and ruled over every performance she took part in with a dictatorial manner that defied contradiction, particularly during her long tenure at Covent Garden. She sang at every major opera house, creating the first Mimi for American audiences at the Metropolitan Opera in 1900, and kept her superb voice until she was well over sixty. Later generations remember her not only through the excellent recordings she made but also because of her particular tastes in food. She gave her name to the thin crispy toast, and the sumptuous dessert with peaches, raspberries and ice cream which the chef of the Savoy Grill is said to have concocted for her, using the only left-overs he could find when she arrived for dinner unexpectedly.

Melchior, Lauritz (1890–1973) Danish tenor who made the transition from his early days as a baritone thanks to the encouragement of his teacher and went on to pursue a highly successful career as 'the world's greatest heldentenor' – a description used of him by many during his lifetime and afterwards. His formative years were spent learning with a number of teachers, paid for by novelist Hugh Walpole who had heard him sing in a Promenade Concert in London and been greatly impressed. He was acknowledged as the best in this field for over quarter of a century, with a brilliantly rich voice supported by a masterful stage presence. It seemed as if the familiarity he achieved with some roles never prevented him from singing each one with the enthusiasm of a premiere performance – an impressive feat when you realize that he sang Tristan over two hundred times! He did sing roles other than Wagner, notably Samson and

Otello, but it was in the heroic Wagner roles that he seemed most comfortable and consequently most impressive. After his retirement from the stage, and as a complete contrast, he made a number of films and proved he was equally at home with light entertainment as well as Wagnerian grandeur.

Menotti, Gian-Carlo Italian composer who maximized the increasing popularity of television to bring a new audience to opera, as well as developing plots which were grimly realistic. The success of his first opera *Amelia al Ballo* prompted NBC to commission him to write *The Old Maid and The Thief* for radio. His serious opera, *The Medium*, showed how powerful and macabre his writing could be, but also how versatile he was, as it was paired with the delightful comic opera *The Telephone*. There was an equal difference between his two best known works written in the early 1950s. *The Consul*, written in 1950, is a sinister indictment of a bureaucracy-ridden, totalitarian regime, whereas *Amahl and the Night Visitors*, commissioned for television in 1951, is a charming story, ideal for children at Christmas. His interest in writing for 'children and those who like children' has also produced the marvellous science fiction opera *Help, Help, the Gobolinks!* and his determination to bring opera to as wide an audience as possible led him to create the Spoleto Festival in 1958, where he still maintains an active role as producer. Menotti is now established as one of this century's leading opera composers whose appeal is extensive thanks to his ability to place operas firmly in the world of his audience.

Merrill, Robert American lyric baritone whose career was based primarily at the Metropolitan Opera in New York, with occasional forays to San Francisco and numerous broadcasts on television and radio. He specialized in the older, more complex roles in the baritone repertoire: Germont in *La Traviata*, Rigoletto, Amonasro in *Aida*, Iago in *Otello* and Scarpia in *Tosca*. His excellent voice and impressive stage presence earned him a loyal and devoted following, most apparent in America and not insubstantial in Europe.

Merry Widow, The (Lehar) FP 1905. A delightful, glittering encounter with high society in late nineteenth-century Paris, full of marvellous melodies with just enough plot to stop it descending into sheer sentimentality. A good choice for an undemanding evening at the theatre.

The widow of the title is Hanna Glawari whose banker husband has died leaving her a substantial fortune. If, however, she chooses to remarry someone who does not hail from her native district of Pontevedro, then the Pontevedrian finances will be thrown into complete turmoil. Her amorous affairs therefore become a matter of national importance, provoking the advice of the Ambassador, Baron Zeta. His attache is the dashingly handsome Count Danilo who is ordered, for the good of the state, to woo Hanna Glawari. Not so difficult, until it emerges that Hanna and Danilo had been lovers in the past and, since she rejected him, he has sworn never again to tell her that he loves her. But Hanna is too smart for him, and in a series of intrigues set against numerous other flirtations, she wins him back and the treasury of Pontevedro is once more secure.

Merry Wives of Windsor, The (Nicolai) FP 1848. Closely based on Shakespeare's play of the same name, this opera retained its popularity in Germany even after the substantial competition posed by *Falstaff*. It has not, however, been anything like so popular outside Germany, in spite of a sparkling overture and many moments of real comedy. The plot is exactly the same as *Falstaff* but the names have been altered. The 'merry wives' are Frau Fluth and Frau Reich, with Frau Fluth taking the more prominent role, corresponding with Mistress Ford. Herr Fluth is her extremely jealous husband and their daughter is called Anne. Anne's choice of husband is called Fenton, as in Verdi's opera, but her father wishes her to marry a man named Slender. The only notable change in the action is that Falstaff is smuggled out of Frau Fluth's home disguised as an old woman, rather than in the celebrated laundry basket.

Messaien, Oliver French composer whose only opera *St Francoise D'Assise* has not found the international acclaim of his other works. Influenced by various forces, from Hindu mysticism to the sounds of nature, Messaien's music is challenging to a newcomer, but merits further study.

Metropolitan Opera House (see New York)

Meyerbeer, Giacomo (1791–1864) German composer who left his wealthy Jewish upbringing to gain entry to the salons of Paris, thanks to his success with one of his earliest operas *Il Crociata in Egitto*. In Paris, he met the librettist Scribe and worked with him on several immensely successful grand operas, notably *Robert le Diable* (1831) and *Les Huguenots* (1836). They continued to work together but their relationship became increasingly fraught as Meyerbeer insisted on revising his music constantly, making the overall result sound self conscious and studied. With the substantial back up of the Paris Opera House, and plenty of diversions such as full scale ballets, massive choruses, vast sets and impressive technical effects, this less-than-wonderful music could be ignored. But with the rise of geniuses such as Verdi and Puccini, whose music came straight from the heart and did not rely on any other effects, Meyerbeer's popularity began to diminish.

Mezzo-soprano The range of voice for female singers which lies between soprano and contralto is called mezzo soprano. Before this category developed in the nineteenth century, sopranos or contraltos would have sung roles now assigned to mezzos, whose range sits most comfortably between the A below middle C to the B flat above the treble stave. The mezzo soprano's tone is usually darker than a top soprano though not as low as a contralto.

Midsummer Marriage, A (Michael Tippett) FP 1955. This is the most frequently performed of all Michael Tippett's operas and serves as a good introduction to the work of this century's leading living opera composer. It combines real life with a spiritual influence, heavy with symbolism which has earned the opera a reputation for obscurity. But the success of a performance can rely very heavily on the style of production rather than the undoubted beauty of the music. It is possible to give the opera such a highly intellectual staging that the basic message – hope for the future from the young people who are at the centre of the cast – is lost.

Mark and Jenifer are to be married on

A Midsummer Night's Dream, by Benjamin Britten. The role of Oberon, King of the Fairies, was the first written specifically for counter-tenor, sung here by Michael Chance. Tytania is sung by Elizabeth Gale.

The Mikado, by Gilbert and Sullivan, in Jonathan Miller's ENO production. Left to right: Maria Bovino, Richard van Allan, Ethna Robinson and Susan Bullock.

Midsummer's Day but moments before the marriage is due to begin, Jenifer announces that she does not feel ready and must gain a greater knowledge of herself before she can commit herself to one man. Jenifer and Mark are transported to a mysterious woodland clearing and separately, they enter a cave. They encounter King Fisher who is Jenifer's father, and the young lovers Bella, a secretary, and Jack. Through a series of Ritual Dances and the eventual death of her father, Jenifer achieves the understanding she seeks and emerges to marry Mark in a final scene of great joy and exhilaration.

Midsummer Night's Dream, A (Benjamin Britten) FP 1960. Britten's opera is an exact telling of the Shakespeare play but is notable as an opera for several reasons. Britten was at the height of his descriptive powers when he wrote the music, for a small chamber orchestra, to conjure up the fairy glen, with its King and Queen. He compares this idyll with the earthly lovers and complements it with marvellous characterizations of the fairies and the mechanicals. The part of Oberon, King of the Fairies was the first role written specifically for a counter-tenor, and the music written for this role provides a wonderfully evocative sense of the supernatural. Finally, Britten introduced a parody of grand opera when writing the play scene for Pyramus and Thisbe, going as far as creating a full blown 'mad scene' for Flute.

Migenes-Johnson, Julia American soprano whose startling good looks and sensuous acting ability led her first to Broadway where she enjoyed a successful early career. She made the transition to opera by singing the role of Maria in Bernstein's *West Side Story* for the Vienna Volksoper and has since proved that she can put her characteristic flair into the more serious operatic roles, particularly those of the contemporary operas. An impressive Lulu and Musetta in *La Bohème*, Migenes-Johnson became an international name when she starred in Franco Rosi's 1984 film of *Carmen* – a role for which she is ideally suited. She now enjoys an active television career as well as performing in operas all over the world.

Milan, La Scala There are actually four other theatres that have presented opera in Milan, hosting among them such notable premieres as *I Pagliacci, L'Elisir d'Amore* by Donizetti, Bellini's works *Anna Bolena* and *La Sonnambula* and Cilea's *Adriana Lecouvreur*. But everyone knows Milan for one of the world's greatest opera houses – La Scala, which was built on the site of a church named Santa Maria della Scala and opened in 1778. Throughout the centuries it has developed its reputation for international excellence, attracting the world's greatest singers, composers and conductors and staging premieres such as *Norma, Falstaff* and *Turandot* and concentrating heavily on the 'core' Italian repertory of Verdi, Rossini, Bellini and Donizetti. Several of the world's finest musicians are indelibly linked with the house – the composer Verdi whose late works *Otello* and *Falstaff* were premiered at the theatre; the conductor Toscanini who was Artistic Director from 1898 to 1903, again from 1906 to 1908 and finally from 1918 to 1929; the producer Luigi Visconti and the singer Maria Callas who was a constant and exciting feature of productions in the theatre during the 1950s.

The theatre was entirely re-built after the Second World War and now boasts one of the most sumptuous and elegant interiors of any opera house. But like other theatres of its size and stature, it has attracted criticism for its phenomenally high seat prices, its espousal of 'sponsorizzazione' and the attendant audience of industrialists and noveau riche who have deposed Milan's fading aristocracy in the stalls and boxes of the theatre. Its questionable artistic standards are now under the control of Riccardo Muti, not always satisfying La Scala's most critical and vociferous audience, the 'loggionisti', who pack the gallery at every performance.

Miles, Alastair English bass, thought to be one of the most exciting young singing talents to have emerged in Great Britain in recent years. He made his professional debut in 1985, and in 1986, aged only 25, won the Kathleen Ferrier prize. Since then he has appeared with all the national opera companies in Britain and with Vancouver Opera. Miles also pursues a busy and successful concert career, performing most of the bass and bass/baritone concert repertoire, and has very exciting future prospects as a singer of international repute.

Miller, Dr Jonathan There can be very few people reading this book who have not already come across Jonathan Miller in one of his many guises: comedian, actor, stage director, neurologist, author, writer, television presenter and personality, and opera director to name but a few. Miller trained as a doctor at Cambridge University where he became involved in the entertainment business through the acclaimed student drama society known as The Footlights. Although over the years he has been tempted back to medicine on a number of occasions, these flirtations with science have been short lived and he has always returned to the theatre.

As one would expect from someone interested in everything from Byzantine art to brain surgery, Miller's opera productions are extraordinarily inventive, and are most successful when he has a team of singers who are also able to act convincingly and put his many ideas into action. Two notable successes have been with English National Opera – the 1950 style New York Mafioso production of Verdi's *Rigoletto*, and the 1930 style old movie treatment of *The Mikado*, designed by Stefanos Lazaridis. Both of these stagings have attracted a wide audience through their showings on British television and have been seen in Houston and Los Angeles.

Milnes, Sherrill American baritone. Recognized throughout the world as possessing one of the most dramatic and thrilling voices now to be heard (described by one critic as 'a he-man voice'), the great American baritone Sherrill Milnes sings in every important opera house in the world, with virtually every orchestra, and in solo recitals in the major music centres. He gives masterclasses, including a series at the Juilliard School in New York, and in recent years has also taken up conducting. He is the leading baritone at the Metropolitan Opera and so tends to sing more in the USA than Europe, although he guests regularly at La Scala, Covent Garden, and with the Vienna State Opera.

Minimalist music (see Glass, Philip)

Minton, Yvonne Australian mezzo-soprano. Yvonne Minton came to England from Australia in 1961. She settled in London and was taken on at Covent Garden, where amongst her many successful roles she has sung Oktavian, Sextus, Dido (*Les Troyens*) Kundry, Brangane and Fricka. She guests at the Met in New York and regularly at Chicago Lyric Opera. She performs as a concert artist almost as much as an opera singer and this is reflected in her varied recording career. Her recordings include *Parsifal*, *La Clemenza di Tito*, Elgar's *The Dream of Gerontius* and *Sea Pictures*.

Mireille (Gounod) FP 1864. One of Gounod's most romantic operas which has two different endings. It concerns the young Mireille whose father, Maitre Ramon, wishes her to marry the bull-keeper Ourrias. But Mireille is in love with Vincent and together they have found a far away secret place where they agree to meet if ever life becomes unbearable. In the first ending, Ourrias succeeds in killing Vincent but then drowns himself and the desperate Mireille dies of exhaustion before reaching her sanctuary. In the second, happy ending, Vincent evades Ourrias's murder and finds Mireille at their sanctuary where her father repents and agrees to the marriage.

Miserables, Les (Claude Michel Schonberg) FP 1985. A controversial choice for inclusion in a book about opera but this phenomenally successful musical has many elements of opera about it. It is ironic how many of the audience who fight to get a ticket for 'Les Mis' (or 'The Glums' as it is affectionately known!) would never dream of trying a 'proper opera' but find over three hours of modern French composition exhilarating and engrossing. The composer readily admits to employing a real operatic structure when writing music for Alain Boubil's text which is closely based on Victor Hugo's epic novel. In doing so, he has created a stepping stone to opera, bringing a huge audience to enjoy a work with no talking, very few jokes, very little colour, very long and which, compared to *La Bohème* or *Madam Butterfly*, rates as a heavier work!

Model Before a set design reaches the stage, but after the concept has been tried out on paper, it has to be seen in three dimensions. This crucial part of the design process is called the model which is usually to the scale of 1:25 and looks to the untrained eye like a fascinating miniature of the set. Every aspect of the design will be reproduced on the model in a reduced size, so that the production team can see how backdrops will be raised and lowered, how particular effects will fit in with the action, whether trap doors may be used and so on. But most importantly, it is at this stage that the management and production team will decide whether the concept can work financially, what the materials will cost, whether saving money on one aspect could lead to problems with another or perhaps create safety difficulties. This consultation process is crucial because once the model has been accepted by everyone, money is spent on constructing the set, by which time it is too late, both financially and practically, to realize a potentially disastrous problem has been overlooked.

Monnaie, La (see Brussels)

Montague, Diana English mezzo-soprano with a highly successful international career. Diana Montague tends to be associated with the Mozart and earlier repertoire, and whilst it is true that her reputation has been built on roles like Cheubino, Zerlina and Prosperina, she has also had great success singing Wagner (Wellgunde and Siegrune in Solti's Ring Cycle at Bayreuth) and she has been engaged to sing Nicklaus and The Fox in a new production of *The Cunning Little Vixen* at Covent Garden.

Monteverdi, Claudio (1567–1643) Italian composer who is credited with being the first composer of operas as we know the term today; a coherent story underpinned by beautiful music which describes the characters and their plights. Nearly four hundred years after his first opera, *La Favola d'Orfeo*, appeared in 1607, three of his operas are still regularly performed in the world's major opera houses. New productions and the pioneering work of specialists such as John Elliott Gardner and the London-based Monteverdi Choir have proved that Monteverdi operas do not need to be enjoyed only by a musical elite. *Orfeo, Il Ritorno d'Ulisse in Patria* and *L'Incoronazione di Poppea* are characteristic of a composer who was profoundly influenced by the magnificence and elegance of music in the Italian church but also excited by the opening of the first public opera

houses (in Venice in 1637), and created music which suited both societies. His composing career was spent in Venice, where he worked as Director of Music at St Mark's and eventually took holy orders there.

Moscow, The Bolshoi Theatre Moscow's leading opera company, renowned for its superb chorus and lavish productions, is housed in the famous Bolshoi Theatre which was opened in 1825. As a complement to the classics presented by the main house, Stanislavsky opened a smaller studio theatre in 1928, designed for the production of more radical works where the acting was as crucial a part of the performance as the singing.

Moses and Aron (Schoenberg) FP 1954 on Hamburg Radio. Unfinished opera by Schoenberg which was not fully staged until 1957, using only the first two acts. Occasionally the third act is included with the words spoken rather than sung with accompanying music by the composer. The role of Moses is written for a 'sprechtstimme' – a method of communication which comes between singing and speech and does not follow any particular pitch.

Moses is fully aware of the might of his God but cannot communicate it to his people. He needs to use his brother Aron as his mouthpiece. Aron goes on to prove God's power by demonstrating miracles and bringing the people to believe more fervently. But during Moses's absence in the wilderness, the Jewish people begin to question their faith and Aron allows them to build a golden calf for them to worship. Furious at this idolatory, Moses crushes the calf and reviles Aron for misleading the people. In the third act, Aron is arrested and left to the judgment of God. He falls dead and Moses comforts the Jews.

Moses in Egypt (Rossini) FP 1818. A complete departure from works such as *The Barber of Seville* or *La Cenerentola*, Rossini proved with this work that he was capable of writing a grand historical drama with superb choruses and powerful characters. The Prayer from this opera was sung at Rossini's funeral to such effect that the mourners demanded an encore!

There are two versions of the opera but the central plot remains the same. It is based on the Biblical story of Moses freeing his people from the Egyptians by leading them across the Red Sea, counterpointed by the more personal story of the love between Amanophis, son the Egyptian Pharoah and Anais, daughter of Moses's sister Miriam.

Moshinsky, Elijah Australian director who now works extensively in Europe and America, notably at Covent Garden where he is an Associate Producer. His stagings are rarely radical but make clever and exciting use of large crowds as well as heightening the drama of the individual characters. Notable productions include *Peter Grimes* and *The Rake's Progress* for Covent Garden, *The Bartered Bride* for English National Opera and *Un Ballo in Maschera* for the Metropolitan Opera.

Mozart, Wolfgang Amadeus (1756–1791) Austrian composer and child prodigy who became one of the world's greatest composers, particularly of opera where many consider him to be unsurpassed. Profoundly influenced by his father, he was taken on a tour of Europe as a young boy and returned to Vienna inspired by the enormous musical range he had encountered in Germany, France and Britain. By the age of twenty, he had composed five operas and a songspiel which, though surpassed by his later works, show the assured confidence of a young musician whose genius was never in doubt. His first major work was *Idomeneo*, written as a commission from the Opera House at Munich. Having married Constanze Webber, he settled in Vienna and wrote *Die Entfuhrung aus dem Serail* and *The Marriage of Figaro*, now both established masterpieces but then barely acclaimed and unable to pay off the composer's considerable debts. But 'Figaro' was far better received in Prague and the theatre there saved Mozart from certain poverty by commissioning his next opera *Don Giovanni* (1787). In the same year, Mozart was appointed composer to the Viennese Court but just as his prospects began to look brighter, Leopold II became Emperor of Austria. Not known for his musical interest, it was he who damned the premiere of *Cosi fan Tutte* in 1790 by announcing that it had 'too many notes'. By 1791, Mozart was gravely ill through malnutrition and overwork. His final two operas

were *La Clemenza di Tito*, written to celebrate Leopold's coronation as King of Bavaria and *The Magic Flute*, in collaboration with the actor manager Schikaneder – again recognized as amongst his best work today but then insufficiently popular to save Mozart from an ignominious pauper's death that same year.

Peter Shaffer's play *Amadeus* has influenced the popular perception of Mozart as little more than a child, reckless and exuberant with undoubted genius but unable to save himself from his own wild personality. Numerous academic studies exist which both support and deny this theory and his true character will remain one of the greatest enigmas in the history of music. What no-one can deny, however, is the brilliance of his operatic writing, the enduring popularity of his work and the flexibility it affords for today's opera producers. The operas of Mozart could serve as a perfect introduction to the whole world of opera, beginning with the dramatic *Don Giovanni*, through the longer but charming *Marriage of Figaro*, the enticing *Magic Flute*, more reflective *Cosi fan Tutte* and *Entfuhrung aus dem Serail* and ending with the most challenging *Idomeneo* and *Clemenza di Tito*. If a new opera goer limits his or her knowledge to these works alone, the experience will surely be a great one.

Muette de Portici, La (Auber) FP 1828. This tale of a deaf and dumb girl and her brother is considered by many to be a fairly insubstantial opera in the early Romantic style. It is notable because it sparked off the Belgian Revolution of 1830, firing the people with anger against their oppressors as mirrored in the plot.

Naples in the late seventeenth century was under the control of Spain. The mute girl Fenela (a role taken by a dancer) has been betrayed by Alfonse, son of the Spanish Viceroy, which has caused great fury amongst Fenela's brother Masaniello and his supporters. They rise up against the Spaniards but Masaniello is prompted to abandon his revolutionary tactics and come to the aid of Alfonse. He helps Alfonse's sister Elvire to escape with her brother and returns to face the wrath of his fellow Neapolitans who murder Masaniello. Unable to face life without her brother, Fenela kills herself.

Murphy, Suzanne Irish soprano who studied in Dublin, and is particularly known for her interpretation of the major roles of Bellini, Verdi and Donizetti. She joined Welsh National Opera from college and has sung with all British national opera companies. In 1987 she made a triumphant debut at the Vienna Staatsoper as Elektra in a new production of *Idomeneo*, conducted by Nicholas Harnoncourt.

Murray, Anne English soprano who has established a formidable reputation as one of Britain's most sought after singers. Her performances are notable for their freshness and frankness, and a beautifully adaptable technique which gives her the freedom to concentrate on the role rather than on the notes. For example she has sung both Mozart, and in contrast, Richard Strauss with equal ease. She is married to the tenor Philip Langridge, but the couple rarely perform together, as they tend to concentrate on different areas of repertoire. They did appear as the title roles of Beatrice and Benedict at the recent production of the Berlioz opera for ENO.

Musgrave, Thea Scottish composer who studied with Nadia Boulanger in Paris. Her seven operas are immensely theatrical and could be of interest to newcomers. The most notable are *Mary, Queen of Scots* and *Harriet, the Woman called Moses*.

Musicals Today, the division between operas and musicals is becoming increasingly blurred as subsidized opera companies in Britain are encouraged to maximize revenue with shows such as *Pacific Overtures* and *Showboat*, while Broadway and the West End have standing room only for three hour, sung extravaganzas based on classic French novels. Traditionally, musicals followed a set form of songs which introduced characters, strung together with a fairly facile dialogue, more songs which furthered the action (usually romantic) between characters, and large set piece numbers to capture the audience's attention lest it has wandered during the solo items. The subject matter of contemporary musicals is increasingly serious and certainly departs from the usual 'boy-meets-girl' formula, frequently with little or no dialogue or humour. But

musicals are currently enjoying unprecedented popularity, no doubt due to the brilliance of composers as diverse as Stephen Sondheim and Andrew Lloyd Webber. The theatrical community, frequently sceptical about anything that can be classed as 'sheer entertainment' has come to respect this new type of musical which can create a performance as serious or demanding as any opera. Perhaps the one major area of difference between opera and musicals lies outside the theatre, out of the control of composers and singers. For with the rise of the 'new musical' has come a type of theatrical promotion which no opera company is in a position to undertake. The 'hype' that now surrounds the mega-musical, as tickets are made scarce as gold dust, every possible merchandising opportunity exploited and every participant elevated to superstar status, calls for marketing budgets of commercial proportions, creating an image of theatre which is light years away from the reality.

Mussorgsky, Modest (1839–1881) Russian composer whose rebellious lifestyle inspired him to create three operas with particularly Russian characteristics, full of fire and individuality – *Boris Godunov* (1874), *Khovanshchina* and *Sorochintsy Fair*. The last two were started in the early 1870s but remained unfinished at the time of his death. Mussorgsky began his career in the Imperial Guard, although he had experimented with composition while at the military school in St Petersburg. There he had met the composer Balakirev who was to exert a great influence on him when he finally abandoned the military life. He never had any formal musical training and his inspiration was constantly dashed by his continuing addiction to alcohol, thus leaving an uneven legacy of compositions. But a work of the stature and power of *Boris Godunov* proves that, had he been able to organize and control his life without losing his inspiration to compose, he would have ranked amongst the greatest of Russian composers.

Muti, Riccardo Italian conductor who now holds one of the most prestigious jobs in international opera – Music Director of La Scala, Milan. Muti developed his impressive reputation over eleven years at the Maggio

Musicale in Florence which he brought to world prominence through notable performances including *L'Africaine* by Meyerbeer and *Guillaume Tell* by Rossini. At the same time, Muti was conducting all over the world, acquiring posts such as Principal Conductor and later Music Director of the Philharmonia Orchestra in London and Music Director of the Philadelphia Orchestra in America, a job he still holds. Dedicated, detailed and highly accomplished, Muti's opera performances are exciting and revealing, even of the best known works.

Muzio, Claudia (1889–1936) Italian soprano who came from a theatrical background to become one of the most popular sopranos of the interwar years, both in Europe and in North and South America. She specialized in the Italian repertory, creating notable performances of Santuzza (*Cavalleria Rusticana*) Violetta (*La Traviata*) and Mimi (*La Bohème*). When the new War Memorial Opera House was opened in San Francisco in 1932, she was invited to sing in the inaugural production of *Tosca*. Her popularity rested on her ability to convey any emotion with passionate intensity, and was therefore particularly beloved of the Italians. She was even able to engross audiences at the end of her life when her singing ability had practically disappeared but her acting prowess was as strong as ever.

Nabucco (Verdi) FP 1842. The success of a performance of *Nabucco* depends very largely on the strength of the chorus, who have some of Verdi's most potent and emotive choral writing to perform. It is often said that 'Va Pensiero' (The Chorus of the Hebrew Slaves) is Italy's unofficial national anthem.

Fenena, daughter of the victorious Babylonian leader, Nabucco, is being held captive by the Hebrew people, who have just lost the war against Nabucco's troops, Fenena has fallen in love with the Hebrew, Ismaele, who allows her to escape back to her father and repulses the advances of Fenena's sister Abigaille, who is also in love with Ismaele. Fenena is left in charge of the Hebrew people while Nabucco returns to the battle front. This incites Abigaille's jealousy further, seeing Fenena with both the power and the lover she wants – particularly when Abigaille

discovers that Fenena is the daughter of slaves and not Nabucco's daughter at all. The struggle between Fenena and Abigaille intensifies as the rumour spreads that Nabucco has been killed in battle but, as Abigaille attempts to seize the crown from Fenena, Nabucco appears. As he crowns himself, proclaiming that he is God, a supernatural force tears the crown from his head and he starts to babble like a mad fool. Abigaille sees her chance and proclaims herself Regent, taunting her desperate father to sign the death warrant for the Hebrew prisoners. Fenena has by now converted to the Hebrew faith and stands to be murdered with the Hebrews. As the prisoners gather by the banks of the Euphrates, they sing the famous chorus, longing for the homeland they have lost and the freedom to practise their faith without fear of persecution. As Nabucco comes round from his temporary insanity, he sees Fenena being led to her death. Torn between loyalty to his kingdom and his wish to save his daughter's life, he prays to the Hebrew God Jehovah to save her. As he arrives at the scene of the execution, he realizes the power of Jehovah and confesses his conversion to the Hebrew faith, thus saving the Hebrews and Fenena among them. The guilty Abigaille takes poison and arrives with time only to call on Jehovah for forgiveness before she dies.

Naples – Teatro San Carlo Naples came to prominence as an opera centre in the late seventeenth century when the composer Alessandro Scarlati was resident in the town and produced operas in the Teatro San Carlo. Since then the theatre has enjoyed periods of prominence in the world of opera, notably when Rossini wrote a selection of serious works for the theatre including *Moses in Egypt* in the early part of the nineteenth century, followed by Donizetti's tenure as Musical Director from 1827 to 1838. Verdi wanted to produce work for the theatre but was hampered by censorship difficulties. The theatre is active now and produces a high standard of opera, under the guidance of Francesco Canessa.

National Endowment for the Arts The NEA is an independent agency of the Federal Government in the United States of America and exists to 'foster the excellence, diversity and validity of the arts in the United States and help broaden the availability and appreciation of the same.' It is the closest equivalent of the Arts Council of Great Britain that exists in America, but with several important differences. While the NEA does have a grant giving function, those grants are miniscule in European terms and prove that the recipient organization has been recognized as having a valid purpose, rather than providing working capital. The Head of the NEA, and the members of the National Council for the Arts who work under him or her, are direct presidential appointments and as such frequently placed in awkward political dilemmas. For example, as party supporters they may feel they have to support cuts in expenditure budgets. But this may cause them to vote for a cut in the arts budget, which the arts lobby look to the NEA to champion. Every arts organization applies to the NEA by means of a detailed application form, followed by an on-site inspection which will be unannounced and may last for several days. In addition to direct grants, the NEA administers a series of 'challenge grants', whereby they will match money raised in a given time span by the arts organizations' own means. The NEA is closely affiliated to the 'discipline committees' who appoint the on-site inspectors, and liaise with the independent service organizations, one each for opera, ballet, drama and orchestras, to whom arts organizations can turn for advice and support. Because the NEA is constrained from being an active lobby for the arts in America, the American Arts Alliance has developed into a powerful voice to champion the cause of the arts in an indifferent and occasionally hostile senate.

National Opera Studio One of the foremost training grounds for young opera singers, with first class links with the world of performing opera in Britain, the National Opera Studio was formed in 1978 to replace the London Opera Centre. The accent is on practical training to equip talented singers for a performing career. The heads of all the major British opera companies are represented on the Board of Management and the Director of the Studio is no less an opera personality than Richard van Allan. He took over from the greatly loved and revered Michael Langdon. The Studio accepts only students who have completed a course at music college and may have sung some professional roles and wish to make that crucial development from minor to principal parts. Tuition is therefore adapted to suit individual needs, with all aspects of a performance covered by professionals in those particular areas of expertise. The Studio is constituted as a charity and funded primarily by the Arts Council of Great Britain, and relies heavily on other forms of private support for its valuable and far sighted work.

Nerves Winston Churchill's famous remark, that the first time he did not feel nervous would be the first time he made a bad speech, is echoed by many opera singers. Even the most experienced and confident will rarely admit to feeling not even the slightest twinge of apprehension before going on – and it is that apprehension which frequently gives a role the sparkle which sets it apart from a run-of-the-mill repertory performance. But singers are presented with a dilemma that is unique to their profession because their 'instrument' is themselves. Thus real, uncontrolled nerves can manifest themselves in cracked notes, intonation slightly sharp, or (every young opera singer's nightmare) opening your mouth and nothing coming out. Achieving that balance between technical confidence and pre-performance apprehension comes with experience and with the routine of preparation before a show which every singer develops individually. Pavarotti is known to read or paint on the day of a performance, talking as little as possible and requiring almost total peace and quiet. Other singers go as far as singing through the whole role and testing out their entrance in an empty auditorium. Some singers prefer to eat only the lightest of food during the day, Josephine Veasey, on the other hand, felt happier going on after a pick-me-up of eggs whipped up in milk with a dash of brandy. Rarely will singers eat a full meal shortly before singing a big role, preferring to eat well after the performance. Because of the scale and length of opera productions, nerves do not end after the first entrance. There may be a particularly difficult staging manoeuvre to accomplish, or a big, famous aria which may not come until the final act. Josephine Barstow described her performance of Salome, where the huge aria and famous 'dance of the seven veils' do not occur until the end of the work, in terms of the difference between rehearsal and performance: 'No rehearsal approaches the circumstances of a performance... I remember lying on the floor the first time I did Salome, after the dance, knowing the final scene was coming up and thinking to myself, Soon we'll all know whether I can sing or not ...'

New Orleans Opera Association French immigrants made up a large part of the population of New Orleans in the nineteenth century and the city's early operatic venture reflect this. American premieres of *Les Huguenots, Lucia di Lammermoor, La Prophete* and *Norma* were all given in the city between 1839 and 1850, as well as the American premiere of *Samson and Delilah* in 1893. The current Opera Association was founded in 1943 and now performs four major works each season, frequently including an example from the heyday of French Romantic opera.

New Year (Tippett) FP 1990. The latest opera from Michael Tippett has recently received its premiere at Houston Grand Opera. One hesitates to describe the opera as his 'last' because that is what Tippett said about *The Ice Break* and now he has written *New Year* at the age of eighty-four. It is highly Americanized opera, featuring jazz, rap and rasta styles of music, all to words by the composer with a strong element of dance thrown in.

The work concerns the maturing of a young girl, Jo Ann, in her abrasive environment of 'Terror Town' (supposedly based on post-war Notting Hill, a mixed race environment in West London), where she is afraid to grow up. She is influenced by Pelegrin, a time traveller from 'Nowhere' whose love helps her develop. And if that sounds alarmingly like contemporary opera meets science fiction, it is perhaps reassuring to know that, in Houston at least, supertitles were being prepared even though the production is to be sung in English. The production has been at Glyndebourne, complete with video screens, computer aided graphics and many other trappings of twentieth-century living, all brought to life by Sir Peter Hall.

New York – The Metropolitan Opera Currently the focus for North American grand opera with an enviable international reputation, the Metropolitan Opera was paid for in 1883 by seventy boxholders whose generosity enabled them to use their boxes on the dress circle level, in an area which came to be known as the 'Family Circle'. The building was constructed as a contrast to the opera company housed in the Academy of Music which, being the preserve of the old elite, was barred to the new industrialists. So the new rich got together to build an opera house bigger and grander than the Academy, but with less thought to the activity on stage. Contrary to expectation, the house proved to be inventive and radical in its early years, staging German operas in the original language at a price the German immigrants in the city could afford. But gradually a wider European influence began to exert itself, and with it, an increasingly conservative attitude as star names were attracted at the expense of inventive productions. Jean de Reske, Dame Nellie Melba, Enrico Caruso, and the conductors Gustav Mahler and Arturo Toscanini brought the house to a peak of activity (occasionally forty-five operas played in a thirty week period), under the guidance of the General Manager Giulio Gatti-Casazza who presided over the house from 1908 to 1935.

During the war, the house was blessed by the dual advantages of attracting singers who could not perform in Europe and access to a currency that was powerful world wide and enabled the management to buy almost anything they pleased. The manager Rudolf Bing harnessed these resources to create productions which were musically magnificent and, for the first time, artistically important. Bing brought international directors to the Met, creating thereby an international recognition for the house which had hitherto looked no further than the limits of its annual tour. Bing also masterminded the move in 1966 to the impressive new theatre on the Lincoln Center Plaza – an area which at the time was considered to be little more than a slum, best known as the home for the Jets and Sharks in *West Side Story*. Now 'the Met' dominates an area which has become chic and humming with artistic activity, flanked on all sides by successful performing arts groups. The theatre boasts some amazing technical gadgetry, from a chandelier which recedes gently into the roof space before each performance, to a series of weights and pulleys which enable Tristan and Isolde to appear to float above the earth in their ecstacy of passion. Such advances create an auditorium which could never be described as intimate but has recreated that stylish, confident glamour which inspired the original building. Under the current Artistic Directorship of James Levine and the management of the Englishman Hugh Southern, the house will no doubt maintain its reputation for staging classic productions such as *Turandot* on a massive set which evoked all Peking, and *La Traviata*, directed by Franco Zeffirelli where the opulence of the first act was outstripped only by decorative indulgence of the penultimate scene.

The patrons of the Metropolitan Opera are enormously supportive of the opera, one lady donating, $1 million annually to sponsor new productions by Franco Zeffirelli. The Met have also brought the opera to a wider audience through regular television and radio broadcasts, video recordings and, as a tribute to the age of mass-consumerism, an extraordinary range of opera-associated merchandise, including Elisir D'Amore Perfume, Tuxedo Truffles and hand painted 'La Boheme' sewing kits retailing at over $250. But, like the city which is its home, the Met is a survivor, adapting to the needs of its audience which may, over the coming years, alter dramatically as new generations emerge.

New York City Opera The relationship between 'NYCO' and the Metropolitan Opera in New York is very similar to that of ENO and the Royal Opera House in London. Even in a city as cosmopolitan and crowded as New York, there would barely be a market for two international 'star-system' houses, or two more avant garde production companies. So NYCO exists to be the 'people's opera', bringing excellent musicianship together with inventive and varied productions, including music theatre and operetta as well as grand opera, at affordable seat prices. It does not pretend to have the overt glamour of the Metropolitan but has created a cachet which is unique to itself, presenting a fashionable contemporary face to opera which young and affluent New Yorkers are

eager to be a part of. The company was started in 1944 as the City Center Opera Company. In 1966 it moved to its present home at the New York State Theater on the Lincoln Center Plaza, literally next door to the Metropolitan. Its season lasts from July to November with a little over one hundred performances each year. One of the tenets of company policy is to provide a forum for about twenty-five young American singers to receive national exposure in each season – over recent decades these have included Sherill Milnes, Carol Vaness, Samuel Ramey and Faith Esham. The repertory of the company is enormously varied, from the old stalwarts (often given radical reworkings) to contemporary American works such as *X – The Life and Times of Malcolm X* by Anthony Davis and *Of Mice and Men* by Carlyle Floyd. In amongst these is a comprehensive selection of music theatre, including *South Pacific*, *The Music Man* and Sondheim's *Sweeny Todd* which the company did much to promote and transferred to Broadway. The company does perform in the original language of the operas, but was the first company to introduce supertitles. Until 1988, the company's General Director was Beverley Sills who made the transition from a superb performing career to an enlightened administrative one with ease and success. In 1987, Sergiu Commissiona was appointed Music Director. Under this leadership, the NYCO has developed as a polished, elegant organization never austere but always professional, where accessibility is a key word which has never been allowed to become patronizing. Such direct friendliness, matched by employing proven talents to teach the emerging ones will stand the company in good stead as one of America's most innovative and accessible opera organisations for years to come.

Niccolini, Ernesto (1834–1898) Talented French tenor one of whose notable accomplishments was to marry the supreme diva, Adelina Patti.

Nielsen, Carl (1865–1931) Denmark's greatest composer whose only grand operatic work was *Saul og David*, which he complemented with a lighter opera buffa called *Maskerade*. 'Saul' has all the orchestral magnificence of Nielsen's massive symphonies but is rarely performed by contemporary houses.

Nilsson, Birgit Swedish soprano whose command of the major Wagnerian soprano roles was masterly, defying any competition from even the most accomplished singers of her generation. Like many great discoveries, Nilsson came to stardom by accident as an emergency substitution in the role of Agathe in *Der Freischutz*. Encouraged by Fritz Busch, she made her international debut in the role of Electra in *Idomeneo* for the 1951 Glyndebourne Festival. By 1954 she had made her Bayreuth debut and remained with the Festival every year until 1970, becoming particularly allied with the roles of Isolde and Brunnhilde. Her career was by now international, encompassing superb performances of heroines in the Richard Strauss operas as well as Wagner. Her voice had phenomenal power, creating performances which seemed effortless and committed, full of subtle intensity which she was able to maintain to the very end of her career. In 1983, at the age of nearly seventy, she sang Isolde's Narration for the Centennial Gala of the Metropolitan Opera, and reports suggest that, even at such an age, her voice had lost little of its awesome magnificence.

Nixon in China (John Adams) FP 1987. Adams is a composer who likes to grasp the world of contemporary politics and place it in an operatic setting. His latest work, to commission for the Glyndebourne Festival among others and a follow-up to 'Nixon' is titled *The Death of Klinghoffer* and deals with the terrorist attack on the cruise ship, the Achile Lauro. Such settings do not dictate sparse sets however – 'Nixon' was produced with aeroplanes on stage, a second act 'ballet' of Red Army guards and even elephants! The plot concerns President Richard Nixon's visit to Mao Tse Tung which was a momentous event for both the Chinese and American nations. Woven into the inevitable culture clash of East-meets-West is an interesting and secondary theme of the sexual tension between Madame Mao and Richard Nixon's wife, Pat.

Nono, Luigi Italian composer who pushes forward the boundaries of opera by incorporating numerous techniques into his scores – the noise of factories, taped interviews with shop floor workers and other devices which involve his passionate commitment to the Communist cause. His best known works are *Intolleranza 1960* and *Al Gran Sole Carico d'Amore*. The latter is a music theatre work, along the lines of the pieces written by Bertold Brecht and Kurt Weill.

Norma (Bellini) FP 1831. The title role in the opera has been described as the 'Hamlet' role for sopranos. It certainly needs a singer of great vocal power and forceful personality to get round the demanding score and emotional variations required of the leading role – a Druid High Priestess at the time of the Roman invasion of Gaul. Almost as important is the role of Adalgisa, Norma's former rival who becomes her closest friend. It is the relationship between these two women that forms the core of the opera.

Norma, despite maintaining a vow of chastity as a High Priestess, has had an affair with Pollione, the Roman Vice Consul, and by him she has had two sons. The beautiful young priestess Adalgisa confides to Norma that she too is in love with a Roman and her lover wishes to take her away to Rome. Norma is at first sympathetic, until she realizes that Adalgisa's lover is none other than Pollione, the father of Norma's children. Distraught, Norma first contemplates murdering her own children in revenge, but cannot bring herself to do it, and turns instead to thoughts of suicide. She takes her children to Adalgisa hoping that she will look after them and provide the home that Norma has never been able to. But Adalgisa realizes that she can place no faith in Pollione who has treated Norma so badly and swears friendship to Norma, renouncing her former lover. Pollione attempts to take Adalgisa by force and in doing so, enters the sacred ground of the Druids. He is about to be murdered by the Druids when Norma seizes on a plan of saving him, by admitting her previous faithlessness to the Druid law. Suicide is now the only course available to her. As she mounts the funeral pyre, Pollione realizes that her sacrifice is truly great and joins her in death.

Norman, Dame Jessye American soprano whose grand physical presence and rich, warm voice have made her one of the most popular and recognizable contemporary singers. Dame Jessye's strength is in finding roles which so exactly suit her personality – strong, commanding but with a vulnerability which is engaging and attractive. Thus she has created a notable Elisabeth in Wagner's *Tannhauser*, a superb Dido and Cassandra in *The Trojans* by Berlioz, a humorous Ariadne and a commanding Aida. Her live operatic performances are rare and therefore extremely popular but her recordings give ample proof of the beauty of her voice.

Nourrit, Adolphe (1802–1839) French tenor who was a mainstay of the Paris Opera from 1820 to 1840. He created the roles of Robert le Diable, Arnold in *Guillaume Tell*, Eleazar in *La Juive* and Raoul in *Les Huguenots*.

Noye's Fludde (Britten) FP 1958. One of the great strengths of Benjamin Britten was his writing for non-professional voices which he made to sound extremely polished by surrounding them with experienced performers. *Noye's Fludde* is perhaps the best example of this.

Its undoubted 'star' is the cast of children (up to three hundred in some productions) who are the chorus of animals and birds. They are kept under control by Mr and Mrs Noye, their sons Shem, Ham and Jaffett and their sons' wives, all of whom are subject to the Voice of God when carrying out the building of the ark. During the performance the congregation are twice included to sing hymns, making the whole opera an engrossing piece of musical theatre, ideal as an introduction for children both as listeners and performers.

Nozze di Figaro (see Marriage of Figaro)

Nucci, Leo Italian baritone who specializes in the Verdi roles, which he performs with ease, thanks to a voice which is as strong in the upper registers as it is rich in the central and lower sections. His career began at La Scala and Vienna, moved to Covent Garden and the Metropolitan Opera and now Nucci is in demand world wide. Notable performances include Miller in *Luisa Miller*, Germont in *La Traviata* and Sharpless in *Madam Butterfly*.

Number opera Not, as might be supposed, a description of some extraordinary contemporary opera technique, a number opera actually describes the style of opera prevalent in the nineteenth century. Operas were then put together by connecting a series of 'numbers' (as we use the word when describing a big show or musical) with recitative or spoken dialogue.

Obbligato Two facts on this musical term which will impress your friends – it is often misspelt with only one 'b', and to use it to mean 'optional' is incorrect. It should only be used to describe an instrumental part in a score which must be included and cannot be cut under any circumstances.

Oberon (Weber) FP 1826. Lush and romantic opera with many of the elements of *A Midsummer Night's Dream*, and a very famous overture. It is very pastoral and anyone wanting a challenging, thought-provoking night out is going to be disappointed. But the music is tuneful and a good production will bring out the more amusing aspects of the work. There are a large number of speaking parts in the cast.

Oberon, King of the Fairies, has spurned his wife Titania, and refuses to accept that there is such a thing as fidelity in marriage. Until he finds a truly faithful couple, he says, he and Titania will not be reunited. So Puck has travelled the world to find such a couple and has come across Sir Juon of Bordeaux who is venturing to Baghdad to find a bride. Oberon joins him and a series of adventures bring together Juon and Reiza and his servant, Sherasmin, and her servant, Fatima. The two couples come through piracy, slavery and shipwreck to end up back in the forest with Oberon who is convinced of their constancy and is reunited with Tatiana.

Oedipus Rex (Stravinsky) FP 1927. Nothing like a conventional opera, Stravinsky's extraordinary work is highly ritualistic, with each scene/tableau being introduced by a narrator, speaking in the language of the audience. The work lasts barely an hour and the sung text is performed in Latin.

The Oracle at Delphi has decreed to Creon that the murderer of Laius, father of King

Noye's Fludde, by Britten, written to bring professional singers together with children. Donald Maxwell and Linda Ormiston (Mr and Mrs Noye) lead a large cast in David Horlock's production for the 1989 Salisbury Festival. *(photo: Alan Wood)*

Opera Factory – renowned for the invention of its operatic productions. Janis Kelly and Christine Botes in *Cosi fan Tutte*.

Oedipus, must be hunted down and punished if the city of Thebes is to be rid of the plague which is destroying its citizens. The seer Tiresias eventually admits to Oedipus that he divines Laius to have been killed by a King. Suspecting a plot against himself, Oedipus turns to his Queen Jocasta, Laius's widow, for help. When she announces that King Laius was killed at a crossroads, Oedipus realizes that the man he murdered on the same road must have been his father. Further revelations prove that Oedipus was an adopted son of Laius. Jocasta hangs herself at this news and Oedipus gouges out his own eyes to avoid his shame.

Offenbach, Jacques (1819–1880) French composer whose association with the Bouffes-Parisiens during the middle years of the nineteenth century produced some of the finest French opera-comique. Offenbach began his musical career as a superb virtuoso cellist, moving on to become conductor of the Theatre Francais in 1850. Five years later he opened the Theatre Marigny under the new name of 'Bouffes-Parisiens' and became its first General Manager. He nurtured the French appetite for light, highly satirical opera over his twelve years with the 'Bouffes', composing *Orpheus in the Underworld* for performance there, as well as producing works by Delibes and Adam. By the time he left in 1862, he was an internationally known composer and such acclaim inspired him to write more works that are regularly found in today's opera repertoire – *La Belle Helene, La Vie Parisienne, La Grande Duchesse de Gerolstein* and *La Perichole*. It was only the outbreak of war with Prussia in 1871 that dampened the French enthusiasm for these witty pieces which lampooned contemporary political figures in a manner not unlike Gilbert and Sullivan, who were greatly inspired by Offenbach's work. As with all great comedy, there is an underlying touch of tragedy in Offenbach's pieces, and his incisive wit directed at nineteenth-century Parisian society is accurate to the point of cruelty. Many regret that Offenbach's final and only serious work *Les Contes d'Hoffmann* does not match his more frivolous operas for invention and tightness of structure. It is still a fine piece, but for Offenbach at his best, it is advisable to start with the operettas.

O'Neill, Dennis Welsh tenor. It is not often that a classical singer has the looks, personality and charisma to persuade the BBC to give him a prime time television series, and it is even more unusual for the series to be so successful that a second is made, and a third planned. This has happened to Dennis O'Neill, whose programmes, mixing the great classical arias and lighter music, are a hit all over Britain and not just in Wales. He comes of an immensely talented musical family – his sister Patricia is also a professional opera singer and his brother Andrew a music producer for the BBC. He has enjoyed a long association with the Royal Opera House, Covent Garden, and also sung many roles for the other British companies, and internationally.

Opera A dangerous undertaking this – to define opera in one or two sentences. Perhaps it is best to confine a definition to facts. Opera must have singers with music to perform, some form of musical accompaniment and there must be more singing than talking. It must be performed in a setting which adds to the description provided by the music and words – if only in the mind of the audience. But it is, of course, far, far more than that. It is Brunnhilde in a breastplate or Carmen in a car-lot, Don Giovanni in a drug-crazed Manhattan ghetto or Albert Herring in an English pastoral idyll. It is *Aida* at an exhibition centre with a cast of thousands or *Falstaff* with a sixteen piece orchestra in a parish church. It is massively varied and open to as many interpretations as there are members of the audience.

Opera America This non-profit making organization acts as a support group for professional opera companies in America. Through Opera America, administrators find courses to attend, the latest opera literature is made available for opera companies and new initiatives are launched, such as the programme 'Opera for the Eighties and Beyond'. In addition, the group has declared aims of increased audiences for opera and heightened awareness of the art form through an active education programme. As the group says in its 1987 Profile: 'Its (Opera America's) goals and objectives are to further the art of opera and to aid each company in becoming the finest opera producer possible. Sharing ideas, problems and solutions makes each company more effective'. While this is particularly true of the United States, where distances between companies may be vast and communication is necessarily difficult, such unity of purpose is valuable and could well be imitated amongst the opera companies of Britain.

Opera ballet A genre of opera popular in late seventeenth-century France where the choral elements of opera were subjugated to the formal ballets which were incorporated into the action. Rameau's opera *Les Indes Galantes* is a fine example of opera ballet.

Opera buffa/opera bouffe The former term is Italian, the latter French and both mean generally the same type of opera – humorous, satirical, with everyday characters set in comic situations. The chief difference between the two is that opera bouffe contains spoken dialogue where opera buffa does not. As a style of opera, it is diametrically opposed to opera seria, relying on ensemble singing rather than individual arias.

Opera comique This is where it starts to get confusing. Opera comique does not necessarily mean comic opera. It refers to an opera which may be on a serious subject but includes spoken dialogue, thus preventing it from being described as grand opera. *Carmen* is an example of nineteenth-century opera comique. In earlier centuries, it was used more literally, to describe lighthearted pieces.

Opera Eighty As Britain's national opera companies were constrained from touring by the prohibitive costs involved, in 1980 the Arts Council decided to create a dedicated small scale touring opera company, hence the eponymous title. The company contracts young artists to create productions which are cost effective to tour and can be assembled quickly in areas which would otherwise receive little or no professional opera. There are no lavish sets or costumes and therefore the productions rely heavily on the invention of the director and the energy and talent of the singers who may undergo punishing

tour schedules of six months or more. Two productions are usually toured together, using the same company of singers in a variety of roles.

Opera Factory Begun in 1973 in Australia by the young theatre director, David Freeman, Opera Factory has grown over the last decade to become an important force in European opera, with bases in Zurich and London as well as Sydney. Freeman describes the company as being, 'devoted to the art of performance', and under his direction the company has evolved an individual approach to the rehearsal and presentation of opera. Freeman's technique relies heavily on ensemble work, with a great deal of improvisation and workshop preparation, leading to energetic, committed, but rarely uncontroversial stagings. The company does not use lavish sets or costumes, preferring to concentrate on the drama of the text and music which is performed to the highest possible standard. Since 1981, Opera Factory has been associated with the London Sinfonietta, now the orchestra for all Opera Factory performances, under the musical leadership of Paul Daniel. Among many notable performances, Opera Factory has staged radical treatments of *La Calisto* by Cavalli, *Cosi fan Tutte* and *Don Giovanni* by Mozart, and the world premieres of Harrison Birtwistle's *Punch and Judy* and *Yan Tan Tethera*.

Opera lyrique This comes between opera comique and grand opera. It describes works that are shorter than grand opera, with fewer choruses and less lavish staging, but has none of the spoken dialogue of opera comique. The masters of opera lyrique were Massenet and Gounod who had the ability to portray simple, heartfelt emotions with sincerity, without the need for grand staging or flippant humour.

Opera North Opera North was founded in 1978 to be a branch of English National Opera serving the northern part of Britain. Its brief was to be inventive, not star orientated but willing to encourage young singers and directors in productions which would start at the company's headquarters in the Grand Theatre, Leeds, but would also tour extensively in a way that English National

Opera was unable to do. The company has proved to be enormously successful, becoming independent from its southern parent after only three years, and now attracts a loyal audience which stretches from Hull in the North to Cheltenham in the South. Led by a new young Music Director Paul Daniel, and an experienced Administrator, Nicholas Payne, Opera North has sufficient reputation to attract singers of international calibre and directors of the prowess of Pierre Audi and Ian Judge. The repertoire varies from the classic to the inventive, such as a production of *The Love of Three Oranges* by Prokofiev which provided 'scratch 'n' sniff' cards for the audience! Opera North also pursues an active education programme, with projects as diverse as a major production of *West Side Story* in a disused mill north of Leeds which involved well over one hundred schoolchildren, to an orchestral placement scheme whereby ten young musicians are selected to play with, and be assessed by, the English Northern Philharmonia, Opera North's permanent orchestra. With Paul Daniel's reputation as a champion of modern music, it seems as if the one gap in Opera North's repertoire – twentieth-century opera and new commissions – will soon be filled.

Opera semiseria A clever style of opera where the comic elements belie a more serious, sometimes tragic undercurrent. A good example is Mozart's *Cosi fan Tutte*.

Opera seria The prevalent style of opera for the seventeenth century for all of Europe except France. Structure, formality and classicism were its principal tenets. There was little room to adapt or improvise, as singers carried out the conventional precepts of the opera, singing complex arias, usually written on a classical theme, with choruses and dances included in the latter part of the century. The characters were primarily mortal nobility or immortal gods, with little reference to everyday personalities. Such rigidity was bound to provoke a reaction, creating the genre of opera buffa as a complete contrast.

Opera workshop An American phenomenon which is fast being copied in Europe. Student opera singers learn their craft by practical application in workshops, often led by professional directors and joined by professional singers. The workshops are then performed to an audience. In this way, premieres of several important works have been given, whilst giving students valuable exposure to the nature of performing opera.

Operetta Literally 'little opera', this term describes works which are part-play, part-musical with plenty of humour and spoken dialogue, an orchestral accompaniment and a light, sometimes farcical plot. Among the best known examples are *The Merry Widow* and *Die Fledermaus*.

Opie, Alan English tenor. A notable actor as well as a fine singer, Alan Opie's skill lies in his ability to portray comic and tragic roles with equal conviction. A highly amusing Figaro in Rossini's opera (performed with many British companies and in Europe) or Sid for a Glyndebourne production of *Albert Herring* he has made equally notable appearances as Beckmesser in *The Mastersingers* and Junius in *The Rape of Lucretia* (both for ENO), Hector in Tippett's *King Priam* for Covent Garden, and Storch in *Intermezzo* for Scottish Opera. He has appeared at the opera houses in Bayreuth, Paris, Brussels and Amsterdam and in Chicago took the role of Messias in *Paradise Lost* by Penderecki.

Orchestra There is an element of 'always the bridesmaid, never the bride' about opera orchestras. The major companies all have resident orchestras who contribute massively to the success (or otherwise) of every performance, but are rarely given the credit accorded to singers or chorus. It has only been since the nineteenth century that orchestras have been placed in a sunken pit in front of the stage – until then the players were placed at the side of the stage with a good view of the action. Not being able to see what is going on (and in Bayreuth the orchestra is completely submerged and covered over) has led many orchestra members to complain of a feeling of isolation. Orchestral players for opera often complain of boredom in playing through repertory operas time and time again, which some believe to be the reason for orchestral musicians to be amongst the most strongly unionized in the profession. There are, too, the physical hazards to be overcome. In a crowded pit, dust and wood fragments can get dislodged and damage a valuable instrument, and the antics on stage may spill over (literally) into the pit (champagne tipped from *Die Fledermaus* and blood from some of the more gory productions.) However, a good conductor can overcome all these problems by recognizing – as Riccardo Muti does – that, 'If it's good in the pit, assuming a minimum level of casting, they can't spoil it up there, If it's bad down here, they can't save it.' Claudio Abbado, at La Scala, Milan, has formed the Scala Philharmonic Orchestra to develop a sense of pride in the orchestra for its own achievements, aside from their support of the singers. Such foresight will reap great rewards for the major opera houses, for a contented orchestra will contribute greatly to the prestige and atmosphere of the performance as a whole.

Orfeo (Monteverdi) FP 1607. Many consider this to be the first 'proper opera' – a contentious definition but it has certainly maintained a place in the twentieth-century repertoire unlike other works written at the same time. It is still not an easy work for a beginner to start with, being fairly static with long recitatives, but has plenty for a more seasoned opera-goer to enjoy.

Just as Orfeo the singer is to be married to Euridice, news has come of her death. Orfeo persuades Caronte to take him to Hades where Euridice lies, and persuades Plutone and Prosperina to permit him to take Euridice back to earth. They agree, but stiplate the famous clause – that he must not look back to see she is following him until they have crossed the river Styx. He is unable to resist a backward glance, and Euridice is taken back to Hades, leaving Orfeo to be consoled by Apollo who reminds him that he and Euridice will be reunited in death.

Orfeo ed Euridice (Gluck) FP 1762. The most important of Gluck's 'reform operas' where he overturned the conventions of opera seria which had been prevalent. He allowed human emotions to be described in lyrical music, with a ballet added in a revision he wrote in 1774. It was Dame Janet Baker who made the role of Orfeo particularly affecting, singing one of the loveliest arias written for the alto voice 'Che faro senza Euridice?'

The story is the same as Monteverdi's version, with two important alterations – Euridice feels she is being ignored by Orfeo as they leave Hades and taunts him into turning round to give her her attention. But once she has returned to Hades, Amor takes Orfeo's side and brings Euridice back to life to general rejoicing.

Orlando (Handel) FP 1733. Avoid this opera until you are completely convinced about your love of the art form. It is an important work but if you want to start with Handel's operas, go for *Julius Caesar* or *Xerxes*. Orlando is torn between his approaching insanity and his human love but submits both passions to his duty in defence of Christendom.

Orpheus in the Underworld (Offenbach) FP 1858. There are certain operas which will briefly be associated with a particular production and this is certainly true of ENO's 1985 production of *Orpheus in the Underworld* with designs by the political satirist Gerald Scarfe. Offenbach's work can only be described as a 'romp', roughly going through the Orpheus legend with some poignant music, particularly John Styx's lament at the start of the last act, some great humour and the finale which incorporates the Can-Can. There can be no better introduction if you are prepared for a rattling good night out, with no intellectual challenge, but masses of fun.

Osawa, Sergei Japanese conductor who studied the techniques of western music at the Toho School in Tokyo and was awarded the coveted Koussevitzkhy Prize for best student conductor at the Tanglewood Music Center in 1960. He went on to study with von Karajan and Leonard Bernstein, working with such notable orchestras as the New York Philharmonic, San Francisco Symphony and Boston Symphony, of which he became Music Director in 1973. He now pursues an active international career on tour with this orchestra as well as conducting many performances of opera. These have taken place at La Scala, Milan, the Vienna Stadtoper, the Royal Opera House, Covent Garden, London, and the Paris Opera, for whom he conducted the world premiere of *St Francis of Assisi* by Olivier

Messaien. His operatic recordings are similarly notable, including a recently acclaimed production of *Carmen* with Jessye Norman in the title role.

Otello (Verdi) FP 1887. Rossini also wrote an opera based on the Shakespeare play (FP 1816) but it is Verdi's masterpiece that remains one of the greatest operas in the current repertory. It is a work of power and beauty, depending heavily on the singers playing the key roles of Iago and Desdemona, but most particularly Otello which is a punishingly difficult tenor role. There is a fine film with Placido Domingo, and spectacularly lavish sets, directed by Franco Zefirelli. But Peter Stein's recent production for Welsh National Opera ranks as one of the most beautiful, engaging productions in contemporary opera, placing the whole compelling drama in sets which look like a Caravaggio picture come to life.

The plot follows Shakespeare closely, as Iago sows the seeds of jealousy in the mind of Otello, first directed against the young nobleman Cassio and ultimately, fatally, against Otello's young wife Desdemona.

Overture The opening of an opera, usually performed with the curtain down, with musical themes which recur during the performance. Such overtures began with the operas of Gluck, earlier composers using quite different music or nothing at all. Weber's overture to *Der Freischutz* was the first to incorporate themes from the opera into the overture.

Owen Wingrave (Britten) FP 1971. Based on a novel by Henry James, but adapted with a realistic libretto by Myfanwy Piper, *Owen Wingrave* is one of the few operas commissioned for television. It develops Britten's life-long commitment to pacificism, telling the story of Owen Wingrave who sets out to reject his family's military background. Branded as a coward, Wingrave loses his fiancée Kate to his principles and feels compelled to prove he has some courage. He offers to sleep overnight in a haunted room but when Kate comes to find him next morning, he is dead on the floor.

Owens, Anne Marie British mezzo soprano. She appears regularly in Britain with all the major companies and is a member of English National Opera. She is also very popular on the concert platform and has appeared several times at the Proms. She has yet to make her mark internationally, but given her undoubted talent and wide repertoire which encompasses an impressive range from Puccini and Wagner, this can only be a matter of time.

Pagliacci, I (Leoncavallo) FP 1892. Inevitably coupled with its lifelong partner, *Cavalleria Rusticana, I Pagliacci* is a superb example of verisimo opera, telling the story of people as they are rather than the fantastical creations of loftier plot writers. The words of the famous prologue reinforce this to the audience – 'Here,' sings the tragic clown Tonio, 'is real life, the dreams and aspirations, loves and losses of everyday country folk.' The theme is a familiar one of a play performed by actors bearing an uncanny resemblance to the events in the actors' lives.

Canio, chief of the actors is married to Nedda who has taken a lover, Silvio. Tonio the clown is attracted to Nedda but she rejects him, thinking him misshapen and repulsive. When Tonio overhears Nedda and Silvio planning to elope together, he warns Canio but is too late to stop Silvio escaping before his identity is known. That evening, the actors begin their performance – the story of Columbine, her jilted husband Pagliaccio and lover Harlequin. The similarity is too much for Canio – coming out of character he demands to know the identity of his wife's lover. Infuriated at her refusal to tell him, he stabs Nedda to death and then kills Silvio, who has re-appeared to help his love. As the curtain falls, Canio closes the action by telling the audience 'the comedy is over'.

Palmer, Felicity English soprano who became a mezzo in the early 1980s. She is a marvellously involved performer with a great sense of dramatic timing put to good use in everything she tackles, principally with English National Opera. Her roles with the company have ranged from Adriano in Wagner's *Rienzi* and Liubov in *Mazeppa* – both highly controversial productions – to the Mother and the Witch in *Hansel and*

Gretel and Katisha in *The Mikado* where she displayed her superb comic timing as well as excellent and distinctive singing ability. She is equally distinguished on the concert platform. She took part in a performance of *The Dream of Gerontius* at the Moscow Conservatoire, conducted by Svetlanov and also sang at the European premiere of Tippett's *The Mask of Time*.

Paris – Paris Opera From the middle of the seventeenth century, the capital of France has enjoyed a fine reputation for opera which ranges from the grand to the absurd and comic. In 1673 the Academie Royale de Musique, which came to be known as the Opera, made its home in the Grand Salle du Palais Royale and it was there that Lully, Rameau and Gluck staged premieres of their important works. During the early part of the nineteenth century, when the Opera had moved to the Rue Lepeltier, a tradition of grand opera began to emerge, with lavish sets, extraordinary lighting effects (electric lights being used for the first time for the 1849 premiere of *Le Prophete* by Meyerbeer) and large casts, culminating in performances of Verdi and Wagner operas (including *Don Carlos* and *Tannhauser*), written with such phenomenal resources in mind. By 1875, the Opera had made its home at the Palais Garnier in the heart of the city, in a magnificent baroque building with a lavish interior which afforded spectacular views of everywhere except the stage. 'Outside it looks like a railway station, inside like a Turkish bath', was how Debussy described it. The Palais Garnier was challenged by the Opera Comique at the Salle Favart where premieres of *Carmen, The Tales of Hoffmann* and *Pelleas and Melisande* were staged, but nevertheless, the house continued to enjoy a reasonable reputation throughout the twentieth century, reaching its height under the joint control of Rolf Liebermann and Sir Georg Solti during the 1970s. But in recent years, that reputation had become tarnished with questionable artistic standards and tedious productions.

Opera Bastille Because of the decline in standards at the Palais Garnier and to prove his personal commitment to the culture life of France, President Mitterand decided to open a new chapter in the life of opera in Paris. He commissioned – at a cost of £30 million – the Opera Bastille, to designs by the young Canadian architect, Carlos Ott, and under the Musical and Artistic Directorship of Daniel Barenboim. The new theatre was to be sited on the Place de la Bastille, site of the infamous prison and considered by many to be the emotional heart of France. Rupert Christiansen, writing in *Opera Now*, one month before Opera Bastille was due to open in 1989, assessed that, 'Since then, the project has been one of almost unmitigated misery.' That may be a little strong, for Paris does now have a superb state-of-the-art opera house where every one of the 2700 seats has a perfect view of the stage and technical facilities that are unrivalled anywhere in the world. What it does not have is an artistic policy in which anyone, music lover or not, has any confidence. Barenboim left under extraordinarily bitter circumstances in January 1989 and was replaced by the young Korean, Myun Whun Chung. Amongst a battery of insults hurled at Barenboim was the valid criticism that his planned programme was unexciting and contained absolutely no French music or artists which is surely inexcusable for such a flagship for the arts in France. Now leadership of the organization is shared by Pierre Berge, former head of the fashion house, Yves Saint Laurent, and Chung who is an exciting, if inexperienced young talent in the opera world. Together they face a hostile French public, many of whom would have preferred the money used to fund the Bastille to go on hospitals or schools, and a sceptical music world, which feels barely reassured by the gala performance given on 13 July 1989 to celebrate the opening of the house. The opening performance of *The Trojans* in March 1990 was generally acclaimed, so it is to be hoped that the action on stage will be more of a talking point than the politics off stage.

Parsifal (Wagner) FP 1882 People who care seriously about opera care passionately about Wagner, and people who care passionately about Wagner tend to go into particular paroxysms of rapture about *Parsifal*. It was Wagner's last opera and developed to the fullest many of the ideas he had tried out previously, most powerfully his idea that the theatrical experience should be almost religious in its intensity. Turning from the heathen legends of The Ring, Wagner used the Christian tale of the search for the Holy Grail as the basis for this opera, which he described as 'ein Buhnenweifestspeil' (the closest translation is 'sacred festival drama'!). For devotees, the first note of *Parsifal* has the same entrancing effect as entering a great cathedral, and the frequent programme request not to clap at the end of the performance seems as unnecessary as a request not to applaud at the end of Holy Communion. *Parsifal* is a sumptuous experience for the really keen, but an acquired taste and not to be recommended for beginners.

Before the opera begins, Amfortas, King of the Holy Grail, has lost the sword of the Grail to the sorcerer Klingsor as punishment for succumbing to the charms of Kundry. Amfortas was irreparably wounded as a result and will only be healed by the touch of 'a guileless fool' who will be sorry for him. He comes, as the opera opens, to seek healing at the lake. There he encounters the young Parsifal and the elder knight Gurnemanz who brings Parsifal to witness the ceremony of the Knights of the Grail. Unaware of the significance of the ceremony, Parsifal attracts the attention of Klingsor who realizes Parsifal may be the redeemer. Klingsor sets Kundry to seduce Parsifal but as she kisses him, Parsifal realizes what happened to Amfortas and rejects Kundry's advances. The spear Klingsor hurls at the young knight stops above Parsifal's head and he bears it away to search for the land of the Holy Grail.

Years later, Amfortas has still not been relieved of his suffering and refuses to extend the life of the Knights by showing them the Grail. The Knights, including Titurel, Amfortas's father, now begin to succumb to mortal death. Finally Amfortas agrees to reveal the Grail as Gurnemanz and the transformed Kundry annoints Parsifal as King of the Knights. But at the last moment Amfortas' resolve weakens and Parsifal is filled with compassion for him. Fulfilling his role as the 'guileless fool', Parsifal touches Amfortas with the spear to heal his wounds, reveals the Grail and rises to assume his noble office as King of the Knights of the Holy Grail.

Patter song A style of singing beloved of Gilbert and Sullivan and certain operetta writers where an extraordinary number of words are set to very fast music (in the style of a tongue-twister), demanding precise annunciation and a excellent sense of rhythm on the part of the singer, who is usually male. Perhaps the best known example is 'I am the very model of a modern Major General' from *The Pirates of Penzance* by Gilbert and Sullivan.

Patti, Adelina (1843–1919) An internationally acclaimed soprano whose reign lasted over fifty years and encompassed the greatest opera houses of the world, but ended, with characteristic eccentricity, in a castle in the valleys of South Wales. The theatre at Craig-y-Nos outside Swansea where she gave her final performances has recently been restored and stands as a fascinating memorial to one of the world's greatest performers. From early days as a child prodigy touring America, through all the quintessentially female roles, from Zerlina (*Don Giovanni*), Lucia, Violetta (*La Traviata*) and Rosina (*The Barber of Seville*) to the first London performance of *Aida* in 1876, Patti was a prima donna in the truest sense, revelling in the public adoration and embellishing her singing with extraordinary agility as well as mastering the lyrical legato style. She never lacked spirit and once sang Rossini's aria 'Una voce poco fa' to the composer complete with her own florid trills and ornamentation. Rossini was not impressed and is supposed to have commented on the originality of the aria and to have asked who composed it!

Pavarotti, Luciano From relatively humble beginnings in Modena, North Italy, where he was devoted to his mama and his pasta, Luciano Pavarotti has gone beyond star opera singer to become one of the most popular tenors ever, with mass appeal and celebrity status. Thousands of people who would not dream of attending an opera performance flock to his concerts, and buy his records in sufficient quantities to push them into the pop charts. His recitals in Madison Square Garden or at the Wembley Arena play to packed houses and he appears on chat shows and television specials alongside the most fashionable film and pop stars. He has been brilliantly marketed, as a larger than life personality, perpetuating every stereotype about the enormous, kind hearted opera singer, complete with aspects of showmanship (like the perennial white handkerchief which accompanies all his performances), with a communicative ability which can reach thousands of people in a vast arena or smaller numbers at the world's greatest opera houses. Thus he is easily differentiated from his fellow tenor and great rival, Placido Domingo. Domingo may have the superstar looks and sensitive acting talents but Pavarotti, 'the King of The High C's', has that irrational, sparkling charisma which fascinates even the least operatic. On the opera stage Pavarotti is not an actor-singer. What little acting ability he has is hampered by his bulk, and his busy schedule means that he has little time to rehearse with a new production from the beginning, so the Pavarotti version of a role gets slotted in to each different production. But he has a marvellous voice and creates superb interpretations of the romantic tenor roles. His operatic performances are increasingly rare and so are not to be missed!

Pearl Fishers, The (Bizet) FP 1863. Bizet began his opera writing career with this work and finished it with *Carmen* and, for the majority of opera goers, might as well have not bothered writing anything in between. On these two works his reputation rests and the only thing that makes *Carmen* the better known of the two is the power of its plot as well as the beauty of the music. *The Pearl Fishers* has marvellous music, but is let down by a rather improbable plot. It also has one of the great tunes of opera – the duet at the end of act one, which would stand as a masterful work in the most dubious of contexts.

Long ago, two pearl fishermen, Nadir and Zurga, quarrelled over a beautiful girl, Leila, who once saved Zurga's life but has now destroyed their friendship. Now Zurga has returned to join Nadir as a fisherman again, but as the priestess approaches to bless their work, Nadir recognizes her as Leila. The couple renew their love and are chastized by the High Priest, Nourabad. Remembering that Leila saved his life and Nadir is once more his friend, Zurga helps the couple escape by setting fire to the village and returns to meet his own death there.

Pears, Peter (1910–1986) English tenor whose distinctive voice made him one of the best known singers of his generation, particularly in the works of his life-long collaborator and friend, Benjamin Britten. Now that we are used to the richer, more fluid tone of tenors like Pavarotti and Domingo, Pears' style can seem almost vulnerable and unsettling. But in context as the sinister Captain Vere in *Billy Budd* or the tortured Aschenbach in *Death in Venice* it is easy to see how the character and the singer are inextricably linked. Pears made his debut in *The Tales of Hoffmann* and had established a reasonable career in the major roles of the Italian repertoire before catapulting into the public eye with the historic first performance of *Peter Grimes* at Sadler's Wells in 1945. Britten went on to write numerous major roles with Pears in mind – Essex in *Gloriana*, the Male Chorus in *The Rape of Lucretia*, Quint in *The Turn of the Screw*, Flute in *A Midsummer Night's Dream*, the Madwoman in *Curlew River*, and Sir Philip in *Owen Wingrave*. Such a range demanded a versatile acting style as well as comprehensive vocal technique, both of which Pears supplied with dignity and intelligence.

Pears, Roberta American soprano whose career was centred on the Metropolitan Opera, New York. Her vivacious stage presence and glittering voice, were admirably suited to the charismatic soprano roles such as Susannah in *The Marriage of Figaro*, Fiakermilli in *Arabella*, Nannetta in *Falstaff*, the Queen of the Night in *The Magic Flute* and Violetta in *La Traviata*. This only gives a small sample of her extensive repertory and versatile acting ability which kept her at the forefront of the principal singers with the Met for over thirty-five seasons. She also performed at Covent Garden, Salzburg and the Bolshoi in Moscow and made many fine recordings.

Pelleas and Melisande (Debussy) FP 1902. It has been said that you can spot when someone is bluffing about opera if they tell you they enjoyed all the good tunes in *Pelleas and Melisande*. This is a deeply romantic piece with very little action and the sort of music it is pleasant to nod off to on a Sunday afternoon in front of the fire. People have sat enraptured on the hard seats of the Albert

Pacific Overtures, by Stephen Sondheim, bridges the gap between musicals and opera. A tale of Western involvement in Japan, it shows how the tables have been turned so that the East now calls the tune.

Peter Grimes, by Britten. Jon Vickers, in the title role, with Heather Harper, as Ellen Orford, at the Royal Opera House, Covent Garden.

Hall balcony for the duration of all five acts, but for the relative new-comer, it is recommended that this one is approached first in the safety of your own home.

Prince Golaud has married the mysterious Melisande and brought her to the house of his grandfather King Arkel. There she meets Golaud's half-brother Pelleas and the attraction between them becomes obvious to everyone at the palace. Golaud's jealousy increases and he sends Ynoid, his son from a previous marriage, to spy on the couple. Ynoid can find no conclusive proof of their infidelity but Golaud's suspicions remain. Pelleas and Melisande declare their love for one another moments before the distracted Golaud murders Pelleas. Melisande is next seen on her death bed, guilt stricken at the grief she has caused her husband. Taunted by Golaud, she maintains she has done nothing of which she should be ashamed and dies in his arms.

Penderecki, Kryzysztof Polish composer whom it is fashionable to term as 'important', which means that only the very few really enjoy his works but everyone remotely interested realizes that his style is bold and creative. Unafraid to break away from the traditional orchestral accompaniments, Penderecki uses all manner of devices from wood saws to typewriters and encourages his singers to hiss, screech, yell and boo, depending on how the mood takes them. If you are fascinated by such an approach, try his best known work, *The Devils of Loudon*.

Pergolesi, Giovanni (1710–1736) Italian composer who wrote seven operas in his short life. Only *La Serva Padrona* is popular today and *Il Maestro di Musica*, which is often attributed to Pergolesi, is not in fact by him.

Peter Grimes (Benjamin Britten) FP 1945. When a new opera is premiered today, it is difficult to assess whether it can ever be heralded as 'an instant success' or whether that praise can only be given with the benefit of hindsight. But every account of the first night of *Peter Grimes*, at Sadler's Wells on 7 June 1945, describes it as such, and today the work has lost none of its power or mystery. It has all the components of great drama, particularly for English audiences – a tortured but sympathetic central figure, a

setting which the composer knew intimately and described with profound affection, unfulfilled love and a sense of nationalism which is bound up with the English affinity to the sea. It is a dark, sinister piece and not the ideal evening for someone looking for light entertainment. But an excellent performance will be engrossing and unforgettable, even for a relative newcomer. If you want an idea of the style of the music, the four Sea Interludes which are interspersed in the opera are available on a separate recording.

The cantankerous fisherman Peter Grimes stands trial in a small English fishing village for having lost his apprentice at sea under suspicious circumstances. Although he is acquitted, he is rejected by the village and only the schoolteacher, Ellen Orford, stands by him. Grimes, supported by Ellen, finds another apprentice and tells Captain Balstrode of his dearest wish – to succeed as a fisherman and to marry Ellen. But the young boy comes to the teacher with torn clothes and badly bruised, and Ellen's suspicions are once more aroused. The villagers mass to confront Grimes, who takes the terrified apprentice to the cliff top to avoid them. But the boy runs too close to the edge and falls to his death. Unable to face the certain condemnation of everyone, Grimes puts out to sea as Balstrode and the villagers search his hut. Suspicions are confirmed as the boy's jersey is washed ashore, followed days later by Grimes who emerges out of the mist, babbling and exhaused. Ellen and Balstrode realize Grimes can have no life in the village now and advise that he sets to sea once more and drown himself by scuttling his own ship. As the lonely figure departs, the village wakes up to prepare for a new day.

Piave, Francesco (1810–1876) Italian librettist who was happy to work under the control of Verdi whose strong opinions on their collaborative work are set out in the letters that went between them. But the results have stood the test of time with works like *Il Due Foscari, Macbeth, Rigoletto, La Traviata* and *Simon Boccanegra*.

Plowright, Rosalind English soprano. Rosalind Plowright's international career was launched in 1979 when she won first prize at the international singing competition in Sofia. Since then she has appeared all over the world from Bern to Buenos Aires. She has given occasional performances with English National Opera, but in Britain you are more likely to hear her at Covent Garden where she sings almost every season. Tall and striking in appearance, and vocally dramatic, she has made many award winning recordings including *Il Trovatore* with Placido Domingo, conducted by Guilini, for Deutsche Gramophone. She is also a regular concert performer.

Plumber's Gift, The (David Blake) FP 1989. The first of a series of seven new operas commissioned by English National Opera, *The Plumber's Gift* was described by some at its opening as an updated *Cosi fan Tutte*. There are certainly some similarities as two couples test each others' fidelity, presided over by a catalyst character not unlike Despina. But this opera is set firmly in contemporary surroundings, described enigmatically in the programme as 'last year' hinting at the timelessness of the problems faced by the main characters.

In the seaside guest house on the South Coast of England, Mrs Worthing's guest house has five visitors. The young couple James and Marian have come to sort out their marriage, the lovers Colin (a plumber) and Sylvia have come for a weekend away on their own, and the retired naval Commander is Mrs Worthing's permanent guest. It transpires that Sylvia and James have had an affair, which James tries to restart and is brusquely rejected by Sylvia. The Commander heightens the tension with his outrageous views and soon James and Colin are pitched against one another. As the tension becomes unbearable, the characters are transformed into a pastoral scene which James attempts to destroy by provoking Colin, once again encouraged by the Commander in the form of a Baron. In their pastoral world, James and Sylvia are reunited and Colin attempts to win her back. He is ultimately successful but is warned by the goddess Astrea that their idyll is nearly over. Back in the real world, James is unable to resolve his difficulties with Marian and resorts to cocaine. When interviewed for a job by James, Colin rejects financial security in return for the ability to practise his gifts as a plumber to strengthen his relationship with Sylvia.

Ponchielli, Amilcare (1834–1886) Only one of Ponchielli's numerous operas has survived into today's repertoire–the lavish *La Gioconda* which shows Italian opera at its most grand. As Professor of Composition at the Milan Conservatory, he took Puccini and Mascagni as pupils.

Ponnelle, Jean-Pierre (1932–1988) French producer and designer who both designed and directed the operas he staged. The resulting work was detailed, carefully thought out and occasionally criticized for being too mannered and introspective. His contribution to opera production was prolific, beginning with a production of *Tristan and Isolde* for Dusseldorf in 1962 and continuing until the late 1980s and his sudden tragic death. His productions of Mozart were particularly notable and included a prestigious cycle of Mozart operas at Cologne but his talents ranged to innovative stagings of Monteverdi operas for Zurich Opera and lavish settings of Rossini's works for La Scala, Milan, including a production of *La Cenerentola* which was subsequently filmed for television.

Ponselle, Rosa (1897–1981) Hugely popular American soprano whose career centred on the Met, with only three seasons at Covent Garden and, from 1951, at the Baltimore Civic Opera. She excelled at the virtuoso roles such as Norma and Violetta with a voice of great range and technical agility. Only an argument with the management of the Met and an increasingly weak top register cut short her career relatively early, though she continued to teach and to record in Baltimore.

Pope, Cathryn English soprano whose youthful looks belie an accomplished voice and sensitive, versatile acting ability. She performs extensively with English National Opera and has been marked out as one of the company's fast rising stars whose career will no doubt extend into opera houses worldwide very soon. Pope has sung notable performances of Miriam in *Moses in Egypt* by Rossini, Gretel in *Hansel and Gretel*, Zerlina in *Don Giovanni*, Sophie in *Werther* and Venus in *Orpheus in the Underworld*. She made her Covent Garden debut as Naiad in *Ariadne auf Naxos* and has featured in recordings of *The Rake's Progress* and *The Marriage of Figaro*.

The Plumber's Gift, by David Blake. Based loosely on *Cosi fan Tutte*, it follows the fortunes of two couples on holiday in Southern England. Ann Howard, Sally Burgess, Peter Coleman-Wright and Philip Doghan.

David Pountney's production of *Carmen*, first seen in 1986, is typical of his exuberant, non-conformist style.

Popp, Lucia Czech soprano who is world famous but most closely associated with the Vienna State Opera which she joined in 1963, after going to Vienna from her native Czechoslovakia. Herbert von Karajan heard her sing and was sufficiently impressed to engage her immediately. She is still a member of the company and excels in the leading Mozart roles. She has appeared regularly at Covent Garden since 1966 and sung in all the great opera houses of the world. Popp's talent extends to the recital of lieder where she is acknowledged to be one of the greatest singers in the world.

Porgy and Bess (George Gershwin) FP 1935. Thanks to Trevor Nunn's superlative production for Glyndebourne in 1986, this work can now hold its head high in the opera house as well as sell out on Broadway. Gershwin's aim with this piece was to set the colloquial speech and speech rhythms of southern black America in the 1920s to a full operatic score, using subject matter that was harsh and realistic. The result was a hybrid that hovers between the musical world and the opera house but which, if the semantic discussions can be ignored, represents an ideal introduction to the world of stage drama and happens to be sung all the way through. The opera is as full of 'numbers' as any musical: 'Summertime', 'Bess You is my Woman Now', 'I Got Plenty O'Nuttin' and 'It ain't necessarily so'.

At a crap game on Catfish Row, the huge and menacing Crown has murdered a man and fled the area, leaving his girl Bess in the company of strangers. Rather than follow Crown and rejecting the 'happy dust' offered by the cocaine dealer Sportin' Life, Bess befriends the crippled Porgy and moves in with him, trying to become assimilated into the tightly knit community. She is gradually accepted and joins her friends on a picnic at Kittiwah Island, leaving a contented Porgy in their home. But on the island she encounters Crown once more and cannot resist his advances. The party returns to Catfish Row without Bess who re-emerges a considerable time latter, obviously very sick. Porgy realizes she has been with Crown and forgives her, but as Crown passes his window, he cannot resist the urge to murder him. Porgy is sent to jail for a week for refusing to identify the body and, alone once more,

Bess is pursued by Sportin' Life and his promises of the wonderful life induced by happy dust. She leaves with him for New York before Porgy returns from jail, but on his return Porgy realizes he cannot stand life without his Bess and sets off to find her.

Poulenc, Francis (1899–1963) French composer whose three operatic works reflect his interest in contemporary social matters, particularly religion and morality. These are *Les Mamelles de Tiresias*, *Dialogue des Carmelites* and, an extraordinary monologue for one singing actress, *La Voix Humaine*.

Pountney, David English director who is Director of Productions for English National Opera and therefore credited with the company's current high artistic status. A director of international status, Pountey's productions have been seen from Amsterdam and Berlin to Chicago and Adelaide, as well as throughout Britain. As Director of Productions for Scottish Opera, he staged acclaimed productions of *Eugene Onegin* and *Die Meistersinger* amongst a prolific output. He also directed the widely praised Janacek cycle, seen in Scotland, Wales and London. Never afraid to shock or provoke by eschewing the conventional, some of Pountney's more controversial productions have included Dvorak's *Rusalka*, set in a Victorian nursery, *Carmen*, featuring nearly forty children and a set of smashed up cars, and a highly symbolic and futuristic *Midsummer Marriage* by Michael Tippett.

Price, Leontyne American soprano whose career was centred on her homeland but spread to Europe where she appeared to great acclaim in Verona, Milan, Vienna and London. A particularly superb Aida, she once stopped the show at a performance at the Met when her singing of the great aria 'O Patria Mia' commanded five minutes of applause in the middle of the opera. Her repertoire encompassed all the great soprano roles including Tatiana in *Eugene Onegin*, Donna Anna in *Don Giovanni*, Tosca and Madam Butterfly but most notable the great roles written for her voice by Verdi. She could also turn her immense talents to contemporary music and sang the title role in the world premiere of *Cleopatra* by Samuel Barber.

Price, Margaret Welsh soprano who performed extensively with Welsh and English National Operas until the early 1970s when her career became international. She now returns to Britain only on very rare occasions, principally to give recitals, but also appearing at Covent Garden in a 1988 production of *Un Ballo in Maschera*. In her early career, she concentrated on interpretations of Mozart roles but, as her voice became stronger and richer, she began to perform the great Verdi heroines and has since made a speciality of these roles. Price now performs regularly at San Francisco, the Metropolitan Opera, Paris and Dusseldorf.

Price – Tickets Opera is expensive to produce and therefore tickets to opera are expensive. Stories frequently hit the press about the ludicrously high top prices for, say, the Royal Opera House which passed the mark of £100 per seat recently, or Glyndebourne which was £50 per seat some time ago. But opera managers are realists and will only price their seats at what they feel the market will bear – they stand to lose more than anyone if everyone stays away. As ever, it is the small minority that grabs the headlines, glossing over the numerous schemes available to bring down opera seat prices. These include seats sold only on the day of the performance for a flat rate (where you may find yourself in the stalls at a highly discounted rate, next to someone who has paid the full price!); subscription schemes with 'six operas for the price of four'; discounts for students, senior citizens, the unwaged, music club members, mailing list members and so on. If you wish to develop an interest in opera, any good box office staff will be happy to take you through these options and it is worth remembering that a full price ticket in the balcony or upper circle for some opera houses will nearly always be cheaper than the equivalent seat in a local cinema.

Prima donna Literally 'first lady', this term is now used rather pejoratively to describe a leading female singer who uses her talent and charm to get her own way over other cast members, managers and back-stage staff. The full prima donna attitude will rarely be tolerated these days. The profession is increasingly full of well-balanced, highly talented musicians who maintain some sort of life away from the opera house, preventing the total, selfish immersion in their own foibles and problems which characterized the prima donnas of past generations.

Prince Igor (Borodin) FP 1890. Borodin's highly militaristic work dealing with battles and campaigns in deepest Russia can be given spectacular productions, like the recent staging at the Royal Opera House, Covent Garden, which can allieviate the rather tedious subject matter. The names of the characters are difficult to get to grips with and some experts think that the music does not fit together particularly well, being finished by Rimsky-Korsakov and the overture added, after the composer's death, by Glasunov. It does possess one extremely well known passage – the Polovtsian, Dances (which to fans of musicals will be familiar as 'Take my hand, I'm a stranger in Paradise'!).

Despite warnings from everyone against the campaign, Prince Igor and his son Vladimir have set out to wage war against the Polovtsi tribe, leaving Igor's wife Yaroslavna to supress a revolt in the Prince's absence. Captured by the enemy Kontchak, Igor and Vladimir are imprisoned and Vladimir falls in love with Kontchak's daughter Kontchakovna. Kontchak offers Igor a bargain – freedom if he will promise to leave the Polovtsi alone. Igor cannot accept such terms and escapes back home without his son. Kontchak gives his daughter to Vladimir as a means of keeping him as a prisoner with the Polovtsi but Igor, spurred on by the rapturous hero's welcome he has received at home, amasses new troops to attack Kontchak at a later stage.

Pritchard, Sir John (1921–1989) An influential force in the world of classical music particularly in Britain but also abroad, Sir John Pritchard was accurately described as 'one of the world's least packaged and promoted conductors'. With quiet dedication and intense professionalism, he provided the musical leadership for some of the world's finest opera houses, notably Glyndebourne from 1969 to 1978, Cologne Opera from 1978, San Francisco Opera from 1986 and Monnaie in Brussels from 1981, holding the last three posts until his death in 1989. In Britain he was also known for his leadership of the major concert orchestras in Liverpool and London, where his work with the London Philharmonic and BBC Symphony Orchestras made him amongst the best known and well-loved concert conductors. His repertoire was extensive, from intelligent interpretations of the Mozart operas at Glyndebourne to the premieres of *A Midsummer Marriage* and *Gloriana* at Covent Garden, to a recent controversial staging of *Lady Macbeth of Mtsensk* in San Francisco. The only composer whose work he rarely performed was Wagner and his otherwise prolific career was not well represented by recordings. But even towards the end of his life, when aided by a stick and sitting to conduct, he led his first 'Last Night of the Proms', with that same determination and faint eccentricity which made him one of the most popular conductors of his generation.

Producer It is fashionable to try to differentiate between a producer and a director in the world of opera, with leaders in the field adhering strictly to one title or the other. In general terms, 'producer' is more frequently used in Europe and 'director' in America. In practice, the terms are interchangeable, both describing the man or woman who is responsible for the overall concept of the opera, telling the singers, on the most simplistic level, where to move and how to react in order to bring a greater depth of understanding of the action to the audience watching the performance. Such an impartial view now competes with a more intrusive type of direction, as radically different interpretations are given to classic works. In commercial theatre and in films, 'producer' describes the person charged with responsibility of finding all the finance for a particular venture and controlling all administrative aspects of it, allowing the 'director' to concentrate on the artistic interpretation.

Prokofiev, Sergei (1891–1953) Do not be tempted to dismiss the operas of Prokofiev as Russian and modern and therefore dissonant and unapproachable. The music may not be immediately tuneful, but the four operas which survive in the modern repertory represent an enormous range of musical styles and witty imagination. *The Love of Three Oranges* is as close to pantomime in its subject matter as opera gets, with music to match. *The Fiery Angel* and *The Gambler* were thought to be controversial by the Soviet authorities and have only found a place recently in the standard opera repertoire. But *War and Peace*, Prokofiev's master work based on the Tolstoy epic, satisfied both the Russians' need for nationalistic grandeur and the opera-lovers' desire for spectacle and power.

Prompter Even the most seasoned opera-goer is sometimes surprised to discover the prompter's box, concealed discreetly at the front of the stage where the singers can see him but, ideally, the audience cannot. The prompter's role is to take the cast through the whole opera, literally mouthing the words and keeping the words of the piece in sequence with the music. Stories abound about a prompter's nightmares. There is a notorious Verdi phrase which occurs in three of his operas. The value of the prompter was recognized by one baritone who, in a momentary lapse of concentration, sang this phrase and led into an aria from *Il Trovatore* instead of the aria in the opera being performed, *La Traviata*. Much hissing of the correct words from the prompter brought him back to the salons of Paris from the gypsy camps of Spain.

Prophete, Le (Meyerbeer) FP 1849. Tremendously popular in the nineteenth century and considered by some to be Meyerbeer's most impressive work, this tale of religious fervour and hypocrisy is rarely performed now. It concerns Jean de Leyde who is prevented from marrying Berthe, the girl of his choice and joins the Anabaptist movement to try to forget her. He rises to be their leader and is acclaimed as their prophet. Misusing the power accorded to him and revelling in his supremacy, he alienates his mother, Fides, and prompts his erstwhile girlfriend to kill herself. Recognizing what he has become, he contrives his own death in a fire which also kills his mother.

Puccini, Giacomo (1858–1924) Italian composer whose career is an object lesson in not accepting initial failure. Puccini's opera writing actually began with *Le Villi* which was a great success and led his public to expect great things of his second work, *Edgar*,

Puccini was perhaps the most successful composer of operas there has ever been. Most of his works are still in the repertoires of opera companies all over the world. This is a selection of some of the original posters issued by Ricordi, the great Milan publishing house.

TURANDOT.

MUSICA DI G. PUCCINI LIBRETTO DI G. ADAMI e R. SIMONI

= EDIZIONI RICORDI =

LA

BOHÈME

QUATTRO QUADRI

DI G. GIACOSA

E L'ILLICA

MUSICA DI

G. PUCCINI

G. RICORDI & C

EDITORI

G. PUCCINI

LA FANCIULLA DEL WEST.

DAL DRAMMA DI DAVID BELASCO

OPERA IN 3 ATTI DI G. CIVININI e C. ZANGARINI

EDITORI G. RICORDI & C. EDITORI

TOSCA

LIBRETTO DI V. SARDOU
L. ILLICA · G. GIACOSA
MUSICA DI G. PUCCINI
G. RICORDI & C. EDITORI

premiered in 1889. But *Edgar* was a colossal failure and Puccini only persevered with his lonely profession by taking immense care and attention from then on over the details of his plots and characters. His plots ranged from the intimacy of love affairs in the garrets of Paris and the shores of Nagasaki to the power of officials and the magnificence of the church in Rome. His characters varied, from the indomitable female, personified by Tosca, to the fateful heroines like Mimi and Butterfly, the hopeless lovers such as Angelo and Pinkerton, to the truly evil Cavaradossi, in a series of works which now reads like 'the greatest hits of opera' including *Manon Lescaut*, *La Bohème*, *Tosca*, *Madam Butterfly* and *La Fanciulla del West*. Bernard Shaw remarked in 1889, having seen *Manon Lescaut* that 'Puccini looks more to me like an heir to Verdi than any of his rivals', and certainly the consecutive careers of these two opera giants gave Italy the unquestioned leadership of the nineteenth-century opera world. Puccini's works were not without controversy – the very realism that makes them so appealing to our modern audience was thought shocking and provocative then, and even the music broke conventions in terms of rhythm and harmony. But Puccini set out to be, and has remained, a composer of popular operas and his works represent a superb introduction to the medium for any new opera goer.

Punch and Judy (Harrison Birtwistle) FP 1968. As with many of the tales which are supposedly designed for children, the fable of Punch and Judy has decidedly sinister overtones which Harrison Birtwistle chooses to develop in this contemporary one-act opera. It was premiered at the Aldeburgh Festival and subsequently given a revolutionary staging by Opera Factory. As in the puppet show, Punch attacks and eventually kills Judy and the baby in order to marry Pretty Polly, but in this version the other characters, the lawyer, the doctor and the master of ceremonies Choregos, meet their ends as well, to the accompaniment of violent, abrasive music.

Purcell, Henry (1659–1695) English composer whose one true opera, *Dido and Aeneas*, is acclaimed as the first masterpiece of English opera with a lyrical beauty which retains its appeal for a twentieth-century audience. Purcell's connections with Church and Crown, as organist, first, of Westminster Abbey and, later, of the Chapel Royal, provided an environment for highly expressive and elaborate music, designed to accompany the courtly masques and pageants, most notably *The Indian Queene* and *The Fairy Queene*. Had the circumstances been appropriate, it is easy to imagine these works away from their regal constraints and developed into full blown operas, although attempts to stage them as such, given the benefits of twentieth-century staging techniques, have not always been successful.

Puritani de Scozia, I (Bellini) FP 1835. The success of a production of *I Puritani* depends largely on the strength not of one particular character but of the central quartet. The action is heavily focussed on them and the plot is not really strong enough to be self-supporting if one of these key players is not up to scratch. Experts tend to rate this work after Bellini's masterpieces *Norma* and *La Sonnambula* but a good performance can still be very exciting, particularly if strong soloists are matched by a powerful chorus. The names of the characters are given in English here – they are given in Italian in original language productions.

At the time of the English Civil War, Elvira, a Protestant, has fallen in love with the Cavalier, Lord Arthur Talbot. Her father, Lord Walton, is furious, hoping that she would marry fellow Protestant, Lord Richard Forth. But seeing how deeply his daughter is in love, he relents and agrees to arrange safe passage for his new son-in-law into the Protestant stronghold. But on his way, Arthur encounters Queen Henrietta, imprisoned widow of the executed King Charles I. He is faced with a terrible dilemma. Should he continue with his marriage and ignore his Queen, or save his Queen and imperil his marriage? He chooses to save the Queen by lending her Elvira's wedding veil and helping her escape disguised as his new bride. But on their way out, they are spotted by the spurned Lord Richard who recognizes the Queen and tells Elvira. Elvira believes Arthur has abandoned her in favour of a royal lover and loses her sanity. Elvira's brother George joins Richard in pledging to avenge Elvira's loss. As their troops amass,

Arthur returns to find his love and explain, although he knows capture will mean certain death. But in one of the quickest conclusions to a complicated plot, a pardon for all prisoners is announced and Elvira, whose sanity has returned, and Arthur are reunited.

Pushkin, Alexander (1799–1837) Russian poet whose gripping stories were turned into magnificent operas by a number of composers including Mussorgsky (*Boris Godunov*), Tchaikovsky (*Eugene Onegin, Mazappa, The Queen of Spades*) and Dargomizhsky (*The Stone Guest* and *Russalka*)

Putnam, Ashley American soprano who won joint first prize in the Metropolitan Opera auditions in 1976 following which work poured in from all over the United States, including five seasons with New York City Opera. She made her European debut at Glyndebourne Festival in 1978 but her career on this side of the Atlantic really developed in the second half of the 1980s. She made her debut at Covent Garden in 1986 as Jenufa in a controversial production which some thought stunning, and others merely contrived. But Putnam was successful enough to be invited back to repeat the role.

Queen of Spades, The (Tchaikovsky) FP 1890. If you have been introduced to the music of Tchaikovsky through his ballets, graduated to his operas through the beauty of *Eugene Onegin* and feel ready for something more meaty, you will not be disappointed by *The Queen of Spades*. It is a typically dark, sinister Russian tale, written by Pushkin and given depth and colour by Tchaikovsky's dramatic music. It depends heavily on the ability of all its principal singers to save it from descending into melodrama.

Herman is torn between two loves – his passion for gambling and his love for Lisa, fiancée of Prince Yeletsky and granddaughter of the extraordinary Countess. The Countess's fame comes from her ability to win at cards thanks to a secret formula she has never divulged. At first, Herman's desire to obtain this secret from the Countess is his means of marrying Lisa, but it soon becomes

an end in itself. By this time, Lisa has fallen deeply in love with him and longs to rid him of his gambling habit. As Herman approaches the Countess to find out her secret, she spies his pistol and dies in terror. Lisa gives Herman one more chance to prove his love for her is stronger than his compulsion to gamble. The ghost of the Countess finally reveals her secret to Herman who is compelled to rush straight to the tables and forget his meeting with Lisa. Realizing she has lost, Lisa throws herself in the river. But the Countess's secret does Herman no good – he loses to Prince Yeletsky and dies, cursing the ghost of the Countess.

Quiet Place, A (Bernstein) FP 1983. This opera was originally written as a sequel to *Trouble in Tahiti* but Bernstein later incorporated the whole of 'Trouble' into *A Quiet Place* in the form of flashbacks. It is an excellent example of a commonplace plot brought to life by exceptional music and proves that opera plots do not have to be extreme or fantastical to be engrossing.

Trouble in Tahiti explores the American Dream, as perpetuated by television commercials, and one couple's attempt to attain that so-called perfection. But Dinah and Sam realize that such a goal is driving them apart and dream of perfect happiness on Tahiti, the paradise island they have seen in the movies. *A Quiet Place* continues Sam's story after Dinah's death. He is joined by Junior, his bisexual son and Dede his daughter. The plot explores the interplay between Junior and Dede and their father, with the added character of Francois who is now Dede's husband and was Junior's lover.

Raimondi, Ruggero Italian bass whose imposing presence, fine acting ability and lyrical voice have earned him a long and distinguished operatic career. His early career was spent in Italy, with performances at La Fenice in Venice and La Scala, Milan. He made his first international appearance as Fiesco in *Simon Boccanegra* at Covent Garden in 1972 and has gone on to take many bass leads, all over the world, including Ramfis in *Aida*, Procida in *The Sicilian Vespers*, Banquo in *Macbeth* and Figaro in *The Marriage of Figaro*. He has also appeared in two notable opera films: *Don Giovanni*, directed by Joseph Losey, and Franco Rosi's *Carmen* when he played Escamillo.

Rake's Progress, The (Stravinsky) FP 1951. This work is a superb composite of a number of styles in both music and words. It makes a fascinating theatrical experience for those who enjoy the staging of operas more than the music. The libretto was written by W. H. Auden and reads as a fine piece of prose when detached from the music. Stravinsky's score is also very enjoyable without any stage action. Listen to it before going to the opera and your enjoyment will be greatly increased. It is also worth finding copies of the Hogarth scenes on which the work is based, as the music brings that dissolute and depraved world vividly to life.

Anne Truelove lives in a world of country bliss with her sweetheart, Tom Rakewell, and her father. But their life is shattered when Tom is lured to the big city by the enigmatic Nick Shadow with the bait that Tom has inherited a fortune. With this money, Tom becomes embroiled in the temptations of city life – shady business dealings, fast women and a generally profligate lifestyle. Rejecting the faithful Anne who comes to look for him, and unable to break from the influence of Nick Shadow, Tom marries Baba the bearded Turkish lady and invests in one last business deal – a machine to turn stones into bread. Naturally it fails and Tom is left penniless and without possessions. In a graveyard, he and Shadow play cards, betting with Tom's soul as the stake. Tom is given one last chance and determines to make it up with Anne. But as Nick Shadow disappears he plays one last trick and deprives Tom of his mind. Anne comes to visit him in Bedlam and, realizing what he has lost, the heartbroken Tom collapses and dies.

Ramey, Samuel American bass who is much in demand all over the world – with a real 'sell-out' voice so far as British audiences are concerned. The operas of Rossini have been a constant element in Ramey's career and he is now strongly identified with the bass roles of Rossini, both in the well known operas and the more obscure. He is a regular performer at the Rossini Festival in Pesaro.

Randle, Thomas American baritone. Thomas Randle began early musical training in conducting and composition but changed emphasis when he won a scholarship to study voice in Los Angeles. He sings both traditional and contemporary music with equal ease and made his European operatic debut in London in 1988 as Tamino in a new production of *The Magic Flute* for ENO. For the same company he creates the role of Dionysus in the world premiere of John Buller's new opera *The Bacchae*.

Rape of Lucretia (Britten) FP 1946. Britten's first attempt at a small scale opera produced this extraordinarily powerful, intimate drama which has a strong moral message.

The story is told through a male and female chorus and concerns the virtuous Lucretia, who has remained faithful to her husband, Collatinus, when all the other Roman wives have been discovered as unfaithful. Such fidelity angers the Roman Prince Tarquinius who becomes determined to shatter Lucretia's reputation. He rides to Rome to find her and rapes her. Deeply ashamed, Lucretia is driven to commit suicide.

Rattle, Simon English conductor whose fire, energy and dedication have revolutionized one of Britain's regional orchestras, the City of Birmingham Symphony Orchestra, bringing it to international prominence and Rattle to superstar status as one of the most exciting contemporary conductors. Accolades have been heaped on him to an almost embarrassing degree, crediting him with everything from the inner-city renaissance of one of Britain's most industrial cities, to the acceptance of classical music by the young-and-trendy, thanks to his unorthodox approach, never-ending enthusiasm and characteristically unconventional appearance. Rattle won the John Player Conducting Competition at the age of nineteen and progressed through senior jobs with orchestras in Bournemouth and Liverpool before coming to Birmingham. He made his operatic debut at Glyndebourne in the late 1970s and has kept a close association with the Festival, making only occasional forays to conduct opera in London. Amongst Rattle's triumphs at Glyndebourne have been the mould-breaking production of *Porgy and Bess*, the first every Glyndebourne production to receive standing ovations and considered by many longstanding opera goers to be the best operatic performance they had ever seen, and a sparkling new production of *The Marriage of Figaro* in 1989. In this, Rattle was described as 'the most rivetting conductor to emerge in over a decade'. He considers himself a 'slow study' preferring two years to get to know an opera well enough to 'feel confident of doing a proper job of it' and insisting on long, thorough rehearsal periods. Such intelligent commitment, from a man who took a sabbatical in 1981 to study English and American literature at Oxford University, underpins his vital and exciting peformances, creating a major force in contemporary music performance.

Recitative Operas are made up of orchestral music where nobody sings at all, recitatives when they sing about things which move the action along in a manner nearest to natural speech, and arias, when they pick up on one thing and sing for some time about that. Then there are choruses, quartets, octets and all manner of other combinations, but it's the 'recits' and the arias which form the bones on which the rest of the musical flesh hangs.

Recordings An excellent introduction to the opera world can be found in the superb range of opera recordings available. It is worth investing in good artists on quality labels. Recordings of highlights and collections are particularly vulnerable to less-than-adequate recording techniques.

Rehearsals The period of rehearsal time allotted to an opera will vary enormously from company to company. In broadest terms it is true to say that new productions will have longer rehearsal periods than revivals. But thereafter the variations are endless. The classic idea of a rehearsal, with singers in costumes, full orchestra, chorus and fully staged set, will only come together after weeks of individual preparation, and will not take place on the theatre stage until maybe a week before the opening night. These 'production rehearsals' are the very last part of a long, complicated and costly

process which starts with individual coaching for singers and sectional rehearsals for players, as designers and set makers are constructing the sets and wardrobe staff are making the costumes. The following rehearsal list for the San Francisco Opera House on 6 October 1981 gives some idea of the complexities of scheduling perhaps eighty chorus, fifteen principals, fifty orchestra members and massive sets with maybe three scene changes with six different operas at various stages of preparation.

Main Stage	*Carmen* – Chorus and orchestra
Third Floor	*Lady Macbeth* – Principals
	Carmen – Off stage orchestra
New Rehearsal Room	*Wozzeck* – first staging
Conference Room	*Le Cid* – Production meeting
Coaching Room	Individual coaching for:
	Die Walkure, Wozzeck, Carmen,
	Lucia di Lammermoor and *Le Cid*.

The Administrator considered this to be a quiet day because there were no costume fittings!

Reimann, Aribert Contemporary German composer whose work is regularly performed in his native land but less so worldwide, with the exception of his 1978 composition *Lear*, based on the Shakespeare play. *Lear*, was composed for the 1978 Munich Festival and for Deitrich Fischer-Dieskau, and considered by many to be climax of Reimann's work. This piece is now in the repertoire of English National Opera. Reimann's music uses unusual techniques which are not easily accessible but his operas do lend themselves to spectacularly innovative productions. He does not belong to any particular musical group or school, his compositions being highly individual and quite different one from another. He earns a living as a freelance composer, pianist and accompanist, often to eminent singers like Fischer-Dieskau. He was Professor of Contemporary Song at the Music Academy in Hamburg (1974–84). His great affinity with music for voice has prompted him to write a number of music theatre pieces.

Reinhardt, Max (1873–1943) Influential German producer whose roots were firmly in the theatre but whose grand designs made a strong impression on opera in Germany at the beginning of the twentieth century. Most notably he worked with Roller on the premiere of *Der Rosenkavalier* in 1911 and laid down the foundations for the Salzburg

Festival which has since become one of Europe's leading musical events.

Remedios, Alberto English tenor. Remedios joined ENO when he was twenty. With the company, he established a reputation as a fine Wagnerian tenor, singing Siegmund, Siegfried, Walter and Lohengrin. He is very popular in Australia (he first toured there in 1965 with Joan Sutherland) and during the latter part of the 1980s was under contract to Australian Opera where he performed Otello, Siegmund, Tristan, Radames and Florestan. He was awarded the CBE in 1981 for services to music.

Rendall, David English tenor who came to prominence through work with Glyndebourne Touring Opera before making his Covent Garden debut in 1975. He has since sung many roles with English National Opera, including a superb Pinkerton in Graham Vick's production of *Madam Butterfly*. In America he has sung with New York City Opera, where he made his debut as Rodolfo in *La Bohème* in 1978, and with the Metropolitan Opera, where his roles have included Alfred in *Die Fledermaus* and Lenski in *Eugene Onegin*. Rendall has that unusual combination of a strong tenor voice matched by versatile acting ability, enabling him to play comic or serious roles with equal ease and conviction.

Repetiteur One of the most talented, diplomatic and unpraised roles in any opera house is that of the repetiteur. Talented because the incumbent must have superb musical ability to accompany all rehearsals on the piano, coaching the singers in all the details of the piece, keeping pace with the conductor, knowing the score intimately to be able to start in mid-bar or mid-phrase and correct any tiny oversight which the conductor will not have time to do. Diplomatic because, along with pub landlords, repetiteurs frequently become a sounding board for the worries, grumbles, posturing and preening that are an inevitable part of any artistic enterprise, all of which must be absorbed and passed on only with the utmost discretion. And unpraised, because as soon as the opera moves from the rehearsal space to the stage and the orchestra moves in, the repetiteur moves aside and, starts a new rehearsal period for a completely different opera, with a different cast and a whole new set of problems.

Repertory The term 'repertory' is more often used to describe companies performing plays rather than operas but several repertory opera companies do exist, notably English National Opera in London and New York City Opera in America. Repertory companies perform a range of operas from their repertoire, performing a different opera every night as singers cannot perform the same work on two consecutive evenings. A repertoire is a collection of productions which companies have built up over a period of time by introducing new productions and reviving old ones. These are then put together in a carefully chosen order to create a season and performed one after the other, with varying degrees of overlap between each one. Thus English National Opera prides itself in having a minimum of two operas (and often as many as three or four) playing alternately at any one time, giving the audience a wide range of operas to see. This accounts for the enormously high cost of running a repertory company, as sets and costumes are constantly being changed over, not only for the nightly performances but for rehearsals on stage for yet a different opera during the day. Scheduling and planning for a repertory company is therefore a logistical nightmare, requiring a very special talent.

Return of Ulysses, The (see Ritorno d'Ulisse)

Revivals An opera house will stage operas of two different kinds – new productions and revivals of old productions. This means literally what it says. Everything in a new production is new – sets, lighting design, costumes, stage direction – and consequently expensive and recipient of the most attention from press and public. But rarely are those new productions designed to be seen once only, the most notable exception being the innovative Norwest Holst season at English National Opera. The size and price of new productions means that they must be incorporated back into future repertoires for years to come, in order to recoup some of their original cost. Because of the need to plan opera schedules years in advance, it is not always possible to wait for the reaction to a new production before scheduling it into future seasons, so every new production must be staged with a view to lasting for many years. Some of the greatest productions actually make it to a second decade – John Copley's production of *Count Ory* for ENO for example, while Zeffirelli's magnificent production of *Tosca* stayed in the repertory at Covent Garden for over thirty years and still, according to many, was as wonderful at the end of its life as it was when it opened. It is interesting to speculate whether the mould-breaking, controversial productions currently being staged will stand such a test of time.

Rheingold, Das (see Ring des Nibelungen)

Ricciarelli, Katia Italian soprano who won the prestigious Palma Verdi Prize in 1970 and made her American debut two years later in the role of Lucrezia in Verdi's *Due Foscari* for Chicago Lyric Opera. Now in international demand, she is particularly notable for the colourful roles written by composers such as Donizetti and Bellini and the darker Verdi heroines. A fine Luisa Miller, Mimi or Micaela, Ricciarelli also starred as Desdemona in the 1986 film of *Otello* directed by Franco Zeffirelli, a role she repeated on stage at Covent Garden in January 1990.

Richter, Hans (1843–1916) German conductor who became indelibly linked with the works of Wagner. He conducted the first *Lohengrin* in Belgium in 1870, the first ever Ring Cycle in 1876, the first *Tristan and Isolde* and *The Mastersingers* in Covent Garden in 1884 and the first Ring Cycle in English in London in 1908. The majority of his working life was spent in Germany but he was known to English audiences as chief conductor of both the Halle and London Symphony Orchestras, and as an eager proponent of an English national opera company.

Ricordi family Dynastic Italian group who exercised great influence on the printing and publishing of operas in Italy for the whole of the nineteenth century. The publishing house was founded by Giovanni Ricordi in 1808 and from 1814 forged a valuable link with the opera house at La Scala, Milan. Giovanni's son Tito (1811–1888) extended the empire beyond Italy and passed a profitable financial operation on to his son Guilio (1840–1912), a trained musician and passionate advocate of Verdi. Guilio overlooked some works by well respected composers such as Leoncavallo, Bizet and Mascagni and caused a divisive argument with Toscanini, but even so his business brilliance combined with his musical intuition propelled the house of Ricordi to the forefront of European music publishing. Recognizing Puccini as heir to Verdi, he nurtured the young composer, deviously obtaining the rights to *Tosca* from another composer in order that Puccini might use it. Sadly his inspiration was not perpetuated by his son Tito (1865–1933) who quarrelled with Puccini and broke many of the allegiances of his forebears. Nevertheless, the house still holds many original scores by Verdi and Puccini and will contest any variations in other published versions.

Rienzi (Wagner) FP 1842. This was the first opera Wagner wrote and is quite different from any of his other works. It is quite challenging for a beginner to get to grips with, and is rarely found in the core repertory of even the more adventurous companies. It was produced by ENO in 1983, (set in Germany in the 1930s) as part of the Norwest Holst series on the understanding that it would be performed for one season and then abandoned. Many thought that production showed what a good opera *Rienzi* is and that it would merit further stagings, but as yet no-one has taken up this challenge.

The plot concerns the rivalry between the noble families of Orsini and Colonna and the intervention of the Papal Notary, Rienzi. Rienzi has a sister, Irene, who is loved by Colonna's son Adriano. When Orsini tries to abduct Irene, Rienzi is furious and leads a successful rebellion against the nobles, joined by Adriano Colonna. Thanks to Adriano's warning, Rienzi survives Orsini's attack on his life. Rienzi rises to lead his people who turn first on the nobles and slaughter them and then on Rienzi himself. As he enters the church, he discovers that the dignitaries are in the process of excommunicating him. Sensing impending danger, Adriano warns Irene of Rienzi's downfall and urges her to run away, but she stands by her brother. The furious mob set

Rigoletto, by Verdi. Brent Ellis, in the title role, and Judith Howarth as Gilda, at the Royal Opera House, Covent Garden, in 1989.

fire to the building where Rienzi and Irene have taken refuge. Realizing they cannot escape, Adriano joins them in the flames, choosing to die with the woman he has always loved.

Rigby, Jean English mezzo-soprano who has become the idol of many would-be singers, moving from selling ice-cream at English National Opera to starring in a number of superb performances which have marked her out as one of the most talented British mezzos of her generation. Rigby trained originally as a music therapist but entered, and won, two prestigious music awards and gained a place at the National Opera Studio. As a member of ENO, she was cast in the challenging role of Lucretia in Britten's *The Rape of Lucretia*. This role proved that her distinctive voice was complemented by a powerful and affecting acting ability and led her to some notable principal roles with the company. These include Amastris in Handel's *Xerxes*, Pitti-Sing in *The Mikado*, Octavian in *Der Rosenkavalier* and the title role in *Carmen*. Her warm personality and attractive stage presence make her one of the most popular members of ENO.

Rigoletto (Verdi) FP 1851. The music for this, one of Verdi's best loved operas, is one long tune from beginning to end, the action never stops and the work is full of engaging characters. It was a subject matter close to Verdi's heart – he had lost his wife and two of his children and could express in haunting phrases the love a father feels for his child.

Rigoletto is a hunchback who lives for his one precious daughter, Gilda. Daily he listens to the woes and worries of everyone who confides in him without ever revealing any of his own problems. He has engendered the hatred of Monterone who has laid a curse on Rigoletto's family. Unbeknown to Rigoletto, Gilda has been courted by a young student who is in fact the notorious womaniser, the Duke of Mantua in disguise. The Duke leads a party of his friends to abduct Gilda, duping Rigoletto into helping them. When father and daughter are reunited and Rigoletto learns that Gilda has been seduced by the Duke, he hires the assassin Sparafucile to murder the Duke. They decide to use Sparafucile's sister Maddalena to lure the Duke to a place where he can be murdered

in secret. Despite only the briefest of flirtations, Maddalena is completely won over by the Duke and works out a plan to save him. She suggests that they kill the next person they encounter and place the body in a sack so Rigoletto will not realize his enemy has been saved. Gilda, who cannot repress her love for the Duke, overhears this plan, disguises herself as a poor tramp and walks straight to certain death. Rigoletto comes to collect his victim, now stabbed to death and wrapped in a sack. But just as he is about to dispose of the sack, he hears the Duke's voice and realizes he has been betrayed. He finds his daughter dying and, with an anguished cry, remembers the curse of Monterone before falling on Gilda's lifeless body.

Rigoletto has been subjected to various stagings away from the historical courts of Italy, most notably, English National Opera's 1982 production when Jonathan Miller decided to update the action to the tenements of 1950s New York and the area known as Little Italy. The jester became a barman, the 'Duke' a Mafia leader turned GI, the chorus, gangsters and their molls, and Sparafucile, an underworld villain. It worked with convincing brilliance, bringing a new audience to an opera which many said could have run as a musical on a commercial basis. The production was not without controversy – when ENO toured America in 1984, the Italian community in New York threatened to boycott the performances at the Metropolitan Opera. But the intelligence and credibility of the staging dominated any critical thoughts and the production was hailed as a triumph. The staging will soon be consigned to the back lot and is unlikely to be seen again after 1991. It is available on video and is one of the few opera productions which looks as good (if not better) on television.

Rimsky-Korsakov, Nikolai (1844–1908) Russian composer. Abandoning an early career in the navy, Rimsky-Korsakov rose to hold the Chair of Composition in the St Petersburg Conservatory by 1871 and composed his first two operas *The Maid of Pskov* and *May Night* during that decade. But his career reached a turning point in 1889 when he heard Wagner's Ring Cycle for the first time and became profoundly influenced by the music of the German composer.

Thereafter his music contained more Wagnerian elements but his subject matter remained firmly rooted in the fairy tales of the Russian folk tradition bringing colour and energy to fantastic tales such as *The Golden Cockerel*, *The Snow Maiden*, *Christmas Eve* and *The Invisible City of Kitezeh*. In *The Tale of the Tsar Saltan*, which he wrote in 1902, Rimsky-Korsakov incorporated his virtuoso piece 'The Flight of the Bumble Bee' – an excellent example of the vibrant and evocative style of music which characterizes much of his operatic composition.

Rinaldo (Handel) FP 1711. The first opera Handel wrote for London audiences concentrates on the battle between the Crusaders, led by Rinaldo and the Saracens led by Argante. Argante's lover, the sorceress Armida, tries to wrest Rinaldo from his lover, Almirena, by witchcraft but Armida's own feelings prevail and she falls in love with Rinaldo. Eventually the Crusaders win out and Argante and Armida are defeated.

Ring des Nibelungen, Der (Wagner) Wagner's massive enterprise is made up of four separate operas, each one of a substantial length. Thus the complete cycle presents a challenge of stamina even to the most seasoned opera goer, but an exhilarating experience for the really keen. A production of the complete Ring Cycle is said to be the ultimate test of any opera company, demanding extraordinary resources for production, and superb singers for the challenging lead roles. Below are only the briefest of synopses, charting the gradual demise of the power of the gods in favour of the mortals. For those tackling a complete performance, Kobbé has by far the most comprehensive summary.

Das Rheingold FP 1869. Alberich, a Nibelung dwarf has stolen a lump of gold which was guarded by the Rhinemaidens. This gold, if made into a ring, will bring immense power to anyone who rejects all forms of love. Alberich comes to Valhalla, home of the gods, where he finds Wotan, the chief god, about to use the goddess Freia as payment for his new fortress which has been built by Fasolt and Fafner. But when Fasolt and Fafner realize the value of Alberich's gold, they agree to take that in payment instead. With the help of Loge the fire

god, Wotan seizes the Ring and the Tarnhelm, a magic helmet, thus incurring a death curse from Alberich. But in order to release Freia, Wotan has to give the Ring and helmet to Fafner. Ignoring the doom predicted by Erda the earth goddess, Wotan and Freia enter Valhalla.

Die Walkure FP 1870. Wotan has visited Erda and she has borne him nine daughters, known as the Valkerie warriors. He can only retrieve the Ring through mortal help and has thus had two children, Siegmund and Sieglinde by a mortal woman. These two have been separated but when reunited feel a strong attraction to one another. They drug Sieglinde's husband Hunding, and Siegmund extracts the magic sword, Nothung, thus giving himself god-like powers. The pair elope but Wotan and his wife Fricka discover their incest and condemn Siegmund to death by fighting with Hunding. Brunnhilde, the eldest Valkerie and Wotan's favourite, disobeys Wotan's wishes and attempts to save her mortal halfbrother Siegmund in the fight, thus incurring Wotan's anger. Hunding kills Siegmund and Sieglinde tells Brunnhilde she is pregnant by Siegmund. They are caught by Wotan who condemns Brunnhilde to a long sleep surrounded by a ring of fire. Any mortal who braves this fire can claim Brunnhilde as his bride.

Siegfried FP 1876. Sieglinde has died in childbirth and her son Siegfried is living with Mime, dwarf brother of Alberich. Nearby, Fafner, now in the shape of a dragon, is guarding the Ring. Siegfried re-forms his father's sword and kills the dragon. By tasting the dragon's blood, he can understand the warning of a bird that he is about to be killed by Mime and slays Mime instead. The bird also urges Siegfried to find Brunnhilde. On his way, he is victorious over Wotan who tries to bar his way and Siegfried claims Brunnhilde as his bride. The mighty Siegfried now has the Ring, the helmet and a wife.

Gotterdamerung (The Twilight of the Gods) FP 1876. Siegfried has left Brunnhilde with the Ring, promising to return, but has fallen in with the evil Gunther and Hagen. They have drugged him and he has forgotten Brunnhilde and fallen in love with Gunther's sister Gutrune. A brainwashed Siegfried brings Brunnhilde to Gunther, trying to pursuade them to marry. Brunnhilde believes Siegfried has rejected her and plots with Hagen to kill him. Hagen kills both Siegfried and Gunther but as he comes to take the Ring from Siegfried's finger, the dead hand attacks him. Brunnhilde rides into a vast funeral pyre which consumes all the gods and the temple of Valhalla. As the Rhine bursts its banks, the Rhinemaidens return to collect their gold.

Rise and Fall of the City of Mahagonny, The (Weill) FP 1930.

In 1927 Kurt Weill had written a songcycle based on poems by Bertolt Brecht about the doom-laden city of Mahagonny (Mahagonny Songspiel) which had been performed with great success as a cabaret piece by Weill's wife Lotte Lenya. By 1930, Brecht developed his songs into an incisive libretto to Weill's catchy music, creating a full-scale opera which stands as a cruel indictment of an acquisitive, egocentric society.

During the American Depression, three convicts on the run, Widow Begbick, Fatty and Trinity Moses, establish a town where the only object will be the pursuit of pleasure – the city of Mahagonny, which means Spider's Web. Such an idyllic existence proves to be a mecca for the disenchanted, among them the prostitute Jenny and her fellow working girls, and the lumberjack from Alaska, Jimmy Mahoney, who arrives with other lumberjacks in tow. As Jenny and the girls arrive, they sing one of Weill's most haunting and well-known tunes, the Alabama song. Jimmy is paired up with Jenny and the quest for hedonism begins, but the sensitive pair realize a life of pure pleasure is only an illusion. Mahagonny is threatened by a hurricane but it passes by and the citizens become more convinced than ever that 'nothing is barred'. One indulgence follows another, gluttony, sex, prize fights and drinking, by the end of which Jimmy has committed the cardinal sin, he has run out of money. In a mock trial, Jim is deserted by his friends and condemned to death. As his execution takes place, the populace unite to agree that 'we can't help ourselves or you or anyone'.

Ritorno d'Ulisse in Patria (Monteverdi) FP 1641.

This score lay undiscovered until fragments of it were unearthed in 1923 in Vienna. Then it raised doubts amongst musical experts as to whether it was actually by Monteverdi at all. Its authenticity has now been established and the version most commonly performed was arranged by Luigi Dallapiccola in 1942.

It concerns the plight of Penelope whose husband Ulysses has not yet returned from the Trojan Wars. She is pursued by numerous other suitors and does not realize that her husband is in fact alive and well and living on Ithaca. He is spurred on by Minerva to return to his palace and is reunited with his son Telemaco. But Ulysses wishes to test his wife's fidelity after his long absence so returns to his palace disguised as a beggar. Penelope has announced that she will marry whichever suitor can draw Ulysses' bow. In the tradition of all good legends, it is only the poor 'beggar' who achieves the feat. He then goes on to slay the other suitors and is eventually recognized by his delighted wife.

Robert le Diable (Meyerbeer) FP 1831.

This opera is very rarely performed today but at the time of its premiere was hailed as a massive success for the Grand Opera in Paris. It certainly has all the lush melody that characterizes grand opera and the sort of plot that has given the whole medium of opera a bad name from the nineteenth century onwards.

Robert is the son of the devil, Bertram, and a human woman, and therefore is constantly torn between the desire to do evil and good. As the opera opens he has been banished to Sicily because of his wrong doing and has fallen in love with Princess Isabella. He attempts to escape from the constant temptations of Betram (who is an early model of Mephistopheles) but ends up losing all his possessions and eventually succumbing to an extraordinary orgy with nuns who have been unfaithful to their vows, as summoned up by Bertram. His pure, devout foster-sister Alice (the personification of good) seeks him out and eventually succeeds in winning him back to the side of the righteous and reunites him with Isabella.

Rodelinda (Handel) FP 1725.

This is one of Handel's finest scores but even so may be a little repetitive for a new-comer. It has some lovely arias, many of which are well known outside the opera.

Rodelinda believes that her husband Bertarido is dead, but in fact he is planning his revenge on his long term adversary Grimoaldo. Grimoaldo tricks Rodelinda into promising to marry him by threatening to kill her son, thus infuriating his betrothed, Eduige, and Bertarido who happens to overhear them. Husband and wife are reunited for a moment before Bertarido is imprisoned. Eduige and Rodelinda are determined to rescue him but find only his bloodstained coat and believe once more that he has been killed. He has in fact escaped and, by a quirk of fate, is moved to save the life of his old adversary, thus gaining the friendship of Grimoaldo and the devotion of his faithful wife Rodelinda.

Robinson, Ethna Irish mezzo-soprano who joined English National Opera straight from the Guildhall School of Music and Drama and has justified the expectations of her early mentors. Her clear voice and versatile acting ability have created excellent performances in *Akhnaten, Moses in Egypt, The Mikado, Hansel and Gretel* and *Orpheus in the Underworld*, all for ENO. Her career seems set to broaden into other opera houses, both nationally and internationally.

Robson, Christopher English countertenor with a wide ranging performing career, encompassing extensive oratorio performances, challenging opera work, particularly in contemporary pieces and session work for pop groups. With English National Opera his performances have covered operas from the early repertoire such as Monteverdi's *Orfeo*, Handel's *Julius Caesar*, taking the title role, and that of Tolomeo which he has also performed at Houston Grand Opera, and the award winning *Xerxes*, also by Handel, seen on British television and now available on video. But, as more contemporary composers choose to write for the counter-tenor voice, Robson has developed a successful career in new commissioned work, taking the lead in the world premiere of *Akhnaten* by Philip Glass in Stuttgart and London. Robson also works extensively with David Freeman's Opera Factory, both in London and Zurich.

Rodgers, Joan English soprano who took a degree in Russian at Liverpool University. In May 1981 she won the Kathleen Ferrier Memorial Scholarship and her career developed in a musical rather than a linguistic direction. Slight, pretty and a captivating singer and actress, much in demand all over Europe, Rodgers is tipped by many knowledgeable opera followers to be one of the great voices of the coming decades. She first came to international attention in 1982 as Pamina at Aix en Provence. She now appears regularly at Covent Garden and at ENO. Her performance of Susanna in *The Marriage of Figaro* in the 1989 Glyndebourne Festival and at a semi-staged production, televised, during the 1989 Proms was heralded internationally as a superb interpretation, both musically and dramatically. Not yet a household name in opera circles in America but there is little doubt that her talent and personality will soon make her one.

Rolfe-Johnson, Anthony English tenor who is one of Britain's finest singers of Handel, Mozart and Bach and as such is in international demand, both as a concert artist and opera performer. His opera repertoire has encompassed many other roles, ranging from *Albert Herring* at Glyndebourne to the Male Chorus in *The Rape of Lucretia* for English National Opera. He has performed extensively in Europe, with opera companies in the Netherlands, Hamburg, Zurich, Brussels, La Scala, Milan, and the Aix en Provence Festival.

Rome Operas have been staged in this city, the capital of Italy, since 1606, but usually for private audiences. The first public opera house, ultimately called the Teatro Apollo, was opened in 1670 and housed the premieres of such great Verdi works as *Il Trovatore* in 1853, and *Un Ballo in Maschera* in 1859. It was destroyed by fire in 1889. Opera was also staged in the Teatro Valle, site of the premiere of *La Cenerentola* by Rossini and in the Teatro Argentina which hosted the first stagings of *The Barber of Seville* by Rossini and *Due Foscari* and *The Battle of Legnano* by Vedi. The current Teatro del'Opera was originally known as the Teatro Costanzi and was opened in 1880. Here the first performances of *Cavalleria Rusticana* and *Tosca* were staged, and, during the reign of the Fascists, Mussolini poured massive resources into the house, determined to make it the greatest in Italy. The head of the organization at that time was Tuillio Serafin who brought the house to standards which rivalled, and occasionally surpassed La Scala, Milan. The house has retained a fine international reputation, in both its winter seasons in the theatre and its summer extravaganza in the Baths of Caracalla. These Roman ruins provide a spectacular backdrop for productions on a lavish scale where audiences of several thousand can marvel at *Aida* staged with herds of live elephants!

Roocroft, Amanda English soprano. Rarely does the cynical music press extol the virtues of a young singer with such unanimity as they did Amanda Roocroft's graduation performance from the Royal Northern College of Music in 1989. Their ebullient praise no doubt created extra pressure for this attractive soprano who was already been wooed by Britain's national companies with promises of star roles, as well as numerous television profiles charting the progress of her embryonic career. Her first professional debut as Sophie in Welsh National Opera's *Der Rosenkavalier* appears to have justified the excitement, and her plans to perform Fiordigli (*Cosi fan Tutte*) for the Glyndebourne Festival, and Pamina (*The Magic Flute*) for the Royal Opera House will be eagerly awaited.

Romeo et Juliette (Gounod) FP 1867. Plenty of good melodies characterize Gounod's faithful setting of the Shakespeare play which sometimes even reverts to the actual Shakespeare text for its libretto. It has been most popular in France, although some good 'pairings' have led to excellent performances outside its country of origin. Among the most notable couples were Adelina Patti and Ernesto Nicolini who sang the roles at the Opera in Paris. Patti was then married to the Marquis de Caux but had her sights firmly set on Nicolini whom she eventually married in 1886. Their obvious affection was not lost on the Paris audience who, it is said, counted twenty-nine 'real' kisses between the pair during the balcony scene.

Rosenkavalier, Der (Richard Strauss) FP 1911. Perhaps the most popular of all Richard Strauss operas, this lovely work lends itself to beautiful productions and provides glamorous vehicles for the female singers. It is a marvellous blend of innocence and sophistication and an excellent choice for those who wish to move on from the 'introductory' operas such as *Carmen* or *Aida*. The only slightly disconcerting aspect for a newcomer is that Octavian, the young knight who is the lover of the Countess (known as the Marschallin), is always sung by a mezzo-soprano. But the intimate scenes between the couple seem effortless and natural, given the lyrical music and sensitive acting by both the singers.

The Marschallin and her young lover Octavian are together in the Marschallin's bedroom enjoying what is quite clearly a post-coital tête-à-tête. They are interrupted by the arrival of the loutish Baron Ochs, a relative of the Marschallin. Octavian cunningly disguises himself as a chamber-maid (a girl singing the part of a boy dressed up as a girl!) to divert the lascivious Baron's attention. Eventually the Baron remembers why he came – he intends to marry the beautiful Sophie von Faninal, many years his junior and asks the Marschallin for her suggestions as to who should present to Sophie the silver rose, the traditional token of love sent to a betrothed. The Marschallin decides that her Octavian would be perfect to carry out this job of 'Rosenkavalier'. Naturally, as soon as Octavian and Sophie meet – in a scene of immense courtly beauty as the rose is presented – their mutual attraction becomes obvious. The moment she sees the Baron, Sophie realizes she cannot contemplate marrying him despite her father's anxious persuasion that marriage to the Baron will save the family finances. She flatly refuses and is banished to a convent. The Baron manages to forget his young fiancée with improper haste when promised a rendezvous with an attractive chamber-maid, arranged by two young courtiers paid by Octavian. The 'chamber-maid' turns out to be Octavian, once more in disguise and she and Ochs carry through a rudimentary courtship scene, to be interrupted by Sophie's father who is naturally alarmed. They are joined by Sophie and by the Marschallin who dismisses Ochs at once. With grace and dignity, the Marschallin recognizes that she has lost Octavian to Sophie and wishes the young couple joy in a stunningly beautiful trio. The curtain falls as the couple leave together.

Rossini, Giochino (1792–1868) Italian composer whose best known work, *The Barber of Seville*, only represents one small part of his enormously varied output. He began his operatic composition in Bologna, writing comic one act operas before embarking on his first serious work *Ciro in Babilonia* which was a critical failure. It was the powerful *Tanncredi* that brought Rossini to prominence away from Italy – success he matched at home with the delightful 'opera buffa', *L'Italiana in Algeri*. During this time he had worked in Milan and Venice before moving to Naples in 1815 to become Music Director of the two opera houses in the city – Teatro San Carlo and Teatro del Fondo. There he met and married the soprano Isabella Colbran who was his inspiration for *Elisabetta, Regina d'Inghliterra*, the first of the more serious works he composed during this period. So serious, in fact, was his version of *Otello*, that the audiences demanded a happy ending be substituted for the performances in Rome. Proving what a versatile composer he was, in the same year that he wrote *Otello* (1816), he penned the comic masterpiece for which he is best known *The Barber of Seville* and followed that up a year later with *La Cenerentola*, a delightful adaptation of the 'Cinderella' story. He maintained this prolific output throughout his stay in Naples, having composed twenty-five operas by the time he was thirty-one. By 1825 he had moved to Paris and staged his epic work *Il Viaggio a Reims* which demanded ten first class soloists and full ballet – such casting makes the work almost impossibly expensive to stage today. The work was commissioned for the Coronation of King Charles X, and Rossini maintained a close relationship with the King, thereby developing his influence at the Paris Opera. Rossini was only at the Paris Opera a short time but there he produced two of his best known works, *Le Comte Ory* and *Guillaume Tell*, reckoned by many to be Rossini's masterpiece. The revolution of 1830 toppled Charles X from his throne and Rossini lived for nearly forty more years in relative obscurity. After his death, his body was returned to Florence and attended by over 6,000 mourners. It is said that when the chorus sang the Prayer from *Moses in Egypt* at the service, the crowd demanded an encore. Such an act would surely have appealed to this composer who could evoke the light beauty of a young girl in love as easily as the tormented power of a great religious leader.

Royal Opera House, Covent Garden (see London)

Rozsa, Vera Hungarian singer who has exerted an enormous influence as a singing teacher over many of the most notable contemporary singers including Nancy Argenta, Anthony Rolfe Johnson, Sarah Walker and Dame Kiri te Kanawa. Her own performing career was distinguished, singing with the Vienna State Opera before coming to the Leeds Festival in 1965, where she was asked to teach at the Royal Northern College of Music. She does not have a particular technique that she imparts to her pupils, but her superb musicianship and imagination is credited with having brought many to the top echelons of their careers. Treating each pupil as an individual with clear strengths and weaknesses, she concentrates on the psychological demands of a professional singing career as well as the musical ones, training singers to cope with the injustices of auditions and rehearsals as well as the successes of superb notices and press attention. Her pupils may remain with her for up to twenty years, often phoning her from thousands of miles away for advice on a certain technique or phrase.

Rudel, Julius Austrian conductor and manager who left his homeland at the age of seventeen to come to New York and joined New York City Opera in 1943. From 1957 to 1979 he worked as Director of the company, pushing forward the boundaries of its work to include much more American opera, using many young, inexperienced singers. He combined this pioneering work with an extensive conducting career, leading the prestigious Wolf Trap Festival and serving as Musical Director of the Kennedy Center between 1971 and 1974.

Runnicles, Donald Scottish conductor, but is best known in Germany. Former Kapellmeister with the Mannheim National Theater and from 1987 Principal Conductor in

Hannover where he conducted at least sixty opera performances a year. He worked for several years at Bayreuth, assisting James Levine on *Parsifal* and Georg Solti on The Ring. The fact that these great conductors have such faith in Runnicles augurs well for his future as an international performer. He made his Met debut at five hours notice conducting the three act version of *Lulu* by Berg – hardly an easy introduction to the USA, but very favourably received.

Russalka Two works based on this fairy tale are found in the contemporary repertory. The earlier is by Dargomijsky, premiered in 1856, the latter by Dvorak, which had its first performance in 1901.

Dargomijsky's work uses a variety of sources for his lighter tale, including 'The Little Mermaid' by Hans Christian Andersen. Dargomijsky's work concerns Natasha, daughter of a miller who has been seduced and left pregnant by a Prince. She is turned into a wood-nymph while her distraught father murders the Prince by throwing him in the river. Dvorak's version begins with the nymph who falls in love with a Prince and is turned into a human being by a witch in order that she might win his love. But he forsakes her and she is condemned to suffer forever unless she can bring herself to kill him. The Prince's conscience proves too much, however, and he returns to Russalka and dies in her arms.

Russlan and Ludmilla (Glinka) FP 1842. Another Russian work based on a fairy tale, full of magic spells, giants, princesses and suitors, with very jolly music and an extremely well-known overture.

The knight Russlan is one of three men after the hand of Ludmilla. His rivals are a poet Ratmir and a warrior Farlaf who has no heart for fighting. Ludmilla has disappeared and each of her suitors seek to find her and thereby win her love. Russlan is helped by the wizard Finn and eventually succeeds in rescuing Ludmilla from the evil dwarf Chernomor by calming a giant, avoiding a vicious fairy and using a magic ring.

Saint Saens, Camille (1835–1921) French composer, teacher, piano virtuoso and organist whose orchestral works were so theatrical and dramatic (for example, the Organ Symphony or the *Carnival of the Animals*) it is difficult to understand why only one of the twelve operas he wrote is still popular today. That one is *Samson and Dalila* which has marvellous melodies and intensely romantic phrases but is still criticized by many eminent musicians for its lack of dramatic content.

Salieri, Antoni (1750–1825) The life of this eighteenth-century court composer has long been of fascination to music lovers, not so much for his own musical ability but because of the theory that Salieri murdered Mozart, as the young genius had crushed the older man's career. Rimsky-Korsakov made this rivalry the subject of the 1898 opera *Mozart and Salieri* and the debate was thrust even more forcefully into the public eye recently in Peter Shaffer's controversial play, *Amadeus*. Salieri became composer to the Austrian Court at Vienna in 1774, rising to Music Director in 1788 before moving to Paris where he became deeply influenced by the operatic reforms that Gluck was suggesting and wrote his opera *Les Danaides* under Gluck's guidance. While his lighter operas were acclaimed by the courts in both Austria and France, they are not so popular with modern audiences.

Salome (Richard Strauss) FP 1905. Strauss was one of several composers to use the biblical tale of Salome and the Dance of the Seven Veils as the subject for an opera, and his version is by far the most notable. It is set to a German translation of a poem by Oscar Wilde, himself no stranger to controversy, and the work caused a sensation at its first performance. The work demands enormous skill of the name part to conquer the punishing singing role and match it with convincingly erotic movements.

John the Baptist (called Jochanaan in the production) has been imprisoned by King Herod for preaching against the King's wife Herodias. Although Herod is angered by this, he has a strange respect for the religious man and cannot bring himself to have Jochanaan murdered. The King's stepdaughter Salome finds Jochanaan equally fascinating for less philosophical reasons and begs to be allowed to exercise her womanly charms on him, driving Narra-

Salome, Richard Strauss's erotic tour de force, with Stephanie Sundine in the title role for Welsh National Opera.

Samson and Dalila, by Saint-Saens. Alberto Remedios and Maureen Guy in the leading roles for Sadler's Wells Opera. *(photo. courtesy of ENO)*

both, who is deeply in love with Salome, to suicide when he witnesses her lascivious behaviour. Exploiting Herod's own infatuation with her, Salome strikes a bargain with her stepfather – if she dances for him, he must grant any wish she asks for. The dance is, of course, the famous scene where she gradually removes each of her seven veils, working Herod into a frenzy of lustful passion. Her demand is to be given the head of Jochanaan to which Herod reluctantly agrees. The murder is heard offstage and the head brought to Salome. Immediately she clasps it to her body, using the head to bring her to a state of erotic frenzy. She kisses the dead lips with passion and Herod can stand no more. Turning to his guards he orders that she be crushed to death by their shields.

Salzburg Austrian city closely linked with its most famous son, Wolfgang Amadeus Mozart, and subsequently with the leader of its Easter Festival and also a native of the city, Herbert von Karajan. The city, the summer home of the Vienna State Opera, now hosts two major music festivals, one in high summer and a second, begun by Karajan in 1966, at Easter. The summer festival was begun in 1917 by Richard Strauss and Hugo von Hoffmannsthal amongst others. Although intended to be primarily a celebration of the works of Mozart, it quickly developed to encompass the German repertory and the first opera, *Fidelio*, was performed in the newly rebuilt Festspielhaus in 1927. During the 1930s, the Festival became increasingly international, with performances led by Toscanini as well as German conductors such as Furtwangler and Bohm who were contracted after Germany invaded Austria in 1938. Furtwangler returned to the Festival after the war and in 1957 handed the leadership to von Karajan who is credited with establishing the Festival as a major international musical event. World premieres at the Festival have included *Danton's Tod* by Einem and *Vanessa* by Samuel Barber. When von Karajan died in July 1989, only eleven days before the opening of the Festival and the new production of *Un Ballo in Maschera* by Verdi, the effect on Salzburg – and on music lovers the world over – was devastating.

The Festival now has three venues. The Old Riding School has been converted to seat over 1500 for open air performances and the original Festspielhaus is now described as the Kleine Festspielhaus (Little Festival Theatre). It was overtaken in size by the building of the massive new Festspielhaus, which opened in 1964 and seats over 2300, with the largest stage area of any theatre in the world.

Samson and Dalila (Saint-Saens) FP 1877. This is the only opera written by Saint-Saens to retain its popularity today. Critics believe that it is actually better suited to a concert performance as the action is fairly static, but anyone who saw Placido Domingo and Agnes Baltsa in the production at the Royal Opera House will need no convincing of the stage drama of the piece, given the right cast. The work contains the heartbreakingly beautiful aria sung by Dalila, 'Softly Wakes my Heart'.

Samson leads his fellow Jews into battle against the Philistines and is victorious. This infuriates the beautiful Dalila, a Philistine woman once in love with Samson. Determined to seek revenge, supported by the High Priest Dagon, she uses her feminine charms on Samson to find out the secret of his strength. Samson confesses that all his power comes from his hair and is shorn and brutally blinded by the enemy. When all seems lost, he prays to God for a final show of strength. His prayer is granted and he brings the pillars of the temple crashing down, crushing the Philistines within.

San Francisco San Francisco is the ideal venue for grand opera – a beautiful city on the Californian coast with an affluent population who take pleasure and pride in their leisure pursuits. The city has always proved popular with touring opera companies since the days of prosperity created by the Gold Rush; but it was not until 1923 that Gaetano Merola created the San Francisco Opera Company, performing Italian works in the main, with the occasional foray into the German repertory. Merola was adroit in timing his two month season to precede the season at the Met in New York, enabling stars from the Met to sing in the San Francisco operas. He oversaw the company's move into the imposing War Memorial Opera House in 1932 and remained in control until his death in 1953, by which time the house and its company had attracted an impressive international reputation. Merola was succeeded by Kurt Adler who maintained the international image of the company but also encouraged young American singers to work alongside established professionals. He provided, through the San Francisco Opera Center, an exciting edge to the established classics which had a tendency to border on the conservative. Adler extended both the season and the repertory, providing works by Cherubini, Massenet and Janacek over a four month period. The international stars still came, including Tito Gobbi, Birgit Nilsson, Elisabeth Schwarzkopf and Renata Tebaldi and by the time Terry McEwen took over from Adler, in 1982, the house rivalled the Met for quality and adventure. The Opera now performs each autumn and has produced a superb Ring Cycle which is surely the aim of any confident and far sighted operatic organization.

Santa Fe A pioneering opera festival takes place each year in the New Mexico city, in an open air auditorium with only the pit and stage under cover. The Festival has a deliberate policy of encouraging new composers and young singers, principally American. American and world premieres since the Festival began in 1857 include *Jakobsleiter* by Schoenberg, *Lulu* by Berg, *The Nose* by Shostakovich, and *Opera* by Berio.

Sass, Marie (1834–1907) Belgian soprano who created the roles of Selika in *L'Africaine* by Meyerbeer, and Elisabeth of Valois in Verdi's *Don Carlos*. But her prima donna attitude during the rehearsals of the Verdi opera infuriated the composer, who refused to allow her to sing Amneris at the premiere of *Aida*.

Satyagraha (Philip Glass) FP 1980. The title comes from the Sanskrit word meaning strength or love. Glass uses Sanskrit with English in the text of the opera which concerns the life of Mahatma Ghandi, from his championing of the Indians in South Africa to his rise to leadership of the Independence struggle in India.

Saul og David (Nielsen) FP 1902. If you know and enjoy the symphonies of Nielsen, with their massive orchestral force and imposing construction, you will not be disappointed by this, the first of his two operas. He chose to portray King Saul as a tortured, involved personality, following his relationship with the young hero David who is friend to Saul's son Jonathan and eventually marries Saul's daughter Mikal. After David defeats Goliath, Saul's affection for the boy turns to jealousy and David is thrown out of the palace, returning to claim the crown after Saul has committed suicide.

Savoy Operas The general term used to describe the operettas with words by W.S. Gilbert and music by Sir Arthur Sullivan, taking the name of the theatre in which many of them were first produced. These operas started with *Trial by Jury* (1875) followed by *The Sorcerer* (1877) *HMS Pinafore* (1878), *The Pirates of Penzance* (1879), *Patience* (1881), *Iolanthe* (1882), *The Mikado* (1885), *Ruddigore* (1887), *The Yeomen of the Guard* (1888) and *The Gondoliers* (1889). The pair's association with Richard D'Oyly Carte, a Victorian impressario, began when he commissioned 'Trial' in 1875 and continued for Gilbert and Sullivan's writing careers. All the works were performed at the Savoy Theatre, which D'Oyly Carte owned and, on Gilbert's death in 1911, the D'Oyly Carte family assumed sole rights to the performances of the operas. To the sadness of all Gilbert and Sullivan aficiandos, the theatre, which is adjacent to the Savoy Hotel in London, has recently been devastated by fire.

Scala, La (see Milan)

Scarlatti, Alessandro (1660–1725) Italian composer. Scarlatti's output hardly ever features in the mainstream repertory of a contemporary opera house but his contribution to the development of opera as an art form is inestimable. He lived at a time when musicians could only succeed thanks to the patronage of the courts of Italy, and therefore had to tailor his output to please the princes and nobles. But that output was massive – one hundred and fifteen operas of which the best known are *Mitridate Eupatore* which he wrote for Ferdinando de' Medici and *Il Trionfo del'Onore* which was ecstatically received by an audience in Rome less hampered by courtly conventions. Scarlatti is credited with developing the da capo aria (where the singer repeats the first section of the aria having sung the whole thing through once) as a feature of 'opera seria'.

Schenck, Otto Austrian producer who took up the post of Chief Stage Director for the Vienna State Opera in 1965, working frequently with Claudio Abbado and Carlos Kleiber. His productions rely less on grandiose concepts than on detailed direction of individual personalities, a successful formula which has brought him into great demand in the world's major opera houses. He produced, amongst other notable productions, the first part of a new Ring Cycle for the Metropolitan Opera in 1986.

Schikaneder, Emanuel (1751–1812) Schikaneder was the actor manager of a highly successful theatre troupe in Austria in the latter part of the eighteenth century and would have remained an obscure figure in the history of popular theatre had it not been for one important collaborative production he undertook in 1791. He joined with Wolfgang Amadeus Mozart to produce the first staging of *Die Zauberflote* (*The Magic Flute*) for which he wrote the libretto and played the first Papageno. He set Mozart's mysterious work firmly in realms of popular theatre (the sequence in the film *Amadeus* brings this out admirably) and it was only later, more intellectual audiences that questioned the deeper meaning behind the references to Freemasonry and the occult in what appears to be a lighthearted and amusing 'singspiel' or pantomime.

Schiller, Friedrich (1759–1805) German playwright and poet whose epic works have been transformed into highly successful operas, including *Don Carlos, Luisa Miller* and *I Masnadieri*, all by Verdi, and *Maria Stuarda* by Donizetti.

Schipa, Tito (1888–1965) Italian tenor who began his career in Europe before moving to America in 1919, making his name with the Chicago and San Francisco Operas as well as at the Metropolitan in New York. He specialized in the lyric roles of romantic leads such as Alfredo in *La Traviata*, Count Almaviva in *The Barber of Seville*, Des Grieux in *Manon* by Massenet and the title role in *Werther* by

Massenet. He returned to Italy in 1929 and spent the remainder of his performing career there. While his voice was not outstandingly strong, his ability to project sincere romantic feeling into every role he played made him one of the most popular tenors of the mid-twentieth century.

Schoenberg, Arnold (1874–1951) If you listen to the music of Schoenberg unprepared, it will confirm all your worst suspicions about contemporary music – harsh, dissonant, spontaneous and definitely no recognizable tunes. His music needs to be approached with caution for the beginner, but stands the test of time because of the revolutionary method of composition he introduced, known as twelve note composition.

Music is usually written in a key, or tone, either major or minor, based on a sequence of eight consecutive notes called a scale. Early in his career, Schoenberg had decided that it was limiting to stick to writing music in one key and decided that his pieces would be written with no particular key as a base – this is called atonal composition (or 'pantonal' as he preferred to call it.) He included the half tones between the eight notes in a scale, making a total of twelve notes. (This is easier to visualize if you think about the seven white notes on a piano and add in the black notes between them.) Using these twelve notes in any order he decided (called a 'note row' or 'series') would become the basis of his composition. Although Schoenberg applied these rules most rigidly in his operas *Von Heute auf Morgen* and the unfinished *Moses und Aron*, his twelve note composition was imitated and adapted by more 'accessible' composers such as William Walton in his violin sonata and Benjamin Britten in his opera *The Turn of the Screw*.

Schorr, Friedrich (1888–1953) Hungarian bass-baritone who created a highly successful international career by specializing in the great Wagner roles of Wotan, the Dutchman, Hans Sachs and Telramund amongst many others. He sang twenty seasons with the Metropolitan Opera as well as frequent appearances at Bayreuth, Covent Garden and San Francisco. He was able to inject individual characteristics into each of the great variety of roles he played with an engagingly lyrical voice that has been well preserved on many recordings.

Schwarzkopf, Elisabeth German soprano who moved from coloratura to lyric roles before finding a small number of parts that were specially suited to her voice. In these she excelled, giving detailed, carefully thought-out performances whose musical excellence occasionally prevented any spontaneous characterization. But nothing could detract from the immense beauty of her voice and her own stunning appearance which made her one of the best loved and most sought after performers of the post war period. From her early work with the Stadtische Opera Berlin, Schwarzkopf moved to work with the Vienna State Opera, where she remained until 1947. Then she moved to London as part of the company at the Royal Opera House, Covent Garden, and by the time she reached Salzburg, where she stayed until 1964, she had perfected a number of roles with which she would ever afterwards be associated. These included the Marschallin from *Der Rosenkavalier* and the Countess from *The Marriage of Figaro*, Donna Elvira from *Don Giovanni*, Alice Ford from *Falstaff* and Fiordigli from *Cosi fan Tutte*. This did not preclude her from contemporary work, and she sang the role of Anne Truelove in the world premiere of *The Rake's Progress* by Stravinsky in 1951, or from Wagner roles which she sang at the 1951 Bayreuth Festival. She retired from performance in 1975 and has since led a series of prestigious masterclasses.

Schweigsame Frau, Die (Richard Strauss) FP 1935. The plot of this work corresponds loosely to *Don Pasquale* by Donizetti. Sir Morosus hates noise of any sort and his barber offers to find him a 'schweigsame frau' (silent woman) for him to marry. Panic descends on the household when Morosus realizes that his nephew Henry has married a very noisy opera singer, Aminta. Henry is disinherited at once and, set on revenge, tricks his uncle into marrying Aminta when she is disguised as 'Timida'. The moment the wedding is over, Aminta's true character is revealed and the desperate doctor agrees to reinstate Henry's fortune in return for his own peace of mind.

Scotti, Antonio (1866–1936) Italian baritone who worked under Toscanini at La Scala where he made his debut in 1898 but thereafter based his career in London and New York. While he performed a wide range of principal roles including Sharpless (*Madam Butterfly*) Marcello (*La Bohème*) and Tonio (*I Pagliacci*), he is best remembered for his performances of Scarpia, the arch villain in Puccini's *Tosca*. He appeared in all but eleven of the performances given of *Tosca* at the Metropolitan Opera during his entire career, (which spanned nearly thirty years) performing the role there a staggering one hundred and fifty-six times. Shortly before he left the Met, he established his own company which was unsuccessful.

Scottish Opera Founded in 1962 by Sir Alexander Gibson, Scottish Opera has developed over the last three decades into a prestigious and inventive opera company with strong and accomplished resident artists and a reputation sufficient to attract singers of international calibre. The company has an adventurous programming policy, staging new productions of contemporary works such as *Candide* by Bernstein and *Street Scene* by Kurt Weill. Such decisions are complemented by high standards in classic productions, particularly of works by Wagner and Britten. The company's home is in the Theatre Royal, Glasgow which takes its place in the forefront of arts venues in a city brimming with excellent artistic initiatives and named in 1990 as the European City of Culture. Much of the success of Scottish Opera is due to the young, forward-looking administration, led by Richard Mantle with the extremely talented American, John Mauceri as Music Director.

Scotto, Renata Italian soprano at her best singing the light, lyric roles written by Bellini, Puccini and the other masters of the romantic Italian repertoire. Scotto made an international impression from these performances, singing all over Europe and America during the early part of her career. By 1974, she felt ready to take on the deeper roles such as Leonora in *Il Trovatore*, Desdemona in *Otello*, Norma and Lady Macbeth, which many believed her voice was not strong enough to sustain. But her excellent sense of musicianship enabled her to produce performances of a high, if not always superb, standard and her sense of theatre led her to direct a production of *Madam Butterfly* for the Met in 1986.

Scribe, Eugene (1791–1861) French librettist who worked with several prominent nineteenth-century composers including Auber for *La Muette de Portici*, Meyerbeer for *L'Africaine* and *Les Huguenots* amongst others and Halevy for *La Juive*. Once Donizetti had abandoned his opera *Duc d'Albe*, Scribe reworked the text and passed it to Verdi who created *The Sicilian Vespers* out of it.

Season, The Conjuring up images of debs, tea dances and charity balls, opera houses still refer to their 'season' to describe the sequence of months in which they do their work. Some play for one long season – English National Opera, for example, roughly follows the academic year from September to June with a break in the summer. The Royal Opera House is less rigid, interspersing ballet with opera throughout the year. The British touring companies refer to their winter, spring or summer seasons, or, occasionally, the town in which they play – the Cardiff or Glasgow season and so on. The Metropolitan Opera in New York runs a system more akin to ENO and there the 'first night of the season' is recognized as a major social event.

Segreto do Susanna, Il (Wolf Ferrari) FP 1909. Susanna's secret is that she is a closet smoker. When her husband sniffs cigarette smoke in the air, he assumes she has taken a lover but eventually Susanna confesses and all is put to rights.

Sellars, Peter American director whose outrageous opera productions have alienated many purists in the opera world but encouraged many others who would otherwise never have thought of attempting to sit through an opera. Like many contemporary directors saddled with the label 'controversial', Sellars will maintain that his work is not controversial, just misunderstood. A regular artist with the now-dissolved Pepsico Summerfest in America, Sellars productions are gradually making their way to Europe. These include a setting of *Don Giovanni* in the drug crazed sub culture of 1980s Manhattan and *The Electrification of the Soviet Union* by Nigel Osborne. Interestingly, of all the British companies who might have commissioned Sellars to work with them, it was the supposedly conservative Glyndebourne Festival Opera which asked him first. He directed 'Electrification' for them and will return for the 1990 Festival to direct *The Magic Flute*. It is advisable not to pre-judge Sellars' work on the almost hysterical media reaction it provokes. Rather base your reaction on whether Sellars' radical interpretations increase your own enjoyment and understanding of the work.

Semele (Handel) FP 1744. This piece can work with equal success as a concert performance in the style of an oratorio or in a full stage presentation. The story is slight and therefore the action in a full staging is minimal. The work contains the famous Handel aria 'Where'er you Walk'.

The god Jupiter, in the form of a man, is in love with the mortal Semele but Juno encourages Semele to ask Jupiter to reveal himself to her as a god. He finally agrees to do so, knowing that the consequences will be tragic. As Semele glimpses the dazzling effect of Jupiter in all his glory, she is consumed in the surrounding fires.

Semiramide (Rossini) FP 1823. Rossini's first 'grand opera' was written for his first wife, the virtuoso singer Isabella Colbran. The plot is confusing, about a mother who falls in love with a young man, not realizing him to be her son.

Semiramide is Queen of Babylon and Prince Assur is in love with her. Together, they have murdered Semiramide's husband, King Nino, but Semiramide's affections have turned from Assur to the youth Arsace. Arsace is in love with the Princess Azema and is told by the priest Orsoe that Semiramide is his mother. Unaware that she is Arsace's mother, Semiramide declares that she will marry Arsace which provokes the ghost of Nino to appear, declaring that the truth will be revealed about his death and that Arsace will accede the throne. The ghost pleads with his son to follow him and they are in turn followed by Assur who is determined to murder his rival. But Semiramide has discovered that Arsace is her son and sets out to protect him. Finding Arsace and Assur locked in battle, Semiramide is stabbed by her son, who intended to strike Assur. The throne is now clear for Arsace, who marries Princess Azema.

Sendak, Maurice American designer and illustrator, Sendak is known principally as an author and illustrator of children's books but his unique and lively style of characterization enchanted the opera-going audience when Oliver Knussen set two of his works *Where the Wild Things Are* and *Higglety Pigglety Pop!* to full operatic scores, leaving Sendak to design the sets and costumes. The productions ran with immense success on both sides of the Atlantic. Sendak has continued his stage work with designs for *The Magic Flute* in Houston, *The Cunning Little Vixen* for New York City Opera and *The Love of Three Oranges* at Glyndebourne.

Senesino (1680–1759) This Italian singer was rarely known by his real name (Francesco Bernardi) but rather by the nickname which was derived from the city of his birth – Siena. He was one of the world's greatest alto-castrati and delighted audiences in London with his creation of many of the major roles in Handel's operas including *Julius Caesar*, *Tamberlaine* and *Rodelinda*.

Serafin, Tullio (1878–1968) Italian conductor whose mastery of the classics of the Italian opera repertoire and encouragement of some of the greatest singers of his day earned him fame throughout the world, particularly in America. He was twice Principal Conductor of La Scala, Milan, from 1909 to 1914 and again from 1917 to 1918, before moving to America for most of the 1920s where in his ten seasons with the Met he conducted the American premieres of *Simon Boccanegra* and *Turandot*. He is credited with being the guiding force behind such notable singers as Dame Joan Sutherland, Rosa Ponselle and Maria Callas.

Serban, Andrei Romanian director. Andre Serban worked as a theatre director in Bucharest before gaining a scholarship to work with the La Mama Experimental Theater Company in New York. In New York he met the international theatre director Peter Brook who invited him to work with him in Paris. Serban's first opera production was *Eugene Onegin* for Welsh National Opera – a staging now considered to be a classic of that company's repertoire. He went on to stage a magnificent Ring Cycle, also for WNO and an often-revived *Turandot* for Covent Garden. His work is now increasingly seen in America where, amongst other work, he has staged *Alcina* and *Norma* for New York City Opera.

Serse (see Xerxes)

Session Before the advent of unions to protect the rights of performers, unscrupulous managers, directors and conductors could arrange endless rehearsals which could take a punishing toll on the physical well-being of a singer or player. Now all rehearsals are divided into sessions, each of which lasts roughly three hours, and after which all performers are entitled to have a break. The session also creates an easy method of payment as each performer will have a 'session rate'. The skill comes in calculating how many sessions will be needed to bring a full cast and orchestra from the first day of rehearsal to a performing standard. It is on the basis of those calculations that performance budgets are set, and extra sessions, particularly if they are scheduled at anti-social times or close to the start of a performance, can prove extremely expensive. It is difficult to split sessions for payment purposes unless the unions are particularly compliant, and occasionally performers will be entitled to a full session payment even if the rehearsal has overrun by only ten minutes.

Sets The set creates the look of an opera, together with the mood and atmosphere which the director and designer together have decided should prevail for the piece. Thus the set makes a powerful impression on the audience, leading either to increased involvement or to gradual alienation from the opera. While every set designer will fiercely defend his or her individuality, there is no doubt that trends do emerge in set design, either through one designer working out a particular theory or several designers exploring variations on one theme. This can sometimes lead to impatience amongst regular opera goers. An intelligently designed set will draw the audience into the production, not necessarily because it is immediately attractive but because it adds another dimension to the performance. Patrick Robinson and Rosemary Vercoe's design for the last act of the 'Mafioso' *Rigoletto* (ENO 1982) is an excellent example of this – a dingy bar in a pool of light with the lowering tenements behind (inspired by an Edward Hopper painting) could not be called attractive by any standards but greatly increased the tension already established by Verdi's magnificent score. Naturally expectations are formed by the reputations of some operas – a monotone *Arabella* or impoverished *Der Rosenkavalier* would be a great disappointment to many. But if the designer and director are convinced by their concept, however radical, it is their responsibility to pass on that vision to the audience and not leave them wondering 'Well it was all very nice to listen to, but why was it set in a corn field?'

Shakespeare, William (1564–1616) English playwright whose massive output became the inspiration for many fine operas. Many have transferred well to the operatic stage but the greatness of Shakespeare's original play needs to be matched by music and a libretto of a similar stature. Of the more successful, one should note *Falstaff* by Verdi (thought by many to be his finest opera), *A Midsummer Night's Dream* by Benjamin Britten and *Otello* by Verdi. Among the less notable, one finds *Hamlet* by Ambroise Thomas and *Liebsverbot* by Wagner, based on *Measure for Measure*.

Shicoff, Neil American tenor who has performed with opera companies in New York, San Francisco and Chicago, with a limited number of performances in Europe. Shicoff's clear strong voice makes him a convincing Rodolfo and Romeo amongst a wide repertoire of roles, though his acting ability is sometimes criticized for its lack of commitment.

Shimell, William English bass. Following a successful ENO debut in 1980 as Masetto in *La Bohème*, Shimell has sung a variety of other roles with this company. In 1985 he appeared in the title role of a new ENO production of *Don Giovanni* directed by Jonathan Miller in which his convincing if effusive portrayal of the Don was much praised. His international career has increased, as his voice matures and develops and he made a very successful debut at La Scala singing the Count in *The Marriage of Figaro*. He makes regular concert appearances throughout Britain and sang in the Glyndebourne production of *The Marriage of Figaro*, televised at the 1989 Proms.

Shirley-Quirk, John English bass-baritone whose distinguished bearing and distinctive voice made him a recognizable feature in many of the first performances of operas by Benjamin Britten. These included the Church Parables, *Death in Venice* and *Owen Wingrave* and his repertoire also included notable performances in *Ariadne auf Naxos* and *The Magic Flute*.

Shostakovich, Dmitri (1906–1975) Russian composer whose operatic output was seriously restricted by the pressure put on him by the Stalinist authorities. His two early operas *The Nose*, written in 1930 and *Lady Macbeth of Mtsensk*, written in 1934 were acclaimed at their premieres but by 1936, he was being attacked in the national press, most notably in an article entitled 'Chaos instead of Music'. Fearing for his own safety, he agreed to conform to the demands of his superiors and thereby deprived the operatic world of the products of his fertile imagination. Once the Stalinist era was over, he returned to opera writing, revising 'Lady Macbeth' under the title *Katerina Ismailova* and penning a lighter work *Moscow, Cheremushki*. He also re-orchestrated two operas by Moussorgsky, *Boris Godunov* and *Kkovanshcina*.

Shore, Andrew English bass-baritone who specializes in the comic roles. Very much in demand all over Britain for these performances and therefore enjoys a prolific performing career. A sample of his engagements for the 1989/90 season included: Dr Bartolo (Glyndebourne Touring, Opera North, Welsh National Opera); Don Pasquale (Opera North); Mr Gedge (Glyndebourne Festival); Papageno, Alfonso, Pooh-Bah, and Frank, in *Die Fledermaus*, (all for ENO).

Sicilian Vespers, The (Verdi) FP 1855. Donizetti had commissioned two writers, Scribe and Duveyrier, to write him a libretto for his opera *Le Duc d'Albe* but by the time their words and his music were approaching completion, Donizetti was dying of syphilis. Verdi, exploiting this opportunity, persuaded the writers to abandon Donizetti's music and adapt their work for his opera instead. The result is one of his richest works, inspired by the French grand opera tradition. As so often with Verdi's works, the central theme revolves around personal love in conflict with family loyalty.

The French, under Montfort, have invaded the island of Sicily. The captured people are planning an uprising against their oppressors. This is to be led by the Duchess Helene, her lover Henri and the revolutionary Jean Procida. But Henri is the illegitimate son of the French leader Montfort and thus feels duty bound to protect his father when the revolutionaries, led by Helene and Procida, come to kill Montfort. The Sicilians are captured and Helen is furious with Henri for betraying them, until she realizes that he is torn between his father and his people. She forgives him and Henri pursuades his father to release the Sicilians and allow him to marry Helene. But Procida cannot abandon his revolutionary aims. At the wedding ceremony, as the bells ring to celebrate the union, Procida leads his men in to slaughter the defenceless French.

Siegfried (see Ring des Nibelungen)

Silja, Anya German soprano who has excelled in two diverse areas of opera – Wagner and contemporary works. Her early career was encouraged by Wieland Wagner and she sang at her first Bayreuth Festival (in the role of Senta in *The Flying Dutchman*) at the age of twenty. Devastated by Wieland Wagner's death, she rejected the Wagner roles altogether and broadened her repertoire to encompass roles as different as The Queen of the Night and Carmen. She felt these did not suit her temperament and moved on to works by Russian composers, by Richard Strauss and by Janacek. It is in these that she now excels and performs internationally, with memorable performances of Salome, Katya Kabanova, Jenufa,

Fidelio and Lady Macbeth of Mtsensk. A strongly committed actress, she welcomes the radical productions of directors like Ruth Berghaus and will soon direct her own opera production. She is married to the Music Director of the Cleveland Philharmonic Orchestra, Christopher Dohnanyi.

Sills, Beverly American soprano who reached the height of her performing career with the New York City Opera and remained there as General Manager after her retirement from the stage. For a decade from her debut with the company in 1955 she sang all the principal soprano roles, attracting a faithful and appreciative audience. By the mid 1960s, her fame had spread to the major European opera houses, including Vienna, La Scala and Covent Garden but it was not until 1975 that she returned home to make her official debut with the Metropolitan Opera. In 1979 she sang in her final performance at New York City Opera, assuming the General Directorship from Julius Rudel in the same year.

Simon Boccanegra (Verdi) FP 1857. Dark and sinister, *Simon Boccanegra* has never been the most popular of Verdi's works and should be left by a new opera-goer until his more accessible works such as *Rigoletto* and *La Traviata* have been seen and enjoyed. Even Verdi described his first version as 'monotonous and cold' and revised it substantially twenty years after its premiere. The plot is divided into two sections, the first taking place twenty-five years before the second.

Simon Boccanegra, a plebian, has fallen in love with Maria, daughter of Jacopo Fiesco, a nobleman, and the couple have had a little girl. Jacopo Fiesco thinks Boccanegra is unsuitable as a son-in-law and has forbidden the couple to marry. Unable to live together, Simon and Maria have left their child with an old woman and now the child has disappeared. Simon is persuaded by fellow plebians Paolo and Pietro that he should stand for the office of Doge which might raise his status in the eyes of Fiesco and enable him to marry Maria. Moments before he is elected, he discovers that Maria has died. Twenty-five years later, Fiesco has changed his name to Andrea and lives with his adopted ward, Amelia. Amelia is in love with Gabriele Adorno, but is loved by the plebian of the previous scene, Paolo. Boccanegra comes to Amelia to ask her to marry Paolo but soon realizes that she is the daughter he, Boccanegra, has lost. He refuses to allow Paolo to marry her. Paolo and Pietro join together in a plan to have Amelia abducted but Adorno thwarts their plan by killing the abductor. Boccanegra does his best to calm the ensuing revolt as Adorno and Fiesco are urged by Paolo to murder Boccanegra. Adorno is led to believe that Boccanegra is Amelia's lover and his jealousy provokes him to attempt the murder. He is unsuccessful and learns that Amelia is Boccanegra's daughter. Paolo is not so easily dissuaded and succeeds in poisoning Boccanegra's drink. As he lies dying, Boccanegra summons Fiesco and shows him the one thing that could have united the two men – Amelia, Boccanegra's daughter and Fiesco's granddaughter. Moments before Boccanegra's death, he and Fiesco forgive one another and Amelia and Adorno are given her father's blessing.

Singspiel Literally 'sing play', this term describes a series of light hearted songs connected by spoken dialogue which was extremely popular in Germany in the eighteenth century. It was the forerunner of the German Romantic Opera movement, developed into full operatic form in works such as *Der Freischutz* by Weber.

Sinopoli, Guiseppi Italian conductor who is principal conductor of the Philharmonia Orchestra in London and pursues an active international opera career, working at the Met in New York, Bayreuth and La Fenice in Venice. A specialist in the Italian repertoire, Sinopoli has proved that conductors can create highly individual interpretations of even the best known works and has roused considerable controversy because of his controversial and exciting approach.

Sitzprobe This 'sitting rehearsal' takes place at the start of every rehearsal period and equates to a read-through for a theatrical play. The chorus and soloists join the orchestra in a complete run through of the opera with all cast members sitting, usually on stage, for the duration of the rehearsal.

Smetana, Bedrich (1824–1884) Czech composer who did much to promote the nationalist sentiments of the Czech people through his operas. His best known work is *The Bartered Bride* which uses tunes which appear to be derived from folk music although they were in fact the fruit of many revisions by the composer. Smetana did not actually learn the Czech language until he was in his mid-twenties but managed to encapsulate the patriotic feeling of his people, even though his musical influences came from numerous sources other than his homeland. For example, *Dalibor*, which he wrote in 1884, is clearly influenced by the music of Wagner (and was criticized as such when it opened). He also looked to Verdi, Gluck and Meyerbeer for his inspiration. Whatever the source or motivation, Smetana will remain in the vanguard of nationalist music.

Smyth, Dame Ethel (1858–1944) English composer who is notable for being one of the very few English women to compose operas. She studied in Germany where one of her works *The Wreckers* was premiered. Perhaps sensing the uncertain reception she would receive at home, she made her music as European in influence as possible, even writing the libretto for *The Wreckers* in French (despite its setting of a fishing village on the West Coast of England!) But taken in total, her music is unmistakably English, relying heavily on English ballads and folk songs in many of her works.

Soderstrom, Elisabeth Swedish soprano. To say that Elisabeth Soderström is something of an institution in the world of opera is not to criticize her, but merely to recognize the great contribution she has made since her debut in the 1950s, reflected by the many honours bestowed on her, both in her native Sweden and elsewhere. She is most famous as The Marschallin in *Der Rosenkavalier* which she first sang for the Royal Opera in Stockholm in 1959 and subsequently for almost every major opera house in the world. In 1981 a performance of *Der Rosenkavalier* in Stockholm was saved from disaster when Soderstrom, singing the Marschallin, substituted for an ailing colleague by appearing as Octavian in the second act while an understudy was found;

she then completed the opera as the Marschallin. Her rare recitals are inevitably sought after by her following all over the world.

Solti, Sir Georg Hungarian conductor whose early career reads like an almost unbelievable combination of luck and courage, resourced by a formidable talent which has brought him to his current status of one of the world's most eminent musicians. With characteristic guts, Solti wrote to Arturo Toscanini at the Salzburg Festival, asking if he might sit in on rehearsals and rapidly fell under the great musician's disciplinarian influence. After a brief time at the Budapest Opera, Solti escaped to Switzerland during the Second World War, opting to move to Munich in 1945 – a brave venture for a Jewish refugee – and gradually gaining an impressive reputation at the opera house there. He made other debuts in Europe and by 1952 had moved on to the Frankfurt Opera, continuing to maintain a now-international reputation, particularly through performances in San Francisco and Salzburg, as well as an acclaimed Ring Cycle for Decca Records. When, in 1959, he was invited to be Music Director of Covent Garden, Bruno Walter advised him to take it saying, 'You will hate the weather, but you will come to love the English and they will love you'. It wasn't quite so simple, Solti finding Covent Garden's standards depressingly amateur and his musicians railing against his tyrannical regime, describing him as 'the screaming skull'! But he brought the house to standards of musical excellence which were world class, working with producers like Zeffirelli, singers like Callas, on productions like *Billy Budd*, *Otello*, and *Moses and Aron* – all of which time has judged to be among the greatest ever. He left in 1971 and has since concentrated on his work with symphony orchestras, notably the Chicago Symphony which he has masterminded to brilliance since 1969. But his continuing and unassailable pre-eminence in the opera world was marked in 1989 when he was asked to take the place of Herbert von Karajan conducting the new production of *Un Ballo in Maschera* at the Salzburg Festival. To take up Karajan's baton at such a time – only weeks after Karajan's death – was a task that would have defeated great men.

With genius backed by confidence, Solti turned the performance into a laudable one, and will conduct the revival in Salzburg in 1990.

Sonnambula, La (Bellini) FP 1831. As with Bellini's other great work, *Norma*, this opera depends heavily on the soprano singing the major role of Amina. As sleepwalking always conjures up such an air of mystery, it makes for thrilling drama if the production has developed the tension throughout the piece, leading to the final dramatic sleepwalk as the villagers look on. Technicians are confronted by a difficulty in this piece – how to make a plank shatter under the heroine without allowing her to fall to the floor.

Amina and Elvino have just become engaged and a stranger has joined them to wish them luck. He is really Count Rodolfo who shows more than a passing interest in Amina, much to Elvino's consternation. Lisa is also in love with Elvino and enters the rooms of Count Rodolfo, fleeing when she hears a noise and leaving her handkerchief behind. Amina, sleepwalking, enters the room as Rodolfo leaves and she is found the next morning by the villagers. As she has been out all night, Elvino suspects she has been with Rodolfo and rejects her, saying he will marry Lisa. Then he realizes Lisa's handkerchief was found in Rodolfo's bedroom and spurns her too. But that night, Elvino sees Amelia sleepwalking on the rooftops of the mill at such danger to herself (as the plank she walks on breaks) that he realizes that her sleepwalking story must be true. He wakes her and begs her forgiveness.

Soprano The highest register of the human voice which can reach the F above a high C in the upper ranges of a coloratura voice. It has many subdivisions from mezzo, describing the lower ranges through lyric, placed in the middle range, to coloratura which encompasses the very top of the register.

Spoleto Festival Known as 'The Festival of the Two Worlds' and located in the small town of Spoleto in Umbria, Italy, this Festival was begun in 1958 by the composer Gian Carlo Menotti. The philosophy behind the

Festival is to perform little known or neglected works using young singers from America and Europe led by experienced directors, including those of the calibre of Visconti and Roman Polanski. The repertoire and productions are exciting and adventurous, encompassing operas by the founder of the Festival as well as those by composers as diverse as Salieri, Prokofiev and Henze.

Sponsorship Fifteen years ago, arts sponsorship in Britain was not unknown but somewhat unusual. Now it is an accepted part of life in any subsidized artistic enterprise. It is still not welcomed in some quarters, attended by much prejudice and destructive rumour, and opinion is still firmly divided as to whether it can be classed as a 'good thing'. It is a fickle form of funding, providing no guarantees and no binding legal agreements. But in the present economic climate, it has worked its way into the minds, if not the hearts of every size of arts group. The situation in America is quite different. The climate for corporate and individual giving is long and firmly held. A sense of civic duty, of 'paying back one debt to society' is prevalent everywhere, with the added social cachet which attends a major donor in New York, Washington or San Francisco. The corporate community has very many positive things to offer the arts world, not only in hard cash. The more enlightened organizations will staff their sponsorship offices with personnel of good calibre who may have an interest in opera or at least a willingness to learn about it. They will develop coherent donations policies and not rely on sponsorship of one new production to change their entire company image. Companies need never feel ill-at-ease when plunged into the business world, as business efficiency, personnel management and constant cost cutting are everyday concerns to a subsidised arts group.

There are many more links between sponsor and sponsored than the oversized cheque and endless photos for the annual report. There are many ways arts and business can get together, through training, secondments, capital projects, education work, new writing – the list is endless – for the benefit of everyone. A certain shyness exists on both sides. Arts groups tend to become defensive about their 'product', believing the sponsor will want to change it, to extract anything controversial, to end up with something which the chairman's wife is bound to enjoy. But even the most senior corporate executive may be daunted by meeting an opera singer or a stage manager or a conductor. 'I can run a senior board meeting at one of London's major financial houses without batting an eyelid but when I met Jessye Norman – my heroine for so many years – I couldn't think of a thing to say.' admitted one.

Staff Producer A thankless job but an excellent training ground for would-be directors, staff producers act as back-up to the main production director and will be responsible for the rehearsals of that production after opening night. The larger companies will employ a number of staff producers to cover the whole repertory, so no director works in isolation. A big new production may have two staff producers working on it. While the overall concept of the production is left to the main director, the staff producer will be expected to contribute ideas during the rehearsal period and listen to the reactions of the cast – the junior members of which may be too shy to communicate their thoughts to the director! Such a combination of inspiration and diplomacy makes the job of staff producer a hard one, but rewarding for those who wish to develop this competitive and oversubscribed career.

Stage Management The capable coper, the still, calm voice in a sea of frenzied egos, the one who simply would not let rip until well inside the pub after the final curtain call is over and the final light has dimmed, the staff of a stage management department are regarded with affection in most theatres. The job virtually defies description – sole charge of all activities backstage during a performance from the moment the 'all-clear' is received from front of house to the final curtain call. It is a massive task of administration for a major opera production, centring on the stage manager's desk (usually stage right with a clear view across the stage) from where he or she must cue the lights, call the principals from the dressing rooms in good time for their entrances, cue all the major scene changes and ensure the chorus is correctly situated throughout. It is the responsibility of the stage manager to ensure that whatever chaos is happening backstage (and a good stage manager will admit to only 'a little local difficulty' even on the most disastrous of performances) is not transmitted in any way to the audience. The stage manager's bible is 'the book', a score with music printed on one side of the page only, leaving the opposite side blank. Here, every move of every person on stage will be noted, together with the position of every prop, in an ever-changing sequence which the stage manager must keep up to date throughout the rehearsal period as the director will constantly refer to it to remind himself of his last brilliant idea. Naturally enough, even a middle scale production cannot rely on one stage manager, but divides the responsibilites between the manager, a deputy (DSM) and an assistant (ASM). Throughout the rehearsal period, the team develops a close working relationship with the cast which is inevitably not without clashes and difficulties but rarely encounters a problem which cannot be solved over a quiet drink in the bar. As one highly experienced singer summed it up: 'I've met plenty of unpleasant singers, a fair few nasty players, and more than one difficult director. But I've never yet met an unfriendly stage manager'.

Stanislavsky, Konstantin (1863–1938) Russian director whose theories on acting style, put forward in his book *Method Acting* have had a profound influence on twentieth-century theatre. Stanislavsky's central theory is that actors should become wholly and utterly identified with the characters they are playing, becoming totally immersed in all aspects of the personality in order to achieve a truly natural performance. He was heavily involved in operatic work, opening the studio of the Bolshoi Theatre as an operatic studio in 1918. Here, he directed performances of (amongst others) *Werther*, *Eugene Onegin*, *Boris Godunov* and *Don Pasquale*, hoping to achieve the same realism in the acting of opera as he attempted in stage drama.

Stevens, Rise American mezzo-soprano whose wide ranging career included per-

formances at all the major houses in America, in several European theatres including notable performances at Glyndebourne and even in a film with Bing Crosby (*Going My Way*)! Her repertoire included excellent interpretations of Cherubino, Carmen and Octavian. She is now a director of the Metropolitan Opera and advisor to their young artists' development programme.

Stockhausen, Karlheinz German composer who was influenced by Messaien in the early part of his career but has gone on to develop a highly individual style which may sound abrasive to the first time listener. His orchestral pieces are all highly theatrical in style, using extraordinary techniques and encouraging the use of 'groups' of sound, where three orchestras with three conductors might create one performance. His only works to be performed in the opera house are part of the Licht cycle which is based on the creation of the world, going through each day in turn. So far, *Samstag* (Saturday) and *Donnerstag* (Thursday) have been staged.

Stone Guest, The (Dargomijsky) FP 1872. Although this is based on a poem by Pushkin, it is clearly the same story as *Don Giovanni* which in turn was based on a poem called 'The Stone Guest' by Giuseppe Gazzaniga. Rimsky-Korsakov provided the orchestration for this opera after the death of the composer.

Don Juan has attempted to seduce the Donna Anna, widow of the Commendatore who was killed by Don Juan. The Don invites the stone statue of the Commendatore to meet him at Donna Anna's house. The statue accepts and condemns the philanderer to hell.

Stratas, Teresa Canadian soprano who broke away from singing in night clubs in down town Toronto but can still give her performances of modern opera that earthy, intriguing quality borne of her early singing career. The first Lulu in the first full staging of Alban Berg's opera in 1979, she has also sung Jenny in *Mahagonny*, Sardulla in *The Last Savage* by Menotti and a range of roles from the classic repertoire. Her voice can be lyric, dramatic, intense, flirtatious or tragic with a fine command of coloratura singing

Karlheinz Stockhausen's contribution to the world of opera is the epic Licht Cycle, planned in seven parts to describe the creation of the world. The dancer, Michele Noiret in a scene from *Donnerstag* at the Royal Opera House.

Richard Strauss's *Der Rosenkavalier* is usually staged classically to emphasize the courtly nature of the opera. Amanda Roocroft as Sophie, and Constance Fee as Octavian, in Welsh National Opera's 1990 production.

Stravinsky's *The Rake's Progress*. David Rendall and Linda Ormiston, in David Hockney's Glyndebourne production, based on the original Hogarth prints.

and an extensive acting ability. She appeared as Violetta in Zeffirelli's 1983 film.

Strauss, Johann (1825–1899) Austrian composer. 'The Waltz King', as he came to be known was initially discouraged from a musical future but overruled his composer father to rise to an illustrious career both in Europe and on tour in America. He was inspired to write opera when he witnessed and admired the success of Offenbach's works in Paris. In *Die Fledermaus*, he achieved a formula which outshone even Offenbach with a witty brilliance (but without Offenbach's political satire) which suited the Viennese admirably and has continued to delight audiences ever since. It was the operatic highlight of his career, with only his later composition *Der Zigeunerbaron* approaching it for popularity. His other operas are hampered by bad libretti, diminishing the effect of his marvellously tuneful music.

Strauss, Richard (1864–1949) German composer, in no way related to the Viennese master of waltzes and light opera. Richard Strauss's operatic output is masterly and consistent in its quality, though extraordinarily varied in its subject matter. He began with *Guntram*, written in 1894, a work which is very Wagnerian in inspiration and followed it with a savage indictment on the cultural attitudes of his native Munich *Feuersnot*. But it was the controversial *Salome*, which was premiered in 1905, which marked his establishment as a major force in opera composition. Here he included new orchestral techniques against a vivid and erotic subject matter, shocking the German establishment with the power of some extremely powerful music. ('Louder, louder' he is supposed to have exhorted the orchestra during rehearsals, 'I can still hear the singers!'). His next offering was the intense psychological drama *Elektra* where his music became even more abrasive. But here he collaborated for the first time with the poet Hugo von Hofmannsthal who is credited with diluting some of the composer's aggression into more gentle works, such as *Der Rosenkavalier*, written in 1911. Many consider this opera to be the height of Strauss's achievement. The pain and anguish so forcibly portrayed in *Salome* and *Elektra* are still there, but introduced with a subtle elegance in the complex character of the Marschallin and coupled for the first time with pure comedy. This lighter vein was developed in *Ariadne auf Naxos* but abandoned completely for *Die Frau Ohne Schatten*, the most Wagnerian of all his works. His final work with Hofmannsthal was *Arabella* first performed in 1933 where he returned to the setting of the salons of Vienna but without the success of *Der Rosenkavalier*. But Hofmannsthal died four years before *Arabella* was premiered and Strauss's opera writing suffered as a result. Despite collaborations with the Jewish writer Stefan Zweig (curtailed because of the advent of Nazism) and Joseph Gregor, none of his later works match the glory of his earlier period. He is remembered as a contentious, arrogant man, full of his own importance and well aware of his contribution to operatic composition. But his talent was prodigious, not only as a composer of both opera and orchestral work and as a discreet and exacting conductor.

Stravinsky, Igor (1882–1971) Russian composer whose best known opera is *The Rake's Progress* written in 1951. But the constraints of classical opera frustrated him and he strove to find alternatives to them. His opera-oratorio *Oedipus Rex* uses chorus and soloists on stage in masks but is too static to be considered an opera, particularly as it is all sung in Latin. *The Soldier's Tale* is words and acting set to music without being sung. His ballet scores *The Firebird*, *Petruska* and *The Rite of Spring*, all written in Russia before 1917, prove his love of effervescent theatricality which never really came to fruition in his opera writing.

Street Scene (Kurt Weill) FP 1946. Weill's 'real-life' drama was originally conceived as a Broadway show and has some distinctly non-operatic elements, including an entire aria on the virtues of ice cream! It charts the loves and lives of the inhabitants of a New York tenement in an atmosphere not dissimilar to Gershwin's *Porgy and Bess*. Life on the street is hard and when one of the chief protagonists is murdered, the heroine is determined to change her life by leaving to find fortune away from New York.

Strepponi, Guiseppina (1815–1897) Italian soprano who created the role of Abigaille in

Verdi's *Nabucco*. Her devotion to Verdi extended beyond the stage however. She moved in with him in 1848, finally marrying him in 1859 and providing him with a secure and happy family background. She is therefore credited with having provided the composer with the best situation in which to compose his finest works.

Sullivan, Sir Arthur (1842–1900) English composer best known for his collaboration with W.S. Gilbert in their series of operettas. He did write one major opera on his own – *Ivanhoe* which was premiered in 1891, after his argument with Gilbert. For full details on the works they wrote together, see 'Gilbert and Sullivan' and 'Savoy Operas'.

Suor Angelica (Puccini) FP 1918. One act opera, the second part of Puccini's 'Trittico' and generally the least popular. Angelica has been confined to a convent for producing an illegitimate baby. She is prevailed on by her aunt to release her share of the family fortune and when she asks about her son, she is told that he has died. Seeing she has no future she poisons herself and has a dying vision of the Virgin Mary carrying her baby towards her.

Subtitles/Supertitles Modern technology meets the opera house in an attempt to relay simultaneous translations of operas sung in their original language via a screen placed above the stage. Hence 'subtitles' is technically incorrect for live performance (though fine for television or cinema) but 'supertitles' always sounds wrong somehow. Following supertitles throughout a performance can leave you wondering what actually went on on stage as it is virtually impossible to watch both things at once, but they can be useful for a quick refresher about what's happening. However, two things can destroy their effect altogether. If the words get out of time with the music, the result can be comic even in the most tragic of scenes and if the translation is unconvincing (particularly in an aria where one phrase may be repeated several times), it is far better to shut your eyes (or concentrate on the stage action) and listen to the music.

Sutherland, Dame Joan Australian soprano who studied in England where she met her husband, the conductor Richard Bonynge. In 1951 Dame Joan joined the company at Covent Garden, singing leading soprano roles such as Desdemona in *Otello*, the title role in *Aida*, and Gilda in *Rigoletto*. But it was her performance in the name part in *Lucia de Lammermoor*, which she sang for the first time in 1959, which rocketed her to international stardom in a manner which is like something out of a fairy tale. Since then, there is no major opera house in the world in which she has not performed, bringing strength and dignity to the major 'bel canto' soprano roles such as Anna Bolena, Norma, and of course Lucia which has come to be her trademark. With her husband, who conducts all of her performances, she has brought many obscure works into more regular performance and has recorded both classics and less popular works with enormous success. Honoured by the governments of Britain and Australia, Dame Joan enjoys a worldwide popularity and the news of her retirement in October 1990 was received with dismay.

Sydney Known all over the world for its extraordinary exterior (finished nine years late and costing $102 million rather than the $7 million originally estimated), the Sydney Opera House symbolizes an operatic tradition which has lasted longer than its current modern setting would imply. During the nineteenth century, Sydney hosted the latest operas on tour from America, presented their famous daughter Dame Nellie Melba in a series of notable performances and, in 1955, launched a national opera company. Renamed Australian Opera in 1971, its reputation so far was not in the top league, but was sufficient to attract two musicians who would make it so, Dame Joan Sutherland and her husband Richard Bonynge. The repertory was created to suit Dame Joan's magnificent voice, effectively precluding any twentieth-century works, but the audiences grew (particularly for 'Opera in the Park', the company's outdoor summer festival) and it came as a surprise to many when the Bonynge partnership was ousted in 1984. But the new administration had the confidence to recognize that their audience could now take more than a diet of classics. The house stages radical new productions of the old favourites as well as more contemporary works, but is still criticized for lack of encouragement to young Australian singers. It is also hampered by insufficient facilities for staging opera in any of the three auditoria in the Opera House complex.

Tabaro Il (Puccini) FP 1918. One act opera which forms the first part of Puccini's 'Trittico'. Giorgetta and Michele live on a barge on the Seine in Paris. Giorgetta is bored and has taken a lover, Luigi, who is one of Michele's barge hands. Michele becomes suspicious, catches Luigi and strangles him. When Giorgetta complains of cold, Michele offers her his cloak (for which the Italian is 'il tabaro') but as she wraps it around herself, she realizes it contains the corpse of Luigi.

Tales of Hoffmann (see Contes d'Hoffmann)

Tamagno, Francesco (1850–1905) Italian tenor who could sing as powerfully at the top of the register as he could in the centre of his range. It was even said that he was happier singing some roles one whole tone higher than they had been written. While the majority of his career was spent specializing in the major roles of the Italian repertoire in his home country, he did make notable appearances abroad in London, New York and Paris, and excelled particularly in the role of Otello.

Tamerlano (Handel) FP 1724. Not a good opera for beginners, this work centres on the trials of the emperor of Tartars, Tamerlano, and his battles against the Turks, led by Bajazet.

Tancredi (Rossini) FP 1813. This was the first of Rossini's serious operas to receive popular acclaim but has not kept its place in the modern repertoire, probably because its subject matter is not particularly intriguing.

Tancredi is in love with Amenaide and returns from the war to realize that she is about to marry Orbazzano. He manages to prevent the wedding. The spurned Orbazzano attempts to prove that Amenaide is betraying her people to the enemy and manages to convince Tancredi that she is guilty. Amenaide is imprisoned and Tan-

credi, against his will, agrees to defend her. He wins the duel against Orbazzano and establishes that Amenaide was innocent all the time, thus enabling the couple to marry.

Tannhauser (Wagner) FP 1845. Although this work had its premiere in Germany, it was substantially revised by the composer after its first performance in Paris in 1861. In these revisions, Wagner challenged the entire French opera establishment by flouting the traditional form of grand opera, where a ballet was placed at the start of the second act to allow patrons to enjoy an extended dinner during the interval. Wagner declared that his new 'ballet' music (called the Venusberg music) should be played at the beginning of act one and that act two should go straight on with the action of the plot. Such controversial opinions caused the opera to be whistled off stage by members of the Jockey Club but now both versions are regularly performed.

The young knight Tannhauser has been taken from the mortal world to enjoy the hedonistic pleasures of the Venusberg where he is attended constantly by Venus and her nymphs. But he has tired of such a life and calls on the Virgin Mary to help him. At the sound of this holy name, the profane Venusberg disappears. Tannhauser finds himself in the company of his old friends including Wolfram and Herman, Landgrave of Thuringia, all of whom welcome him back after a year's absence. They come to the Landgrave's castle at Wartburg where Elizabeth, the Landgrave's niece, is delighted to see Tannhauser again. A song contest on the theme of love is announced. Wolfram's offering praises the pure virtues of chaste affection, while Tannhauser's song revels in the explicit detail of the type of passion he encountered at the Venusberg. The listeners are horrified and prepare to attack Tannhauser but he is saved by Elizabeth and sent to seek absolution from the Pope. Months later, Elizabeth is pining for her errant knight and Wolfram pining for Elizabeth. A distraught Tannhauser enters – his absolution has been refused and he has no option but to return to the Venusberg. Elizabeth can bear it no longer and dies of a broken heart. As her cortege approaches Tannhauser too collapses and is carried away with her. But the final symbol of hope is offered – a staff belonging to the Pope has sprung into leaf, signifying that God has forgiven the erring Tannhauser.

Tate, Jeffrey English conductor who has triumphed over a debilitating disability to become one of the most admired international conductors, with a wide ranging repertoire that includes a particular affinity for Mozart's operas. Tate was appointed Covent Garden's first ever Principal Conductor in 1987, an accolade which extends his other professional qualification – that of a doctor.

Tauber, Richard (1891–1949) German tenor who became a British subject in 1940. Tauber proved to everyone that with a sound classical training and excellent sense of musicianship, even the lightest of operettas can sound meaningful. His was a truly classical education, studying in Frankfurt and Freiburg before being contracted to the Dresden and Vienna State Operas where he specialized in the romantic tenor roles and in Mozart. In 1922 he was cast in *Frasquita* by Lehar and found that operetta was his true metier. He went on to attract a wide audience through his films such as *Blossom Time* and was widely mourned when he died suddenly of cancer.

Taverner (Maxwell Davies) FP 1972. Highly intellectual piece by Peter Maxwell Davies which discusses the dual merits of religious faith and a more opportunist outlook as exemplified by the sixteenth-century English musician John Taverner. Taverner was imprisoned for the Protestant heresy contained in his sublime Church music. He later abandoned all forms of musical scholarship and dedicated his life to ransacking the Christian monasteries.

Tchaikovsky, Peter (1840–1893) Bureaucracy's loss was music's gain as Russia's foremost composer abandoned an administrative career to pursue his love of the stage. He began writing operas in 1869 but it was not until 1879 that he wrote the first of his operas to survive in today's repertory, *Eugene Onegin*. By this time he had survived the trauma of his mother's death, had been heavily influenced by performances of *Carmen* in Paris, and by Wagner in Bayreuth, emerged from a loveless marriage as a con-

firmed homosexual, and found in Madame von Meck a patron who was to exert a profound influence on him. It is hardly surprising then that *Eugene Onegin* contains such a welter of deeply felt emotion! Three further operas followed with mixed success (including the nationalist-inspired *Mazeppa*) before his penultimate opera *The Queen of Spades*. Once again using Pushkin as his source, Tchaikovsky achieved the balance between individual lyricism and dynamic theatrical effect in an opera which is as gripping today as it was in the time of the composer. His final opera *Iolanta* was quite different – a delightful one act fairy tale intended to accompany *The Nutcracker*.

Tear, Robert English tenor. Since 1961 when Tear left Cambridge where he was a choral scholar, he has repeatedly shown his versatility and great talent as one of the world's leading tenors. Within eight years he had sung with such conductors as von Karajan, Bernstein, and Guilini. His repertoire is very varied, ranging from Monteverdi and Dowland to Stravinsky and Tippett. He is a regular guest at the Royal Opera House, Covent Garden, at the Metropolitan Opera New York and as a recital artist all over the world.

Teatro Colon, El (see Buenos Aires)

Tebaldi, Renata Italian soprano who excelled in Italian opera in the post war period, starting with more than ten years in the reopened La Scala, Milan; ranging then to Rome and Florence then to London and New York and finally to Paris, Vienna, Berlin, Tokyo and Osaka. Dramatic, versatile, an excellent actress and an attractive personality offstage, Tebaldi was greatly missed by her loyal public when she retired from performance in 1976.

Te Kanawa, Dame Kiri New Zealand soprano whose warmth, charm, extraordinary musical ability and distinguished acting style make her one of the greatest and most popular contemporary singers. She made her professional debut in England, with an opera company in Newcastle in the role of Carmen. A steady progress through engagements in and around London led to a debut at Covent Garden in 1971, followed a year later by a series of international performances as the Countess in *The Marriage of Figaro*. This brought her to the attention of management all over the world, as did her debut at the Metropolitan Opera in New York, substituting at three hours notice as Desdemona in *Otello* in 1974. Over the last fifteen years she has risen to become perhaps the most popular soprano on the international circuit, in demand worldwide and seen by millions when she sang at the wedding of the Prince and Princess of Wales in 1981. Film appearances include Donna Elvira in Joseph Losey's film of *Don Giovanni*.

Telephone, The (Menotti) FP 1947. Menotti wrote this comic one act opera to act as an 'intermezzo', being played either between the two acts of longer piece or as a 'curtain raiser' for one shorter work. The music is pleasant and the action slight.

Lucy is in her flat with her boyfriend Ben. Ben seems anxious to ask Lucy something but is constantly interrupted by telephone calls. Lucy seems irrepressibly drawn to chatter in response to calls or make them herself, forcing the desperate Ben to go out to a phone box and ring her in order to have time enough to ask her to marry him. She accepts, on the condition that he will always remember one thing about her – her telephone number!

Tenor Of the range of voices that come naturally to a male singer, the tenor range is the highest, spanning two octaves from the C below middle C to the C above. Like other voices, it is subdivided into numerous categories including heroic tenor (or 'heldentenor' in German) and lyric tenor. The present generation is fortunate in having two world-class tenors currently performing: Placido Domingo and Luciano Pavarotti.

Terfl, Bryn Welsh bass-baritone who has left his sheep farm in North Wales to concentrate on a promising international career which has already brought him to the final of the 1989 Cardiff Young Singer of the World and won the prestigious Kathleen Ferrier Memorial Scholarship. His rich voice and pleasing stage presence have attracted the attention of national companies and debuts are planned at both Welsh and English National Operas.

Teseo (Handel) FP 1713. The third opera Handel wrote for London audiences. Teseo is the estranged son of King Egeo and is in love with Agilea. The sorceress Medea is anxious to break up this partnership and have Teseo for herself but she is unsuccessful and Teseo is restored to his rightful throne.

Tessitura From the Italian meaning 'texture', tessitura has come to describe the range of notes most commonly used in one particular role or the range of voice in which a singer is most comfortable. Thus Francesco Tamagno, who asked for pieces to be transposed up in order for him to sing them more comfortably, would be described as having a particularly high tessitura whereas the role Dido in Purcell's *Dido and Aeneas* is principally written in the lower part of the soprano range – a low tessitura.

Tetrazzini, Luisa (1871–1940) Italian soprano who shot to fame with a performance of Violetta at Covent Garden in 1907 and went on to command $3,000 a performance at the height of her career. She had a true coloratura voice, vibrant and so exciting in itself that audiences were prepared to overlook her portly figure and lack of acting ability. During the First World War she concentrated on performing for troops at the Front and never returned to the opera stage, preferring to concentrate on her concert performances. It was said that she earned over £5 million during her career, but died in poverty in Milan.

Teyte, Dame Maggie (1888–1976) English soprano who studied in France at the start of her career and went on to specialize in the French repertory. She became almost better known on the French stage than in her homeland, adding notable performances of French song to her operatic repertoire.

Thaïs (Massenet) FP 1894. This opera is considered to be less satisfying than Massenet's great works *Werther* and *Manon*, but has some lovely moments in it. It reverts to one of Massenet's favourite themes, that of a religious man struggling against human desires.

In fourth century Alexandria, Thaïs is one of the most beautiful, highly regarded prostitutes. The monk Athanael had known her in his younger days but has now turned to God and is determined to convert Thaïs from her chosen way of life. He enlists the help of Nicias who has bought Thaïs' love for a week and Nicias brings the monk and the prostitute together. In a long scene, Athanael pursuades Thaïs to join a convent. But once he has achieved his aim, he cannot be satisfied. He realizes that he did not want to save her for her own good but rather to prevent other men from having her, as he is himself in love with her. He goes to her convent to confess his love for her but finds she is dying. With her last breath she sees the glory of God and Athanael is left alone.

Thieving Magpie, The (Donizetti) FP 1817. A very well known overture, a very slight plot and a great showcase for a coloratura soprano make this opera hardly the most profound in the repertoire but nevertheless very jolly. 'Things of startling originality were presented in a manner that anybody could follow and understand' was how it was first described, which has to be an excellent introduction for a new opera goer. It is rarely performed in full these days, except by music colleges and amateurs. The story concerns the village girl Ninetta who is sentenced to death for stealing a silver spoon but is reprieved when it turns out that the magpie stole it.

Threepenny Opera, The (Weill) FP 1928. Weill was heavily influenced by the political forces of the time he was writing. The emergence of Fascism in Germany heightened his interest in the role of the working classes and the morality of cities like Berlin at the time made him question the wider aspects of man's humanity (and inhumanity) to his fellow kind. He was rather unkindly dubbed 'the people's Verdi' by a fellow composer. So to take John Gay's work *The Beggar's Opera*, set it in the slums of Victorian England, add some lyrics by Kipling but most by Berthold Brecht and write the whole with a knowledge of the Café Society of the late twenties Berlin, results in a work of considerable political message, more a play with music than a full-blown opera.

Mack the Knife is married to Polly Peacham, daughter of a Soho underworld boss. He is betrayed by the Jenny the prostitute and by Polly's family, taken to prison where he escapes thanks to the help of Lucy, daughter of Tiger Brown, the corrupt police chief. After his recapture, he is condemned to hang but pardoned by the personal intervention of Queen Victoria as a magnanimous gesture on the day of her coronation.

Through-composed The opposite to a number opera, this term described works which have a continuous line of action all described in song, rather than being divided into individual 'numbers' with recitatives and arias. Modern musicals (such as *Les Miserables*) are occasionally described as being 'through-sung', meaning there is no speech in them.

Tippett, Sir Michael English composer and one of the world's leading living opera composers. Tippett was Director of Music for Morley College in London from 1940 to 1951 when he wrote the strongly pacificst oratorio *A Child of Our Time* for which he received international praise. Such concern for the rights of the individual against his governing society has been a constant theme in Tippett's subsequent works, expressed with a passionate commitment. His first opera was *A Midsummer Marriage*, written in 1955. Tippett's music is both traditional and contemporary, deliberately mixing styles to create highly descriptive passages of writing. His operas are less easy for a first-time opera goer to enjoy than perhaps the lightest of Britten's works, but they certainly merit deeper study for anyone who wishes to develop a strong interest in opera. Now aged over eighty and still composing, Tippett's operas to date include *A Midsummer Marriage, King Priam, The Knot Garden, The Ice Break* and *New Year*.

Tomlinson, John English bass. A very popular, talented, committed performer, who joined ENO in 1974 and remained with them until 1981. He has also sung regularly with the Royal Opera and Opera North and is becoming increasingly popular in Europe, notably at Bayreuth where he has recently made a highly successful debut. His sensitive dramatic skills have been used to full effect in some memorable productions, especially at the Coliseum where ENO has exploited Tomlinson's adaptibility and willingness to be part of an ensemble, often in very different, daring production styles, for example Mephistopheles (*Faust*), and the title role in a modern dress production of Rossini's *Moses in Egypt*.

Tomowa-Sintow, Anna Bulgarian soprano who was encouraged by Herbert von Karajan to develop her career in the strong soprano roles including the Countess in *The Marriage of Figaro*, the title roles in *Arabella* and *Madam Butterfly*, Violetta in *La Traviata* and Donna Anna in *Don Giovanni*. She first sang for Karajan in the 1973 Salzburg Easter Festival and is now in international demand.

Tornrak (John Metcalf) FP 1990. Commissioned by Welsh National Opera, this opera has the unusual setting of the frozen wastes of the Arctic in the nineteenth century for its first act. The word 'tornrak' means the animal spirit guardian which protects each of the natives of the Arctic, thus requiring one singer to take the form of a polar bear. Highly topical for a year when conservation and the power of nature were uppermost in many people's minds, the opera, which includes throat-singing as practised by the Inuit people, was enthusiastically greeted at its first professional staging in 1990.

The British sailor Michael has been shipwrecked in the Arctic and is rescued by the Inuit woman Milak. He takes Milak back to England where, separated from her country and her people, she is treated as something of a freak. She is adopted as an academic exhibit, used in a circus and finally hanged for stealing sheep to feed the starving people she finds throughout England. Michael returns to the Arctic where he meets Milak's tornrak and is reunited with her in death as he freezes on the Arctic wastes.

Toronto – Canadian Opera Company The capital of Canada has hosted some of the world's finest opera companies on tour since the 1850s but the Canadian Opera Company was only founded in 1959. It is now based at the O'Keefe Center, a forbidding arts centre in down-town Toronto which suffers from the architects of the 1960s predilection for pre-stressed concrete. Such uncongenial surroundings are quickly forgotten, however, by the company's loyal audience and, in the relatively short time of its existence, the company has developed an excellent artistic reputation. Their repertory covers the standard works, with occasional premieres of Canadian works such as *Heloise and Abelard* by Charles Wilson (1972) and artists of the calibre of Teresa Stratas and Jon Vickers regularly perform with the company. During the summer, the company move from their concrete bunker and perform a series of outdoor performances known affectionately as 'Opera-in-a-Tent'.

Tosca (Puccini) FP 1900 One of the most popular operas of all time with all the ingredients of success – lavish settings, a towering love story, one truly evil character, a sensual and engaging heroine and a thread of tension which a good director can develop into an atmosphere to rival Hitchcock. Many singers regard it to be the 'Macbeth' of the opera world, with stories abounding about mishaps at the most dramatic moments. Read the synopsis first to convince yourself of the brilliance of the opera – which would be ideal for a first-timer – then read the anecdotes and realize why they can shatter the tension so dramatically.

The painter Cavaradossi is engaged on a commission in the church of San Andrea della Valle where he has encountered the political prisoner, Cesare Angelotti. In a whispered conversation, he offers the prisoner sanctuary in his villa, but the conversation is overheard by Cavaradossi's lover, Floria Tosca, who suspects him of having an affair. Cavaradossi says nothing about the prisoner but, as soon as Tosca leaves, manages to smuggle Angelotti away to his villa, before Scarpia, chief of police, comes to search the church. Clues are found implicating Cavaradossi in aiding the escape and Scarpia determines to track both men down. As Tosca re-enters, her suspicions of Cavaradossi's infidelity are aroused again, and exploited by Scarpia who has a fervent passion for Tosca. He persuades her to follow Cavaradossi home to see if he has another lover. The act closes with a magnificent Church service, contrasting the grandeur of Roman Catholic ceremony with the individual anguish of the major characters.

In the Farnese Palace, Scarpia can hear Tosca serenading visitors at a victory banquet. Cavaradossi is brought in and

Tosca, one of the greatest of Puccini's operas. Josephine Barstow, as Tosca, with Neil Howlett as the evil Scarpia, in the dramatic confrontation at the core of the opera.

questioned about his knowledge of Angelotti. He is taken away for 'further questioning' as Tosca is brought in to Scarpia's room. In a scene of powerful intensity, Scarpia begins to question Tosca on her knowledge of the escaped prisoner. (Tosca now knows the full story, having seen Cavaradossi and Angelotti at the villa.) But she starts to deny everything when suddenly Cavaradossi's anguished screams can be heard – he is being tortured and his cries are intended to make Tosca weaken. Taunted beyond all endurance by the sound of her lover undergoing such agony, she collapses and admits that Angelotti is hidden in a well in Cavaradossi's garden. Guards are sent to seek him out and Cavaradossi is condemned to death. Scarpia offers Tosca a bargain – Cavaradossi's life will be saved if Tosca will yield to Scarpia's passion for her. In a magnificent, tormented aria ('Vissi D'Arte') Tosca wrestles with her conscience when news arrives that Angelotti has committed suicide. Realizing that she now stands between her lover and death, she silently consents to Scarpia's advances. He appears to arrange for Cavaradossi's release before taking Tosca in his arms. But she has managed to pick up the knife lying on the desk and with the famous line 'It is thus that Tosca kisses' she stabs him and he falls to the floor. Extracting the note of safe conduct from the dead man's fingers, she places a lighted candle on either side of his head and slips from the room.

The scene changes to the Castle San Angelo just before dawn. Cavaradossi is bravely facing death when he is reunited with his beloved Tosca who shows him the safe conduct and whispers her bargain with the murdered Scarpia. The execution will only be a mock one, she explains. He must pretend to fall and lie still until the soldiers have left – then they will be free to leave together. He faces the firing squad and falls with such conviction that Tosca comments on his acting ability! The soldiers leave and Tosca calls excitedly for Cavaradossi to rise and flee. But he is dead. Scarpia has tricked them both, and rather than face the ensuing furore, Tosca throws herself from the parapet of the castle.

From first to last, *Tosca* is magnificent, unrelenting drama so the following anecdotes must in no way spoil your enjoyment of such a wonderful work. The best known is the 'trampoline story', attributed to numerous sopranos who have angered the stage management. Rather than place a nice receptive mattress to cushion her fall from the castle ramparts, stage management placed a very well sprung trampoline so that the audience could hardly imagine that the diva had crashed lifeless to the ground when she re-appeared bouncing back up the ramparts several times. . . .! Almost as awful is the tale of the Tosca whose anger at Scarpia was as real off stage as on. She laid the candles at each side of his head ever so slightly too close to his powdered wig and, as the curtain came down slowly at the end of the act, the audience witnessed a very lively Scarpia rush across stage with hair aflame!

Toscanini, Arturo (1876–1957) Italian conductor who started his musical career as a cellist and only discovered the joys of the baton when asked to deputize at short notice. His first major post was as Music Director under Gatti-Casazza at La Scala from 1898 to 1903 and again from 1906 to 1908. The two men moved together to America to head the Metropolitan Opera where Toscanini conducted the American premieres of *Boris Godunov, Armide, Ariane et Barbe Bleu* and the world premiere of *La Fanciulla del West* as well as extensively widening the repertory of the Met. Arguments with Gatti caused Toscanini to return to Europe where, in 1930 he became the first non-German to conduct at Bayreuth while maintaining the position of Artistic Director at his old home at La Scala. But the rise of Fascism forced him back to America where he made many notable recordings with NBC. He returned to Italy once before his death, to conduct the opening concert at La Scala after its restoration in 1946.

Stories abound about Toscanini's tyrannical treatment of players, his relentless perfectionism and his autocratic behaviour in the pursuit of performances which strove to be as true as possible to the composers' original intentions. But, as his numerous recordings prove, his performances had a spark of genius which few other conductors could emulate. His friendship with Verdi symbolized a deep seated commitment to the whole Italian opera repertory while his performances of *Fidelio* are considered by many to be unsurpassed.

Traviata, La (Verdi) FP 1853. La Traviata is variously translated to mean 'the fallen woman' or, with rather more subtlety, 'the strayed one'. But that conveys the general idea of the opera, which is based on the story by Alexandre Dumas *La Dame Aux Camelias*. It is a perfect subject for an opera, being highly romantic and not too complicated and the music suits this atmosphere excellently. The work is full of well known tunes, particularly the overture and drinking song ('Brindisi') at the beginning. But the work should never be dismissed as light sentimentality as it provides telling descriptions of individual relationships, particularly that between father and son.

In a glittering salon in Paris, a party given by the high society courtesan Violetta is in full swing. But Violetta has tired of the round of admirers and has fallen deeply in love with one man, Alfredo Germont. She moves with him to a country estate and for a while is blissfully happy. But the scandal of Alfredo living with an ex-prostitute will prevent his sister from making an acceptable marriage; so Alfredo's father, Giorgio, pleads with Violetta to leave his son and return to her life in Paris. Aware that she has tuberculosis and that life without Alfredo will probably kill her, Violetta nevertheless agrees and returns to live with her former lover, Baron Douphol. Alfredo believes he has been rejected in favour of another lover and challenges Douphol to a duel in which Douphol is wounded. But in a scene of immense beauty, the father confesses to his son the sacrifice he provoked Violetta to make. The lovers are reunited for a brief moment before Violetta dies.

Tristan und Isolde (Wagner) FP 1865. 'The greatest setting of a love story for the lyric stage' is how Kobbé describes this towering piece of writing by Wagner. It is somewhat superficial to talk about plot with a work of this nature. Certainly there is a story but it is so heavily concerned with the thoughts and emotions of the two major characters that the opera develops into more of a psychological study than an action packed drama. Many versions exist of the 'Tristan' legend, whereby Tristan and Isolde forget their previous enmity having drunk a love potion and fall passionately in love, to be reunited in death. Wagner changes this slightly by developing a mutual attraction between the couple before they take the love potion. The potion therefore acts as a catalyst rather than a cause of their passions.

Tristan once killed Morold, the lover of the Irish Princess Isolde and is now bringing Isolde back to Cornwall to marry King Marke, who is Tristan's uncle. In the battle with Morold, Tristan was wounded and cared for by Isolde, who never disclosed who she was, because she found herself falling in love with Tristan. He developed a similar affection for her, but both kept silent because they believed their love would not be reciprocated. Isolde believes Tristan will never love her and resolves to kill herself with poison which Tristan agrees to share with her. But Isolde's attendant Brangane changes the cup to a love potion and, believing they are both about to die, Tristan and Isolde pour out their long repressed passion. Encouraged by the love potion, their passion continues in Cornwall where they are discovered by King Marke and Tristan is wounded by the jealous courtier, Melot. Tristan is taken to Brittany by his friend Kurwenal and joined there by Isolde who arrives just as Tristan dies. Longing for death so she can be reunited with her lover, Isolde sings the famous 'Liebestod' before falling dead on Tristan's body.

Trittico, Il (Puccini) Comprising *Il Tabaro*, *Suor Angelica* and *Gianni Schicchi*, these operas are often performed individually but were originally written as a contrasting three part work. A complete performance of all three is planned by the Metropolitan Opera in New York.

Trojans, The (Berlioz) First complete performance 1890, although part two only was premiered in 1863. Berlioz must have found *The Trojans* an extraordinarily frustrating experience. He had always been fascinated by Virgil's *Aeneid* and brought his love of grandeur and scale in musical form to create this mighty enterprise, *The Aeneid*, as an opera in five acts lasting, by his own estimation, nearly four and a half hours. But this was at a time when Paris was enjoying the heyday of French grand opera, with Gounod and Bizet dominating the stages and the satire of Offenbach only round the corner. Berlioz could find no theatre willing to produce his work in its entirety during his lifetime, and therefore had to be content with splitting the work in two and seeing the second part only staged in 1863. Its massive scale has daunted producers (and accountants!) ever since but it stands as a masterpiece of French drama, possibly the greatest composition Berlioz ever wrote and comparable with Wagner's Ring Cycle in scale and consistency. The recent production shared by Welsh and Scottish Operas with Opera North proved that the work can be engrossing for modern audiences. Full details of the plot are best read in Kobbé, save to say that the first part of the work deals with the sack of Troy by Greek soldiers emerging from the Trojan horse and the second charts the love between Dido and Aeneas.

Trouble in Tahiti (see Quiet Place, A)

Trouser role (see Hosenrole)

Trovatore, Il (Verdi) FP 1853. This is not the best Verdi opera to introduce a newcomer to opera. There are some excellent musical moments, most notably the 'Anvil Chorus', beloved of male voice choirs all over the world. But the plot is so complicated ('the acme of absurdity' as Kobbé puts it) as to be very unconvincing. A very important part of the action has taken place before the curtain rises (see Antefatto) and the setting is rather gloomy.

This is the antefatto. In fifteenth-century Spain, a gypsy has been burnt at the stake for supposed witchcraft, having been implicated in causing the illness of one of the Count of Luna's infant sons. The gypsy's daughter, Azucena, is determined to avenge her mother's death. She steals one of the Count's baby sons from the palace, intending to kill him but, crazed by the heat of the moment, sacrifices her own baby son instead. She then rears the Count's son as her own, calling him Manrico. Her desire for vengeance against the Luna family is as strong as ever.

The opera opens with Manrico grown up and his brother installed as the new Count of Luna. They are both in love with the same girl, the Duchess Leonora. Leonora favours Manrico. The two men, who do not realize they are brothers, meet beneath her window and are forced into a duel. Manrico wins but

spares the Count's life and returns to his home at the gypsy camp. A messenger informs Manrico that Leonora believes he has been killed in a battle and that she has become a nun. Manrico sets off to find her and encounters Luna who is attempting to abduct Leonora. Manrico saves her and they escape together. As they are about to marry, news is brought that Azucena is about to be burnt at the stake, accused of the murder of the Count of Luna's brother. Torn between his would-be wife and his supposed mother, Manrico chooses to save his mother (singing a magnificent aria which reaches right up to a top C, the height of the tenor register), but fails. Manrico and Azucena are imprisoned and Leonora bargains with the Count – she will marry him if Manrico is released. The Count agrees, but rather than face marriage, Leonora poisons herself and dies in Manrico's arms. Realizing he has been tricked, the Count orders Manrico's execution and makes Azucena watch it. As Manrico's head rolls from the block, Azucena turns to Luna in anguished triumph. He has murdered his own brother and Azucena has had her revenge.

Troyanos, Tatiana Mezzo-soprano of Greek and American parentage, Troyanos has a commanding stage presence and an exciting voice of vibrant clarity and power. She is thus in great demand world wide for roles which demand intuitive acting ability as well as musical prowess, for example Carmen, Princess Eboli in *Don Carlos* or Poppea in *The Coronation of Poppea*. But Troyanos also possesses the sensitivity to portray seemingly less dominating roles such as Charlotte in *Werther*, Octavian in *Der Rosenkavalier* or the Composer in *Ariadne auf Naxos*. Troyanos is a regular performer at the Metropolitan Opera, New York where she has appeared since 1976 and has also featured in productions in Chicago and San Francisco. In Europe she has performed in Paris, Salzburg, Milan, and the Aix en Provence Festival. Her work spreads beyond the world of opera to include her role as Anita in the recording made of Leonard Bernstein's *West Side Story* with Dame Kiri Te Kanawa and José Carreras.

Troyens, Les (see The Trojans)

Tucker, Richard (1913–1975) American tenor who performed with the Metropolitan Opera Company for nearly forty years specializing in the romantic leads such as Rodolfo (*La Bohème*), Don José (*Carmen*) and Des Grieux (*Manon Lescaut*). Away from New York, he sang with the companies in Chicago and San Francisco. In 1947 he made his European debut in the Arena at Verona on the same night as Maria Callas made her Italian debut. His death is notable in two respects. He must be the only reputable opera singer to have passed away in the wonderfully named town of Kalamazoo and he is certainly the only singer to have been given the honour of a funeral on the stage of the Metropolitan Opera House.

Turandot There are in fact two operas on this subject, one by Busoni which was premiered in 1917, and the more famous version by Puccini, first staged in 1926. Their stories are virtually identical but the Busoni version is hardly ever performed today. It is an unusual and exotic story and would make an interesting introduction to opera for those not seeking the classic grandeur of the most popular works. Some find the opera unsatisfying, however, as Turandot is clearly such an unpleasant character compared with the devoted Liu and it therefore seems improbable that Calaf will go to such lengths to win her.

The beautiful Princess Turandot will only love the man who can answer three riddles. Anyone who tries and fails will be killed. The Tartar Prince Calaf resolves to try, even though his father Timur and the slave girl Liu who loves him want to stop him. He answers the riddles correctly but Turandot reneges on her promise and refuses to marry him. Calaf offers her one more chance. If she can guess his name by morning, he will die just as if he had not answered one of the riddles. All night, Turandot dispatches her envoys to find out Calaf's name while Calaf sings the great tune of the opera 'Nessun Dorma' ('None shall sleep'). Though confident that only he can reveal his secret, Calaf reckons without Turandot's cunning in torturing Liu to reveal the name. Liu stabs herself rather than betray the man she loves. In the morning, Calaf comes to Turandot and kisses her passionately depriving her of all power to resist him. She consents to marry him, revealing to her court that the stranger's name is love.

Turner, Dame Eva (1892–1990) English soprano. Dame Eva was certainly one of the 'grande-dames' of the opera world, maintaining an active interest in opera until her death at the age of ninety-eight. At the height of her career, from 1924 to 1948 she performed chiefly in Covent Garden and in the great theatres of Italy, where she was known for her performances above all of Turandot, as well as Aida, Amelia and several of the major Wagner heroines. She sang opposite many of the greatest male singers including Laurence Melchoir and Benjamin Gigli. Dame Eva never sang at the Met, but moved to America after the war to become Professor of Voice at the University of Oklahoma. Until recently, she maintained an active teaching career with pupils rising fast to the height of their own operatic careers, thanks to the guidance and extensive experience of their great singer and coach.

Turn of the Screw (Britten) FP 1954. One of Britten's most sinister works, based on the novel by Henry James adapted into a libretto by Myfanwy Piper. In it, he creates one of his most powerful female characters – the governess. The opera is structured as a continuous series of sixteen scenes which are written as musical variations of the same twelve note phrase. Here Britten used the influence of Schoenberg (see entry)

Miles and Flora, the children of a great country house in nineteenth-century England, are put into the care of a new governess who is given complete control over them. But Miles is dismissed from school for harming one of his friends and the governess soon realizes the house is full of sinister shadows and feelings. She describes the mysterious figure she has glimpsed to Mrs Grose, the housekeeper, who identifies him as Peter Quint, former manservant and controller of the household, now dead. It becomes obvious that the children have fallen under the spell of the ghosts of Quint and of the former housekeeper, Miss Jessel, with whom Quint had an affair. The opera develops into a battle between the governess, determined to save the children, and the ghostly tormentors but as she finally demands that Miles identify the ghost, the little boy falls dead.

Twilight of the Gods (see Ring des Nibelungen)

Turandot, by Puccini. Dame Gwynneth Jones in the title role, with Franco Bonisolli (Prince Calaf) in the final scene of the Covent Garden production which also toured the Los Angeles Opera Center.

Unger, Caroline (1803–1877) Hungarian mezzo-soprano with a phenomenal range of voice which enabled her to sing soprano roles as well. She created a sensation in the title role of Donizetti's *Lucrezia Borgia* and sang in the premiere performance of Beethoven's Ninth Symphony. It is she who is credited with having turned the totally deaf Beethoven round to face the audience at the end of the performance so that he might see, if not hear, the applause.

Ursuleac, Viorica (1894–1985) Romanian soprano who created many of the leading roles in the operas of Richard Strauss who thought that her expressive and dramatic voice was ideal for his compositions. These roles included Arabella, and the Countess in *Capriccio*.

Valkyrie (see Ring des Nibelungen)

van Allan, Richard English bass who appears regularly with English National Opera, having been a policeman, a miner and a teacher before deciding to become an opera singer! Van Allan is one of the most distinguished and experienced opera singers currently performing in opera houses all over Britain, Europe and America with a wide variety of roles to his credit. He has made notable performances of both Don Giovanni and Leporello in Mozart's opera, Collatinus in Britten's *The Rape of Lucretia* and a superbly regal Phillip II in *Don Carlos* by Verdi. As Pooh Bah in ENO's production of *The Mikado*, van Allan showed that his comic timing and dancing ability are every bit as effective as his sensitive portrayals of the more serious roles! While maintaining an active performing career, he is putting his experience to valuable use as Director of the prestigious National Opera Studio, based in London.

van Damm, Jose Belgian bass whose range encompasses some baritone roles. Van Damm's career developed from a period with the Geneva Opera to larger roles with the Deutsche Oper in Berlin with whom he sang a notable Leporello (*Don Giovanni*) and Don Alfonso (*Cosi fan Tutte*). He now appears all over the world, making a speciality of the brooding bass roles for which his physical presence and sonorous voice are ideally suited. These roles have included the title roles in *Wozzeck* and *The Flying Dutchman*, and Jochanaan in *Salome*.

Vaness, Carol American soprano who sings extensively with NYCO and Metropolitan Opera, as well as acclaimed performances at Glyndebourne and for Australian Opera. A vivacious singer-actress, Vaness came to prominence through a performance in 1977 of Vitellia in Mozart's *Clemenza di Tito* at San Francisco and this has remained a favourite role ever since. Particularly strong in Mozart roles, Vaness has also sung excellent performances of the Israelite woman in *Samson and Dalila* by Saint-Saens and Leila in Bizet's *The Pearl Fishers*.

Vanessa (Samuel Barber) FP 1958. Using a libretto by Gian Carlo Menotti, Samuel Barber created a lyrical opera which has become a standard feature in American houses but is rarely performed in Europe.

The lovely Vanessa has waited for more than two decades for the return of her lover. Eventually, she is put out of her suspense by the arrival of Anatol who claims to be her lover's son and tells her that her lover is dead. Anatol remains in Vanessa's house and seduces Vanessa's niece Erika, who falls hopelessly in love with him. But Anatol's designs are set on Vanessa herself whom he marries and takes to Paris, leaving Erika to wait for her lover's return, as Vanessa had done a generation earlier.

Vaughan-Williams, Ralph (1872–1958) English composer who can be considered amongst the most nationalist of British music writers. He collected large numbers of English folk songs and adapted them into pieces which have become classics of the choral repertoire. But this popularity did not extend into his six operas which are rarely performed by professional companies today, although they are often given excellent stagings by the music colleges. Many consider his one act opera *Riders to the Sea* to be the best of the six. The others are *Sir John in Love* (based on the story of Falstaff), *The Shepherds of the Delectable Mountains*, *Hugh the Drover*, *The Poisoned Kiss* and *The Pilgrim's Progress*.

Venice – La Fenice 'The most beautiful theatre in the world', is how Stravinsky's wife described the tiny jewel of a theatre called La Fenice, Venice's only surviving theatre dedicated principally to opera. The city of the first public opera house, Venice has a long illustrious tradition of opera performances from the first ever opera performance in 1630, on the site of what is now the Danieli Hotel, to the Fenice which underwent its most recent restoration in 1934. This theatre has staged the world premieres of *Rigoletto*, *La Traviata* and *Simon Boccanegra*, amongst a number of Verdi operas and, in this century *The Rake's Progress* by Stravinsky in 1951 and Britten's *The Turn of the Screw* in 1954 and now presents opera as the ultimate social spectacle. The audience have a perfect view of each other across the tiers of boxes, glittering with gold fretwork highlighted by delicate paintwork and twinkling lights. They also enjoy excellent acoustics and unusually good sight lines, given the shape of the auditorium. But such social cachet does not prevent the house from staging an adventurous repertory which is not always backed up by suitably confident productions. But the attractions of the glorious theatre and the beautiful setting ensure that La Fenice can always attract some of the world's greatest singers to perform there.

Verdi, Guiseppe (1813–1901) Italian composer who was rejected by the Milan Conservatory for being 'insufficiently talented' and went on to become the most celebrated operatic composer in Italy. His works read like a list of the highlights of the operatic repertoire with a series of themes running through them which have come to characterize Verdi's works. The most prominent of these are his intense patriotism and love of Italy and his fascination with the actions of individuals shaping the destinies of large numbers of people. His compositions span more than half a century, from the earliest work *Rocester*, composed in 1836 and now mislaid, to his last opera *Falstaff* which he wrote in 1893 at the age of eighty! Verdi is the ideal composer for a first time opera-goer to start with. His melodies are expansive, his characters engaging and his plots (on the whole) quite credible. His opera writing falls into three clear periods. Of his early period, *Nabucco*, premiered in 1842, was the first work to achieve massive public acclaim, coinciding exactly with the movement to

unify Italy under the leadership of Vittorio Emmanuele. The Chorus of the Hebrew Slaves yearning for their freedom from Babylonian captivity, was taken up by every fervent Italian patriot and Verdi's own name was used as an acroymn for the political struggle (V.ittorio E.mmanuele, R.e-D.'I.talia). It was a profound experience for the composer who went on to become a Deputy in the first Italian Parliament in 1861 and was nominated as a Senator in 1874. His other notable operas from this period include *Ernani* (1844), *Macbeth* (1847) and *Luisa Miller* (1849). His middle period produced his most dramatic works which the modern audience arguably find most enjoyable, beginning with *Rigoletto* (1851), *Il Trovatore* (1853) and *La Traviata* (1853) – a colossal failure at the first performance. The plots of these three operas alone prove how versatile he was in adapting a myriad of different situations to convey powerful and affecting drama. It is satisfying to attribute this to a stability in his private life, as he finally recovered from the loss of both his wife and daughter (which had occurred before he started to write *Nabucco*) and settled in Paris with the singer Guiseppina Strepponi whom he finally married after living with her for over ten years. Between 1855 and 1871, he composed his grandest works, including *Simon Boccanegra*, *Un Ballo in Maschera*, *Don Carlos* and *Aida*, before abandoning composition to live the life of a country gentleman in Busseto. Only the combined persuasion of his wife, his publisher Ricordi and the librettist Arrigo Boito persuaded him to write scores for Boito's libretti of *Otello* and *Falstaff*, thereby creating two operas which many consider to be the pinnacle of his achievement.

Verisimo Adjective meaning realism which has come to describe a style of opera which was prevalent in Italy of the late nineteenth century and is typified by *Cavalleria Rusticana* by Mascagni. Verisimo operas deal with the realities of life, derived from folk tales, where passions are high and money is short and the chief protagonists come from the lower ranks of society.

Verona Although Verona has staged opera in theatres from the eighteenth century, it is now best known for the open air performances in the magnificent Roman Arena in the centre of the town. This had been used to stage occasional performances in the mid-nineteenth century but was transformed into a regular performance space in 1913, thanks to the work of the tenor Giovanni Zenatello and his supporters. The Arena seats over 25,000 and therefore lends itself to large and spectacular productions, much like the Baths of Caracalla in Rome. It attracts singers from all over the world for its summer seasons which have taken place every year since 1913, except for the war years.

Verrett, Shirley American mezzo-soprano whose repertoire also includes soprano roles. A dignified presence on stage combined with a sonorous voice enables Verrett to instill a passionate intensity into her roles which include Eboli (*Don Carlos*), Azucena (*Il Trovatore*), Dido (*The Trojans*) and the title roles in *Norma* and *Tosca*. Amongst numerous appearances worldwide, she appeared as Carmen at the Bolshoi in Moscow where she was the first black singer ever to perform.

Viaggio a Reims, Il (Rossini) FP 1825. Even though this opera only lasts for one act, it ranks as one of the most expensive works to produce, demanding ten principals of excellent calibre to undertake each of the roles. It was composed for the coronation of Charles X and was a consummate failure at its first performance. It was produced with great success in 1985 and has since been recorded.

The plot follows a group of travellers from numerous countries on their way to the coronation, charting their various intrigues and amorous encounters and their ultimate frustration at not being able to continue because of lack of coach horses. They are comforted by the promise of the celebrations they will enjoy in Paris once the coronation is over.

Viardot, Pauline (1821–1910) French mezzo-soprano who created the roles of Fides in *Le Prophete* by Meyerbeer and the title role in *Sapho* by Gounod. She is notable for her prominence in the intellectual circles on nineteenth-century Paris, her friendship with the Russian novelist Ivan Turgenev and

for her own operetta compositions to libretti by Turgenev.

Vibrato In the most general terms, it is true to say that vibrato is attractive on a string and unattractive when you sing. The term (from the Italian meaning 'vibrated') describes a rapid, regular fluctuation of pitch which on a violin or cello can produce a rich, vivid sound and can also sound pleasing if quickly controlled as a descriptive part of a singer's performance. More often, however, it is employed by singers who are unable to achieve a purer tone and resort to an unpleasant 'wobble'.

Vick, Graham English director whose productions have been staged in venues as diverse as La Fenice in Venice and a disused warehouse outside Leeds. Such versatility is the key to Vick's success as he approaches each new project with the same degree of imagination and enthusiasm, regardless of whether he is working with world class opera professionals or recalcitrant school-children on an opera-in-education project. Vick's career began at Scottish Opera where he worked as Director of Opera-go-Round, devising community based projects to widen the opera audience. His work has subsequently been seen in the opera festivals at Wexford and Battignano in Italy, for Opera North where he directed an intensely moving *Katya Kabanova* and for English National Opera where his petal-strewn *Madam Butterfly* has become a classic of ENO's repertoire. A passionate advocate of opera for all, Vick is also Artistic Director of the innovative City of Birmingham Touring Opera, bringing excellent small scale opera productions to a wide range of touring venues.

Vickers, Jon Canadian tenor whose career developed during a ten year residency at Covent Garden, during which time he sang roles including Radames (*Aida*), the title roles in *Don Carlos* and *Peter Grimes*, Florestan in *Fidelio* and Canio in *I Pagliacci*. By 1960 he was in international demand, singing in the Bayreuth Festival, at the Metropolitan Opera, in San Francisco, Chicago, Milan and Salzburg. His massive physical presence and well supported heldentenor range have created highly individual performances which many believe to be virtually definitive and he has frequently been compared with Enrico Caruso. His greatest roles are Tristan, Otello and Peter Grimes.

Video As with opera on television, a massive new audience has come to opera over the last decade thanks to the availability of excellent productions on video. Performances from the Royal Opera House, English National Opera, The Metropolitan Opera in New York and even the Arena at Verona are available at the touch of a button (still at a considerable price, though this will doubtless change). As interest has increased, so techniques for shooting videos of opera performances have become more sophisticated, as directors appreciate that it is not enough simply to film the stage action. Adaptations have to be made for the performance to retain its effect on the small screen. The most important consideration is that of lighting. The lamps needed to flood a stage the size of the Arena at Verona with bright light will render a video of the performance there virtually invisible. Make-up will need to be adapted for close-ups, as will costumes and stagings, particularly if dancing is involved. A singer in full flight, whose voice aims to fill an auditorium full of 25,000 people will not look particularly attractive if filmed at close quarters for the television screen. But a superbly shot video of an opera will heighten the drama of any performance if the camera is used as a part of the action, rather than an unwelcome extra. Close-ups need to be used judiciously and the scale of the performance should not be lost by transferring it to a small screen.

Vienna Austria's capital city with an illustrious history of opera premieres in a number of different theatres before the opening of the current Staatsoper. Mozart's works *The Abduction from the Seraglio*, *The Marriage of Figaro*, *Cosi fan Tutte* and *The Magic Flute* all had the first stagings in Vienna. *Fidelio* by Beethoven and, naturally, *Die Fledermaus* by Johann Strauss were first performed in this city. But it was the opening of the Court Opera in 1869 that gave Vienna an international opera centre, whose reputation was consolidated and enhanced by the leadership first of Gustav Mahler from 1897 to 1907 and then of Richard Strauss from 1919 to 1924. Renamed the Staatsoper in 1918, the

house is now ranked amongst the best in the world, with a social reputation that matches its artistic one. The annual Opera Ball in 1990 caused riots throughout the city as the differences between the opera audience and the poor and unemployed in Vienna flared into angry violence. Tempers are only a little less frayed when discussions ensue about the Opera Director, one of the most notoriously difficult jobs to hold down in the entire spectrum of professional music. Herbert von Karajan stimulated many such arguments during his time there (1956 to 1964) but assuaged them with definitive performances (particularly of Wagner) featuring international singers such as Birgit Nilsson and Hans Hotter. Under Karajan the Vienna Philharmonic rose to become one of the world's finest orchestras, providing reliably superb performances when the house was without a music director after Karajan's resignation. Now the house is led by Claudio Abbado as Musical Director and Claus Helmut Drese who will oversee the administrative merger with the Volksoper in 1991. The repertoire concentrates on the classic, particularly Mozart and the house plans to present the entire Mozart repertory for the 1991 Vienna Festival.

Vie Parisienne, La (Offenbach) FP 1868. Exactly as its title suggests, Offenbach's satirical opera deals with life in Paris during the Second Empire and compares with *Orpheus in the Underworld* for wit and jollity.

Village Romeo and Juliet, A (Delius) FP 1907. The theme of this opera has echoes of Shakespeare's play – two lovers unable to continue their relationship because of a feud between the families, but there the similarity ends. The opera contains the very well known section 'Walk to the Paradise Garden'.

The plot is set in Switzerland and concerns Sali, the son of one farmer and Vrenchen, the daughter of another. The farmers have argued about rights to a certain piece of land, but in secret the children have met and fallen in love. The continuing feud ruins both families financially but further drama occurs when the lovers are discovered by Vrenchen's father. Sali strikes him to the ground and the father loses his senses. Realizing their love has no future, Sali and

Vreli take a boat out to the middle of the lake and drown themselves.

Villi, Le (Puccini) FP 1884 This two act opera was the first ever written by Puccini, who originally condensed all the action into one act. It echoes the ballet by Adam called *Giselle*. 'Le Villi' is the Italian for 'the witches', although in this case it refers more to spirits.

Anna has been jilted by her lover Roberto and has died of the resulting heartache. Her spirit joins the willis, who are ghosts of lovers who have been abandoned over the years and return to plague their former partners. Anna and the willis are exhorted by Anna's grief-stricken father, Gugliemo, to pursue Roberto who is driven mad by their attentions and dies in a frenzied fit.

Visconti, Luchino (1906–1976) Italian producer and designer who is best known for his work at La Scala and for the productions he designed for Maria Callas, including *La Vestale*, *La Sonnambula*, *La Traviata* and *Anna Bolena*. Authenticity was the key note to Visconti's style and he was relentless in pursuing the exact details to create the effect he desired, even to the extent of using nineteenth-century sets when required. His productions were noted for this powerful stylization (the 'Black and White *Tosca*' or 'Art Deco *Rosenkavalier*' for example) but the stagings were never allowed to dominate the dramatic intensity of the singing.

Vishnevskaya, Galina Russian soprano who excelled at the core of soprano repertoire while a principal artist at the Bolshoi from 1953 to 1974, particularly in the female leads written by Russian composers. In 1974, she and her husband, the cellist Mstislav Rostropovitch settled in America and she appeared in the 1975 production of *Tosca* at the Metropolitan Opera. Vishnevskaya made several appearances in Western theatres while resident in Russia and though no-one could fault the power and beauty of her voice, her acting ability seemed dated when placed in the context of western artists.

Vivaldi, Antonio (1678–1741) Although Vivaldi's orchestral output is amongst the most popular in the twentieth-century repertoire (*The Four Seasons* remains a constant best seller of classical music records), his extensive operatic work is rarely seen. Vivaldi actually wrote forty-six operas, but only twenty-one scores survive.

Voix Humaine, La (Poulenc) FP 1959. A tour-de-force for one singing actress to convey in forty-five minutes a telephone conversation with her lover who is in the process of ending their affair. The work was written for the acclaimed French soprano Denise Duval and stands as a masterpiece of intense and beautiful composition.

von Dohnany, Christoph German conductor who trained in his home country and in America with his grandfather, the composer Erno von Dohnanyi. Director of the Cleveland Orchestra, he is known internationally for both his concert and opera work.

von Karajan, Herbert (1908–1989) Austrian conductor who became pre-eminent in the world of opera through his work with many of the world's finest ensembles, and was a particular specialist in operas by Wagner Verdi, Strauss and Mozart. As conductor of the Berlin Philharmonic from 1955, he brought the orchestra to recognition as one of the most prestigious in the world. Von Karajan held the notoriously difficult post of Artistic Director of the Vienna Staatsoper from 1957 to 1964 when he inaugurated a collaboration between Vienna and La Scala, Milan, creating a supremely powerful force in international opera. He left Vienna under difficult circumstances and assumed the Directorship of the Salzburg Festival, a post he held until his death. His orchestra, the Berlin Philharmonic, is resident at von Karajan's great innovation, the Salzburg Easter Festival which he began in 1967. All the while, he was conducting with orchestras worldwide – at Bayreuth, in London, in New York, with particularly acclaimed performances of *Die Walkure* and *Das Rheingold* which he had produced for the Salzburg Festival.

Enigmatic, charismatic and dogmatic, von Karajan was without doubt one of the world's greatest conductors. An unstinting professional, demanding of his artists and rigorous in his rehearsals, von Karajan would become so thoroughly acquainted with his score that by the time of a performance he would conduct with his eyes closed and become totally immersed in the whole sound. At Salzburg he produced nearly all the operas he conducted, showing an active interest in the technical aspects, as he did when any of his performances were being recorded. Von Karajan belied the notion that artists are only recognized as famous after their deaths, leaving an estate valued at several million pounds and a vast furore amongst those who claimed rights to it. A prodigious recording artist, von Karajan's works are planned to be produced in their entirety on video disk, leaving the world with a lasting legacy of a great musician.

von Stade, Frederica American mezzo-soprano who is as well known on the concert platform as on the opera stage. Her career developed when she moved to Europe in 1973 where she created an enchanting performance of Cherubino (*The Marriage of Figaro*) for the opera houses of Paris, Salzburg and Glyndebourne. Thereafter she has sung all over the world, and is particularly known for Cherubino, Hansel, Rosina in *The Barber of Seville* and Zerlina in *Don Giovanni*. von Stade's strong features and rich voice make her an admirable choice particularly for hosenrole which she makes convincing without losing her essential femininity.

Wagner, Cosima (1837–1930) Richard Wagner's second wife and daughter of the composer Franz Liszt. She bore Wagner three illegitimate children, Isolde, Eva and Siegfried (the inspiration for Wagner's beautiful short work, the *Siegfried Idyll*) before divorcing her first husband (the conductor Hans von Bulow) and marrying Wagner in 1870. After Wagner's death she continued as Principal of the Bayreuth Festival, implementing his ideas to the finest detail without absorbing the new and imaginative theatrical ideas of the subsequent generation. When the Festival was handed on to her son Siegfried in 1906 therefore, it was musically supreme but artistically static.

Wagner, Richard (1813–1883) German composer. Richard Wagner was far more than a composer of operas. He devised a theory of performance which was radical and uncompromising at a time when Europe was content was the grandeur of Italian

opera or the cynicism and satire of French opera. Before Wagner, audiences came to the opera to socialize, dress up, eat and drink well and be amazed by lavish spectacle and rich melodies. But Wagner believed that operas should be composed and staged so that the audience would be challenged, engrossed and so profoundly moved that to clap at the end of a performance would seem irreverent. The audience should be a part of a 'gesamkunstwerk' (literally together-art-work). From early beginnings with a work like *Die Feen* which was influenced by Beethoven, *Das Liebsverbot* where the French influence is apparent and *Rienzi* which is close to 'grand opera' in the accepted sense, Wagner moved on to carve out a particularly individual style. He took risks with melodies by expanding the size of the orchestra, developing themes to characterize people and emotions (leitmotifs) and creating one musical structure for a whole opera, rather than creating an opera from a series of different styles and episodes. Holding fast to these ideas he composed *Tannhauser* (1845) and *Lohengrin* (1850) before being forced into a decade of exile in Switzerland from 1850, after his role in a political uprising in Dresden a year earlier.

Wagner's intense, demanding style of opera was not popular but even the most recalcitrant opera-goer would grudgingly admit that Wagner was a composer of profound intellectual stature and radical genius. *Tannhauser* was given a notoriously bad reception in Paris in 1861 but by 1864 Wagner was back in Germany under the patronage of King Ludwig of Bavaria and was able to concentrate on refining the works which were to be recognized as his masterpieces. *Tristan and Isolde* and *Der Meistersinger* were premiered in 1865 and 1868 respectively. By 1876 Wagner's epic creation the Ring Cycle had had its first full staging in a theatre specifically designed for the performance of Wagner's works – the Festival Theatre at Bayreuth in Bavaria. Wagner's final opera *Parsifal* was premiered at Bayreuth in 1882 and the composer died in Venice barely six months later.

Newcomers to opera are usually advised to avoid Wagner like the plague, which is actually a ridiculous generalization. Anyone who finds something like *The Barber of Seville* totally implausible may relish the all-encompassing power of a Wagner performance, where music, words and action are designed to fuse together to create a totally absorbing performance. The facts are straightforward – Wagner operas are very long, the action is minimal, the music includes some superb melodies, together with less engaging writing, and the characters have, in the past, been represented by the worst aspects of opera production. But if you are willing to do some preparatory work by listening to recordings and reading some of Wagner's detailed, carefully thought out stage directions, you will begin to understand the depth of passion that committed Wagnerians feel about this extraordinary composer.

Wagner, Siegfried (1869–1930) The only son of Richard and Cosima Wagner, he studied with Humperdinck and conducted his first major opera at Bayreuth before the age of thirty. He began to produce operas there in 1901 while creating fifteen compositions of his own, none of which has achieved much popularity. Always involved in the Festival with his mother, he was officially named Artistic Director in 1908 but Cosima continued to exert a powerful influence over productions at the Festival, thus depriving Siegfried from developing any more advanced ideas. He married the English girl Winifred Evans and produced two sons, Wieland and Wolfgang. He died barely four months after his mother.

Wagner, Wieland (1917–1966) The elder of Siegfried Wagner's two sons, Wieland had the courage to break the mould of traditional productions at Bayreuth in favour of a more direct approach, less hide-bound by the pageantry and convention that Cosima Wagner had insisted on. In doing so, Wieland believed he was returning to his grandfather's original intentions whilst retaining the excitement of new productions by declaring 'Every new production is a step on the way to an unknown goal'. His ideas were not uncontroversial but widely influential and characterized the style of Wagnerian productions in Germany and abroad for many years. He reached the height of his influence as Director of the Bayreuth Festival from 1951 to 1966, a post he shared with his brother Wolfgang.

Wagner, Wolfgang Wolfgang has combined an ability to stage his grandfather's operas with an acute business sense which enabled the Bayreuth Festival to attain financial security as well as artistic prestige. His productions did not quite have the flair of his elder brother but were nevertheless influenced by the more modern approach to staging. After their successful joint tenure of the Festival ended with Wieland's death in 1966, Wolfgang has continued there, opening out the directorial opportunities to artists from all over the world. While the results of such a bold policy were not always successful, his strategy has brought the Festival to a high international status, respected all over the opera world.

Walker, Sarah English mezzo-soprano whose repertoire stretches from Bach to Berio and from Gounod to Gershwin. Her popularity is correspondingly wide and appreciative of her sparkling voice, matched by an effervescent personality and consummate acting ability. She has performed with the Royal Opera Covent Garden, English National Opera (including performances with the company at the Metropolitan Opera New York), the Vienna Stadtsoper, San Francisco Opera, Chicago Lyric Opera and Glyndebourne. Her memorable performances include a superb interpretation of Elizabeth I in the ENO's production of *Gloriana* by Benjamin Britten, the Countess in Tchaikovsky's *The Queen of Spades*, Katisha in *The Mikado* (all for ENO) and Dido in *The Trojans* by Bizet for Vienna. She is known to non-opera goers for superb concert performances, notably at the Last Night of the Proms where she can be relied upon to match (or exceed!) the humour of the ebullient audience and through her singing of cabaret songs and classical lieder with the pianist Roger Vignoles.

Walkure, Die (see Ring des Nibelungen)

Wally, La (Catalani) FP 1892. Set in Switzerland and requiring a full scale avalanche at the end of the performance, *La Wally* is rarely performed partly because of its technical requirements and partly because of the lack of music of an outstanding quality. There is one superb aria which was used extensively in the French detective film *Diva*.

Wally is a peasant girl who loves Hagenbach but has been rejected by him and now plans to murder him. Wally's new suitor Gellner offers to help her by pushing Hagenbach down a ravine but once he has done so, Wally is filled with remorse and sets off to rescue Hagenbach. She finds him and he declares that he does love her after all, but it is too late. A distant rumble heralds an avalanche which kills them both.

Walter, Bruno (1876–1962) German conductor who gave a particularly personal interpretation to his orchestral leadership, making his work well loved and admired. He studied in Berlin and Cologne, before coming to Hamburg to work with Mahler. Thereafter the great opera houses of the world opened up to him – he held the Music Directorships of Munich and Vienna and performed extensively at Covent Garden, Salzburg and the Metropolitan Opera in New York. His speciality was the German repertoire, particularly *Fidelio* and *Der Zauberflote*.

Walton, William (1902–1983) English composer whose two operas are rarely given professional performances today. *Troilus and Cressida* is a lush and romantic interpretation of the classical tale and *The Bear* is a highly enjoyable comic piece in one act. The most evocative music by Walton is found not in his writing for the opera stage but for films, in scores such as *Henry V* for the film starring Laurence Olivier.

War and Peace (Prokofiev) FP 1944. Prokofiev's epic work in five acts which chronicles Russia's struggle from peace to war waged by Napoleon and his troops. The project succeeds thanks to evocative music and engrossing action. It requires enormous resources on the part of the producing company with over twelve major roles, large choruses and technical effects ranging from lavish balls in St Petersburg to the burning of Moscow by the French troops. The opera is arranged in two parts, Peace and War, and in thirteen scenes – scenes one to seven in Peace, and scenes eight to thirteen in War.

Peace introduces the principal characters as they declare their intention to defend Russia against the French invader. Natasha Rostova meets Prince Andrei at a ball and they fall in love. But she is badly received by his family and he joins the troops at the front. Natasha is pursued by Anatol who, although married, attempts to elope with her. He is unsuccessful and Pierre, Natasha's close family friend, tells her that Anatol is married. In doing so, Pierre realizes that he is in love with Natasha, but all incipient romance is held at the announcement of the outbreak of war. War opens as Andrei is assessing his campaign and longing for death on the battle field. In the French camp, Napoleon feels uneasy about the campaign ahead but the Russian General Kutuzov feels worse and takes the decision to retreat to Moscow. The French army sets fire to the deserted city and Natasha finds Andrei, dying amid the decimated Russian army. But the French are finally forced into retreat, not because of the might of the opposing army but through the severity of the Russian winter.

Washington Opera Surprisingly for America's capital city, a full time opera company was not established in the city until 1956, under the title of the Opera Society of Washington. The company is now housed in the elegant surroundings of the Kennedy Center where it performs both in the main auditorium (where performances have also been staged by the Paris Opera and La Scala, Milan) and smaller Terrace Theatre. The company has staged notable American premieres of Stravinsky's *Oedipus Rex* conducted by the composer, *A Village Romeo and Juliet* by Delius, and Monteverdi's *The Return of Ulysses*. Now under the pioneering leadership of Martin Feinstein, the company enjoys a strong artistic reputation.

Watson, Lillian English soprano. Since her Covent Garden debut in 1971 Lillian Watson has returned there every season and appears regularly with WNO, ENO, Scottish Opera and at Glyndebourne. She is most popular in lighter roles – Susanna, Despina etc, which suit her quicksilver personality and diminutive stature. Not yet well-known in the United States, she sings regularly in Europe and has made several records (including Janacek's *The Cunning Little Vixen* with Samuel Ramey) and television recordings.

Weber, Carl Maria von (1786–1826) German composer. Only two of Weber's operas are regularly found in today's repertoire – *Der Freischutz* written in 1821 and *Oberon* (1826). *Euryanthe*, which Weber wrote in 1823, is given the occasional professional staging but suffers from an appallingly bad libretto. But Weber is credited with having been the father of the Romantic opera movement in Germany, producing music which was lyrical, rich in tone and highly descriptive, using themes to describe certain characters, echoed many years later by Wagner's 'leitmotivs'. Weber's operas exerted a profound influence on Wagner who developed the style of opera that Weber had begun – a satisfying fusion of music, words and action rather than being an amalgamation of solo items, to engross the audience entirely rather than allow them to drift in and out for the favourite moments. Weber died of consumption at the age of forty, leaving his final opera *Die Drei Pintos* unfinished. It was completed by Mahler but has not found popularity in the modern repertoire.

Weill, Kurt (1900–1950) The operas of Kurt Weill stand as a fascinating record of one man's immersion in the social and political activities of Europe betewen the First and Second World Wars. Weill studied in Germany and became immersed in the café society of inter-war Berlin on which he based many of his characters so vividly portrayed in his music. His work is contemporary opera that speaks powerfully to its audience of corruption, dictatorship, poverty, hardship and the individual against the state, with words often written by the great poet and dramatist, Berthold Brecht. But the political message is not hammered home unmercifully, depriving the audience of even the slightest good tune or moment of humour. By the time Hitler came to power in 1933, Weill could stand Germany no more and fled to Paris and thereafter to America, with his wife, cabaret singer Lotte Lenya. There he continued his composition before his death in 1950.

Weill's music has found an appreciative audience way beyond the opera house ('The Alabama Song' from *Mahagonny* was recorded by David Bowie), particularly amongst jazz musicians and cabaret singers. Because it is difficult to classify his operas critics have been wary about their place in the opera house. Perhaps the most operatic is *The Rise and Fall of the City of Mahagonny*, but *The Threepenny Opera* and *Streetscene* have been given professional performances by opera companies and been greatly enjoyed by opera goers. For anyone interested in the work of Kurt Weill, these three productions are the best ones to start with, together with his last work, *Down in the Valley*, written in 1948, a year after *Streetscene*.

Weir, Judith Scottish composer whose first opera *A Night at the Chinese Opera* proved to many in its audience that new opera is not always abrasive and difficult for a first timer to enjoy. It was staged with enormous success by Kent Opera in 1987, having been commissioned by the BBC. So great was its popularity that it has been revived several times and was premiered in America in July 1989. Weir studied at Cambridge University and in America where she won the prestigious Koussevitsky Scholarship to study at Tanglewood. She is now Guinness Composer in Residence at the Royal Scottish Academy of Music and Drama and is working on new operas to commissions from Scottish Opera, English National Opera and the Royal Opera House, Covent Garden.

Welsh National Opera The beginnings of Welsh National Opera seem almost unbearably romantic but the current success of the company seems to point towards a fairy tale outcome. It was extraordinary that the Land of Song did not have a national opera company but singing in Wales had long been the preserve of the enthusiastic, highly talented amateur and professional musicians were viewed with some suspicion. Thus the origins of the company were strictly amateur. At a meeting in a chapel in Cardiff in 1943, twenty-eight volunteers met together to establish what was to be called the Lyrian Grand Opera. By the end of the meeting, it was agreed to produce six operas in three years from an entirely amateur cast and crew but directed professionally, in order to give the singers of Wales a chance to perform the classic opera repertoire on stage. It was also agreed to change the name to the Welsh National Opera Company. The first Music Director was Idloes Owen, a local choir master and singing teacher, the company's business dealings were handled by the prosperous and well-connected garage proprietor, Bill Smith, all other offices were manned by volunteers. The company's first production was *Cavalleria Rusticana* and *I Pagliacci*. Nearly forty-five years later, the company enjoys an international reputation, can attract the world's greatest singers and producers, sells out on its infrequent performances in London, enjoyed a spectacular debut in New York, has royal patronage and is about to make its home in a purpose built opera house in the centre of Cardiff. The main stage productions range from the lavish to the spartan, and the classic to the controversial. There has been a much praised cycle of operas by Janacek (in association with Britain's other national opera companies), notorious productions of *Carmen* set in a circus (directed by Lucian Pintille) and *Don Giovanni* (with a set that defies description!), directed by Ruth Berghaus, a powerful staging of *Otello* by German theatre director Peter Stein, a highly acclaimed Ring Cycle, and classic interpretations of the great Verdi operas which give the outstanding chorus (which only became professional in 1968) the opportunity to take centre stage. Such internationalism is complemented by an active touring policy around Wales and Western England including productions which may only include a few singers and a piano and take place in a schoolhall. There is too a commendable policy of encouraging young talent and such established singers as Josephine Barstow, Thomas Allen, Helen Field and Arthur Davies have all developed their careers through work with the company.

Werther (Massenet) FP 1892. Massenet's lyrical and romantic opera is based on the story by Goethe of a young man's love turning into a fanatical obsession. The work is occasionally dismissed as shallow sentimentality, as the central character appears to be his own worst enemy and completely incapable of getting out of the predicament he has created for himself. But the music is magnificent, and sensitive actors can bring out the agony of such a frustrated love affair.

Werther has fallen passionately in love with Charlotte, daughter of the local Magistrate. She is engaged to Albert and, determined to reach Charlotte in any way he can, Werther befriends his rival. But it does no good. Werther cannot shake Charlotte from

his mind and determines to leave the town. On his travels, he writes her a series of tender, loving letters and she realizes that she cannot forget him either. In a climatic scene, the two pour out their long-repressed love for one another before Werther insists on leaving her once more. Albert's suspicions are aroused and when Werther asks if he might borrow his pistols, Albert readily agrees, sensing what might be about to happen. Charlotte reaches Werther just as he has shot himself and he dies in her arms.

Wexford In this small Irish town, an opera festival has developed from small beginnings in 1951, to enjoy international prestige by producing rarely performed and neglected operas by composers whose repertoire also includes classic works. For example, Rossini also wrote an opera based on Shakespeare's *Othello* which was presented at Wexford, as was *Medea* by Mayr and *I Due Foscari* by Verdi, which has now found popularity with a wider audience. Wexford also encourages young singers from whom the delightful Theatre Royal provides a comfortable singing space. One of Wexford's most illustrious 'finds' was Mirella Freni.

Where the Wild Things Are (Knussen) FP 1980. Based on the popular tale by Maurice Sendak, this opera was written in one act by Oliver Knussen and presented at the Glyndebourne Festival as a double bill with another Sendak tale *Higgledy Piggledy Pop!*. It is an enchanting work, perfect for introducing children to opera (and hence a slightly strange choice for Glyndebourne!) and much enhanced by Sendak's colourful designs.

The little boy Max has been banished to his room without supper because of his bad temper. There he dreams that he is transported to a magic forest where he becomes king of all the beasts that live there before taking his leave on a ship which brings him home.

White, Willard Jamaican bass with an extraordinary singing and speaking voice, great good looks and acting ability. A scholarship to the USA in 1968 marked the start of his professional career at New York City Opera. Since his European operatic debut in 1976 he has appeared with all major companies in the UK and on the continent. Highly acclaimed for his interpretation of Porgy in Trevor Nunn's outstanding production of *Porgy and Bess* at the 1986 and 1987 Glyndebourne Festivals. He has recorded this role with the Cleveland Orchestra, conducted by Lorin Maazel, and made another recording with the original Glyndebourne cast. His level of accomplishment as an actor is indicated by his performances in Shakespeare's *Othello* with The Royal Shakespeare Company in the 1988/9 season.

William Tell (see Guillaume Tell)

Wolf-Ferrari, Ermanno (1876–1948) Italian composer who abandoned a career as a painter to develop his opera composition. His two best known works are *Il Segreto di Susanna*, a comic opera in one act and *I Gioielli di Madonna*, an example of real-life drama among the peasants of Italy. They are quite different from each other in style, characterizing a composer whose principal works are humorous but with 'verisimo opera' overtones. Five of his works were based on plays by the Italian comic writer Goldoni, including *I Quattro Rusteghi* (1906) *Gli Amanti Sposi* (1925) and *Le Donne Curiose* (1930) but 'Susanna' shows that his own comic invention was excellent. 'I Gioielli' on the other hand can veer towards unconvincing drama and great sentimentality and is not a good example of opera portraying real life.

Workshops A style of teaching opera which is very popular in the United States and is increasingly used in Europe, particularly at training colleges such as the National Opera Studio in London. The theme is learning by experience, as student singers are encouraged to explore the potential of a range of performance techniques under the guidance of more experienced teachers. In an informal setting, students can try out various ways of expressing themselves, explore which sorts of action suit their characters, learning both from their teachers and from each other. Workshops may only include a very few people working on a small excerpt from an opera or may expand up to a complete opera, given in performance in front of an audience.

Wortham Center (see Houston)

Wozzeck (Berg) FP 1925. From its very first performance, when the public in Berlin had a chance to hear fragments of the opera eighteen months before the official premiere, *Wozzeck* has caused controversy. Quite simply, it is unlike any other opera because of its structure, content and style and therefore it cannot be compared with anything and has to be judged on its individual merits and defects. No less an opera personality than Tito Gobbi described the character of Wozzeck as 'a tragic torn off rag of humanity'. But there are as many opinions as there are members of an audience and if you are broad minded and interested in opera as theatre, seek out a performance. It is not, however, for those who wish to leave the theatre without their senses being assaulted and their attitudes challenged. Berg intended the work to provoke and to shock and in that, he has been highly successful.

The soldier Wozzeck earns his money from co-operating in medical experiments with the Doctor and submitting to the influence of the Captain. He uses this money to support his lover Marie and their young son. But Marie wants to leave Wozzeck, fearing his extraordinary mood swings as a result of the Doctor's experiments, and has begun an affair with the Drum Major. When Wozzeck discovers this, he murders Marie and throws the knife he has used into the lake. But he finds he is unable to forget his crime and returns to the lake to find the weapon he used. As he reaches the lake, he walks further and further in, eventually losing his life in the water. All that is left of the tragic couple is their little boy who is told by the children of the village that his mother is dead.

Wunderlich, Fritz (1930–1966) German tenor who worked in the major German opera houses including Stuttgart, Frankfurt and Munich, establishing a reputation as a superb lyric tenor who could sing as convincingly in grand opera as he could in operetta. His performances of Mozart were most notable and many felt his career was only just coming to fruition when he was killed in an accident at the age of thirty-six, barely two weeks before his American debut.

Xerxes (Handel) FP 1738. An excellent choice for someone wishing to get to know

Xerxes, by Handel, considered one of the least accessible of Handel's operas, until Nicholas Hytner's 1985 ENO production, subsequently seen in Russia. Valerie Masterson as Romilda.

Yan Tan Tethera, by Birtwistle, chronicling the plight of a shepherd, sung by Omar Ebrahim, at the premiere of the work, produced by Opera Factory at the Queen Elizabeth Hall, London, in 1986.

Handel's operas, *Xerxes* has an absorbing plot, plenty of comic moments and many good tunes, including the aria known as 'Handel's Largo' or 'Ombra Mai Fu', to give it its correct description. It was given a particularly good production by English National Opera to celebrate the Handel Tercentenary in 1985, which brought out every moment of wit and elegance in the work. The plot is complicated, and the women singing male roles can seem disconcerting at first, but the characters are so attractive that by the last act, it seems completely plausible to have a princess dressing up as a man to win back her fiancé, the king, who happens to be sung by a woman!

Xerxes, Emperor of Persia is engaged to the Princess Amastre. But he has encountered Romilda, the fiancée of his brother Arsamene, and has decided that Romilda is to be his wife. This delights Romilda's sister Atalanta who has always been in love with Arsamene and will devise any cunning plot to get him back. Romilda rejects the King's advances but a misdirected letter makes Arsamene believe Romilda has been unfaithful and the couple's argument gives Atalanta yet more chance to attract Arsamene. Twists and turns result in a final showdown as all the protagonists unweave their various relationships, the King recognizes his duty and returns to the Princess, Romilda and Arsamene are reunited and only the wily Atalanta is left alone to fight another day.

Yan Tan Tehtera (Birtwistle) FP 1986. The London based Opera Factory presented the world premier of Birtwistle's small scale opera which is centred on the shepherds of Wiltshire. 'Yan (one), tan (two), tethera (three). . .' is an ancient method of counting sheep.

The central characters are Alan and Caleb Raven, both shepherds. Alan has come to Wiltshire from the north and would like to return but the imminent labour of his sheep prevent him from doing so. He is more successful as a shepherd than Caleb, who resents Alan and calls on the help of the Bad 'Un. Together they capture Alan and kidnap his new born twins, leaving Caleb to woo Hannah, Alan's deserted wife. It takes Alan and the twins seven years to be reunited with Hannah, thanks to the magic northern

shepherd's spell which begins 'Yan, tan, tethera. . .'

Zaide (Mozart) FP 1866. An unfinished opera by Mozart which he composed in 1779 but at his death in 1791 only amounted to a collection of musical numbers. It was adapted for performance by Anton Andre and seems to be a precursor of *The Abduction from the Seraglio*.

Zaide is the chief of the Harem of the Sultan of Turkey but has sympathy for the prisoner Gometz. She helps him escape by giving him money but, despite the efforts of the Sultan's erstwhile servant Allazim, Gometz is recaptured and taken back to the Harem.

Zandonai, Riccardo (1883–1944) Italian composer who was thought at one stage to be the successor to Puccini and was taken on by the publishing house of Ricordi. However only one of his twelve operas, *Francesca da Rimini*, is still regularly performed and while the other eleven are good examples of verisimo opera, they do not fulfil the hopes that Ricordi had of the composer.

Zarzuela A style of Spanish folk operetta, extremely lively in performance with plenty of dancing as well as singing and a large amount of spoken dialogue, much of which is updated for contemporary audiences. The best performances are given in the large theatres, built specially for zarzuela in Madrid where the audience contribute as much as the performers.

Zauberflote (see The Magic Flute)

Zeffirelli, Franco Italian director and designer whose productions are characterized by their lavish grandeur, massive scale and authentic detail. Zeffirelli was profoundly influenced by his teacher Visconti with whom he worked from 1949 to 1952, before designing *L'Italiana in Alghieri* for La Scala, Milan, in 1953. He made his Covent Garden debut directing *Lucia de Lammermoor* with Joan Sutherland in 1959. Since 1964, Zeffirelli has been closely associated with the Metropolitan Opera, New York where audiences eagerly await his increasingly opulent stagings, including *Otello* in 1972, *Tosca* in 1985 and *Turandot* in 1987. He has broadened the audience to opera through his spectacular films such as *La Traviata* and *Otello*.

Zemlinsky Alexander von (1871–1942) Austrian composer and conductor whose operas have revived in popularity recently, although they should be approached with caution by a new opera goer. His style is tonal and he exerted a profound influence on Schoenberg who was both his pupil and son-in-law.